FOUNDING THE AMERICAN COLONIES

THE NEW AMERICAN NATION SERIES

Edited by HENRY STEELE COMMAGER and
RICHARD B. MORRIS

* In preparation

FOUNDING THE AMERICAN COLONIES

1583 ★ 1660

By JOHN E. POMFRET

with FLOYD M. SHUMWAY

ILLUSTRATED

HARPER TORCHBOOKS
Harper & Row, Publishers
New York • Evanston • San Francisco • London

To
Dedicated scholars, past and present
who molded the
Institute of Early American History,
Williamsburg, Virginia

Contents

Illustrations

ix

MAPS

Editors' Introduction

"I WONDER nobody has ever presented the world with a tolerable account of our Plantations," remarked Robert Beverley, the colonial historian of Virginia. If Captain John Smith, Bradford, Winthrop, and Edward Johnson prudently chose to write about specific colonies largely out of their own experience, their more modern successors have provided us with comprehensive treatments dealing with settlement and institutional origins and conforming to the canons of historical scholarship prevailing in our own day. More particularly are present-day historians indebted to Herbert L. Osgood and Charles M. Andrews for their magisterial multi-volume accounts of the founding of the British Empire in America.

During the past generation notable monographic studies have probed the socio-economic bases of colonization; portrayed the early colonial leaders; contributed an added dimension to the history of Puritanism in America and to our understanding of its covenant theology: psychoanalyzed Anne Hutchinson; put nonconformity and dissent in proper seventeenth-century perspective; analyzed Indian-white relations; argued over the moment when slavery was established in the colonies; focused on the common man and on white labor, free and indentured; traced the origins of public support for education and the beginnings of science and medicine; and considered the transplantation of English law to America and its adaptation to indigenous conditions. More recently scholars have delved into family and demographic problems related to early settlement, have examined social mobility, the structure of colonial society and the degree of stratification, searched out the evidence on the accumulation and distribution of wealth, and reconsidered the case for political democracy in early America.

This volume, *Founding the American Colonies, 1583–1660*, re-examines, in the light of twentieth-century scholarship, the story of early America, from the ventures of Gilbert and Raleigh down to the restoration of the Stuarts. During these years Englishmen, who once regarded the North Atlantic seaboard as a site for exotic adventure and great riches, came to accept it as a continent for serious settlement. Englishmen in comparatively large numbers left to colonize the New World, not only the mainland colonies but the Caribbean periphery which is herein considered as well. The colonies slowly formed a patchwork pattern of emerging empire and were governed in a variety of ways—by business corporations, by proprietors, as self-governing colonies, and under royal authority. How much authority the King possessed, how much Parliament, were issues that still remained moot, and were hardly settled by the Restoration, which climaxed a titanic struggle between Crown and Parliament for control of the state.

What does emerge, however, is a nucleus of quasi-democratic societies and institutions of government—the New England town, the Virginia parish, the representative assemblies, a comparatively liberal land system in all the English colonies—and a group of small or middling freeholding farmers, with New Netherland providing the glaring exception. The bases of prosperity were firmly established, with the tobacco staple uniquely distinguishing the economy of Maryland and Virginia, and New England moving swiftly to exploit its advantages for fishing and shipping.

Founding the American Colonies, 1583–1660, constitutes a volume in The New American Nation Series, a comprehensive and cooperative study of the history of the area now embraced in the United States from the days of discovery to our own time. Wallace Notestein has already examined the English bases of colonization. David B. Quinn will consider, in a forthcoming volume, the problem of early exploration of the areas herein under review; while a volume by Wilcomb E. Washburn will explore in full detail the course of Indian-white relations, a topic which has been considered here only peripherally. Finally, Louis B. Wright has interpreted the cultural life of the era in a volume already published in this series.

HENRY STEELE COMMAGER
RICHARD B. MORRIS

Preface

THE founding of the American colonies has fascinated historians for scores of years, as a voluminous library testifies. This volume recounts the absorbing story in the light of recent research, covering the years between 1583 and 1660 and describing colonizing efforts from Newfoundland to southern Virginia and the British West Indies. After many faltering starts in the late sixteenth century and not a few outright failures, hardy English adventurers succeeded in founding their first permanent settlement in 1607. By 1660 seven colonies were flourishing on the mainland, the islands were thriving, and the population, especially in Virginia and Massachusetts, was increasing by leaps and bounds.

The earliest colonists brought much of their social and political heritage with them from England. The impulse to retain and enlarge self-government was strong, because many of these men valued government by consent of the governed. Fortune favored them in their aspiration because England, preoccupied after 1640 with political troubles of its own, allowed the colonists considerable latitude. From the start, too, the colonists discarded feudal forms that had shackled them in England for generations. They wanted to hold their land, wherever possible, in fee simple and rid themselves of feudal encumbrances. Thus the proprietors of Maryland had to modify their manorial plans, while Sir Ferdinando Gorges, who strove for years to establish a feudal fief in New England, was completely thwarted.

Religion loomed large in the founding and development of the American colonies: the Virginia Company, following Spain's example, attempted to Christianize the Indians; Lord Baltimore endeavored to attract other than Roman Catholics to Maryland, thus launching a unique experiment in that colony; the Puritans of Massachusetts sought a new environment in which to build a City of God free from the restraints of an impure church; and the Pilgrims of Plymouth and the Independents of Rhode Island satisfied their religious cravings by molding beliefs and churches to suit their own inclinations. Clearly, "Americanization" was at work in the sphere of religion as well as in patterns of government and landholding.

During the first two generations, the colonists made substantial economic progress. They began to produce money crops: tobacco in the South and grain and livestock in New England. While most of the settlers devoted themselves to agriculture, there was also substantial development of trade and commerce, from town to town, from inlet to inlet, and finally across the ocean. New England, and Boston especially, took the lead with exports of fish, cattle, and grain. By 1660 Boston teemed with marketing and shipping activities, and her merchants and shipowners were reaching out to Virginia and Maryland, to the West Indies, and above all to England. Cash crops and shipping had endowed these young colonies with a source of wealth greater than the gold of Peru and the fabled pearls of the Indies.

In a general account such as this, the indebtedness of the writers is overwhelmingly great. As the bibliography reveals, there has been a large interest in the early American colonies during the past two decades. Our greatest debt is to the late Charles M. Andrews, whose four-volume work, *The Colonial Period of American History,* has influenced every historian who has followed him in this field. We are indebted to the writings of A. L. Rowse and David B. Quinn for preliminary material, to Richard B. Morton for his study of colonial Virginia, to Perry Miller and Edmund S. Morgan for their work on the Puritans, to Darrett B. Rutman for his contributions on the Massachusetts economy, to Wesley Frank Craven for his writing on the Southern Colonies, and to many others. Samuel Eliot Morison, John Jennings of the Virginia Historical Society, and William A. Parish of the Huntington Library have given assistance with the illustrations. I am especially grateful to Dr. Floyd Shumway for his collaboration. His assistance in elaborating the manuscript and enriching the bibliographical material has been invaluable. Dr. Richard B. Morris, himself an authority in this field, has been a most helpful and forbearing editor. I am indebted also to the reference staffs of the Henry E. Huntington Library, San Marino, and the Harrison Memorial Library, Carmel, and to my wife, Sara Wise Pomfret, for aid in checking and proofreading.

Carmel, California   JOHN E. POMFRET

CHAPTER 1

Prelude to Settlement

WHEN the great era of exploration began early in the fifteenth century, England showed no interest in the quest for sea routes to the Orient. The nation was exhausted at the beginning of the period after its efforts in the Hundred Years' War, and it shortly suffered the double affliction of economic depression and the Wars of the Roses. England shook off the worst of its economic troubles by the end of the century, and the Tudor dynasty restored domestic tranquillity, but the new rulers were at first too busy consolidating their control to concern themselves with the possibility of profitable overseas adventure.[1]

Meanwhile the Portuguese, led by Prince Henry the Navigator, pushed southward along the east coast of Africa, rounded the Cape of Good Hope in 1487, and shortly thereafter established a monopolistic direct trade with the Far East. Spain retaliated by exploring westward, and Columbus' discoveries were at first believed to be part of the Asian continent. Under Cortés, Pizarro, and other military leaders, the Spanish soon spread-eagled the West Indies, Peru, and Mexico and fanned out from these bases to explore the South

---

[1] A. L. Rowse argues in "Tudor Expansion: The Transition from Medieval to Modern History," *William and Mary Quarterly*, XIV (July, 1957), 309–316, that the Tudors had to pull England out of the Middle Ages and create a vigorous centralized government before the nation could undertake colonization in the New World.

American coast from the Orinoco to the Rio de la Plata. The pope forestalled a struggle for overseas supremacy between these two Catholic powers by dividing the New World between them, awarding Brazil to Portugal and reserving the rest for Spain.[2]

Like England, France was content to lag, although its fishermen, particularly those from the Basque provinces, developed some familiarity with the banks off Newfoundland. Not until 1524 did Verrazano, an Italian navigator in the French service, undertake a voyage that carried him from Florida to Newfoundland, and in the 1530's Cartier of Saint-Malo made his two exploratory visits to the St. Lawrence that assured France an undisputed claim to Canada. Admiral Gaspard de Coligny, the only French statesman dedicated to overseas expansion, encouraged Jean Ribault to establish Huguenot colonies in Carolina and Florida in 1562 and 1564, but this venture had no permanent consequences, because the Spanish wiped out both settlements within a short time.[3]

The first of England's Tudor monarchs, Henry VII, encouraged foreign trade, but his interest in exploration was limited to sponsorship of the voyages of the Cabots. In 1497 John Cabot touched at Cape Breton, explored the coast of Nova Scotia, and came within sight of Newfoundland, and the next year he sailed south along the coast as far as Chesapeake Bay. These are the earliest occasions on which English vessels are conclusively known to have touched the American mainland, although there is some likelihood that Bristol merchants had previously reached the "island of Brazil." John Cabot's son, Sebastian, apparently discovered Hudson Strait in 1508–9, but his later claim that he had found a Northwest Passage to the Orient stirred little interest in England, and in discouragement he accepted employment in the service of Spain.[4]

---

[2] Charles M. Andrews, *The Colonial Period of American History* (4 vols., New Haven, Conn., 1934–38), I, 6–17, gives a succinct account of the early Portuguese and Spanish overseas activity. For more extensive treatments of the entire outward thrust by the European nations, see Arthur P. Newton (ed.), *The Great Age of Discovery* (London, 1932), and John H. Parry, *The Age of Reconaissance* (2d ed., New York, 1964).

[3] A. L. Rowse, *The Elizabethans and America* (New York, 1959), pp. 6–9, discusses French overseas activity during these years, stressing that lack of support by the royal family predestined the effort to relative failure.

[4] There are several excellent Cabot biographies. Henry Harrisse, *John Cabot, the Discoverer of North-America, and Sebastian His Son: A Chapter in the Maritime History of England Under the Tudors, 1496–1557* (London, 1896), is

Restless, energetic Henry VIII never found time for involvement in any sort of exploring activity, but during the brief reign of his successor, Edward VI, there was some revival of interest, encouraged by Northumberland and founded on the belief that an Arctic route to the northeast would lead to Cathay and fabulous riches. In 1553, the year that Queen Mary came to the throne, Sir Hugh Willoughby set out to chart the Northeast Passage, accompanied by Richard Chancellor as his chief pilot. Willoughby perished when his ship became icebound in Icelandic waters, but Chancellor went on to the mouth of the Dvina in another ship and then made his way on land to Moscow. There he obtained an audience with the czar and was able to establish trade routes from England to Russia and beyond.[5] English merchants founded the Muscovy Company in 1555 to exploit this opportunity, and two years later its remarkable agent, Anthony Jenkinson, reached Bokhara, making contacts that eventually led to overland trade with China. Jenkinson served England in Russia until 1572.[6] Meanwhile, others tried their luck with the Northeast Passage. In 1556 Stephen Burrough navigated as far as the Vaigatz Islands at the mouth of the Ob River, and Arthur Pet and Charles Jackman penetrated a little beyond that point in 1580.[7] The quest was becoming manifestly hopeless, and English mariners lost interest for the time being in exploration in that direction.

England made another foray during this period along the western coast of Africa. Bristol merchants already had some modest familiarity with sea routes to the south, having previously ventured as far as Spain, the Canaries, and the Madeiras. Defying the Portuguese monopoly, which had the support of papal bulls and was also buttressed by Hispanic-Portuguese treaties, venturesome Eng-

---

thorough, whereas Charles R. Beazley, *John and Sebastian Cabot: The Discovery of North America* (London, 1908; reprinted New York, 1964), is somewhat more readable. The most current and scholarly work is James A. Williamson, *The Cabot Voyages and Bristol Discovery Under Henry VII* (Cambridge, England, 1962), which incorporates new information unearthed since his *The Voyages of the Cabots and the English Discovery of North America Under Henry VII and Henry VIII* (London, 1929).

5 Sir William Foster, *England's Quest for Eastern Trade* (London, 1933), is the best account of the Willoughby-Chancellor expedition.

6 Douglas Bell, *Elizabethan Seamen* (Philadelphia, 1936), pp. 20–22.

7 *Ibid.*, pp. 19–20, 22–28.

lish captains now began sailing farther and farther from home in search of commercial opportunity. The most successful of these navigators, Thomas Windham, made his first trip in 1551, and he succeeded in establishing not only a Barbary trade in sugar and fruit but also a Gold Coast trade in gold, pepper, and ivory. This activity continued after and in spite of Mary's marriage to Philip of Spain.[8]

English exploration during the reigns of the early Tudors was sporadic, unsystematic, and largely unrewarding, but when Elizabeth I became queen in 1558, a new mood gave promise of new and more effective effort. The public, it is true, remained unaware of the significance of overseas enterprise, but a number of influential people were becoming actively concerned. There was growing interest in court circles, even though Sir William Cecil (Lord Burghley after 1581) was a dampening influence, and the queen herself was anxious to encourage discovery and colonization. Sir Walter Raleigh, the Earl of Leicester, and Leicester's illegitimate son, Robert Dudley, were active enthusiasts, as in lesser measure were Sir Francis Walsingham, Sir Christopher Hatton, and Sir Edward Dyer.[9] Intellectual leaders like the two Richard Hakluyts, who were cousins, and Thomas Hariot and John Dee were busily publicizing the latest geographical, mathematical, and navigational knowledge. The younger Hakluyt spent five years in Paris writing *The Principal Navigations, Voyages, Traffiques and Discoveries of the English Nation . . .* , which he dedicated in 1589 to Mr. Secretary Walsingham.[10] Allusions to new lands began appearing in plays such as *Macbeth, Othello,* and *The Tempest* and in other forms of popular literature.

Not only was there a new mood, but a variety of changed conditions combined to make overseas activity attractive and even urgent. More capital was available for investment than heretofore, much of it derived from the sale of monasteries. An increasing number of

[8] James A. Williamson, *Maritime Enterprise, 1485–1558* (Oxford, 1913), pp. 274–284, gives detailed information about Windham's adventures.

[9] Drake renamed his flagship the *Golden Hind* to pay tribute to Hatton, whose crest contained that mythical creature. For biographical treatments, see Eric St. John Brooks, *Sir Christopher Hatton: Queen Elizabeth's Favourite* (London, 1947), and Ralph M. Sargent, *At the Court of Queen Elizabeth: The Life and Lyrics of Sir Edward Dyer* (London, 1935).

[10] (London, 1589; reprinted in full, 12 vols., Glasgow, 1903–5; now in 2 vols., Cambridge, England, 1965).

men were engaged in importing and exporting, and their trading companies were now well enough developed to undertake exploration and eventually colonization. Some of these merchants not only were ambitious and alert to beckoning opportunity abroad but possessed considerable organizational ability. Foremost in their ranks was Sir Thomas Smythe of London, who became the driving force in the founding of the East India Company and of the corporations responsible for settling Virginia and Bermuda. There were even people available for colonization, because the enclosure of fields, which drove farmers off the land, and an increase in the birth rate had combined to produce a surplus population, and acute unemployment between 1530 and 1635 added to the attractiveness of emigration. In addition to capital, technique, and manpower, the nation possessed a large fishing fleet, manned by experienced captains and seamen. If England needed justification for its entrance into the competition for trade routes and overseas possessions, it could fall back on the new theory of mercantilism, which taught that every country should increase its supply of bullion by increasing exports, taxing imports, and developing colonies to serve as suppliers of its raw materials and markets for its manufactures.[11]

The early Tudor monarchs encouraged a close alliance with Spain and took no steps that would have challenged Spanish overseas domination, but Elizabeth reversed this policy. She did not inaugurate her new program abruptly, but she did give prompt evidence of her point of view toward expansion, when at the start of her reign she encouraged full-scale resumption of the African trade. The queen at first replied softly to Portuguese and Spanish protests, but eventually she refused flatly to halt the trade, and in 1580 Cecil informed Spain's ambassador that England recognized neither the papal lines of demarcation nor the Spanish-Portuguese treaties. English policy thereafter stood for freedom of the seas and permanent occupation as the test of ownership of overseas territory. Elizabeth also claimed the entire North American mainland on the basis of John Cabot's discoveries.[12]

Elizabeth's reign quickly won renown for exploration and com-

11 James A. Williamson, *The Tudor Age* (New York, 1953), provides an outstanding analysis of early English expansion and the forces that caused it.

12 Max Savelle, "The International Approach of Early Angloamerican History," in Ray A. Billington (ed.), *The Reinterpretation of Early American History* (San Marino, Calif., 1966), pp. 201–209, discusses this complex subject.

mercial activity. Initiating a chain of great English enterprises were Sir John Hawkins' three voyages between 1562 and 1569. The son of a notable Plymouth merchant seaman who had been the first of his countrymen to visit Guinea and Brazil, Hawkins began his career by continuing his father's regular trade with the Canary Islands. He became aware that Spanish colonists in the West Indies needed laborers and were endeavoring to supplement the inadequate native Indian supply by importing Negro slaves from Africa. Deciding to participate in this activity, which at the time impressed nobody as inhumane,[13] Hawkins sailed to Guinea, picked up about three hundred slaves, and delivered them to the West Indies, where he sold them at great profit in spite of Spanish orders that the colonists were to avoid dealing with the Englishman. Thwarted in the hope that the Spanish king would give him official approval, Hawkins gave up the pretense that he operated in the king's service and advertised thereafter that he represented his own monarch. His second voyage in 1565 was as successful as the first, and he also took the opportunity of exploring the whole Florida coastline. On the way home after the third profitable visit to the West Indies in 1569, Hawkins took his ten-ship squadron into the port of Mexico, San Juan de Ulloa (now Vera Cruz), in order to make repairs. The new viceroy, Don Martin Enríquez, arrived with a large Spanish fleet and secured permission to enter the harbor by assuring Hawkins of his peaceful intentions. Enríquez then attacked the English, killing and imprisoning more than one hundred seamen. The *Minion* escaped with two hundred aboard, and young Francis Drake got away successfully on the little *Judith*.[14]

England under Elizabeth had been moving cautiously toward greater diplomatic independence of Spain, but this treacherous assault now ended abruptly a friendship dating back to Henry VII. To the ensuing struggle for world power England brought the twin advantages of youth and vigor. In contrast, Spain had already begun

[13] For the equation in English minds of African Negroes and slavery, see Winthrop D. Jordan, *White Over Black* (Chapel Hill, N.C., 1968), pp. 60 *et seq*.

[14] James A. Williamson has written two biographies, *Sir John Hawkins: The Time and the Man* (Oxford, 1927), and *Hawkins of Plymouth: A New History of Sir John Hawkins and of Other Members of His Family Prominent in Tudor England* (London, 1949). See also Sir Clements R. Markham (ed.), *The Hawkins' Voyages During the Reigns of Henry VIII, Queen Elizabeth, and James I* (London, 1878).

to lapse into crippling rigidities, conspicuous among which was religious intolerance, epitomized by the inquisitions. The Duke of Alva's suppression of revolt in the Netherlands in 1567, which included 18,000 executions, outraged Protestants all over Europe, and San Juan de Ulloa and Antwerp combined to unite the Protestant nations in common cause against Spain.[15] Between the time of Enríquez' attack and 1577, English privateers contrived to keep the Spanish colonies in the West Indies in turmoil. Sent out by the Hawkins brothers in 1570–71, Drake raided Venta de las Cruces, and he came back from his 1572–73 trip with £40,000 in stolen treasure, enabling the Hawkins family to recover in part the great loss they had suffered at San Juan.[16]

Drake's West Indian raids earned him notoriety, but he soon went on to greater fame as a navigator and explorer. Rumor had it that somewhere in the southern waters of the Pacific lay Terra Australis, a large land mass rich in precious metals, and Sir Richard Grenville, William Hawkins, and other Englishmen became interested in sending out an expedition to find it. They purchased two ships for that purpose but could take no immediate action, because the queen refused permission. Elizabeth changed her mind three years later, and Drake, with her backing as well as that of Leicester, Walsingham, Hawkins, and others, took command of what in reality became a significant national enterprise. While the queen busied herself quieting the suspicions of Philip II of Spain, Drake set sail in 1579, maintaining secrecy by not revealing to the crew that they were bound for the Pacific until they reached the equator. Passing through the Strait of Magellan in record time, Drake then hit strong winds that prevented him from continuing westward. He therefore proceeded up the west coast of South America and captured the rich treasure ship Cacafuego off Panama. He stated frankly to his Spanish captives that his motive was to revenge San Juan and to regain the £2 million his cousins, the Hawkinses, had lost there.

15 Rowse, Elizabethans and America, pp. 10–11, 31–32, is a particularly penetrating discussion of England's change of attitude toward Spain.
16 Arthur P. Newton, The European Nations in the West Indies, 1493–1688 (London, 1933, reprinted New York, 1967), pp. 95–107, is a detailed account of English privateering exploits in that area between 1573 and 1590. Rowse, Expansion of Elizabethan England, pp. 179–180, describes Drake's visits that began the raids on the Spanish Main.

He proposed to continue his attacks until Spain agreed to relinquish its trade monopoly and recognize the right of other nations to plant settlements in lands not yet occupied by any white men. Drake continued on up the west coast of North America to British Columbia, where rough water compelled him to give up his search for the fabled Strait of Anian. On his return, near the Golden Gate, he proclaimed California a dominion of the queen under the name of New Albion. He then sailed around the world by way of the Spice Islands, South Africa, and the Gold Coast. The first Englishman to cross the Pacific, following in the wake only of Magellan and Saavedra, and the first to enter the Indian Ocean, navigated previously only by the Portuguese Vasco da Gama early in 1498, Drake added enormously to England's seafaring prestige. The queen saw fit to ignore mounting Spanish protests about her navigator's accomplishment.[17]

The Drake voyage provoked a flurry of subsequent undertakings. Several Englishmen attempted to repeat his circumnavigation of the globe, but only Thomas Cavendish succeeded, making the trip in 1586–87 and capturing the Manila galleon with a rich cargo along the way. Cavendish's luck ran out in 1591 when he and John Davis encountered fierce weather in the Pacific. Famine and disease began to cut down the crew, and Cavendish himself was among those who died. After leaving California, Davis tried to find a Northwest Passage around Asia, but a mounting death toll and an increasingly unseaworthy ship forced him to turn homeward. By the time he

[17] It is scarcely surprising that a number of able biographers have chosen Drake as a subject. Sir Julian S. Corbett, *Drake and the Tudor Navy: With a History of the Rise of England as a Maritime Power* (2 vols., London, 1898–99; reprinted, New York, 1965), retains interest and value in spite of its age. Zelia Nuttall (trans. and ed.), *New Light on Drake: A Collection of Documents Relating to His Voyage of Circumnavigation, 1577–1580* (London, 1914), introduced new evidence about the voyage. William C. H. Wood, *Elizabethan Sea-Dogs: A Chronicle of Drake and His Companions* (3d ed., New Haven, Conn., 1921), is a lively account. More scholarly and comprehensive is Henry R. Wagner, *Sir Francis Drake's Voyage Around the World: Its Aims and Its Achievements* (San Francisco, 1926). John D. Upcott, *Sir Francis Drake and the Beginnings of English Sea Power* (London, 1927), is intended more for popular consumption, as is Edward F. Benson, *Sir Francis Drake* (New York, 1927). That able saltwater historian, James A. Williamson, has provided two studies, *The Age of Drake* (4th ed., London, 1960), which considers the man and his period, and *Sir Francis Drake* (2d ed., London, 1966), which emphasizes the man himself.

finally reached England, only sixteen men were still alive. Richard Hawkins, son of Sir John, was the last of the Elizabethans to enter the Pacific, but by then the Spanish were on the alert, and they captured young Hawkins and kept him prisoner for many years.[18]

The Northwest Passage had powerful advocates. The great Humphrey Gilbert, arguing the matter before the queen, finally won over Anthony Jenkinson, chief proponent of the Northeast Passage; together these two men petitioned for a monopoly of the passage, the right to govern whatever territory they discovered, and generous trading privileges. Gilbert's "Discourse to Prove a Passage by the North-West to Cathay and the East-Indies," circulated in manuscript in 1576 just when the discouraged Muscovy Company was about ready to give up looking for a Northeast Passage, played a part in initiating the Forbisher expedition that year.[19]

Martin Forbisher sailed with the queen's blessing, although characteristically she did not invest in what appeared to be an unpromising venture. He rounded the southern tip of Greenland and crossed over into Baffin Bay, believing that the broad channel leading into Hudson Bay was the long-sought-for passage. The public exhibited interest when he brought home samples of a black ore, and this made it easy to finance a second voyage, the queen herself contributing £500 and a ship. Frobisher paid little attention to exploration on this visit but returned carrying 200 tons of the ore in his hold, further stimulating the general mood of speculation. The queen now put up £1,350 for a larger expedition. The young Earl of Oxford contributed £2,000, and even his father-in-law, the prudent Lord Burghley, subscribed £100. Fifteen ships sailed west in 1578, stopping to pick up forty-one miners at Plymouth. Frobisher once again penetrated Hudson Strait, convinced that he had found the true passage, but his main preoccupation was gathering more ore. Unfortunately, the ore turned out to be valueless, and the queen and her fellow investors lost all the money they had ventured. Frobisher fell into temporary obscurity, and his wife and

---

[18] Rowse, *Expansion of Elizabethan England*, pp. 188–190.
[19] George B. Manhart, *The English Search for a Northwest Passage in the Time of Queen Elizabeth* (Philadelphia, 1924), pp. 3–30, discusses all the arguments advanced to prove that there was such a route to the Orient, of which Gilbert's was the most influential.

children were reduced to actual want. For the next few years enthusiasm for a Northwest Passage was at a low ebb.[20]

Adrian Gilbert, Humphrey's brother, obtained patents in 1585 authorizing him to explore and trade in the direction of the Northwest Passage, and he selected his friend and neighbor, the able navigator John Davis, to conduct the voyages that began that year. Before Davis sailed, he and Gilbert discussed the proposed route with John Dee, the famous protoscientist. This first expedition reached Baffin Land, 66 degrees north, where Davis and his crew visited the Eskimos and saw thousands of tons of the black ore. They returned a year later but added little data because of unfavorable weather. They spent a good deal of the time observing the Eskimos, whose witchcraft and enchantments interested them and whom they found to be clever thieves as well as formidable wrestlers. The Englishmen did manage to bring home a cargo of sealskins, and they made one final voyage to latitude 73 north, but interest lapsed again, for this was Armada time, and the Spanish war preempted men's attention.[21]

The last English attempts to find the Northwest Passage during this period were partly a response to Dutch commercial rivalry which began with the coming of peace in 1604. While employed by the Dutch East India Company in 1609, Henry Hudson failed to persuade his crew to continue through the fog and ice toward what he hoped was the Northeast Passage. Making the best of the situation, he then turned westward to attempt the Northwest Passage. This change of plan resulted in the famous voyage of the *Half Moon* from the Chesapeake to the coast of Maine and the first penetration into the Delaware and Hudson rivers. Sir Thomas Smythe and some of his English merchant friends became interested and backed Hudson's next voyage in 1610, when Hudson proceeded successfully through Hudson Strait to the great bay that

[20] Two men familiar with the sea have written about Frobisher. William McFee, *The Life of Sir Martin Frobisher* (New York, 1928), is a fine biography. Vilhjalmur Stefansson (ed.), *The Three Voyages of Martin Frobisher in Search of a passage to Cathay and India by the North-West, A.D. 1576–8* (2 vols., London, 1938), reprints seven contemporary records and adds valuable comment about Frobisher and other explorers of that period.

[21] Sir Albert Hastings Markham, *Voyages and Works of John Davis the Navigator* (London, 1880), and Sir Clements R. Markham, *Life of John Davis* (London, 1891).

bears his name. His ship became frozen in the ice in James Bay, the southern inlet. After surviving the cold months, Hudson's crew mutinied and cast him adrift in a small boat in June, 1611, and left him to perish.[22] Smythe, however, was not easily discouraged, and he later sent out expeditions under William Baffin, who in 1616 reached Davis Strait at latitude 78 degrees north, the farthest point yet achieved.[23]

The English were slow to make their way around the Cape of Good Hope to India and the East Indies. While they indulged in their extensive and futile search for a Northwest Passage, the Portuguese were pioneering the route around Africa and were developing the thousand-ton carrack, twice the size of English merchantmen and several times as practical for long-haul cargo voyages. Then at the beginning of the seventeenth century the enterprising Dutch made overseas commerce a national goal, and they soon impinged upon the Portuguese route around the Cape. They became students of navigation and shipbuilding and experts in maintaining the health and welfare of their crews. The English were at a serious disadvantage when they finally became interested in using the southern route to reach the Far East.

The indefatigable Sir Thomas Smythe and his London friends organized and backed the first English voyages around the Cape of Good Hope, and they employed adventurous sea captains to find ways to inaugurate trade with the Orient. Queen Elizabeth authorized a trip to the East Indies by three ships under the command of James Lancaster in 1591, in response to a petition by London merchants. Shortly after rounding the Cape, Lancaster lost two of his ships, and by the time he reached Ceylon his crew was ridden with sickness and scurvy. At that point he turned back and audaciously sailed west toward Brazil. Making for the West Indies because of starvation, he underwent hardships in the Caribbean but finally reached Bermuda far to the north, becoming the

[22] Llewelyn Powys, *Henry Hudson* (New York, 1928), is the best of several useful biographies, and Lawrence J. Burpee, "The Fate of Henry Hudson," *Canadian Historical Review*, XXI (Dec., 1940), 401–406, contains the best available information about Hudson's death.

[23] Sir Clements R. Markham (ed.), *The Voyages of William Baffin, 1612–1622* (London, 1881). For a brief account see Nellis M. Crouse, *In Quest of the Western Ocean* (New York, 1928), pp. 179–184, or John B. Brebner, *The Explorers of North America, 1492–1806* (3d ed., Cleveland, 1964), p. 177.

first Englishman to touch there. Some of the company made off with the ship, leaving Lancaster and the remainder of his associates to return aboard a French vessel.[24] But the English were not to be denied, for there was rich treasure in the East and many prizes to be taken. In 1592 Sir Robert Dudley equipped three ships, but one went down off the Cape of Good Hope, another on the Malay coast, and the third in the Indian Ocean.[25] Encouraged by the queen, Lancaster then sailed four ships to the East Indies, taking a great cargo of pepper aboard in Sumatra and Java and capturing a rich carrack. He established a "factory" and then brought all four ships safely home, thus beginning England's trade with the Indies. In 1601 Sir Henry Middleton became the first to reach the Moluccas.[26] By this time the English were engaged in rivalry with the Dutch, who themselves were striving to break Portugal's monopoly.

Parliament chartered the East India Company in 1600 and gave it a trade monopoly in the entire Eastern Hemisphere, but Dutch dominance in the Spice Islands caused the English to concentrate on India. John Mildenhall traveled there on the overland route by way of Aleppo, and in spite of Portuguese opposition, he was able to secure trading privileges. In 1607 the company sent out William Hawkins, who established an English "trading factory" on the west coast at Surat. To combat powerful Portuguese influence, Sir Thomas Smythe managed the appointment of a special ambassador, Sir Thomas Roe, who took a strong stance and put on a show of naval strength at Goa, thereby obtaining a grant authorizing permanent trade. Starting in 1608, the East India Company sent out ships annually. The opening of a factory at Pasulipatam enabled trade to expand north to Bengal and south to Madras. In 1612 the English reached Siam and the Shan states and soon touched Japan. In short, in the course of a single generation England caught up with Spain and Portugal, the nations that had shared monopoly of the seas for a century.[27]

24 Sir William Foster (ed.), *The Voyages of Sir James Lancaster to Brazil and the East Indies, 1591–1603* (rev. ed., London, 1940), contains contemporary accounts by participants. See also Sir Clements R. Markham, *The Voyages of Sir James Lancaster, Kt., to the East Indies . . .* (London, 1877).

25 Rowse, *Expansion of Elizabethan England*, pp. 201–202.

26 Sir William Foster (ed.), *The Voyage of Sir Henry Middleton to the Moluccas, 1604–1606* (London, 1943).

27 Sir William Foster has edited two books on England's establishment of

For long years the English thought of America merely as an obstacle blocking the way to the Indies. But two small groups—men of action like Humphrey Gilbert, Walter Raleigh, and Richard Grenville, and thoughtful men like John Dee, the Hakluyts, and Adrian Gilbert—took the view that the New World might be important to England for its own sake. These enthusiasts had access to the queen and her minister, Sir Francis Walsingham, who gave them a sympathetic hearing, yet actual progress was painfully slow. Following his first Florida expedition, Jean Ribault came to England in 1562 and published his report, the first document issued there dealing with a North American enterprise. A plan for a joint Anglo-French undertaking under Ribault fell through, however, as did a projected Florida colony under Sir Richard Hawkins. Then Sir Humphrey Gilbert advocated still another colony in California "that would care for such needy people of our country which now trouble the commonwealth." Meanwhile, during the 1570's English fishermen followed the Basques and Bretons to Newfoundland waters. Anthony Parkhurst, who had been on the St. Lawrence on behalf of Bristol merchants, made a plea for a permanent settlement in Newfoundland to protect the English fisheries, which had expanded from thirty to fifty sail in four years. He argued that this could be done without difficulty, since the English ships were better armed than those of their rivals. True, when the war with Spain broke out, Bernard Drake was able to take the whole Spanish Basque fishing fleet, but the Basques and Bretons proved more tenacious than Parkhurst expected them to be.

There was no real possibility of progress until the late seventies, because until then the time was not ripe and the future leaders were too young. During those earlier years Adrian Gilbert was studying maps and learning all he could about geography, to which his cousin, the elder Hakluyt, had introduced him as a boy. The younger Hakluyt was at Christ Church, Oxford, absorbed in mathematics and geography. There he met such scholars as Thomas

trade with India, *Early Travels in India, 1583–1619* (London, 1921), and *The Embassy of Sir Thomas Roe to the Court of the Great Mogul, 1615–1619, as Narrated in His Journal and Correspondence* (2 vols. in 1, reprinted Nendeln, Liechtenstein, 1967).

Hariot and Thomas Warner, and while working later (1583–88) at the Paris embassy, he immersed himself in continental geographical knowledge.[28] In 1580 Hakluyt began issuing tract after tract advocating "western planting." He gathered and disseminated minute information about the early English voyages to America.[29] The younger Hakluyt was highly conscious of the rivalry with Spain, and in *Divers Voyages Touching the Discoverie of America and the Island Adjacent* he urged England to take possession of all North American territory as yet unoccupied by the Spaniards. In his dedicatory epistle to Philip Sidney, he bewailed his country's failure, after ninety years, to have occupied "the firm and temperate places" not yet taken by the Spanish and Portuguese. Contending that Philip II was overextended and that Spain's population could not support such a great empire, he claimed that Spanish initiative was visibly weakening and that England's opportunity was at hand.[30]

The adventurous men were busy, too. Queen Elizabeth granted Humphrey Gilbert letters patent in 1578 authorizing him to occupy lands not possessed by other sovereigns and to keep for himself or his assigns an area 200 leagues (600 miles) in extent. Gilbert received the right to govern and to make any laws provided they were not contrary to the laws of England. To accomplish his purpose of founding a colony, Gilbert was destined to expend his own fortune and that of his wife. Toward the close of the six-year period of grace allowed him to get a colony launched, Gilbert marshaled five small ships, one of which was supplied by Raleigh, then a favorite of the queen. Elizabeth doubted Gilbert's ability to command the expedition, because despite his dedication he was prone to spells of rage and bad judgment. This was clearly a colonizing and not a commercial

28 Henry Stevens, *Thomas Hariot, the Mathematician, the Philosopher and the Scholar* . . . (London, 1900).

29 *The Principal Navigations, Voyages, Traffiques and Discoveries of the English Nation* . . . (London, 1589; reprinted in 2 vols., Cambridge, England, 1965). For selected highlights from this large work, see Edward J. Payne and Charles R. Beazley (eds.), *Voyages of the Elizabethan Seamen to America: Selected Narratives From the 'Principal Navigations' of Hakluyt* (Oxford, 1907).

30 George B. Parks, *Richard Hakluyt and the English Voyages* (2d ed., New York, 1961), is an excellent biography, and there is a good, briefer treatment in the introduction of Eva G. R. Taylor (ed.), *The Original Writings & Correspondence of the Two Richard Hakluyts* (2 vols., London, 1935).

expedition, since the cadre of 260 men included carpenters and masons as well as miners and metal refiners. The ships carried trinkets and other gifts with which to win over the natives. Gilbert made a landing at St. Johns, Newfoundland, in 1583, and he took possession in the queen's name, making Newfoundland the first and oldest overseas colony. Moving southward along the coast, Gilbert encountered one misfortune after another. A ship foundered, with a loss of many supplies and one hundred lives, and then a second ship went down, and this time Gilbert himself was lost.[31]

Sir Walter Raleigh took over where his half-brother, Sir Humphrey, left off. A complex man combining many attractive and some disagreeable qualities, Raleigh shared Gilbert's imagination and daring.[32] When not in close attendance on the queen, he occupied himself in planning an expedition to the Atlantic seaboard, and to this end he obtained a royal charter bestowing even greater powers than Sir Humphrey had enjoyed. Although Elizabeth refused to contribute funds, her moral support was of great help, and she agreed to let him name the plantation Virginia in her honor. As soon as the charter was granted in 1584, Raleigh sent two small ships on a scouting expedition to the Carolina coast, and his captains reported an earthly paradise—fertile soil, plentiful fishing, and friendly natives. Two attractive young Indian chieftains, Manteo and Wanchese, came back to London as partial proof of the good report.

The first English colony in America was founded in 1585 under Raleigh's direction but without his direct participation. To his disappointment the queen would not permit him to leave the court, and so his cousin, Sir Richard Grenville, went in his place, commanding three ships of 100 to 150 tons and another of 50 tons.

---

31 William G. Gosling, *The Life of Sir Humphrey Gilbert* (London, 1911), remains scholarly and useful in spite of its age. David B. Quinn (ed.), *The Voyages and Colonizing Enterprises of Sir Humphrey Gilbert* (2 vols., London, 1940), includes a fine sketch and the major documents relating to his career.

32 There have been many good biographies of Raleigh. Edward Edwards, *Life of Sir Walter Raleigh* (London, 1868), and William Stebbing, *Sir Walter Raleigh: A Biography* (Oxford, 1899), both remain valuable in spite of their age, particularly the latter work. More recent books, all of them superior, are Milton Waldman, *Sir Walter Raleigh* (New York, 1943); Ernest A. Strathman, *Sir Walter Raleigh: A Study in Elizabethan Skepticism* (New York, 1951); Willard M. Wallace, *Sir Walter Raleigh* (Princeton, N.J., 1959); and A. L. Rowse, *Sir Walter Raleigh, His Family and Private Life* (New York, 1962).

Grenville successfully planted his passengers at Roanoke Island on Pimlico Sound, and the importance of what he did lies in the fact that it was the first of a number of related attempts to found a permanent English settlement.[33] This expedition, like others that followed, carried a number of notables: John White, whose maps and illustrations have established him as the first English watercolor painter;[34] Thomas Hariot, author of *Brief and True Report* (1588), the first scientific observation of America by an Englishman; Ralph Lane, one of the queen's equerries; and young Thomas Cavendish, who in 1586–88 was to repeat Drake's trip around the globe.

Grenville did not stay to administer the settlement he had founded. He landed his colonists, together with livestock brought from the West Indies, and then, after exploring to the south, he returned to England to obtain supplies and reinforcements for the next year. Ralph Lane remained behind in charge of one hundred men. Because dangerous shoals surrounded Roanoke and it possessed no deep anchorage, Lane explored northward toward Chesapeake Bay, the area favored by Hakluyt and destined to become the site of the first permanent settlement. Competition for the meager food supply available in the area irritated the Indians and resulted in several killings. Nevertheless Lane wrote home cheerfully, praising the soil and climate and stating that more horses and cattle would solve most of such few problems as confronted the colony. He advocated an expedition against Hispaniola and Puerto Rico to cut the Spanish lifeline.[35]

The original Roanoke settlement did not survive long. On his way home from a West Indian raid, Sir Francis Drake touched there and offered to give the settlers a boat and some supplies, because Grenville was long overdue. Before he could make delivery, a sudden hurricane came up, and Drake had to put to sea. This headlong withdrawal prompted the settlers to decide quickly to return to England with Drake while there was still time. Shortly after that,

[33] David B. Quinn (ed.), *The Roanoke Voyages, 1584–1590* (2 vols., London, 1955), is the authoritative reference for the brief career of the Roanoke settlement.

[34] *American Drawings of John White, 1577–1590* . . . (Chapel Hill, N.C., 1964).

[35] David B. Quinn, *Raleigh and the British Empire* (London, 1947), pp. 65–96. This book is another of the good Raleigh biographies, but its particular purpose is to relate the man's contributions to imperial development.

a ship sent by Raleigh arrived at the abandoned colony, and several weeks later Grenville himself came with additional men and supplies. Grenville, unfortunately, had lingered too long in the West Indies on the lookout for prizes. Disappointed, he sailed away, leaving fifteen men behind as a holding operation until he could reestablish the colony.[36]

In 1587 Raleigh dispatched an expedition of more than one hundred men and seventeen women to the colony under John White as governor. He ordered his captains first to search for survivors, then to sail north and settle in the Chesapeake Bay area. When the expedition reached Roanoke Island, the English found only abandoned houses. They learned from Manteo, then living on nearby Croatan Island, that Wanchese had driven the colonists from Roanoke. For his loyalty they granted Manteo the sacrament of baptism and named him Lord of Croatan. White left the new colonists at Roanoke without effective leadership and returned home for supplies. Undaunted, Raleigh and Grenville made preparations for an even larger expedition, but misfortune dogged their efforts. First, two little pinnaces were unable to get across the Atlantic, and then later, when Grenville was equipping his ships, he was ordered to Plymouth to fight the Armada. Being occupied with many things in 1587, Raleigh vested control of the colony in a governor and twelve assistants, and two years later he transferred the whole enterprise to a group of London merchants headed by Sir Thomas Smythe and William Sanderson.[37]

When John White finally arrived back at Roanoke with a three-ship expedition in 1590, he found the settlement deserted. A previously agreed-upon signal informed him that the colonists had taken refuge with friendly Croatans, but there was also clear evidence of looting by Indians. A storm blew up, White found it necessary to move his ships to the open sea, and he never made any effort to continue his search. Sir Francis Bacon commented scornfully, "It is the sinfullest thing in the world to forsake or destitute a plantation once in forwardness; for besides the dishonour, it is the guiltiness of blood of many commiserable persons."[38] There

---

36 A. L. Rowse, *Sir Richard Grenville of the Revenge* (2d ed., London, 1949).
37 Quinn, *Raleigh and the British Empire*, pp. 97–128.
38 Clark Sutherland Northrup (ed.), *The Essays of Francis Bacon* (Boston, 1908), p. 109.

has been conjecture ever since regarding the fate of the settlers. Some believe they perished on their way to the Chesapeake; others, that they were all killed; and others, that the few survivors were eventually absorbed by the Indians. The Lost Colony was one of the tragedies of English colonization in America, and it had the effect of postponing further efforts for a whole decade.

The Spaniards were aware of England's colonizing ambition and were disinclined to let it go unchallenged. They had reconnoitered Chesapeake Bay in 1572 and had a greater familiarity with the whole Atlantic coast than is generally recognized, and the possibility of invasion of what they called Florida alarmed them. To protect their interest, they decided to build a series of posts up the coast and to destroy any colony the English tried to establish. In 1588 Pedro Menéndez scouted as far north as the Chesapeake but discovered no English settlement. He strongly advised King Philip to conquer North America, lest some other nation, gaining the friendship of the natives, do so, pointing out that once the English secured a foothold, it would be difficult to dislodge them. All Spanish activity, however, came to a halt with the outbreak of war. Then the Armada sapped Spain's vitality, and Menéndez was unable to revive Spanish interest in North America. In 1599 Queen Elizabeth pressed for the principle of the open door in America, but no agreement was reached. The Spanish refused to accept the English position that there should be freedom of trade in all areas not effectively occupied. The English said nothing about colonization "beyond the [pope's] line," because they had no intention whatsoever of paying any heed to that restriction.[39]

The French under Henry IV, free of the war with Spain in 1598, resumed their interest in the New World. In 1603 the king gave a license to settle anywhere between 40 and 46 degrees north to Pierre du Guast, Sieur de Monts, and a year later that nobleman founded Port Royal in Acadia. The great Champlain, too, was

[39] David B. Quinn, "Some Spanish Reactions to Elizabethan Colonial Enterprises," Royal Historical Society *Transactions*, 5th ser., I (1951), 1–23. Irene A. Wright has edited and translated three volumes of documents which give illuminating evidence of Spanish reaction to English expansion: *Spanish Documents Concerning English Voyages to the Caribbean, 1527–1568* (London, 1929); *Documents Concerning English Voyages to the Spanish Main, 1569–1580* (London, 1932); and *Further English Voyages to Spanish America, 1583–1594* (London, 1951).

exploring these northern coasts, and in 1608 he consolidated French suzerainty in the St. Lawrence by founding Quebec. The French were actively challenging Spain's claim to North America, but their future rival was destined to be England.

The Roanoke disaster cooled English expansionist ardor briefly, but by the turn of the century that lusty nation was in the mood for new adventures. Captain Bartholomew Gosnold and Bartholomew Gilbert explored the Maine coast, Cape Cod, and Martha's Vineyard in 1602, and that same year Raleigh sent Samuel Mace to the Roanoke coast. In 1603 Gilbert took a ship to the Chesapeake to look for Lost Colony survivors and was killed by the Indians.[40] A number of men continued their active sponsorship of colonizing ventures, including the well-known Lord Arundel and the Earl of Southampton.[41] Two groups never lost interest: the London merchants, led by Sir Thomas Smythe, and the West Country fisheries and fur trading men, whose leader was Sir Ferdinando Gorges. From one was to spring Virginia; from the other, New England.

Merchants like Smythe and dreamers of empire like Gorges were relatively new types, made possible only because England had been transformed by an economic revolution that started about the middle of the fourteenth century and was finally terminating as the seventeenth century began. The transformation was initiated when English landowners, recognizing a rising demand for woolen clothing throughout Europe, decided to raise more sheep. To make this possible, they turned considerable land formerly cultivated by serfs into enclosed pastures. This change reduced the need for agricultural workers, but those who remained were able to escape from serfdom to become independent yeomen, tenant farmers, or hired laborers. Those serfs who were evicted moved into towns to try to learn new ways of supporting themselves, and the large number who could not make that

40 Rowse, *Elizabethans and America*, p. 62. This book and his *Expansion of Elizabethan England* are particularly useful for this entire period. For more information about Gosnold, see Warner Gookin, "Who Was Bartholomew Gosnold?" *William and Mary Quarterly*, VI (July, 1949), 398–415, and John Brereton, *A Briefe and True Relation* (London, 1602), which describes the 1602 expedition.
41 A. L. Rowse, *Shakespeare's Southampton, Patron of Virginia* (London, 1965).

transition successfully ended up as homeless vagrants. Enterprising Englishmen began organizing trading companies to take advantage of the increasing volume of business, and after 1600 there was ready capital available to invest in their ventures. This new class of merchants, of whom Sir Thomas Smythe was an outstanding example, gradually took the place of the foreigners who had in the past conducted such trade as had then existed.[42]

The long economic revolution was essentially complete at the beginning of the seventeenth century, but new forces kept the nation in economic ferment, and new theories were abroad in the world. Contributing factors included an unusually long period of peace starting in 1603, a rising standard of living for almost everyone except the very poor, and technological changes resulting from development of new manufacturing and trading methods.[43] The new economic philosophy, which by the eighteenth century became known as mercantilism, was widely accepted throughout Europe. In England it took the practical form of a set of laws designed to make the country economically self-sufficient, to bring maximum profits to English businessmen, and to enlarge royal revenue to the greatest extent possible.

In 1607, the year Englishmen founded their first permanent colony, they probably numbered altogether somewhat over 4,000,-000, a sharp increase from the 3,000,000 of 1485. Approximately 70 per cent of them lived in rural areas, and a large majority were concentrated in the southern counties. Only $1\frac{1}{2}$ per cent, according to Carl Bridenbaugh's estimate, were members of the gentry and nobility, while the yeomanry accounted for slightly

[42] The best explanation of the agricultural change will be found in R. H. Tawney, *The Agricultural Problem in the Sixteenth Century* (New York, 1912). John U. Nef has also made substantial contributions to our understanding of the intricate economic revolution during this period. See particularly his *Industry and Government in France and England, 1540–1640* (Philadelphia, 1940), and *The United States and Civilization* (Chicago, 1942). Wallace Notestein, *The English People on the Eve of Colonization, 1603–1630* (New York, 1954), pp. 108–115, 250–266, discusses the new business class, emphasizing that it was dominated by Puritans, and he provides a compact description of their earliest trading companies.

[43] Carl Bridenbaugh, *Vexed and Troubled Englishmen, 1590–1642* (New York, 1968), pp. 201–22. Much of the analysis of early seventeenth-century England in the paragraphs that follow is based on this recent and perceptive book and on Notestein, *English People*.

more than 7½ per cent, so that at least nine Englishmen in ten belonged to the lower orders. Although the classes were clearly defined, there was considerable social mobility. There was also a good deal of geographical mobility, and a long series of migrations from the Continent had produced an ethnically mixed people.[44]

How Englishmen lived depended largely on class and place of residence. Country people suffered from limited diet, periodic regional famine, disease, and a shortage of fuel, but they found pleasure in dancing, music, the fellowship of the tavern, and sports, some of which they insisted on playing in churchyards. Life for the rural poor was dull at best, and although yeomen were much better off, even they expended most of their energy on brutalizing labor. Town existence was comparatively varied and sophisticated, but urban residents had to put up with generally poor housing, filthy streets, frequent fires, increasing crime, and a shortage of water. Compensating factors included some handsome public buildings, particularly churches, increasingly well-furnished dwellings, the stimulus found only where people crowd together, and greater access to the types of entertainment enjoyed by their country cousins. Bristol, Norwich, Exeter, Salisbury, York, and Newcastle all contained between eight and twelve thousand inhabitants, and in 1605 the great and growing city of London had a population of 224,275.[45]

Regardless of his station in life or where he lived, no Englishman was untouched by some part of local government. Country people had witnessed the evolution of the parishes during the sixteenth century, and they now had ample opportunity to observe their local vestries and churchwardens performing a mixture of ecclesiastical and civic duties, assisted by petty constables, surveyors of highways, overseers of the poor, and a number of other lesser officials.[46] The administration of incorporated towns developed along different lines, so that each of them had a mayor,

44 Bridenbaugh, *Vexed and Troubled Englishmen*, pp. 16–25. Thoughtful analyses of the lives led by the gentry, nobility, yeomanry, and farm laborers will be found in Notestein, *English People*, pp. 36–60, 70–85.

45 Bridenbaugh, *Vexed and Troubled Englishmen*, pp. 46–200.

46 *Ibid.*, pp. 243–252. Notestein, *English People*, pp. 228–249, reviews the duties and problems of wardens and constables.

aldermen, a common council, and an underlayer of minor office-holders similar to that found in the rural parishes.[47] Everyone was familiar with sheriffs and justices of the peace, royal appointees who served their home counties without pay. The justices, whose duties were both administrative and judicial, were particularly busy and useful, and they constituted the main link between London and every corner of the realm.[48]

The central government seemed infinitely remote to all but a handful of subjects, but there was growing pride in some of the advantages it offered, such as the idea of representation and the protection provided by the common law. For reasons such as these and because of their nation's increasing vigor, Englishmen had recently developed a new sense of patriotism, even though many of them found themselves increasingly displeased by the actions of their ruler and his Privy Council.[49]

Cultural and educational accomplishments as well as political advantages underlay national pride. Italy still ranked ahead of all other countries in painting, sculpture, and architecture, but English music, theater, and poetry had become the world's best. Italy also maintained its position as Europe's intellectual center, but Germany and France were rapidly closing the gap, and so was England, as an outpouring of books and pamphlets proved.[50] English educational methods and institutions also compared favorably with those of other nations. Parents gave serious attention to training their children, and the petty schools for youngsters were improving rapidly.[51] Latin grammar schools, a sixteenth-century innovation, had suffered a setback when Henry VIII closed the monasteries with which many of these schools were affiliated, but new and excellent ones had opened during the reign of Queen Elizabeth.[52] The two great universities, Oxford and Cambridge, had

[47] Bridenbaugh, *Vexed and Troubled Englishmen*, pp. 202–255.
[48] *Ibid.*, pp. 255–258; Notestein, *English People*, pp. 202–227.
[49] Notestein, *English People*, pp. 4–10, amplifies on the causes of the new national pride; pp. 172–184 describes the role of sovereign and Privy Council at this time; pp. 185–201 explains the start of Puritan opposition in Parliament during the reign of Elizabeth I and its increase during the time of James I and Charles I.
[50] *Ibid.*, pp. 25–27; Bridenbaugh, *Vexed and Troubled Englishmen*, pp. 339–354.
[51] Bridenbaugh, *Vexed and Troubled Englishmen*, pp. 311–327.
[52] *Ibid.*, pp. 327–339; Notestein, *English People*, pp. 116–128.

good buildings and equipment and ample financing, and they were turning out increasing numbers of scholars.[53] Education for women received comparatively little attention, of course, but a number of private schools for females were founded shortly after the beginning of the seventeenth century.[54]

England was not without its darker side, one aspect of which was an increase in poor manners and misconduct. The new spirit of adventure had as one of its least attractive by-products a tendency toward pretentiousness and gaudy display. Regardless of their station in life, Englishmen were apt to be quarrelsome, litigious, and disorderly. Dishonesty and fraud were encountered frequently, and so, too, were drunkenness and sexual laxity. There was a great deal of crime, and it was not confined, as one might have expected, to the abject and desperate poor.[55]

In spite of rampant vulgarity and immorality, this was a religious age, and community life everywhere continued to revolve around the church. On the whole, however, the lower classes were not devout, particularly in the rural areas, and a large part of the ministry was poorly trained and indifferent to responsibility. Puritanism arose during the reign of Elizabeth I, partly as a reaction to irreverence and partly as a response to the queen's attempt to turn the Church of England into a bland state institution with no strong religious convictions. The dissident movement grew under the early Stuarts, until by about 1620 the Puritans were strong enough to launch a quiet but well-organized and sustained campaign to take over the Church from within and reorganize it according to their principles. Eventually Puritanism broke in two, the Presbyterian element finding some advantages in centralized control, while the men variously called Brownists, Separatists, Independents, and Congregationalists opted for congregations united only by shared faith. Although Puritanism thus divided its religious force and in the long run lost its political power, Wallace Notestein maintains that it contributed crucially to the molding of the English people. "An English thing in its origins

---

[53] Notestein, *English People*, pp. 130–145; and for a description of the training of lawyers and physicians, pp. 86–107.

[54] *Ibid.*, pp. 128–129.

[55] *Ibid.*, pp. 13–14, 20–24; Bridenbaugh, *Vexed and Troubled Englishmen*, pp. 240, 357–392.

and evolution," he states, "it affected the character of the English. More than any other single factor it explains the differentiation of them from their continental cousins."[56]

A restlessness crept over England during the final years of Elizabeth's reign and increased under the early Stuarts. Dissatisfaction with the Church of England partially explains this mood, but there was much more to it than that. Enclosures and depressions created poverty, unemployment, and class unrest, and even the financially secure could not escape the effects of fuel shortages, crop failures, and periodic epidemics. As the Stuarts stumbled into foolish military adventures, their subjects had to submit to impressment, forced loans, and the billeting of troops on householders. The purposes and methods of James I and Charles I irritated the majority of the people and added to their list of grievances, some political and others ecclesiastical, until in time they became what Carl Bridenbaugh calls "vexed and troubled Englishmen," ready to consider an alternative to life at home. This state of mind was an important factor in England's emergence as a colonizing nation in the years between 1607 and 1660.[57]

[56] Notestein, *English People*, pp. 61–69, 130–145, 170–171; Bridenbaugh, *Vexed and Troubled Englishmen*, pp. 274–276, 286–291, 305–309.

[57] Bridenbaugh, *Vexed and Troubled Englishmen*, pp. 95–106, 259–262, 264–273, 355–356.

CHAPTER 2

The Founding of Virginia

ENGLAND'S earliest attempts at colonialization all ended disastrously, and pessimists might have argued that the nation apparently lacked the ability to build an overseas empire. Those initial frustrating experiences were not without some value, however, because men interested in expansion gradually found out how to go about accomplishing their purposes. The success of Virginia, the first English colony that survived and grew, can in fact be traced in no small measure to lessons learned during the time of Sir Walter Raleigh.

When Raleigh became discouraged by his failure to establish a permanent settlement at Roanoke, he transferred his interests in Virginia to a number of London merchants, among whom was the dynamic and influential Sir Thomas Smythe. Raleigh did, however, reserve to himself and his heirs one-fifth of all gold and silver that might be found in Virginia, inasmuch as the notion persisted then and for long afterward that precious metal could be found in North America.[1] The London merchants accomplished nothing for a number of years, the times being unsettled. When peace with Spain did finally come, England was ripe for colonization, and the leading men of business both in London and in Bristol became enthusiastic about the prospects.

[1] Philip A. Bruce describes the English colonists' long-sustained interest in gold and silver. *Economic History of Virginia in the Seventeenth Century* (2 vols., New York, 1895, reprinted 1935), I, 10–21.

Organization had to precede colonization, and the first step was taken in 1605. A group including Richard Hakluyt, Raleigh Gilbert, Sir Thomas Gates, Sir George Somers, and George Popham drew up a petition that year, requesting permission to incorporate two companies, one based in London and the other in Plymouth, whose purpose would be to plant colonies along the North American seacoast. King James I obliged them on April 10, 1606, chartering two Virginia Companies and granting them all the land between 34 degrees north (Cape Fear River) and 45 degrees north (Passamaquoddy Bay) and extending inland one hundred miles. The Londoners were instructed to settle south of the forty-first parallel, while the Plymouth men were to stay north of the thirty-eighth. The effect of this arrangement was to create a strip available to both groups between the thirty-eighth and forty-first parallels, but no settlements there were to be located within one hundred miles of one another, a requirement designed to avoid the possibility of conflict. A central governing board located in England and appointed by the king was to have general supervision over the entire project, but a local council would have immediate jurisdiction over each individual colony. Each thirteen-man local council would elect its own president and had the power to remove him or any other councillor. The charter guaranteed colonists all the liberties, privileges, and immunities of native-born Englishmen, including such rights as trial by jury.[2]

Equipped with this authorization, the London merchants made prompt preparations to send a colonizing expedition to the New World. They assembled a small fleet consisting of the hundred-ton *Susan Constant,* the forty-ton *Goodspeed,* and the twenty-ton *Discovery,* and they selected Captain Christopher Newport to be the officer in charge during the voyage. Once the settlers reached Virginia, they were to open a box containing the names of the local councillors, and the men thus appointed would elect one of their number president.[3] The expedition had instructions to settle

[2] Herbert L. Osgood, *The American Colonies in the Seventeenth Century* (3 vols., New York, 1904–07), I, 26–29.

[3] Captain John Smith, *A True Relation of Such Occurences and Accidents of Noate as Hath Happened in Virginia* . . . (London, 1608), reprinted in Edward Arber and A. G. Bradley, eds., *Captain John Smith, Travels and Works* (2 vols., Edinburgh, 1910), p. 90.

inland on a river that might lead to the East India Sea and then to divide into three groups, one to fortify the town and build a storehouse, another to plant vegetables, and the third to explore up the river assessing the possibilities for trade.[4] Some of the investors hoped for precious metals and a lucrative trade with the Orient; others expected a much-needed supply of masts, tar, pitch, and resin, but to all of them the enterprise was clearly a commercial venture.[5] In line with the prevailing mercantilist theory, it was also anticipated that the colonists would eventually become purchasers of English exports.

The expedition left London on December 20, 1606, carrying 144 colonists. After encountering some delay, the three little ships sailed by way of the Canaries and West Indies the usual route at that time, and Virginia was sighted on April 26, 1607. The colonists searched the area carefully and then settled on May 13 on the Jamestown peninsula (now Jamestown Island), thirty miles above Hampton Roads, at a spot where the shoreside was so deep that the ships could anchor under the trees.[6]

When the sealed box was opened, it was learned that the councillors appointed by the company in England were Bartholomew Gosnold, George Kendall, John Martin, Christopher Newport, John Ratcliffe, John Smith, and Edward Wingfield. This group then awarded the presidency to Wingfield, the only settler whose name appeared on the charter. The original council included men with a variety of talents. Newport was an experienced sea captain who had forayed against the Spanish, and Gosnold was an able administrator who had sailed the New England coast for Raleigh. The most capable of the councillors, and certainly the most colorful, was Captain John Smith, the adventurous son of a tenant farmer. Although still only twenty-seven years of age, he had traveled widely in Europe as a soldier. He had fought the Turks in Transylvania and Hungary, had been captured, and had spent some time as a slave in Turkey. During the voyage to

[4] Anonymous, *A Relation of the Discovery of Our River* . . . (1607), reprinted in Bradley-Arber ed., *Captain John Smith, Travels and Works*, pp. xxxiv–xxxv.
[5] George L. Beer, *Origins of the British Colonial System* (New York, 1908), p. 86.
[6] The expedition is ably described in Richard Lee Morton, *Colonial Virginia* (2 vols., Chapel Hill, N.C., 1960), I, 7–9.

America, he had been suspected of plotting to usurp the government, and he was under arrest when the fleet reached Virginia, but his associates released him when they learned that he was to be one of the councillors and they permitted him to take his place among the appointed leaders.[7]

Settlement began in an orderly way, but soon discord and mismanagement contributed to widespread hardship. The colonists built a fort at Jamestown, planted a garden there, made nets, and began manufacturing clapboards for export. Newport explored the James River as far as the falls, at what is now Richmond, and then sailed for England. Meanwhile the councillors had become suspicious of one another, and presently a jury tried Kendall for conspiracy and ordered him shot. Wingfield was expelled for favoritism, Ratcliffe, an incorporator of the company, replacing him as president.[8]

The settlers, whose ranks included a number of gentlemen, a surgeon, a minister, and some artisans such as carpenters and bricklayers, needed better leadership than they were receiving, because they were unequipped both physically and mentally for the hardships that lay ahead of them.[9] Soon food became scarce and disease prevalent, so that by September half the colonists had perished, including Councillor Gosnold. During this period of crisis the colonists almost lost the invaluable Captain John Smith. Captured while exploring the Chickahominy River by Powhatan, the most powerful Indian chief in the area, the Englishman's life

[7] Ibid., pp. 9–11. The able but boastful and possibly unreliable Captain John Smith has captured the attention of a number of biographers. Edward K. Chatterton, Captain John Smith (New York, 1927), long a standard work, has been joined by several more recent studies, including Bradford Smith, Captain John Smith: His Life & Legend (Philadelphia, 1953), and the carefully researched and judicious Philip L. Barbour, The Three Worlds of Captain John Smith (Boston, 1964). Henry Wharton, The Life of John Smith, English Soldier,, ed. Laura Polanyi Striker (Chapel Hill, N.C., 1957), is a translation from the original Latin of a manuscript written in 1685. Paul Lewis, The Great Rogue: A Biography of Captain John Smith (New York, 1966) stresses the romantic and sensational and addresses itself to a popular audience.

[8] Smith, True Relation, reprinted in Bradley-Arber ed., Captain John Smith, Travels and Works, pp. 6–9, 95–97.

[9] Ibid., pp. 93–94. See also Thomas J. Wertenbaker, Patrician and Plebeian in Virginia: Or, The Origin and Development of the Social Classes in the Old Dominion (Charlottesville, Va., 1910), p. 7.

was spared, and he was released when, according to Smith, the chief's daughter, Pocahontas, interceded on his behalf.[10]

On January 8, 1608, when only thirty-eight settlers were still alive, Smith got back to Jamestown from his adventure among the Indians. That same day Newport sailed in from England, and so it seemed momentarily that the crisis might have passed. However, a fire destroyed all but three of the houses in the town a few days later, leaving few provisions for the new settlers and for the ship's crew. Smith managed to obtain bread, corn, fish, and meat through Powhatan and he resolutely set about rebuilding the community and planting corn. These efforts were of vital importance, as was the arrival of another ship, the *Phoenix*, bringing food from the West Indies, but the winter nevertheless brought great suffering. While Smith was away on another exploratory trip, this time to the Potomac and the head of Chesapeake Bay, the other councillors bickered among themselves, and first Ratcliffe and then Scrivener, a new member, were removed from office.[11]

The council finally had the good sense to elect the energetic

10 Smith, *True Relation*, reprinted in Bradley-Arber ed., *Captain John Smith, Travels and Works*, pp. 94–98, his virtually contemporary account, describes his capture by the Indians but makes absolutely no reference to Pocahontas. The romantic story of how she allegedly saved him from execution was not introduced until many years later in his *The Generall Historie of Virginia, New-England, and the Summer Isles . . .* (London, 1624), reprinted in Bradley-Arber ed., *Captain John Smith*, p. 398. The historian Henry Adams printed portions of the two accounts side by side in his essay, "Captaine John Smith," in 1867 and showed that no other descriptions of pioneer life in Virginia written prior to 1624 alluded in any way to Pocahontas as Smith's savior. Adams' famous article, which is reprinted in Elizabeth Stevenson (ed.), *A Henry Adams Reader* (Garden City, N.Y., 1958), caused a drop in the reputation of the adventurous captain, who came to be regarded as little more than a self-promoting liar. Recent scholars have done much to restore his reputation by showing that his accurate observations far outnumbered his inconsistencies and seeming inventions. Edwin C. Rozwence pointed this fact out in "Captain John Smith's Image of America," *William and Mary Quarterly*, XVI (Jan., 1959), 27–36. See also Richard S. Dunn, "Seventeenth-Century English Historians of America," in *Seventeenth-Century America: Essays in Colonial History*, ed. James Morton Smith (Chapel Hill, N.C., 1959), and Morton, *Colonial Virginia*, I, 13.

11 Smith, *True Relation*, reprinted in Bradley-Arber ed., *Captain John Smith, Travels and Works*, pp. 100–105.

Captain John Smith president in September, 1608, and almost immediately conditions began to improve.[12] Newport returned from England in October, bringing provisions and gifts for the Indians and also seventy immigrants, among whom were eight artificers from Holland and Poland and two women, the first to come to Jamestown. When Newport left in December, his ship carried timber instead of the precious metal he had hoped to find. Smith kept everyone busy procuring food, building houses, and strengthening the Jamestown fortifications, and he employed the foreign craftsmen in the manufacture of pitch, tar, soap, and glass. Rats from the visiting ship consumed most of the food supply, but Smith met this new misfortune by sending out hunting and fishing parties and distributing some of the colonists temporarily among Indians who were willing to feed them. Largely because of this superb leadership, only seven out of two hundred settlers died that winter. Meanwhile the *Phoenix* reached England with a map of the new colony and with Smith's *True Relation*, which gave a vivid account of the colonists' adventures.[13] Publication of this manuscript, which was done without the author's knowledge, added to the already considerable interest in Virginia and made Smith a celebrity.

The infant colony had survived thus far, but it was still critically weak and lacking in economic self-sufficiency, and a number of unresolved underlying problems threatened its future. There was much sickness, and the food supply remained uncertain. Leadership, except during Captain John Smith's regime, ranged from mediocre to miserable, and the ordinary settlers were a shiftless lot who had to be driven merely to keep themselves alive.[14] Despite outbursts of animosity, the Indians had been generally helpful, but their interests and those of the colonists by no means coincided. Powhatan, in the process of solidifying political control over some thirty Algonquian-speaking tribes in coastal Virginia, saw an advantage in having the English as military allies, but he had no intention

[12] *Ibid.*, p. 121; Morton, *Colonial Virginia*, I, 15.
[13] Smith, *True Relation*, reprinted in Bradley-Arber ed., *Captain John Smith, Travels and Works*, pp. 3–39.
[14] Thomas J. Wertenbaker, *Virginia Under the Stuarts, 1607–1688* (Princeton, N.J., 1914), pp. 1–2.

of letting them create a regional power greater than his.[15] Finally, the colony's governmental structure, more appropriate for rapid looting operations than for promoting slow growth, was proving unsuitable to existent conditions.[16]

More than anyone else it was Sir Edwin Sandys, a Virginia Company councillor and former member of the House of Commons, who recognized the need for a general reorganization.[17] Sandys took the lead in procuring the revised charter of 1609, which set up a joint-stock company whose ownership was shared by fifty-six city of London firms and 659 individuals. Under the new arrangements the council and its head, the treasurer, exercised absolute control, while the general court of stockholders had only the single duty of electing the council members. The new charter placed executive authority in Virginia in the hands of a lord governor, appointed for life and subject only to the council in London, who was authorized to appoint all members of the local council and all subordinate officials. The charter also increased the boundaries of the colony to 200 miles north and south of Point Comfort. Its territory was to extend "west and northwest" from sea to sea, a provision reflecting geographical ignorance rather than imperialistic ambition.[18]

The reorganization produced new leadership, and further changes occurred during the next few years. The crown gave the treasurership to fifty-one-year-old Sir Thomas Smythe, long active in all the great overseas enterprises and since 1600 governor of the East India Company.[19] The governorship of the colony went to Sir Thomas West, Lord De la Warr, a privy councillor under both Elizabeth I and James I. He remained nominally the governor until his death in June, 1618, but residing for the most part in England,

15 Nancy O. Lurie, "Indian Cultural Adjustment to European Civilization," in *Seventeenth-Century America: Essays in Colonial History*, ed. James Morton Smith (Chapel Hill, N.C., 1959), pp. 37–46.

16 Sigmund Diamond, "From Organization to Society: Virginia in the Seventeenth Century," *American Journal of Sociology*, LXIII (1958), 461–463.

17 Charles M. Andrews, *The Colonial Period in American History* (4 vols., New Haven, Conn., 1934–38), I, 102–103.

18 Percy S. Flippin, *The Royal Government in Virginia, 1624–1775* (New York, 1919), p. 60. See also Osgood, *American Colonies*, I, 56.

19 A recent commentator, A. L. Rowse, identifies Smythe as the individual most responsible for keeping the colony from complete collapse. *The Expansion of Elizabethan England* (London, 1955), p. 230.

he was generally represented in Virginia by a series of deputy governors.

As the result of a further reorganization in 1612, provoked by stockholders' demands, the whole body of the stockholders meeting quarterly assumed active control and the company was put on a regular joint-stock basis. One share of stock, costing £12 10s., not only conveyed membership but entitled the owner to one hundred acres of Virginia land. At this same time Bermuda was formally added to Virginia, and the king authorized lotteries. The lotteries were unsuccessful until the shrewd Sir Thomas Smythe created public confidence by having local officials in communities throughout England supervise the sale of tickets. The device of raising money by this means was thereafter of great assistance, some sales producing as much as £1,000, enough to send a well-supplied ship to Virginia.[20]

Efforts on behalf of the colony could be increased because of the 1609 reorganization, and nine vessels sailed that year carrying five hundred men, women, and children to Virginia. Sir George Somers was admiral of the fleet, and his vice-admiral was Christopher Newport. The passenger list included Sir Thomas Gates, an old soldier who had been designated deputy governor, and Sir Thomas Dale, a comrade-in-arms who was to be his assistant. A hurricane scattered the fleet on July 25 and wrecked the ship in Bermuda that was carrying Somers, Newport, and Gates. Providentially, nobody was lost, and the incident later inspired Shakespeare to write *The Tempest*, but the arrival of these key figures in Virginia was delayed by many months. Meanwhile the rest of the fleet managed to regroup and make its way to Jamestown, where the colonists were found to be in the midst of new discord.[21] Captain John Smith had managed to fend off an attack by three disgruntled councillors, but he was upset and in discomfort because of a wound suffered when gunpowder exploded accidentally, and he left Virginia when the fleet sailed home. He published his remarkable *Map of Virginia with a Description of the Country* . . . in 1612, and he continued

---

20 An excellent description of the lotteries will be found in Robert C. Johnson, "The Lotteries of the Virginia Company, 1612–1621," *Virginia Magazine of History and Biography*, LXX (1966), 260–290.

21 Gabriel Archer, "Letter Announcing Arrival of the Third Supply," reprinted in Bradley-Arber ed., *Captain John Smith*, pp. xciv–xcvi.

to be a supporter of the colony, but he was a hard man to replace.[22]

Conditions deteriorated promptly under George Percy, who succeeded Captain John Smith as president. Attacks by Indians under Powhatan made matters worse by driving the settlers back onto unhealthy Jamestown, where great numbers of them died from hunger and from malaria and dysentery. The dreadful winter of 1609–10, during which one man was executed for cannibalism, was remembered as the "Starving Time." When Gates finally arrived from Bermuda in May, 1610, bringing with him 175 people but very little food, he found that only 60 out of 490 settlers had survived. Judging that it would be impossible to keep the colony going, Gates reluctantly loaded everyone onto ships and was headed down Chesapeake Bay when he met Governor De la Warr coming in from England with 300 new settlers. Together Gates and De la Warr sailed back to the abandoned town and reoccupied it. The colony was saved, but the times of trouble were not yet ended. An expedition to the West Indies procured some provisions, but food remained in short supply. De la Warr became ill and went home. Disease continued at an epidemic rate, and there were soon fewer than 150 surviving residents in the Virginia Colony.[23]

The turning point came in 1611. Sir Thomas Dale arrived in May, bringing with him more colonists and a one-year supply of food, and he promptly put everyone to work planting corn, felling timber, repairing houses, and effecting other improvements. In order to promote discipline he instituted a severe set of laws which he enforced rigorously. Deputy Governor Gates came in August, bringing enough more immigrants so that the total reaching Virginia that year amounted to five hundred men and twenty women.[24]

Gates and Dale thereafter worked together closely and with good

---

[22] Smith's 1612 account is reprinted in Bradley-Arber ed., *Captain John Smith*, pp. 40–84.

[23] Wesley Frank Craven, *The Southern Colonies in the Seventeenth Century, 1607–1689* (Baton Rouge, La., 1949), presents an authoritative account of Virginia's early years in Chap. III and IV. See pp. 97 ff. for a detailed description of the hardships of the winter of 1609–10. Clifford Dowdey, *The Great Plantation: A Profile of Berkeley Hundred and Plantation, Virginia, from Jamestown to Appomattox* (New York, 1957), pp. 8–9, points out that disease took such a toll in the earliest period that of the 800 settlers who came in the years between 1607 and 1610, not five have left descendants in Virginia.

[24] Ralph Hamor, *A True Discourse of the Present State of Virginia* . . . (London, 1615, reprinted 1957), pp. 26–27.

results. The colony at last began to grow. Hostile Indian tribes were subdued and pacified by 1614. John Rolfe proved that tobacco could be grown successfully as a cash crop, and he took his bride Pocahontas to England on a good-will trip in 1614. Their ship also carried Indian children on their way to be educated abroad, and the cargo included such samples of Virginia produce as sassafras, pitch, potash, sturgeon, and, of course, tobacco. Pocahontas won many friends for Virginia in England before her untimely death there prior to Rolfe's return in 1617. Meanwhile Captain John Smith, John Pory, Ralph Hamor, and the Reverend Alexander Whitaker were publicizing the colony with accounts of their adventures there.[25]

Rolfe is remembered as the husband of Pocahontas, but his real fame rests on his achievement in developing tobacco as the staple crop Virginia needed so badly.[26] Early explorers had discovered that the Indians prized tobacco highly and used it in their ceremonies. Drake introduced it into England from the West Indies in 1586, and Raleigh made it fashionable. The custom of smoking spread in spite of James I's famous anonymous tract called *Counter-Blaste to Tobacco* (1604), and any colony able to grow a plant of acceptable quality had the certainty of a lucrative business with the mother country. The plant native to Virginia was so poor that no tobacco could be exported until after Rolfe experimented successfully with varieties from the West Indies and the Orinoco. Starting with an initial shipment of four barrels to Sir Thomas Smythe in 1614, exports increased from 2,300 pounds in 1616 to 49,500 pounds in 1618. Virginians finally had a cash crop permitting them to establish credit in England for the purchase of clothes and other necessities, but emphasis on the new crop was not an unmixed blessing. When Rolfe returned in 1617 with the new deputy governor, Samuel Argall, Jamestown was almost deserted, because the population had dispersed to raise tobacco.[27] To make

---

[25] Hamor, the son of an important investor in the company, spent several years in the colony, acting part of that time as clerk to the council. His *A True Discourse of the Present State of Virginia* . . . (London, 1615, reprinted 1957), is a valuable contemporary source, as is *Good Newes from Virginia* (London, 1612, reprinted 1936), by Whitaker, who was the minister at Henrico.

[26] Hamor, *True Discourse*, p. 24.

[27] John Smith, *Generall Historie* (London, 1624), reprinted in Bradley-Arber ed., *Captain John Smith, Travels and Works*, p. 535.

sure that there would be a food supply, Argall had to insist on the planting of two acres of corn for every one of tobacco. With the discovery that tobacco was better cured by stringing it instead of piling it up like hay, further impetus was given to its culture, and as early as 1627 Charles I observed that Virginia was "wholly built upon smoke."[28]

After a decade of existence, the company had nothing more to show for its efforts than a struggling colony whose population in 1616 amounted to only 351 people.[29] Two hundred five of the settlers were officials and laborers occupying company land. Another eighty-one men were tenant farmers, and there were also sixty-five women and children. Some artificers employed by the company raised their own crops, but most of the laborers drew food from a common supply, a system that encouraged shiftlessness by giving equal rewards to everyone regardless of the amount of energy expended. When the terms of the seven-year indentured servants began to expire in 1614, some returned to England, but others preferred to stay on as free laborers. The development of tobacco increased the number of tenant farmers, who raised just that one crop and exchanged it at the company magazine for food, clothing, and other necessities. Dale stimulated immigration by promising every newcomer a rent-free house for one year, together with a twelve-acre plot planted in vegetables and stocked with poultry.[30] Food became plentiful and more varied as people took advantage of this offer, and there was a great increase in the number of livestock. At the same time the company land gradually became deserted.

Land titles followed English precedents to some extent, but new conditions made it necessary to adopt certain innovations. All land assigned to the Virginia Company by the king was considered to be held on a freehold basis under the arrangement known as free and common socage that was in use on the manor of East Greenwich in

[28] Descriptions of the development of the tobacco trade include George L. Beer, *The Origins of the British Colonial System, 1578–1660* (New York, 1908), pp. 81–94; Bruce, *Economic History*, I, 211–212; and Thomas J. Wertenbaker, *The Planters of Colonial Virginia* (Princeton, N.J., 1922), pp. 21–27.

[29] Sigmund Diamond emphasizes in "From Organization to Society," p. 468, that the reforms instituted in 1609 were insufficient to increase the flow of migration or to motivate the planters who were already in Virginia.

[30] Hamor, *True Discourse*, p. 19.

the county of Kent.[31] Title to individual parcels of land in the colony was obtained from the Indians by treaty or purchase prior to 1622 and by expropriation after that date. Two methods were used to make permanent grants of land to colonists, the more popular of which all during the seventeenth century was the so-called headright system. Under this arrangement, which proved a mighty stimulus to migration, the company gave fifty acres to anyone who would cross the Atlantic and settle at his own expense. The method was not without its abuses, because some men who crossed the ocean more than once managed to acquire headrights for their additional voyages, and crafty sea captains were not above claiming headrights for their sailors and passengers.[32] The other land-distribution system, which also enjoyed some popularity, was the "particular" or subsidiary plantation grant. A group of associates would receive a substantial grant of land in return for financing the transporting of a party of colonists and settling them on what was known as a particular plantation.[33]

Observing that there had been a breakdown of morale, Deputy Governor Samuel Argall began his rule in 1617 by putting into effect The Lawes Divine, Morall and Martial, a code that was on the whole strict rather than cruel.[34] It halted private bartering with Indians, forbade employing them to shoot game, and made it a misdemeanor to teach an Indian how to shoot a gun. Argall's stern measures irritated some lax planters, and his frankness antagonized certain members of the council in London.[35] He charged that the company officials in England underpaid the colonists for tobacco, overcharged them for company goods, sent over the wrong tools, and issued too many special commissions for trade. A crop failure in 1618 provided a convenient excuse for Argall's recall, and he went home to England that year. Lord De la Warr, nominal governor since the charter reorganization, decided to go to Virginia to become governor in fact, but he died on the way.

31 Marshall D. Harris, *Origin of the Land Tenure System in the United States* (Ames, Iowa, 1953), p. 83.

32 *Ibid.*, p. 207.

33 Andrews, *Colonial Period*, I, 127–133, explains the origins and characteristics of particular plantations.

34 The code can be found in Peter Force, *Tracts . . .* (reprinted New York, 1947), III, No. 2.

35 Morton, *Colonial Virginia*, I, 50.

Company leaders, particularly Sir Thomas Smythe, Sir Edwin Sandys, and John and Nicholas Ferrar, recognized that strong measures should be taken to restore confidence and put the colony on a sounder footing. Largely at the urging of Sandys, who replaced Smythe as treasurer before the end of 1618, they conceived a program of sweeping reform and sent Sir George Yeardley to Virginia to execute it as the new governor.[36] Yeardley, an old soldier who knew the colony and had once served briefly as its deputy governor, was a firm but temperate executive, and he turned out to be both an effective and a popular choice.[37] Sent with him as secretary was his wife's cousin, the versatile John Pory, whose experience included six years in Parliament.

The new governor reached Virginia early in 1619, bringing detailed written instructions describing the changes he was to effect. A new body of laws was introduced, and martial law was completely eliminated. Yeardley was to retain Argall's innovation of dividing the colony for administrative purposes into four parts, which later became the four original counties. He was also directed to continue the headright system, liberalizing it so as to include servants who had ended their terms of service.[38] Property was to be set aside for a number of specific purposes, including a glass factory, shipyard, and ironworks. Land was also reserved for schools, and 10,000 acres at Henrico was earmarked for "a University and College" that was never built. Finally, the governor's instructions called for establishment of a general assembly consisting of councillors chosen by him and burgesses elected by the people. All male inhabitants could vote, making the franchise vastly more liberal than it was in England. The assembly, meeting annually, was to make laws, advise on matters relating to the welfare of the colony, and serve as a court of justice. The governor had veto power, and no law could continue in force without company ratification. Conversely, the company stipulated that none of its orders would be binding without ratification by the assembly, a promise that was not always kept.[39]

36 For changes in agreements with the colonists during the charter periods, see Diamond, "From Organization to Society," pp. 457–475.

37 Flippin, *Royal Government*, p. 103.

38 Harris, *Land Tenure*, p. 200.

39 Yeardley's instructions appear in Susan Myra Kingsbury (ed.), *The Records of the Virginia Company of London* (4 vols., Washington, D.C., 1906–35), III, 98–109.

The general assembly, the first representative legislative body ever to convene in British North America, met in the church at Jamestown on July 30, 1619. Governor Yeardley was present and active, and Secretary John Pory, who was also a councillor, served as the speaker. The six appointed councillors and twenty-two elected burgesses sat as one house, two burgesses representing each of the eleven districts. After considering possible charter revisions that it might ask the company to make, the assembly recommended further liberalization of the land distribution system and measures designed to stimulate immigration. It also adopted legislation giving effect to the governor's instructions and improving conditions in the colony. It passed laws, for example, protecting Indians and regulating all dealings with them. The company magazine was put under better control, and everyone was required to grow food crops. The sale price of tobacco was fixed, and all inferior leaves were to be burned. Other new regulations defined the status of servants and tenants. Church attendance twice every Sabbath became mandatory, and penalties were assigned for swearing, idleness, gaming, drunkenness, and excess in apparel. Then, converting itself into a court, the assembly sentenced a notorious indentured servant to stand in the pillory. These pioneer legislators—the governor, councillors, and burgesses—adjourned after sitting for six days and setting a significant precedent in colonial history.[40]

Owing in large measure to the efforts of Sandys in London and Yeardley in Jamestown, a brief period of activity and expansion began in 1619. More than 1,200 immigrants arrived that year to join the 1,900 people who were already there.[41] The newcomers were described as "choice men, born and bred up to labour and industry," and the group included ninety young women who came as prospective wives for colonists. Cattle and grain also came over from England in 1619, and ships visited New England and Newfoundland to procure fish. During the next several years the company arranged for the construction of ironworks, sawmills, and

---

[40] See Craven, *Southern Colonies*, Chap. III, for a detailed treatment of the first session of the general assembly. The records of this session appear in Virginia General Assembly, Joint Committee on the State Library, *Colonial Records of Virginia* (Baltimore, 1964), pp. 9–32.

[41] But Andrews, *Colonial Period*, I, 136, points out that a high death rate cut heavily into the population in the years immediately after 1619.

shipyards, and Sandys continued to send skilled foreign workers in the vain hope of establishing silk, wine, and glass industries.

Interest in particular plantations reached its climax during these years. More than half of the 1619 immigrants came to settle on new tracts being developed on this basis. By the middle of 1622 the company had issued a total of seventy patents, twenty-six of them during the previous twelve months. Every particular plantation was a self-contained unit with its own trading privileges, manorial jurisdiction, and local governments. One of the most unusual of these groups was John Peirce and his Associates, English Separatists who came in 1620 and who also helped finance the Pilgrims. Seven particular plantations were important enough to be represented at the first general assembly, but the majority were unsuccessful, and the system was abandoned after 1624.[42]

Because Virginia did not initially attract settlers in sufficient numbers, the company resorted to unusual devices to supplement the trickle of volunteer migration. Sandys provoked "grateful" applause in the House of Commons by suggesting the transportation of paupers to the colony, and the city of London obliged by sending over occasional shipments of dependent children.[43] The company was at first less enthusiastic about accepting convicts, but it soon changed its mind, and in 1615 James I issued a commission inaugurating the transfer to Virginia of persons guilty of any felonies except murder, rape, witchcraft, or burglary.[44] Convicts were transported from that time on, but not in sizable numbers until the second half of the century.[45] A larger element in the early population consisted of indentured servants who contracted to work for a master for a term of years, at the end of which they received clothing, tools, and other equipment with which to begin a new life. Some of these people, along with other settlers who had migrated at their own expense, became tenants on land leased from the company, which made them North America's first farmers. The most gifted, or at least the most durable, of all these people

[42] *Ibid.*, pp. 127–133, is an excellent explanation of particular plantations.

[43] Beer, *Origins*, pp. 46–47.

[44] Richard B. Morris, *Government and Labor in Early America* (New York, 1946), p. 323. This book contains a wealth of information on the lot of workers of all categories throughout the colonial period in Virginia and elsewhere.

[45] Diamond, "From Organization to Society," p. 464.

survived to become the founders of Virginia's colonial middle class.[46]

The company would have preferred to colonize Virginia with complete families, but few chose to migrate, and so single men formed the predominant element in the population. A few women did come, the first two arriving in 1608, but the supply of unmarried females, both volunteer settlers and indentured servants, never came close to meeting the demand. In 1620 a subordinate joint-stock company, organized in London specifically for the purpose, undertook to ship women to Jamestown on a businesslike basis. It was careful to pick candidates with satisfactory character, and it placed them in good homes until they married. When that time came, the company collected 120 pounds of prime leaf tobacco from the successful suitor as reimbursement for the expenses of the passage. The young women were not turned into servants prior to marriage, and they were not forced to marry against their will. To protect prospective bridegrooms, the assembly made it illegal to become engaged to more than one man at a time.[47]

Negroes appeared early in Virginia, but their number remained small for some time, and the institution of slavery took many years to develop. A Dutch man-of-war put in at Jamestown late in August, 1619, and sold the colonists what Captain John Smith described in his writing as twenty "Negars."[48] Importation of African natives continued at a very slow rate, and there were only about 300 of them in Virginia at midcentury, when the white population amounted to 15,000. There were still as few as 2,000 Negroes in 1670, but by 1700 their total jumped to 6,000, and by then they formed a substantial part of the working force.[49] There was no such thing as slavery in earliest Virginia, and its first Negroes had substantially the same status as white indentured servants. They

[46] Wertenbaker, *Patrician and Plebeian*, pp. 143–215, traces the rise of the Virginia middle class.

[47] Morton, *Colonial Virginia*, I, 70–71. See also Diamond, "From Organization to Society," p. 470.

[48] Reprinted in Bradley-Arber ed., *Captain John Smith, Travels and Works*, p. 541.

[49] James H. Brewer, "Negro Property Owners in Seventeenth-Century America," *William and Mary Quarterly*, XII (Oct., 1955), 575. Wertenbaker, *Planters of Colonial Virginia*, contends that slavery was not the predominant form of labor in the seventeenth century. See also Morris, *Government and Labor*, p. 313.

were, in fact, listed as indentured servants in the census records of 1623 and 1624. As late as 1651 Negroes who had completed their terms of servitude were receiving grants of land in the same manner as white men. By the middle of the century the white colonists were beginning to take advantage of the opportunity for exploitation of the blacks, and the records began to show evidence of Negro servants and their children in servitude for life.[50] It seems impossible to say precisely when slavery started, but a 1660 law relating to runaway servants makes mention of people who had become slaves prior to that date.[51]

Virginia seemed to be prospering more than ever before when, in 1621, the wise and well-intentioned Sir Francis Wyatt assumed the governorship, but the colony was shortly devastated by unforeseen calamities.[52] The first blow fell on Good Friday, March 22, 1622, when the hitherto peaceful Indians infiltrated the white settlements, pretending to be offering provisions for sale, and then suddenly fell on the inhabitants, first killing whomever they found in the houses and later going into the fields to slay the workers there. On that single day the natives massacred 350 people, including six councillors, one of whom was John Rolfe. The savages spared no males but carried away twenty women as prisoners. The death total would have been much higher had it not been for a friendly Indian boy, Chanco, whose timely warning to his master in Jamestown saved the people of that community.[53]

[50] John Hope Franklin, *From Slavery to Freedom: A History of American Negroes* (New York, 1950; 2nd ed., 1956), pp. 70–71.

[51] The origin of the institution of slavery has aroused much controversy. Oscar and Mary Handlin, "Origins of the Southern Labor System," *William and Mary Quarterly*, VII (1950), 199–222, take the position that until the decade following 1660 Negroes had the status of servants and that the gradual development of slavery generated racism. Carl N. Degler, "Slavery and the Genesis of American Race Prejudice," *Comparative Studies in Society and History*, II (Oct., 1959), 49–66, refutes the Handlins, maintaining that there was racial prejudice from the start and that this attitude quickly led to the Negro's enslavement. Winthrop D. Jordan, "Modern Tensions and the Origins of American Slavery," *Journal of Southern History*, XXVIII (Feb., 1962), 18–30, seeks to reconcile these contentions by suggesting that slavery and prejudice were facets of a general debasement of the Negro. Stanley Elkins, *Slavery: A Problem in American Institutional and Intellectual Life* (Chicago, 1959), pp. 2–26, provides an excellent bibliographical essay on slavery.

[52] Flippin, *Royal Government*, pp. 102–103.

[53] Morton, *Colonial Virginia*, I, 73–76.

The colonists had made themselves particularly vulnerable to attack by falling into the habit of going about unarmed, something they should never have done considering the scattered pattern of their settlements and the recent mood of the Indians. Although there was certainly no reason to expect open warfare, relations between the races had undeniably been deteriorating since 1618, when Powhatan died and Opechancanough succeeded him. Competition for land caused the underlying strain, and the gradual increase in the white population finally convinced the new Indian leader that only a war of extermination could save his people. He miscalculated his chances; the aroused English struck back savagely, slaughtering the natives, burning their villages, and destroying their crops. The colonists kept up this devastation for two years, and by the end of that time they had scattered the tribes and broken their power.[54]

The colonists mounted this vigorous counterattack despite attrition from disease, which was again sweeping through Virginia. At one time only 180 men were fit to resist the Indians, and only 80 of that number were well enough to engage in actual combat. George Sandys wrote in 1623 that the living were hardly able to bury the dead, and a total of between five and six hundred people died during this epidemic.[55] Malaria was endemic in Virginia, but it was not as lethal as the diseases that broke out on shipboard during the voyage from England—scurvy, dysentery, typhus, typhoid fever, and cholera. Much of the suffering resulted from the fact that the company was then sending over ship after ship in rapid succession, so overcrowded that the passengers arrived worn out, lack-

54 Lurie, "Indian Cultural Adjustment to European Civilization," pp. 48–49. Wilcomb E. Washburn maintains that the English were more treacherous than the Indians and that they pounced upon the massacre as an excuse for their bloody counterattack. "The Moral and Legal Justifications for Dispossessing the Indians," in James Morton Smith (ed.), *Seventeenth-Century America: Essays in Colonial History* (Chapel Hill, N.C., 1959), pp. 19–21.

55 The "Great Mortality" left a population of only 1,095 in 1624 out of a total of 7,549 who had entered the colony since 1607. W. B. Blanton, Virginia medical historian, asserts that in the absence of any large incidence of malaria, smallpox, scarlet fever, diphtheria, and even the plague, deaths at Jamestown for the most part were caused by the deficiency diseases, the toxic effect of rotted grain, burning fevers during the summers, the respiratory diseases of the winter, and unsanitary conditions caused by living within the crowded fort. See *Colonial Medicine Symposium* (Richmond, Va., 1957), pp. 64–71.

ing resistance to disease if not already ill. Sir Edwin Sandy's greatest blunder was trying to solve the colony's problems by building up the population too rapidly.[56]

The difficulties in London were even worse than those in the colony. The Virginia Company, long in poor condition financially, was now on the verge of bankruptcy, owing in no small measure to the fact that in 1621 King James forced it to discontinue its income-producing lotteries. The stockholders had never received a single dividend, and it was becoming clear that few if any results could be expected from recent efforts to establish viniculture, silkmaking, and naval stores as profitable industries. The owners of the company were in a sullen mood, and in this state of mind they accused the colonists of neglecting worship while preoccupying themselves with rich food and fancy clothing. Governor Wyatt defended his people and made counter-accusations against the company. It was easy to criticize the London management, which had repeatedly sent unfit settlers to Virginia in the wrong ships at inappropriate times, poorly provided with food and clothing and insufficiently housed upon arrival. Captain Nathaniel Butler, formerly governor of Bermuda and brother-in-law of Captain John Smith, brought complaints before the stockholders at a meeting held in April, 1623, addressing them on the subject of "The Unmasked Face of our Colony in Virginia, as it was in the Winter of the year 1622." By then the leadership was split by factional strife, the end result of which was a quarrel with the king over the tobacco contract.[57]

Tobacco had developed into a profitable crop, but it involved serious risks. England collected duty beginning in 1619 on all products imported from Virginia, and there was always the danger that a greedy government might increase the rate. Appointed monopolists known as "farmers" conducted all of England's import business, and they were capable of victimizing colonial planters. Then, too, King James disliked tobacco, and he had the power to forbid its importation. Virginians were acutely aware of these hazards, but they refused to acknowledge that overspecialization and

[56] Diamond, "From Organization to Society," p. 470.
[57] Wesley Frank Craven, *The Dissolution of the Virginia Company: The Failure of a Colonial Experiment* (New York, 1932, reprinted Gloucester, Mass., 1964), is the classic account. See particularly Chap. VIII, "The Tobacco Contract."

overproduction might ultimately work to their disadvantage. Inasmuch as tobacco fetched 3s. a pound while grain earned only 2s. 6d., Captain John Smith pointed out that no sensible man would grow anything except tobacco. When Sir Edwin Sandys advocated greater attention to hemp, silk, and the grapevine, the colonists answered that tobacco production was so demanding that there was no time to experiment with other crops. Planters in both Virginia and Bermuda refused to consider greater diversification even when Sir Edwin revealed in July, 1621, that the king had voiced his disapproval of the raising of tobacco in the colonies.[58]

The company sought a change in government regulations to end what it considered discrimination against tobacco planters. The existing regulations stipulated that all tobacco exported from Virginia must be shipped directly to England. Customs duties were collected there, even though some tobacco was later reshipped to other countries. Exporters of English goods had an advantage over colonial tobacco producers, because they could make sales wherever in the world they could get the best prices, and their merchandise did not have duties levied against it as it left England. The Privy Council was disinclined to make concessions, fearing loss of revenue for the king. Finally, in response to continual pressure, it offered a contract to the Virginia and Bermuda companies, awarding them a monopoly on tobacco importation into England and Ireland, in both of which countries the raising of that crop was forbidden. The companies were to supply their own output and at least 40,000 pounds of Spanish tobacco from Venezuela annually, and all deliveries were to be made in London at company expense. The king would bear one-third of the subsequent distribution costs, including customs duties, and would receive one-third of the revenue from sales.[59]

Many stockholders disliked the terms of the proposed contract, objecting to the inclusion of Spanish tobacco and to the amount of money to be paid to the crown. Sandys, on the other hand, considered the offer acceptable and manipulated acceptance of the contract at a joint meeting of the two interested parties in Novem-

[58] Beer, *Origins*, pp. 117–133, describes the tobacco regulations and the subsequent disruption of the company.
[59] Morton, *Colonial Virginia*, I, 92–97, is a good treatment of these events.

ber, 1622. This vote enraged and solidified the opposition, and Robert Johnson, Sir Thomas Smythe's son-in-law, began cooperating with the Earl of Warwick and the latter's cousin, Sir Nathaniel Rich, in efforts to undermine Sandys. The Smythe-Warwick faction appealed to the government for an improvement in the terms of the contract and secured a hearing, which was held in March, 1623. The bitterness of the testimony by the two warring factions focused official attention on colonial affairs, and in April the Privy Council created a commission headed by Sir William Jones to investigate conditions in Virginia and Bermuda. At the same time, to the delight of Sandys' enemies, the government canceled the tobacco contract.

Lack of funds and internal dissension had by then rendered the Virginia Company virtually inoperative, and in July, 1623, the Privy Council assumed temporary jurisdiction over the colony. The special commission shortly recommended abolishing the charter and placing the Virginia government permanently and directly in the king's hands. James agreed and ordered the company to vote on acceptance of the proposal. With many members conspicuously absent, the company voted 60 to 9 to reject the arrangement. The attorney general thereupon commenced legal proceedings on November 4, 1623, aimed at dissolving the company.[60]

The Privy Council meanwhile decided to look into conditions in America. It appointed a five-man investigating commission, and at least four of its members were Virginia residents, former residents, or men with business interests there. Two of this number, John Pory, former colonial secretary, and John Harvey, a ship captain who later became governor, came over from England in February, 1624, bringing news that the Privy Council contemplated giving the crown direct authority over Virginia. The general assembly reacted unfavorably, arguing that what the settlers really needed was greater freedom under the existing system and blaming much of the past trouble on the misrule of Sir Thomas Smythe. Ignoring the fact that the commissioners officially represented the home government, the assembly addressed a petition to the Privy Council, pleading for retention of their legislature, greater control over their affairs, some flexibility in interpreting orders from England, and

60 Andrews, *Colonial Period*, I, 172–178.

certain limits on gubernatorial authority. One of the five commissioners, Captain Samuel Mathews, was also an assembly member, and he placed himself in a distinctly ambiguous position by agreeing to become one of the signers of the petition. The commissioners wrote a report approving the king's desire to revoke the charter and to obliterate self-government in the colony. The assembly understandably refused to sign its copy of the report, declaring that James had been greatly misinformed about Virginia, "one of the goodlyest partes of the earth," and most worthy of the king's care. Unimpressed, John Pory went back to England convinced that the company's efforts to establish a successful colony had failed.[61]

Virginians were appalled at the possibility of losing their general assembly, for which they had developed considerable respect. In spite of what settlers believed to be disinterest and even antipathy on the company's part, the people's representatives had built up a body of legislation designed to protect the public and strengthen the colony. They had required the governor to ask their approval before levying taxes or requisitioning labor. They had taken measures to provide for the worship of God, the payment of ministers, and the preservation of morals. Other laws established public granaries and a gunpowder supply and arranged for defense against the Indians. In the interest of security, it was enacted that in perilous times no person might disobey the government, just as no servant might disobey his master.

The government action against the company was tried in the Court of King's Bench in May, 1624, and Chief Justice James Ley rendered a decision in favor of the monarch. The charter was declared vacated. The company was dissolved, and Virginia became England's first royal colony. A new commission headed by Sir John Mandeville, president of the Privy Council, and including Sir Nathaniel Rich, Robert Johnson, Captain Samuel Argall, and John Pory, then undertook to reorganize the political structure of Virginia. This group decided on complete concentration of power, subject only to direction by the Privy Council, in the hands of a governor appointed by the king, assisted by a twelve-man council. No provision was made for continuation of the general assembly.

[61] Craven, *Dissolution of the Virginia Company*, Chap. IX, "The Royal Investigation of 1623," and Chap. X, "The Dissolution of the Company."

In August Sir Francis Wyatt was reappointed governor, and council members were selected.[62]

Some authorities have maintained that King James took the action he did because of animosity toward Sir Edwin Sandys, a liberal-minded member of Parliament, with which the king was feuding, and because of Parliament, the king found this apparent trend toward self-government in Virginia uncongenial. It is more generally accepted, however, that James's objective was peaceful and efficient government in the colony. According to this theory, the king destroyed the company simply because it was incapable of establishing an economically and politically stable plantation.[63]

The death of James I in March, 1625, automatically terminated the Mandeville commission along with all other activities being conducted under royal directive. The Privy Council appointed two new committees to deal with Virginia, one to continue with arrangements for its government and the other to study the tobacco import problem. The change of rulers gave the now defunct Virginia Company one last brief reprieve, because the new king, Charles I, liked Sandys and agreed to reconsider the matter of the charter. The Sandys faction excoriated their opponents at a Privy Council hearing and demanded that the company be given a patent confirmed by Parliament or at least that the colony be placed in the hands of a committee favorable to Sandys and his followers. This intemperance convinced Charles that the previous ruling had been wise, and on May 13 he refused to revive the Virginia Company.[64]

The company had based its organization on several misconceptions which made eventual failure inevitable. Its limited financial resources would have been adequate only if a quick and easy profit could have been taken out of Virginia. This was an impossibility, there being no potential trade with the natives and no readily available product of great value to loot and ship home to England. The only alternative was to build the colony inch by inch to the point where it could support itself and return a profit. The management lacked not only the money but the experience and wisdom to achieve this objective. The result was that it lost control on both sides of the Atlantic. The stockholders became impatient and

62 Flippin, *Royal Government*, p. 31.
63 *Ibid.*, p. 31; Morton *Colonial Virginia*, I, 105–109.
64 Andrews, *Colonial Period*, I, 193.

created dissension in London, while the colonists got absorbed in their own developing world with its increasingly complex relationships, to the point where their primary concern was no longer their affiliation with the company.[65] As one recent observer has commented, "It was the Company's fate to have created a country and to have destroyed itself in the process."[66]

The English government should have learned from its experience with Virginia in the years prior to 1624 that a business corporation was not ideally equipped to administer a colony. The manifest inadequacy of the Virginia Company established without doubt that some other form of organization was to be preferred when future colonizing ventures were undertaken. The men who ran England closed their eyes to the implications of Virginia, however, and soon erected a similar corporate structure to undertake the settlement of Massachusetts Bay.

[65] *Ibid.*, pp. 178–179.
[66] Diamond, "From Organization to Society," p. 473.

CHAPTER 3

Virginia, Royal Colony

THE new royal government in England was calculated to prove more effective than the previous regime, and it was well that this should be so, because the colony had to contend with many grave problems. Tobacco had established itself as a profitable cash crop, but sole reliance on it could be risky. Some geographical expansion seemed inevitable, but it would have to be regulated to maintain administrative control and to avoid disagreements with the Indians. Local government would have to become more complex as the population burgeoned and spread out, and, if possible, the new rulers would have to find ways to please the colonists as well as the king in England.

There was considerable danger that representative government would come to an end after just a few years of usefulness, because the new arrangements made no provision for further meetings of the general assembly. Governor Wyatt did, however, summon what he called a "convention" of elected delegates in 1625 to discuss the current situation with him and to give advice. Similar nonlegislative meetings in 1628 and most years thereafter debated matters of current interest, thereby continuing the tradition of representative gatherings. Finally in 1639 the king obliged the anxious Virginians and ended fifteen years of uncertainty by giving formal consent to the calling of annual general assemblies.[1] Virginia's persistence

[1] Charles M. Andrews, *The Colonial Period in American History* (4 vols., New Haven, 1934–38), I, 194–205, gives a perceptive analysis of these meetings. The

thus turned a royal colony into a self-governing colony with a governor and council appointed in England and a representative legislature chosen by the people.[2] The inhabitants of any royal colony
were assured thereafter of the right to help make laws, levy taxes,
and direct local affairs. Virginia's victory came at a time, curiously,
when King Charles was attempting to govern England without
Parliament.

The census of 1625 listed 1,478 inhabitants, of whom 269 were
females and 23 were Negroes, and there was thereafter a slow but
steady growth for a number of years. The largest population con-
centrations were in James City County and at Hampton. Plantations
had by then spread all along both sides of the James River, and the
fishing and saltmaking outpost still existed on the Eastern Shore.
The colonists pressed their attacks on the Indians, whom they
displaced by steadily absorbing their land. Gains were being
made, but hard-core difficulties and weaknesses remained, as Wyatt
pointed out at the end of his first term.

Sir John Harvey arrived to take over the governorship in 1630.
His visit to Virginia in 1623 as one of the commissioners had
familiarized him with the colony, and his intentions appear to
have been good. Unfortunately, his pride, stubbornness, bad temper,
and lack of humor predestined him to failure.[3] Before leaving
England he had attempted to get permission from the Privy Council
to call a general assembly to confirm the settlers in the ownership of
their land. This request was denied, because the ownership question
was to be settled in England, but the colonists were allowed to elect
representatives to adopt laws which the king could approve at his
pleasure. When the new governor convened the meeting in the

---

author contends that Virginia was kept in a state of uncertainty, not because
the home government chose to be perverse, but rather because it was unable
until 1638 to decide what form of government would be most suitable for the
colony.

[2] All inhabitants were eligible to vote for burgesses until 1655, when a law
was passed limiting the franchise to all housekeepers, whether freeholders,
leaseholders, or other tenants. Richard B. Morris, *Government and Labor in
Early America* (New York, 1946), p. 504.

[3] There is universal agreement that Harvey had an unfortunate personality,
but Herbert Osgood, *The American Colonies in the Seventeenth Century* (3
vols., New York, 1904–7), III, 97, attributes some of his difficulties to greed and
the mishandling of funds.

spring of 1630 soon after his arrival, both the representatives and
the council turned out to be querulous. Harvey found himself
caught between the king and Privy Council on the one hand
and a strong-willed, able group of colonists on the other. The latter
gave full expression to their exasperation, outraged by what they
felt to be impractical instructions from London.

No small part of Harvey's trouble was caused by a man named
William Capps. This eccentric former burgess returned from a
visit to England armed with a letter signed by the king, which
directed the governor and his council to develop new industries and
to make use of Capp's skill as a consultant while so doing. The
nettled governor reported back to London that Virginia possessed
the initiative to undertake production of new commodities but that
it lacked the means. A meeting of elected representatives of the
settlers supported Harvey by addressing a report to the king asserting
that production of new staples could not be undertaken without
proper equipment. The report also stated that great harm had been
done to the colony by the rumor that tobacco would shortly be
monopolized in England.[4]

Harvey then went to England to set matters right, deputizing a
councillor, Dr. John Pott, to act as governor during his absence.
When Harvey returned, he preferred numerous charges against Pott,
removed him, deprived him of his plantation near Williamsburg,
and imprisoned him. This highhanded course of action alienated
many council members and made a bad impression in London. A
group of English officials came to the conclusion that Pott had
been convicted on insufficient evidence and prevailed on the king
to set him free and restore his property.

Rigidity and lack of charm would have made Sir John Harvey
an indifferent administrator at best, but it was his poor luck to have
a council made up of ambitious, self-seeking men. He could not
dominate them, and they delighted in reminding him that the king
had promised that all important decisions should be made with
their advice. Harvey complained that his authority in the council
had been reduced to a "bare casting voice," and he begged the king
to differentiate between his powers and those of the council. Un-

4 Richard Lee Morton, *Colonial Virginia* (2 vols., Chapel Hill, N.C., 1960),
I, 117.

aware of the meaning of this internecine struggle, the Privy Council commanded both parties to stop quarreling and to govern the people in peace. The governor and his councillors thereupon signed an agreement to work in harmony, but they had by no means composed their discord, and their truce was bound to be of short duration.

A recent scholar has suggested that a radical shift in the social organization of Virginia underlay Governor Harvey's difficulties.[5] When Virginia and the later colonies were founded, the settlers accepted without question the close relationship between social structure and political authority that had prevailed in England from time immemorial. The superior class monopolized riches, dignity, and power, and this superiority was indivisible. A man was not a political figure or a social entity; if he was one, he was inevitably both. The squire thus enforced the statutes, decrees, and local ordinances, and he also distributed the benefices to the clergy and fixed the terms of the tenancies and leaseholds. This "amateur competence" made possible the continuing identity in England between political and social authority, and a man living there did not pass easily from the lower to the upper class. In Virginia during the first generation, in other words until about 1630, these same conditions prevailed, the leaders being drawn from the upper echelons of British society. Eight of the twenty men who were councillors in 1621 had attended Oxford University. They were in touch with the political and intellectual currents of the age, and several of them were actively interested in natural history and in literary pursuits. During this earliest period, the Virginia leadership was characteristic of what was normally found anywhere in the English-speaking world.

This small coterie of rulers began to disappear shortly thereafter, some dying and others returning to England. By 1630 they had all departed one way or another, and no men of their type remained in Virginia to succeed them. The council then fell into the hands of the hardiest and most ambitious of the surviving early planters, who coveted membership, not because they accepted it as a natural

---

[5] Bernard Bailyn, "Politics and Social Structure in Virginia," in James Morton Smith (ed.), *Seventeenth-Century America: Essays in Colonial History* (Chapel Hill, N.C., 1959), pp. 90–97.

obligation, but because it exempted them from taxation. These men had risen from obscurity by virtue of hard work and shrewd manipulation, and they were an unsentimental, quick-tempered, crudely ambitious lot. They had earned their new authority because of their ability to exploit the wilderness, and they continued to concern themselves with profits, including landed wealth, but not with the graces of life. Lacking the attributes of social authority and enjoying a tenuous dominance that had to be sustained by continuous achievement, they did not qualify as a true ruling class. Because they were a new breed, they also lacked that sense of responsibility to the public that rests upon a deep identification with the land and the people. The objectives of such men as Samuel Mathews, Sr., George Menefie, John Utie, Abraham Wood, and William Spencer were essentially selfish, and for this reason they urged unrestricted access to land, autonomous local jurisdiction, and an aggressive expansion of settlement. They remained the most substantial figures in Virginia until 1650, and in their capacities as councillors they exercised a considerable influence over public events.

The ambitions of this clique clashed with Sir John Harvey's policies. The governor questioned the legality of land grants made prior to his regime, and he wanted land returned to the public which had once been the property of the Virginia Company. He also limited territorial expansion in order to stabilize relations with the Indians. Furthermore, he did not favor William Claiborne's claim to Kent Island in Maryland or the monopoly of the Chesapeake trade or unrestricted commerce with the Dutch. His sponsorship of crop diversification annoyed planters whose new prosperity derived entirely from tobacco cultivation, and they were further offended by his favorable attitude toward the establishment of an English monopoly over that profitable crop. Harvey argued that the governorship involved more than merely the chairmanship of the council. His quarrel with the planter cabal deteriorated into a personal feud, and he was eventually undone by the unreasonableness of his actions.

The Indian massacre of 1622 temporarily discouraged expansion toward the frontier, and the settlers even abandoned Henrico and the Charles City district for a brief time. The population continued to inch upward, however, and the burgeoning tobacco culture demanded fresh lands. The lower James being already occupied,

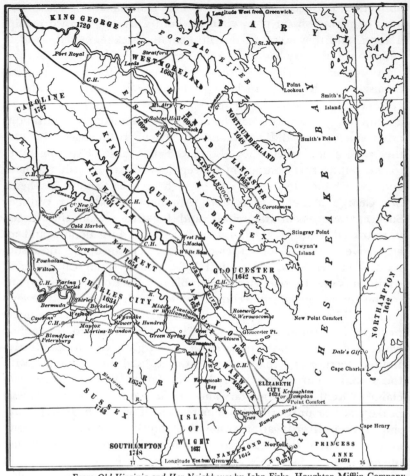

From *Old Virginia and Her Neighbours* by John Fiske, Houghton Mifflin Company

TIDEWATER VIRGINIA

planters began to consider Chiskiack on the south side of the York, a few miles upriver from where Yorktown now stands. The Chiskiack location, if fortified and colonized, it was felt, would provide protection against the Indians living across the river. Accordingly, the council offered a fifty-acre grant in October, 1630, to anyone who would settle there within a year. The famous palisade stretching across the peninsula from Archer Hope Creek, a tributary of the James, to the York soon guaranteed planters there some measure of security. Middle Plantation, later renamed Williamsburg, was founded at this time midway between the James and the York.[6] In 1631 William Claiborne, who had been driven by Lord Baltimore from Kent Island, his trading post in Maryland at the head of the Chesapeake, received a grant on the Pamunkey River, near the head of the York.

Renewed expansion was accompanied by an increased flow of immigration, and by 1635 the population was nearly 5,000, approximately double that of 1630.[7] Every family had its house, its garden and orchard, and a field for raising cattle and hogs. Tobacco culture required many hands, and hundreds of indentured servants arrived every year from England. Their masters paid for their passage and received under the headright system a fifty-acre grant for each person so transported.

Increasing population required a more decentralized administrative organization, and by 1634 the colony converted the four general plantations and the seven leading particular plantations into eight counties. The six counties on the James River, beginning at its mouth, were Elizabeth City, Warrasqueoc (now Isle of Wight), Warwick River (later Warwick), James City, Charles City, and Henrico. The last-named county, located at the falls of the river, extended indefinitely westward. The occupied territory on the York River was organized as Charles River County (now York), and the Eastern Shore area became Accomack County. Most of these early counties straddled streams, which provided the principal transportation routes, but roads later replaced waterways, and some boundaries were altered accordingly. Elizabeth City County originally spanned Hampton Roads, but in 1636 the part of it lying south of the Roads became New Norfolk, which was eventually divided into Upper Norfolk (now Nansemond) and Lower Norfolk (later Norfolk and Princess Anne). Accomack County became Northamp-

---

[6] Morton, *Colonial Virginia*, I, 122–124.

[7] Evarts B. Greene and Virginia D. Harrington, *American Population Before the Federal Census of 1790* (New York, 1932), p. 136. In answer to the controversial question why the Virginia population increased so slowly, to a mere 33,000 in 1660, Wyndham B. Blanton concludes that the main reason was that less than a fifth of the immigrants arriving before 1660 were women. *Colonial Medicine Symposium* (Richmond, Va., 1957), pp. 71–72.

ton in 1643. Twenty years later it was split into two units, the southern section retaining the name Northampton, while the northern section revived the name Accomack. In 1652 the south side of James City became Surry County.[8]

Other counties were added as new land was occupied. Northumberland, located in the Northern Neck between the Rappahannock and the Potomac, dates from 1648. In 1651 its southern portion became the principal part of newly organized Lancaster County. Gloucester, between the York and the Rappahannock, was created that same year. By 1654 the Claiborne grant on the Pamunkey became New Kent County.[9] Virginia expanded by 1660 far beyond the confines of the original eight counties into the Pamunkey Valley and along the coastline of the Chesapeake from the Potomac to Hampton Roads. In a number of places the settlements were approaching the fall line.

Local government took on fixed institutional forms following the organization of counties. Officials formerly known as commissioners became justices of the peace. The governor and council appointed the justices, along with sheriffs, constables, clerks, and coroners. Single justices had jurisdiction in petty cases, both civil and criminal, but where more was involved, several justices sat together, such meetings being regularized in 1643 as the county court. Every defendant was entitled to a jury trial, and he could appeal its decision to the general court, consisting of the governor and council, which sat quarterly in judicial session at Jamestown. Punishments included jail terms as well as the use of the whipping post, pillory, and ducking stool, and in certain cases public confession in church was required.[10] The justices also had a variety of administrative duties, as did their counterparts in England. Their responsibilities included maintaining the public peace and the general welfare, probating wills, granting letters of administration, supervising ferries and establishing ferry rates, licensing inns and

8 Osgood, *American Colonies*, III, 80–81; Susie M. Ames (ed.), *County Court Records of Accomack-Northampton, Virginia, 1632–1640* (Washington, 1954), pp. xvii–xlix.

9 Morton, *Colonial Virginia*, I, 127.

10 *Ibid.*, pp. 127–129. See also Andrews, *Colonial Period*, I, 127–129, which points out that most convictions involved the servant class in Virginia, a situation that was true throughout the colonies. Cf. Morris, *Government and Labor*, pp. 461–512.

regulating liquor prices, and laying out parishes as directed by the assembly. The justices, one of whom in each county also acted as sheriff, were influential men who received only expenses for their services. The church, too, performed certain public functions, such as caring for the poor, and churchwardens were charged with delivering a true presentment of any misdemeanors coming to their attention. The assembly in 1632 made provision for the building and maintenance of highways, which were to be laid out as the justices in each county or the parishioners in each parish agreed. Governor Harvey, anxious to uphold his prerogative and provoked by his council, did not have an easy time during the last three years of his administration, 1636 to 1639. Like every royal governor, he was plagued by the problem of keeping a working balance between the wishes of the crown and the demands of a pioneer community. In addition he faced the unusual problems relating to tobacco. The Virginia planters had to contend with periodic gluts in the English market, lack of regulation in the quantity and quality of the product, and all the shortcomings of a one-crop agricultural system. Prior to this time Charles I had excluded Spanish tobacco from England and had attempted to create a monopoly of the trade from Virginia and the Bermudas. The colony agreed tentatively to the policy but then found the suggested conditions thoroughly unacceptable. The governor and council wrote in March, 1628, that the very word "contract" discouraged the colony, and the assembly remained so opposed to the contract idea that no attempt was made to impose one during Harvey's administration.

Although the king had ordered Virginia to diversify agriculture back in 1627, Governor Harvey complained that more tobacco was being grown than ever before, to the point where an actual food shortage developed. Concurrently, the price of tobacco fell to less than a penny a pound, the lowest level ever experienced. Harvey would have rooted out this "stinking commodity," but he admitted ruefully that without it the economy would collapse. An effort was consequently made to tighten controls, and, following instructions, the assembly codified its tobacco laws in 1633. The new legislation stipulated that no one might grow more than fifteen hundred plants and that only the finer grades could be raised. All tobacco must thereafter be brought to Jamestown, where all tobacco contracts would be made and where a set price would be determined.

The governor ordered the planting of two acres of corn per settler, and in 1634 he was able to report that tobacco planting had decreased. The price of the commodity did not improve, however, and the rapid expansion of the outlying districts made many of the restrictions ineffective. In 1640, after Harvey left office, the government ordered the destruction of half of all the good tobacco in order to limit the crop to two and a half million pounds. The price of tobacco was fixed at that time, and debtors were relieved for a three-year period from paying more than two-thirds of what they owed. In spite of all these measures, the good prices of the earlier days never returned.[11]

The founding of Maryland was another problem with which Virginia had to contend, because it not only pushed back the northern limits of Virginia but brought a new tobacco competitor into existence. Lord Baltimore arrived in Virginia in 1628 from his colony in Newfoundland, bringing with him his family and a retinue of friends. He intended to plant a new colony in a climate milder than the one from which he had come, and it seemed for a time that he would settle in Virginia. Dr. John Pott, who was then the acting governor, tendered the party the usual oaths of supremacy and allegiance, but Baltimore and his followers refused to take them, because they were Roman Catholics.[12] Baltimore returned to England, where he renewed his request for a haven for members of his faith. He died before a grant could be made, so it was to his son, Cecilius Calvert, that the Maryland charter was issued in 1632.

The council of Virginia was so much disturbed at the prospect of a Roman Catholic colony within territory it regarded as its own that it dispatched William Claiborne, councillor and secretary of the colony, to England to remonstrate. Claiborne, a member of the council cabal, had a special interest in the land at stake, because he and a number of associates had already made a settle-

11 George L. Beer treats the subject of tobacco regulations fully in his *Origins of the British Colonial System* (New York, 1908), Chap. VI. For a description of the colony's activities seen as part of the imperial tobacco problem, see Charles M. MacInnes, *The Early English Tobacco Trade* (London, 1926).

12 Thomas J. Wertenbaker, *Virginia Under the Stuarts, 1607–1688* (Princeton, N.J., 1914), p. 69, maintains that Pott's action was deliberately intended to drive Baltimore out of Virginia.

ment on Kent Island, which was represented in the House of Burgesses. Virginians petitioned vainly that they not be deprived of such a large portion of their heritage.

The ill feeling between Governor Harvey and the council came to a head in 1635. Word reached him in April of that year that Captain Francis Pott, brother of the former acting governor, had read a paper directed against him and had then delivered a series of inflammatory speeches. Without consulting his council, Harvey imprisoned the Potts brothers and several others presumed to be their supporters, put them in irons, and made plans to dispose of them by martial law. The council met and demanded a legal trial for the prisoners. Harvey's response was to demand that each councillor put in writing what punishment he thought suitable for men who attempted to provoke disobedience of "their Majesty's substitute." The council cabal declined to do this, basing their stand on the fact that the governor had refused to send the assembly's answer about the tobacco monopoly to England. Samuel Mathews, Sr., a leading councillor, told Harvey that he had better go to England to seek redress for the people's complaints, warning him that the colonists would not be appeased until he did so.[13] Harvey replied haughtily that he had no intention of returning until the king called him. The feuding parties were now past the point where any compromise remained possible. The councillors framed a set of propositions for the governor to sign, but he refused. Harvey then demanded that the assembly members go home, but instead they composed a list of grievances addressed to the Lords of Trade and the Plantations.[14] On April 28, 1635, they "thrust out" Harvey, and the council, acting on its own initiative, chose as his successor John West, an old planter and brother of Lord De la Warr.[15]

Denouncing West as a usurper, Harvey sailed for England, sharing passage from necessity with two of the alleged mutineers, Francis Pott and Thomas Harwood, who were carrying letters to the king

---

[13] Ivor Noël Hume, chief archaeologist of Colonial Williamsburg, has unearthed a fine collection of plantation artifacts of the second quarter of the seventeenth century at Denbigh Plantation, which was owned by Mathews (died *ca.* 1657), the father of Governor Samuel Mathews.

[14] A committee of the Privy Council.

[15] This whole series of events is well treated in Osgood, *American Colonies*, III, 98–101.

in which the Mathews faction stated its case. Upon arrival at Plymouth on July 14, Harvey persuaded the mayor of that city to seize the letters and to imprison his enemies. He then requested the lords commissioners to settle the Virginia dispute promptly, but the Privy Council was determined to hear both sides. Not permitted to answer the charges against him until December, 1635, Harvey denied the accusations, admitting only that he had assumed authority over the council, and finally he was acquitted and given a new commission as governor. This bitter experience improved neither his temper nor his discretion, and as soon as he returned to Virginia in January, 1637, he charged his enemies with treason and shipped West, Mathews, and others to England to be tried by the Court of Star Chamber. He then began seizing his opponents' property, but on appeal, because several of them were prisoners in England, he was compelled to restore their land. His quarrels and arbitrary actions finally exhausted the patience of the Privy Council, which removed him from office in 1639. Sir Francis Wyatt was reappointed governor, retaining the council which had effected Harvey's downfall. After two uneventful years, Wyatt was supplanted in February, 1642, by Sir William Berkeley, Virginia's best-known colonial ruler.[16]

Well connected, well traveled, and a well-educated graduate of Merton College, Oxford, Governor Berkeley was thirty-four years old at the time of his appointment, and he was known personally to King Charles. In spite of the fact that he was a staunch believer in divine-right rule, he did not encounter any great acrimony during his long first term of ten years. He brought a congenial personality to his task and succeeded in reconciling factions in the council and in the assembly, and because his instructions were identical with those previously given Wyatt, there was no sharp break in policy. Berkeley sympathized to some extent with men who wished to see the province expanded, and he had no intention of disturbing the status of the yearly legislative meetings, trial by jury, or the right of petition. Adding to the general feeling of security was the king's announcement in July, 1642, that he did not plan to change

<hr />

16 *Ibid.*, pp. 101–104. Osgood contends that by 1642, when Berkeley became governor, the colony had for all practical purposes reached its full development as a royal province.

the form of government which had, as was evident, given satisfaction throughout the colony.

There was considerable progress during the early years of Berkeley's rule. With his approval, the colony repealed the poll tax paid annually to the governor, and it made peace with the Indians and reached an agreement with Maryland concerning trade in Chesapeake Bay. The authorities altered tax assessments so that they corresponded to the value of land and the ability to pay, and they followed English law as closely as possible in court proceedings. No appropriations were made or taxes levied without approval by the assembly. Relief was granted indigent debtors in prison, and rapacious attorneys were removed from office. In 1645 Virginia limited the number of burgesses to four from each county, except the capital county, James City, which was allowed five. That same year the assembly arranged to have the freemen elect vestrymen. The colony made an attempt to replace tobacco, which suffered from periodic price fluctuations, with coins as the medium of exchange. When the civil war in England put an end to Berkeley's salary as royal governor, the assembly voted him an allowance, and when he visited England in 1644, it arranged to pay his expenses. During Berkeley's one-year absence, Richard Kemp acted as governor.

Sir William was under instructions to maintain the establishment of the Church of England.[17] There being few Catholics in the colony, there was little to fear from that quarter. There were Puritans in southside Virginia, but they were not inclined toward the passionate disputes which threatened to engulf England. Seventy of them did send a petition to Boston in 1642, requesting that three ministers be sent to Upper Norfolk (Nansemond) County. The Boston church elders selected John Knowles, William Thompson, and Thomas James, all men of good education, and they received a warm welcome when they arrived to begin their work. In 1643, however, the assembly reacted to events in England by passing a law requiring all clergymen to conform to the practices of the Church of England. At the same time it ordered all nonconformists to leave the colony. James and Knowles obeyed, but Thompson, an Oxford graduate, decided to stay, and he attracted many followers,

17 William H. Seiler, "The Anglican Parish in Virginia," in Smith (ed.), *Seventeenth-Century America: Essays in Colonial History*, pp. 119–142, describes the organization and operation of the parishes during this period.

including the Reverend Thomas Harrison of the Elizabeth River parish. In April, 1645, Harrison was presented by his wardens for refusing to read the Book of Common Prayer, but the governor allowed him to stay on for another three years. Later, when Harrison's parishioners complained to Parliament that their minister had finally been banished, Cromwell's Council of State reminded Berkeley that the use of the Book of Common Prayer had been forbidden by law. Harrison should consequently be restored, it was pointed out, but no such action was taken, because the minister decided to return to England at that time. Considering Berkeley's loyalty to King Charles, whom the English Puritans had been fighting for six years, his relations with the local Puritans were not overly oppressive. Consequently, many people leaning toward non-conformity remained in Virginia until 1649, when several hundred migrated to Maryland, where a strong Puritan faction had arisen.[18]

The last concerted Indian attack during this period took place on April 18, 1644. It affected principally the settlers living south of the James rather than the colony as a whole, and yet the death toll reached five hundred, a total greater than the losses during the 1622 massacre. During the years since that earlier disaster, the colonists' desire for profits had overcome their prudence, and they had increasingly ignored the regulations governing trade with the natives. Although Opechancanough had by this time become feeble, it was he who engineered the attack from his seat on Pamunkey Neck (now West Point). John Winthrop and his Massachusetts associates regarded the tragedy as punishment visited upon Virginia for driving out the ministers they had sent. A contemporary account, *A Perfect Description of Virginia,* claimed that Opechancanough roused his people to action because he learned that there was strife and a consequent weakening of control in England.[19] The most logical explanation would appear to be that the native leader regarded this as an opportune moment, possibly one of the last that would be available, to halt the white man's inexorable advance into the Indian hunting grounds.

[18] Fully discussed in Babette Levy, "Puritanism in the Southern and Island Colonies," American Antiquarian Society *Proceedings*, LXX, Pt. I (1960), 122–134.

[19] (London, 1649), reprinted in Force, *Tracts*, II.

The colonists who survived the attack fled into older districts but then rallied quickly under Berkeley and drove the Indians back, killing many and destroying their villages and crops. When Berkeley made his trip to England, Acting Governor Kemp, former secretary of the colony, took over direction of the war with the help of able military leaders. In October the assembly decided it was safe for the settlers to move back to their homes, providing there were at least ten able-bodied men near every habitation. Opechancanough was taken prisoner and moved to Jamestown, where he was killed by a soldier. The Indians sued for peace, and in October, 1646, Chief Necotowance agreed to terms, acknowledging that he held his territory from the king of England and arranging to pay an annual tribute of twenty beaver skins. The colonists gave all the land north of the York River to the Indians, who in turn "ceded" the whole peninsula from the falls to Hampton Roads. Trading was to be limited in the future to certain forts, and neither party would be permitted to enter the other's territory. Unstable as it was, this peace lasted until 1676.[20]

The Indian war merely delayed the inevitable westward march, which had always interested the government as well as land speculators and influential planters. The possibilities improved when Berkeley came, because he favored expansion, whereas Harvey had resisted it. Four prominent colonists petitioned the assembly in 1641 for permission to undertake discovery of a river west and south of Appomattox, and two years later the legislature granted this request, while reserving the "royal fifth" from any ore mined. Though the massacre intervened, this agreement set a precedent for future action. Later governors awarded a trade monopoly for fourteen years and stipulated that, when the grantees made their choice of newly discovered land, they must make the remainder available to others.

After the Indian uprising was suppressed, the assembly voted to build four forts located at the falls of the James, the forks of the York, the ridge of the Chickahominy, and the falls of the Appomattox. The men assigned as commanders received title to the forts and to adjacent land. Fort Henry, the name given to the establish-

---

[20] Wilcomb E. Washburn, "The Moral and Legal Justifications for Dispossessing the Indians," in Smith (ed.), *Seventeenth-Century America: Essays in Colonial History*, pp. 15–32, discusses the case of the Indian.

ment of the Appomattox location, was intended to protect the south side of the James, and it has since become Petersburg. Captain Abraham Wood, who was in charge of its forty-five-man garrison for thirty years, built it into a trading post of great importance. Similarly Henry Fleet traded from the head of the Potomac tidewater, and William Byrd conducted his commercial activity at the falls of the James. The development of these military outposts opened up Indian trade in the interior, utilizing packhorses to carry guns, ammunition, hardware, and trinkets to be traded for furs and other forest products. It was a profitable but at the same time a hazardous pursuit.[21]

In 1650 Abraham Wood, Edward Bland, and five other men set out on horseback toward the southwest, far beyond the fringes of settlement. Berkeley was interested in their venture and had himself planned two years previously to explore in the same region. Virginians had never ceased to hope that some day they would find great deposits of precious minerals or at least rich resources in furs. Wood's expedition crossed the Nottaway and reached the falls of the Roanoke, but the members returned to Fort Henry after only a four-day trip because they encountered so many indications of possible Indian hostility. The travelers were convinced that they had found a route to the "Great Sea," which the Indians told them was but a few days' journey beyond. Bland accordingly secured an order from the legislature authorizing him to conduct further explorations, provided he would take one hundred well-armed men with him. He died before carrying out the plan, and another trip by Wood to the Roanoke, hardly more than one hundred miles from Jamestown, was the most ambitious expedition into the wilderness before 1660.[22]

Meanwhile, Charles I, who had ascended the throne a year after the dissolution of the Virginia Company, was in deep trouble at home. His arbitrary rule had led to the Petition of Right in 1628. The following year Charles dismissed Parliament and then, thanks to foreign subsidies, was able to govern England without the legislature for eleven years. When Parliament finally did reconvene in

[21] Clarence W. Alvord and Lee Bidgood, *The First Explorations of the Trans-Allegheny Region by the Virginians, 1650–1674* (Cleveland, 1912), pp. 32–33.
[22] *Ibid.*, pp. 47–51.

November, 1640, strife broke out again. In August, 1642, Charles raised his standard at Nottingham, supported by an army, and seven years of civil war began. England was destined for military rule for eleven years, and the Stuarts had to wait until 1660 to regain the throne.

Governor Berkeley sided with the king, and so did the colonists, who remembered how he had managed the dissolution of the Virginia Company and the Harvey mutiny without injury to them. Moreover, he had more than tacitly approved their system of representative government, and he never took any action against such Puritanism as manifested itself in Virginia. The settlers were remote from the center of the struggle, with the result that the support they offered Charles was based on broad loyalty rather than on an understanding of precisely what was happening.[23]

Events in England bewildered Virginians and created considerable suspicion. Early in the war both sides placed an embargo on such items as arms, ammunition, and shoes, all of which were sorely needed in the colony. Soon after Charles' execution in January, 1649, the Council of State transmitted a notice of the change of government and demanded obedience to the Commonwealth. That fall it recommended that Parliament appoint commissioners to Virginia with power to take over its affairs and select a governor and council. The Virginia legislature responded in October by asserting that the authority of Parliament was null and void. It added that anyone defending the proceedings against Charles I would be prosecuted as an accessory to the king's execution, that speaking evil of the king was punishable at the discretion of the governor and council, and that it was high treason to question the authority of the Virginia government in any way or to propose any change in that government. The assembly echoed these sentiments by declaring that the proceedings against the king were malicious and contrary to the laws of the kingdom as well as to the laws of God himself.[24]

The war had an important effect on the population of Virginia.

23 Philip A. Bruce, *Institutional History of Virginia in the Seventeenth Century* (2 vols., New York, 1910; reprinted Gloucester, Mass., 1964), I, 274–277.

24 Wesley Frank Craven, *The Southern Colonies in the Seventeenth Century, 1607–1689* (Baton Rouge, La., 1949), Chap. VII, gives a detailed account of Virginia's course during the Civil War.

Many planters who had gone home to England returned to the colony during this period, and after Prince Charles' defeat at Worcester in 1651, more than a thousand royalist prisoners were given leave to migrate there. Royalist newcomers like Colonel Richard Lee, Edward Digges, William Randolph, Colonel George Mason, and John Page founded distinguished families. Governor Berkeley welcomed these "distressed cavaliers" and appointed some of them to office.[25]

England's antiroyalist government was initially too involved in more urgent matters to undertake the subjugation of colonies loyal to the king, such as Virginia, Barbados, Bermuda, and Antigua. In May, 1649, however, the Rump Parliament, in its Act Establishing the Commonwealth, assumed authority over all colonies and territories. Shortly thereafter, in October, 1650, Parliament prohibited trade between its colonies and all foreign countries, except when conducted by specially licensed ships.[26] By 1653, after Virginia came under Cromwell's control, the home government relaxed its embargo on arms, ammunition, and other imports and, fearing Dutch commercial competition, made an effort to supply the colonies with their needs. Parliament made it clear to the colonists that they owed their very existence to English money, effort, and protection and that ignoring its authority amounted to treason. When news of this declaration reached Virginia, Berkeley addressed the assembly, accusing Parliament of depriving Virginians of their liberties of speech and conscience and of their freedom of trade. Announcing that he would "not submit to murderers," he pleaded with the settlers to follow him to victory, come what might.[27] The assembly adopted a strong declaration, reiterating its loyalty to the king, praying for restoration of the monarchy, and demanding that their merchants be permitted to trade with all nations approved of by the late King Charles I.

Virginians could not resist drawing frequent comparisons between

25 Morton, Colonial Virginia, I, 166–168, gives sketches of a number of these immigrants. For their effect on Virginia, see also Philip A. Bruce, Social Life in Virginia in the Seventeenth Century (2d ed., Lynchburg, Va., 1927), pp. 76, 79, and Thomas J. Wertenbaker, Patrician and Plebeian in Virginia, or The Origin and Development of the Social Classes of the Old Dominion (Charlottesville, Va., 1910), pp. 20–28.

26 Andrews, Colonial Period, IV, 35–41.

27 Morton, Colonial Virginia, I, 169.

the Dutch merchants who had helped them in time of necessity and the English merchants who had neglected them. These references irritated both the Rump Parliament and the London trading community and were in some measure responsible for passage of the first of the famous Navigation Acts in October, 1651. Though far less restrictive than subsequent similar legislation in 1660 and 1663, this first step toward commercial control forbade importation of foreign goods into England or her colonies, except in English vessels or vessels of the country producing the goods and imported directly from that country. The main purpose of the law was to keep the Dutch out, and otherwise it had little effect on the trade of the colonies.[28]

Because Virginia remained unwilling to submit to the Commonwealth government, Parliament finally sent four commissioners to the colony with instructions to work out a peaceful settlement. These four men, all well known there, were Robert Dennis, who commanded the fleet, and William Claiborne, Richard Bennett, and Thomas Stagg. Claiborne, of Kent Island fame, had for years been a leading politician and land speculator. Bennett was a moderate Puritan who had once lived briefly with his coreligionists in Maryland, but he had a much longer familiarity with Virginia, where he had held or was to hold in the future nearly every important office including the governorship. Stagg was a planter, merchant, and shipbuilder who divided his time between London and Virginia. The commissioners were realistic and hardheaded, and they realized how important it was for Virginia, where they held large interests, to avoid rebellion. At the same time they recognized that it would be difficult to talk the colonial government into adopting measures abolishing the kingship, the House of Lords, and the Book of Common Prayer. Parliament gave the commissioners the power to grant or withhold pardons and sent them off protected by a strong military force and supplied with goods that were much needed by the settlers. Dennis and Stagg were lost in a storm during the passage, but most of the fleet got through, including Claiborne and Bennett, and reached America in midwinter of 1651–52.

---

28 Lawrence A. Harper, *The English Navigation Laws. A Seventeenth-Century Experiment in Social Engineering* (New York, 1939), is the standard source for the origins, enforcement, and effects of these acts of trade.

After a delay of several months the commissioners received a conciliatory letter which set the stage for a meeting with the assembly at Jamestown. By that time the colonists had cooled off, and they began to understand the almost certain destruction confronting them if they remained adamant. The assembly, too, determined to avoid bloodshed if possible. After a long debate, the House of Burgesses agreed to disband Governor Berkeley's army and then signed articles of surrender, renouncing its former government and promising obedience to the Commonwealth. The new situation was not punitive, because control of affairs was placed in the hands of the assembly. No taxes, customs, or dues could be imposed without its consent, and Virginians were permitted to retain the rights and privileges of Englishmen. Persons unwilling to take the oath of allegiance were allowed a year to remove themselves and their property from the colony. Should a majority of the people of a parish desire to read the Book of Common Prayer, they might do so for a period of one year. Finally, Virginians could trade freely with all nations in accordance with the laws of the Commonwealth.

The general assembly held a second meeting with the commissioners in April, 1652, and together they agreed upon a provisional government. Their appointments to the positions of governor and secretary of state were, respectively, Richard Bennett and William Claiborne, both commissioners and both members of the faction that had successfully curbed Governor Harvey. Councillors and justices of the peace were chosen for one-year terms. The governor and councillors derived their powers from the burgesses and were to sit with them in the legislature. The burgesses, as representatives of the people, had the right to choose all colonial officers, except that the council retained the power to appoint justices on the nomination of the county courts. Richard Bennett, who undoubtedly owed his selection as governor to the Council of State in England, retained his post until March, 1655, when he went to London as Virginia's colonial agent.[29]

Sir William Berkeley, who had been so successful as governor, had the great wisdom to keep his peace during this critical period. He remained loyal to the Stuart family as long as he lived, because he had been a personal friend of Charles I, who had trusted him

[29] Craven, *Southern Colonies*, Chap. VIII, treats Virginia from 1652 to 1660.

to follow suitable policies in Virginia. Berkeley's intense interest in the welfare of the province had, during his ten years in office, won him a popular following. More than anyone else he was responsible for the loyalty Virginians felt toward the crown following the king's execution. Berkeley now retired to his estate at Green Spring, near Williamsburg, and for the time being withdrew from public affairs.

The transition from the old to the new form of government ran smoothly. The Council of State, sending instructions from England, reappointed ten of Berkeley's council members. In March, 1655, the assembly elected Edward Digges to succeed the departing Bennett as governor. The new official, thirty-five years old at the time, was the son of a man who had been Master of the Rolls under Charles I. During his three-year term the assembly dealt principally with Indian relations and a revision of the laws.

After a long interval, the assembly turned its attention again in 1653 to the matter of expansion into Indian territory. To encourage expeditions under adventurous men like Wood and Claiborne for the purpose of discovering minerals, fur supplies, and good land, the assembly adopted an act similar to the one in effect a decade earlier. It also offered special inducements to anyone willing to settle on the Roanoke or south of the Chowan River.

The colony also attempted major adjustments within the settled areas where the two races lived in close proximity to each other. Indian reservations were established in two counties, Gloucester and Lancaster, inaugurating a system that continued for more than three centuries. The assembly worked out a plan in 1656 calculated to discourage the Indians from going on the warpath. Hoping to indoctrinate the natives in the meaning of private property, the lawmakers directed that for every eight wolves' heads brought in, a chief would receive a cow. The theory was that once Indians acquired possessions of their own, they would come to respect the property of others. Other legislation stipulated that Indian children held as hostages would henceforth be instructed in Christianity and a trade and would no longer be treated as slaves. To protect Indians further, it became illegal to sell off or trade any of their land without permission from the assembly. Some of the strict laws of 1646 were modified at this time. All freemen might now trade with the natives, for example, and it ceased to be lawful to shoot an Indian simply because he had entered English territory without wearing a recognition badge. Finally, since it had been the custom to fire arms in case of sudden attack, the legislature decreed that henceforth "social shootings" should not take place except in connection with wedding celebrations.

In December, 1656, the assembly arranged to send Governor Digges to England as agent, with instructions to assure the lord protector that Virginia would not interfere with Maryland and also to endeavor to promote a higher price for tobacco. Digges, who went to join Richard Bennett in London, was to assure the English merchants that the assembly was taking steps to decrease tobacco output while improving its quality. These efforts would come to naught, he was to explain, unless the merchants would offer a more satisfactory price, because farmers raised only inferior crops when the price was low. Before Digges left for London in March, 1657, the assembly selected Samuel Mathews, Jr., to be his replacement.

The wealthy and well-connected new governor was still in his twenties, but he was experienced in public affairs, having served as burgess while his father sat in the council. When the legislature met in March, 1658, it continued the governor and his councillors in office subject to the approval of the protector, although there was a certain amount of restiveness because the governor seemed inclined to assert his authority beyond the limits set by the commissioners in 1652. The assembly reaffirmed its right to appoint all officers and restated the powers vested in it by the commissioners, and it took pains, whenever differences arose, to defer to the wishes of the lord protector.

The comprehensive revision of the laws embodied in 131 acts passed in March, 1658, together with the proceedings of the March, 1659, session, provide an insight into many facets of mid-seventeenth-century colonial life. The management of the church was wisely left in the hands of the parishioners, and parishes continued to cooperate with local courts in suppressing drunkenness, blasphemy, and similar offenses. As in other American colonies, officials were responsible for seeing that servants attended religious services, for curbing the firing of guns on the Sabbath, and for preventing the loading of ships or traveling on the Lord's Day except in cases of necessity. To protect immigrants during their long voyage, shipmasters were required to carry a four-month supply of provisions and to see that passengers did not lack food or clothing.[30] Other laws protected poor debtors and servants who worked for harsh masters. Runaway servants, on the other hand, were to be branded when they were caught and then returned. Legislation typical of the period also provided for naturalization of foreigners and regulated millers, innkeepers, physicians, surveyors, and tobacco planters. Provision was made for construction and maintenance of highways from county to county, for indemnity for farmers from damage done by stray animals, and for destruction of wolves.

The assembly had trouble curbing Governor Mathews' independent spirit. In order to clarify their prerogatives, the burgesses decided to discuss all proposals separately before taking them up with the executive and his council. They repealed a law providing each of the councillors with a £200 fee for attendance at the quarterly courts and legislative meetings, while concurrently declining to limit their own number to two from each county, an economy move proposed by Mathews and the cabal in the council. Mathews forthwith dissolved the assembly, only to meet with a declaration that this action was illegal. The burgesses refused to dissolve, and after angry debate the governor withdrew his order, leaving the lord protector to rule on its legality. The assembly made a claim that final authority rested with the burgesses and that neither the governor nor any other power could dissolve one of their meetings. The lower house then adopted the reports of its committee that Mathews be retained as governor but that the burgesses should sit with him in choosing new councillors. It furthermore demanded that the governor appear before it and take the prescribed oath of office. The burgesses then made a conciliatory gesture by reappointing the secretary of state and all the former councillors.

Governor Mathews and his burgesses managed for a while to exist together in a state of concord. The very next assembly meeting produced evidence of the new mood, when word arrived that Oliver Cromwell had died and had been succeeded as lord protector by his son, Richard. The lower house, supported by both the governor and his councillors, drew up an address requesting the

---

30 John Duffy, "The Passage to the Colonies," *Mississippi Valley Historical Review*, XXXVIII (1951), 21–36, describes vividly the difficulties of sea travel in the early colonial period.

new protector to acknowledge that the Virginia legislature would retain the power to choose governors and other colonial officials. The assembly of March, 1659, adopted a provision requiring one legislative meeting at least every two years and another reappointing Mathews governor for two years and the councillors for life. This amiability did not last, however; in March, 1660, the burgesses adopted "An Act for the Annihilation of the Councillors," a forceful program that was interrupted by the death of Governor Mathews.

From September, 1658, when Oliver Cromwell died, until May, 1660, when Charles II landed at Dover, England was in a state of uncertainty and instability. The Virginia Assembly met in March, 1660, knowing only that England had been thrown into a crisis, and it promptly restated its conviction that the supreme governmental control in the colony remained in the assembly until reversed or amended by lawful commands from London. Since the legislature had adjourned before Mathews died, the council took the initiative in arranging for his replacement, choosing Sir William Berkeley as acting governor, subject to ratification by the assembly.

Selection of a royalist governor, particularly one who had been dismissed from that post by the Commonwealth government, created a unique situation, but Berkeley was a natural choice, because he had proved his ability and had earned the respect of his fellow Virginians. In a vigorous show of independence, the next assembly ratified his election and adopted written instructions, directing him to govern in accordance with the ancient laws of England and the established laws of Virginia. Berkeley was enjoined to call a meeting of the assembly at least once in every biennium and was forbidden to dissolve it without the assent of a majority of the members. He might choose his secretary of the province and the members of the council, but the assembly had to approve. In accepting the post, Sir William made it clear that his earlier resignation had been forced by the Commonwealth government and that he had at that time written to the exiled Charles II, craving his pardon for surrendering the government to the rebels. He later explained to his king that he had agreed to serve in 1660 only to save Virginia from factionalism. In taking office he swore to uphold the Commonwealth government, but the people of Virginia knew full well that he was a royalist.

Although there was some economic and political growth during the eight years that Virginia was under the Commonwealth, life on the surface appeared to change very little. Trade remained relatively free from interference, and the colony became during this period to all intents and purposes an independent commonwealth. Her population had risen steadily to about 30,000. Virginia had to face several crises in government, but it managed to resolve them in ways that did not build lingering discontent. There was no bloodshed and no revolution.[31]

And yet, beneath this calm surface, a change destined to have vast consequences was in progress. Displaced or made restless by the civil war, a new sort of immigrant was arriving in Virginia during this period, founding most of the colony's great eighteenth-century families and laying the groundwork for what became in time "the most celebrated oligarchy in American history." Many of these newcomers were younger sons, well connected in government and business circles. Some had inherited company shares or had claims to Virginia lands, while others were sons of wealthy merchants who could afford to purchase property in the Tidewater. Governor Berkeley himself was a good example of the type, being a younger son whose family's interest in Virginia dated from the 'twenties. These men, to the manner born, were ambitious to establish themselves in Virginia. They understood public as well as imperial responsibility, and they brought with them social eminence and political authority at the county level. Armed with these resources, they gradually dominated and then absorbed the exploiting group that had previously displaced Governor Harvey and assumed control.

In time there grew up an inner circle of privilege, a system of patronage, and the custom of intermarriage destined to last for two centuries. Local offices fell into the hands of the leading families, who had access to the council. As the number of counties increased, their magistrates sought a voice in colony management and found it in burgess representation. Originally regarded merely as a supplement to the council, the burgesses gained supreme power in the fifties and began meeting by themselves in 1663. Bacon's Rebellion

31 Morton, *Colonial Virginia*, I, 122–190, contains a balanced narrative of Virginia's history from 1640 to 1660. See W. F. Craven, *The Colonies in Transition, 1660–1713* (New York, 1968) for this more conservative population estimate.

later threatened the stability of this new class, but once matters
settled down again, there was again full acceptance of the English
tradition that certain families should be distinguished from others
in wealth, dignity, and access to political authority. These leading
families largely dominated the history of Virginia in the years
after 1660.[32]

[32] See again the perceptive essay by Bailyn, "Politics and Social Structure,"
especially pp. 98–115, in *loc. cit.*, and read Louis B. Wright, *The First Gentlemen
of Virginia* (San Marino, Calif., 1940, reissued in paperback, Charlottesville,
Va., 1964), for a discussion of the qualities and tastes of the nascent aristocracy.
Both Bruce, *Social Life*, pp. 255–261, and Daniel J. Boorstin, *The Americans:
The Colonial Experience* (New York, 1958), p. 100, stress Virginia's self-conscious
attempt to reproduce the social and political structure of England.

CHAPTER 4

Maryland

THE issue of political loyalty complicated the religious problem in England, posing for the state the question of how best to dispose of recalcitrant groups. The discordant elements were of several types, because Queen Elizabeth I had broken with the Catholics on the right, the Presbyterians in the center, and the Separatists on the left. Conformity was the ideal, and "obedience joins, disorder separates" was the maxim of her statesmen. The dissident groups early saw America as a refuge, just as the persecuted Huguenots in France, prior to the Edict of Nantes, sought asylum in Brazil, Florida, and South Carolina. In England there was concern that the queen would lose many loyal subjects if religious dissenters began to leave the country, and, indeed, many of the potential exiles anxiously protested their loyalty to the crown. It was nevertheless felt that laws were needed to control the rising tide of nonconformists who, in the words of a secretary of state, "called themselves Reformers, and we commonly called Puritans."

John Whitgift, Archbishop of Canterbury, began a policy of repression in 1583 by expelling all Protestants within the Church and dealing harshly with all outside it. Even before that date, however, the ill-fated Roman Catholics had sought some solution for themselves. In 1570 Sir Thomas Gerrard proposed to settle a body of Catholics in Ireland, who could prove their political loyalty by coping with the rebellious natives there. A Puritan-minded member of Parliament recommended to Lord Burghley that three thousand

Puritans be sent to Ireland for the same purpose. Thus began a long debate, with many advances and many retreats, to reconcile the claims of conscience in religious matters and the demands of the state. The founding of Plymouth in 1620 and of Maryland in 1632 must be counted among the early advances.

The penalty for embracing Catholicism could be severe. Not only were Catholics prohibited from hearing mass, but they were fined for not attending state-approved churches. Though the law was applied only intermittently, when the authorities did choose to use it, nonattendance could cost a Catholic gentleman as much as £240 per year for each member of his family. It is understandable that even Catholics who insisted they were good Englishmen might occasionally give thought to emigration. Sir Thomas Gerrard and Sir George Peckham drew up a proposal in 1582 to settle in Narragansett Bay, but Peckham found few subscribers for estates of from 2,000 to 16,000 acres, and Sir Humphrey Gilbert, who was associated in the venture, was lost at sea in 1583. Even Archbishop Whitgift's death in 1604 brought no relief for either Protestant or Catholic, except where the queen had made an exception. It was in this sort of environment that the Catholic colony of Maryland was launched.[1]

Unlike Virginia, the founding of Maryland was the achievement of a single proprietor, George Calvert, who acted entirely on his own initiative. A long apprenticeship prepared him for his accomplishment, and only his death at the age of fifty-two prevented him from actually planting a colony. Calvert, born in Yorkshire, entered Oxford as a boy of fourteen and was graduated from Trinity College in 1597. Later he spent some time on the Continent, where he learned French, Spanish, and Italian. In 1606 he became private secretary to Sir Robert Cecil, secretary of state under James I. Under Cecil's patronage, Calvert rose rapidly and won the confidence of the king. He held a judicial post in Ireland, where he owned estates. From there he moved to a clerkship in the Privy Council, and he was knighted in 1617. Two years later, though the Duke of Buckingham opposed the appointment, he became principal secretary of state. In this office, which made him also a member of the Privy Council, Sir George defended the king's unpopular

[1] David B. Quinn, "The First Pilgrims," *William and Mary Quarterly*, XXIII (July, 1966), 359–366.

policies. Not unexpectedly, but in the face of pending measures for the persecution of Catholics, Calvert announced his conversion to that faith and resigned his secretaryship. In spite of this, James retained him on the Privy Council and created him Baron of Baltimore in the Kingdom of Ireland.[2]

Through his first wife's relatives, among them the Earl of Warwick and Sir Nathaniel Rich, Calvert fell in with the gentlemen adventurers of the day. He subscribed to stock of the Virginia Company, although he was never active in its affairs. He also formed a friendship with a Roman Catholic named Sir Thomas Arundel, whose daughter married his son Cecilius, and through Arundel he became a member of the council of the New England Company in 1622. Two years before that date Calvert purchased part of the peninsula of Avalon in the southeastern part of Newfoundland. Avalon, by royal charter, was erected into a province on the model of the county palatine of Durham, whose lord bishop in the fourteenth century exercised truly regal powers.[3] A small colony was established at Ferryland in 1620, but it did not flourish. Baltimore visited Ferryland in both 1627 and 1628, but, discouraged by the severity of the Newfoundland climate, he petitioned for a grant in Virginia.

Without waiting for a reply to his petition, Calvert embarked for Virginia in 1628 with his wife and children, "where the winters would be shorter and less vigorous," and where he hoped to find a suitable location south of Jamestown. The Virginia authorities welcomed Baltimore and hoped he would settle among them, but he refused to take the oath of supremacy, and he returned home determined to obtain a separate colony.[4] Charles I, who like his father was friendly to Calvert, tried to dissuade him on the ground that his scheme was impracticable. Calvert was not to be deterred,

[2] Biographical treatments of George Calvert will be found in William P. Browne, *George Calvert and Cecilius Calvert, Barons Baltimore of Baltimore* (New York, 1890), and Clayton C. Hall, *The Lords Baltimore and the Maryland Palatinate* (Baltimore, 1904). A more recent account is in Matthew P. Andrews, *The Founding of Maryland* (New York, 1933).

[3] For an explanation of the development of the county palatine and its powers, see Gaillard T. Lapsley, *The County Palatine of Durham: A Study in Constitutional History* (New York, 1900).

[4] The rivalry that developed between Virginia and the colony created by Calvert is described in John H. Latané, *Early Relations Between Maryland and Virginia* (Baltimore, 1895).

however, because the Arundel group was dedicated to establishing a haven for persecuted Catholics.

King Charles granted Calvert territory in 1632 extending from the James to the Roanoke and west to the mountains. When the members of the defunct Virginia Company learned of this gift, they raised such a clamor that the bill had to be withdrawn. A new warrant was prepared designating "Mariland," the territory east of Chesapeake Bay from Delaware Bay to Cape Charles, as a patent for Baltimore, perhaps in the hope of staving off the Dutch in New Netherland.[5] Thus the original Maryland encompassed only the Eastern Shore. Again there were outcries from the Virginia adherents, who objected to the southern boundary. Subsequently that boundary was altered to run from the mouth of the Potomac across the Chesapeake to Watkins Point, thence to the Atlantic Ocean, leaving part of the Eastern Shore for Virginia.

Baltimore, who died April 15, 1632, left his estates and his patent to his son Cecilius, whose interest in colonization was persistent and abiding and whose views on religion remained tolerant in a violent age. Cecilius was only twenty-six years old when the patent was in its final phases.[6] A fourth warrant was prepared that not only pushed the northern boundary to the fortieth parallel, where Philadelphia is now located, but extended it westward to the source of the Potomac. This was the last warrant in these drawn-out proceedings, for on June 30, 1632, the government finally issued the charter.

The instrument creating Maryland was unique even among proprietary charters in that it represented a type of government and landholding that England itself had largely outgrown. The governmental provisions followed those of the Avalon grant except that the type of tenure was changed from knight service to free and common socage.[7] The alteration was included because Baltimore

[5] Wesley Frank Craven, *The Southern Colonies in the Seventeenth Century, 1607–1689* (Baton Rouge, La., 1949), pp. 188–189.

[6] His name was actually Cecil, but we know him today by the Latinized version that he used when signing documents. M. P. Andrews, *Founding of Maryland*, p. 36. Browne, *George Calvert and Cecilius Calvert*, and C. C. Hall, *The Lords Baltimore*, give biographical data.

[7] Charles M. Andrews, *The Colonial Period of American History* (4 vols., New Haven, Conn., 1934–38), II, 202. Knight service bestowed feudal rights that were more trouble than they were worth. Free and common socage was more vital, permitting both an oath of allegiance and the imposition of quitrents.

had learned from his Irish experience that he did not wish to be burdened with knight service. Familiar with procedures in chancery, he fashioned his original petition so as to yield a maximum of rights and a minimum of obligations. As in the Avalon patent, there was a stipulation that he was to hold his lands in the same manner and exercise the same authority as the Bishop of Durham. In this way Baltimore successfully obtained the very special privileges accorded in ancient times to an English lord charged with the heavy burden of maintaining security on a dangerous frontier. He received absolute power over the administration and defense of his province. All writs were issued in his name instead of that of the king, and confirmation of laws rested in him. The Statute of Quia Emptores, forbidding feudal subdivision except with the king's assent, did not apply to his proprietary, and he could fix rents and services on whatever manors he created. Added to these prerogatives was a clause to the effect that every interpretation of the charter terms would be favorable to the patentee. From the point of view of English law, the palatinate of Maryland was as free from royal intervention and control as the palatinates of the fourteenth century on the Welsh and Scottish borders. Thus the king carved the province of Maryland out of the territory granted to the Virginia Company in 1621, a reassignment of the land which he felt free to make after annulment of the company charter in 1624.[8]

There was bitter opposition when the terms of Lord Baltimore's charter became known. The Virginia planters were the first to protest, and their petition was referred to the Privy Council. During this period there were other petitions for land patents to both the north and the south of Virginia, such as the Plowden patent of 1632, the Withers petition, and the Heath patent for Carolina in 1629.[9] The Privy Council's legal adviser quickly pointed out that it was not only awkward but dangerous to bestow so many powers upon the Calverts, particularly since some of them had not been granted to Virginia. He also objected to the charter on broader grounds and emphasized that the privileges granted could jeopardize the rights of Englishmen in the colony.

[8] A thorough discussion of the terms of the Maryland charter will be found in M. P. Andrews, *Founding of Maryland*, pp. 36–46.
[9] C. M. Andrews, *Colonial Period*, II, 222, 223–224, 284 n.

Following issuance of the charter, Lord Baltimore advertised his colonization plans carefully and widely, and he announced that his first expedition would depart in June, 1633.[10] He hoped that maximum publicity would clarify his religious objective and serve to counteract false rumors, but in spite of these efforts, the number of applicants was not large. The Jesuits were permitted to sponsor the undertaking, so the proposed colony was sure to be strongly Catholic. A number of Catholic gentlemen agreed to go and take their servants, and they probably shared in the considerable expenses of the expedition, which must have cost at least £10,000. The Maryland assembly later made some effort to compensate Cecilius for his own large and continuing outlay. The Virginians tried to thwart the departure of his first settlers not only by appeals to the Privy Council but even by hiring his seamen.

The Privy Council did hold up the expedition from August 20 until November 22, 1633, on the ground that certain passengers had not taken the oath of allegiance. Since the oath required denial of papal authority, it is thought that a number of priests and Catholic laymen avoided taking it by concealing themselves or by boarding the two ships, the *Ark* and the *Dove,* below London. In the long run, only 128 out of several hundred passengers ever did take the oath. The ships sailed from Cowes on November 22 but were soon separated by a storm, which forced the *Dove,* a pinnace of only sixty tons, to return to the Scilly Islands. Both vessels finally proceeded by way of the Canaries and West Indies, where they rejoined one another at Barbados. Here the company rested, and the ships replenished their water and provisions. After separating again, they arrived together at the Virginia Capes on February 27, 1634. Though the Virginians were far from cordial, the emigrants were well received by Governor John Harvey, who helped them obtain provisions they sorely needed.[11]

On March 3 the colonists started up Chesapeake Bay and landed on an island now called Blakiston on the northern side of the Potomac. On the twenty-fifth they celebrated mass and took formal

---

[10] *A Relation of Maryland* (London, 1635), reprinted in Clayton C. Hall (ed.), *Narratives of Early Maryland* (New York, 1910), pp. 70–112, draws on the experiences of the Virginia colonists. A translation of the charter is contained in the *Relation.*

[11] Bernard C. Steiner, *Beginnings of Maryland, 1631–1639* (Baltimore, 1903), pp. 15–40, gives details of the voyage and the arrival in the New World.

)ossession of the country. Later they moved southward to the Indian own of Yoacomico, which they renamed St. Mary's. Here they)ought land from friendly Indians in exchange for axes, hatchets, 1oes, and clothing. They built a small fort, a storehouse, and a :hapel and began to erect small cabins for homes. They existed nitially on their shipborne provisions and on food furnished by he natives. Since part of the land they purchased had been pre-•iously cleared, they were able to plant corn and other crops and hus escaped the "starving time" that had beset Virginia.

Between two and three hundred settlers reached Maryland at his time. Accompanying the expedition were two Jesuits, Fathers 1ndrew White and John Altham, and two lay brothers named 3ervase and Wood.[12] There were also sixteen gentlemen-adventurers vith their families and more than two hundred other persons, prin-:ipally handicraftsmen, laborers, servants, and a few of the farmer-yeoman class. Possibly the majority of these were members of the Church of England. Many who came later were indentured servants who were brought over by planters or who were purchased on 1rrival. Cecilius Calvert maintained a London office open to all who might wish to emigrate. Land was assigned immediately, and this practice continued for the next half-century. The Jesuits and some of the Catholic gentry, to protect themselves, obtained their land, as they had done in England, under assumed names.

Even though as late as January, 1634, the younger Lord Calvert had intended to accompany the first expedition, he wrote finally that he had again been delayed by the pressure of business. His all-consuming purpose was to protect his interest against any un-toward circumstance in England, and though he lived until 1675, he never felt free enough, from either the care of his estates or the intrigues of his enemies, to get away. We know that he had a troublesome land dispute in 1642 with his brother-in-law, William Arundel, and that in 1647 he nearly lost his charter at the hands of Parliament when he was forced to appeal against an order vacat-ing it. He was thus compelled to govern from England, sending over men, equipment, instructions, commissions, rules for land dis-tribution, and letters to his brother, the governor, and others to whom he delegated authority.

12 White was the author of *A Briefe Relation of the Voyage unto Maryland* (1634), reprinted in Hall (ed.), *Narratives of Early Maryland*, pp. 27–35.

The proprietor entrusted the governorship of the colony t
Leonard Calvert, who was twenty-eight years of age in 1634. H
had served as captain of a ship lent to Lord Baltimore by the kin
for the purpose of carrying provisions to Ferryland. Before th
Maryland sailing, Cecilius gave his brother and his commissione
instructions which above all disclosed his firm intent of creatin
a colony in which Catholics and Protestants might reside togethe
in harmony, an ideal as exemplary as that of William Penn's Ho
Experiment fifty years later. The Catholic adventurers, he charge
must maintain a friendly understanding with their Protestant ass
ciates and keep silent on all occasions when there were religiou
disputations. Unfortunately, he was unable to control the religiou
enthusiasm of his Catholic followers. The activities of the Jesui
aroused fears and fostered complaints in an age when animosit
was easily awakened and when popish recusancy in England wa
illegal. Nevertheless Maryland is unique in early English coloniz
tion, because it was the only plantation whose stated goal was t
enable Catholics and Protestants to live together in equality, amit
and forbearance. This effort had to be made, since there were to
few Catholics to support a colony by themselves. The first Lor
Baltimore was constrained, in order to attract settlers to Marylan
to promise full religious toleration. That he did so freely and tha
his son willingly carried out his father's wishes prove the father
honesty and the son's loyalty.[13]

Giving his colony close attention, Cecilius Calvert strove perpetu
ally for peace and harmony. He was well aware of the enmity o
William Claiborne of Virginia, who had established a post on Ken
Island on the upper Chesapeake opposite present-day Annapolis
Claiborne had already journeyed to England for the avowed pur
pose of preventing the issuance of the Maryland charter. Leonar
Calvert wrote to Claiborne, hoping to clarify matters for his brother
He proposed to Governor John Winthrop of Massachusetts Bay a
exchange of corn for fish and other commodities. Later he sen
Governor William Kieft of New Netherland a tender of friendshi
and an inquiry concerning the renting of ships. The Calverts wer
indefatigable in seeking peace with Maryland's neighbors.

Leonard Calvert and his commissioners proceeded to carry ou

[13] C. M. Andrews, *Colonial Period*, II, 290–297.

ecilius' instructions relative to settling the area below the Patapsco
River, where Baltimore is now located. The earliest districts planted
ere the northern bank of the Potomac, both shores of the Patuxent,
nd Kent Island. Maryland was developed as a great barony with the
roprietor standing in a feudal relationship with his lords of the
manors and with his freeholders and their land. From 1635 to
665 the proprietor issued many detailed instructions that con-
ormed to types of landholding known to the proprietary class in
ngland. There were great manors with lesser manors within, as
well as freeholds and copyholds, all with their customary tenurial
nd judicial obligations. These peculiarly manorial grants did not
utlast the seventeenth century and were on their way out even
efore 1660.[14] But in the early period of Maryland's history there
re many references to baronies and honors. Even so, the baronies in
Maryland never had the reality of those in South Carolina. Sir
Ferdinando Gorges, whose charter was not as strong as Baltimore's,
wished to install the manorial system in Maine after 1639, but his
owers were inadequate.

The proprietor created more than sixty manors during the sev-
nteenth century, not including his own or those of his relatives.
The latter, known as proprietary manors, comprised 6,000 acres
ach. The manors held of the lord proprietor varied from one to
,000 acres in size and were endowed with the rights and privileges
elonging to a manor in England. For example, the manorial lord
ad a right to hold courts leet and baron for the trial of petty
misdemeanors. As required by the condition of free and common
ocage, the mesne lord was obligated to pay the proprietor a rent,
usually in corn or tobacco. He also had to take an oath of fidelity
o the proprietor, but it was not until 1656 that he was required to
promise fealty to the English government—then the Commonwealth
—and not until 1684 did he promise allegiance to the king. It was
proposed in 1639 that a lord of the manor should be tried only by
his peers, but the bill never became a law.

Both manorial lords and freeholders paid the proprietor an

14 Some manorial courts did function for a time, and the records of St.
Clement's Manor have survived for the years 1659-72. J. H. Johnson, "Old
Maryland Manors," *Johns Hopkins University Studies in History and Political
Science*, ser. I, no. 7, 31. For the court baron of St. Gabriel's Manor, see J. L.
Bozman, *The History of Maryland* . . . (2 vols., Baltimore, 1837), II, 581.

annual quitrent of one shilling for every hundred acres, and quit
rents made up a large part of the proprietor's income from the
province.[15] During the early years many lords of manors and many
freeholders received town land in the hamlet of St. Mary's, a system
which also appeared in other colonies. Through the distribution
of free town land, it was hoped to build up at least two towns,
one at St. Mary's and the other on Kent Island. Although men
talked of laying out additional towns, nothing came of this hoped
for boom during the early seventeenth century. Freeholders, who
possessed up to a thousand acres, were far more numerous than the
manor lords. Although some freeholds were larger than manors,
their owners enjoyed no manorial rights, because only a patent
issued by the proprietor could create such privileges. Nevertheless,
just as manors bore names, so did most of the freehold plantations.
As mentioned above, freeholders paid quitrents, the amount varying with the size of the freehold. For example, one William Smoote,
with 300 acres, paid a quitrent of three bushels of corn, or six
shillings in sterling. Sometimes the rent was paid in barrels of
Indian corn at five bushels to the barrel. It was customary in Maryland to state the amount in sterling with the equivalent in tobacco
or corn.

Estimates of Maryland's early population are only guesses, but
a figure of 2,000 in 1640 seems reasonably accurate. This total
compares with 8,000 for Virginia, 12,000 for Massachusetts Bay,
1,000 for Plymouth, 2,000 for Connecticut, 300 for Rhode Island,
and 1,500 for New Haven. The West Indian populations were larger
at that time, Barbados having 8,000, St. Kitts 13,000, St. Nevis
4,000, and Bermuda 3,000. Maryland never experienced a spectacular growth, for the estimates for 1660, twenty years later, vary from
8,000 to 12,000.[16]

---

[15] A quitrent, small in amount, usually a penny or halfpenny per acre, or a
shilling per hundred acres, was paid to one's feudal superior in commutation
of feudal services. It was common in the proprietary colonies.

[16] Evarts B. Greene and Virginia D. Harrington, *American Population before
the Federal Census of 1790* (New York, 1932), *passim*, and W. F. Craven, *Southern
Colonies*, pp. 177, 183, and 302. Population estimates for this period vary
widely, and Arthur E. Karinen, "Maryland Population, 1631–1730," *Maryland
Historical Magazine*, LIV (Dec., 1959), 371, suggests that the figures given above
for 1660 are probably both too high, with 6,000 more accurate. On the un-
reliability of the West India Islands figures, see Bridenbaugh, *Vexed and Troubled
Englishmen, 1590–1642* (New York; 1968), pp. 427–428.

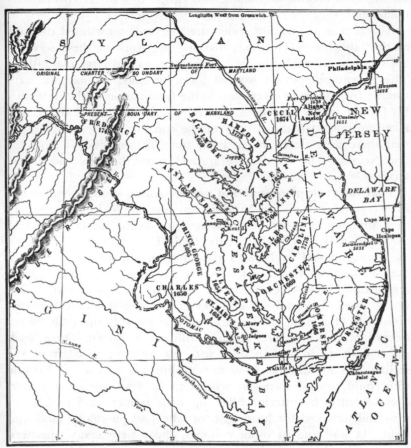

From *Old Virginia and Her Neighbours* by John Fiske, Houghton Mifflin Company

THE PALATINATE OF MARYLAND

Maryland's steady increase was due in some measure to good climate and soil, excellent water transportation, and a liberal land policy. Its agricultural system paralleled that of Virginia to some degree. Most of the plantations and farms were on or near waterways, and the ships that carried the colony's tobacco to England brought back clothing, shoes, farm equipment, and assorted wares. As a matter of fact, Maryland's agriculture was somewhat more diversified during the early years than Virginia's, for there were substantial crops of wheat, corn, vegetables, and fruit. But tobacco raising soon became dominant, and efforts to halt its growth were ineffectual.[17]

As was true in Virginia, indentured servants constituted the bulk of the labor force. Overseers directed the work of these servants, both male and female, on most of the manors and large plantations. The indentured person worked for a specified number of years, usually from three to seven, and at the termination of the indenture his former master gave him a year's supply of corn, clothing, and farm equipment—"the custom of the country." It seems doubtful that there were slaves in the labor force before 1660; in fact, the few Negroes who lived in Maryland were there as indentured servants.[18]

That the great plantation did not become as strongly entrenched in Maryland as it did in Virginia was not due to lack of effort in that direction, and the manorial system was the special form that the effort took. To qualify as the lord of a manor of 2,000 acres, the applicant had by 1638 to guarantee to import five workers, a number that was raised to ten in 1642. Likewise, the terms regarding headrights were restricted. In 1638, for example, Cecilius Calvert granted one hundred acres to each individual who transported himself to Maryland, one hundred acres to his wife and each domestic servant, and fifty acres to each child under sixteen. These headrights were cut in half in 1642, with the quitrent raised from one shilling per hundred acres to one shilling per fifty acres. No one who could pay his own way wished to be a servant on a manor. Consequently the interior filled up with farmers and ex-servants who had qualified for headrights or who had purchased land outright. As was true in other colonies, there were many squatters. After serving his term, the indentured servant received land of his own, thus adding to the number of freemen in the colony.[19] Inas-

---

[17] Avery O. Craven, *Soil Exhaustion as a Factor in the Agricultural History of Virginia and Maryland, 1606–1860* (Urbana, Ill., 1926), pp. 34, 162, points out that in both colonies crude tools and poor labor applied to a dominant crop soon caused yields to decline and the soil to become exhausted.

[18] W. F. Craven, *Southern Colonies*, p. 215; M. P. Andrews, *Founding of Maryland*, pp. 175–177.

[19] A Maryland servant who had completed his service could obtain a grant by showing the authorities his certificate of freedom, but Abbot E. Smith believes that less than a tenth of the servants who entered the colony were able eventually to take advantage of this opportunity. *Colonists in Bondage: White Servitude and Convict Labor in America, 1607–1776* (Chapel Hill, N.C., 1947), pp. 298–299.

much as all economic activity was rooted in agriculture, the skilled workers were to be found on the plantations, and Cecilius, Lord Baltimore tried in vain to develop thriving towns.

No such form of seignorial life characterized any other English colony to such a degree, and no such thorough transplanting of any manorial system took place elsewhere in America. Planting tobacco gave Maryland agriculture a uniform quality that lent itself readily to the forms of feudal landholding. Manors and plantations dominated the land, and their owners soon formed an exclusive class.[20] At the very top stood the proprietary family and its coterie. As the prevailing faith was Roman Catholicism, there were priests, chapels, and services on the larger plantations. If the aim of the colony was both proprietary and feudal, the system that the Baltimores chose to maintain was, as Charles M. Andrews has demonstrated, too inelastic to survive in its original form.[21]

The view that there existed in Maryland a large aristocracy of blood based on immigration is entirely unfounded. Leonard Calvert and his gentlemen made up only a small group. They brought no great wealth with them; indeed, their wealth consisted of land given to them by Baltimore. A few men whose fortunes were on the wane, or who were younger sons, ventured to Maryland after the founding years, but most of the landholders were simply Englishmen of the upper middle class. Most of the immigrants who attained status during the period from 1637 to 1676 enjoyed a kind of luster by virtue of having adventured to America at their own expense. They constituted a larger group than the inner circle attached to the Calvert family. This upper class remained rather constant in numbers for about ten years, after which an indigenous gentry began to emerge. Its members achieved distinction because they exhibited initiative and the capacity to create wealth in a new environment. They amassed land, and that in itself lent an aura of gentility. Their rise was more rapid than it could have

20 W. F. Craven, *Southern Colonies*, p. 209, suggests that a good many of these large properties were not actually being cultivated at this time, warning that "title to 1,500 or 2,000 acres does not of itself prove that a plantation of that extent was actually in operation." On the question of how large plantations really were, see Vertrees J. Wyckoff, "The Sizes of Plantations in Seventeenth-Century Maryland," *Maryland Historical Magazine*, XXXII (December, 1937), 331–339.

21 C. M. Andrews, *Colonial Period*, II, 296–298.

been at home, because in England one could not span this gap in a single lifetime.

Wealth, then, became one measure of social status. William A. Reavis illustrates this point by showing that, on the average, a member of the gentry grew about five times as much tobacco as a commoner. The difference between those two groups was not, however, based on wealth alone, and the surest path to higher social position for the commoner was through officeholding. In two-thirds of the cases in which a man's name eventually was preceded by "Mr." or followed by "Gent." or "Esq.," he used this method to elevate himself. The nature of the settlement permitted ambitious men in a frontier environment to occupy many posts in new hundreds and counties. During this period, which reached its apex by 1660, the indigenous gentry came into its own. Before 1643, gentlemen sitting as judges decided cases in the provincial court; after that time they were decided by jurors, practically all of whom were commoners. Only in the event of a heinous crime was the gentleman class thereafter drawn upon exclusively. By 1676 Maryland had stratified into an upper and a lower class.[22]

The struggle of the settlers to eliminate proprietary controls was constant, the processes of transformation imperceptible, but from time to time there was a violent eruption, because there was unquestionably a rising tide of popular opposition. The colony was divided for judicial purposes into hundreds and counties.[23] The parish, each in the hands of its own vestry, was the ecclesiastical unit. The proprietor held both the judicial and the ecclesiastical powers under the terms of the charter, but he delegated them to his deputy, Leonard Calvert, who exercised them until his death in 1647. The powers granted to Calvert were practically absolute, he being concurrently lieutenant governor, admiral, and chief captain, and all officials of the colony had to recognize his authority and submit to his will. He had full power to regulate commerce, to use the great seal for issuing writs, licenses, and pardons, and to hear all final appeals, except in rare cases which were reserved for

[22] William A. Reavis, "The Maryland Gentry and Social Mobility, 1637–1676," *William and Mary Quarterly*, XIV (July, 1957), 418–428.
[23] Maryland during the seventeenth century made greater use than any other colony of the English county subdivision called the hundred. W. F. Craven, *Southern Colonies*, pp. 201–202.

the proprietor. Leonard Calvert was chancellor, chief justice, and chief magistrate, with authority to appoint all judicial officers. He appointed all members of the council. In case of absence or disability, he could delegate his powers to anyone he pleased. He was, in fine, an autocrat, and though the commissions were in the name of the proprietor, Leonard often issued them himself.[24]

By his commission of 1637, Leonard Calvert was required to convene the freemen or their representatives and to issue laws with their advice and consent. He need summon them only when he wished, however, and he could adjourn and dissolve them at will. Leonard held that by the terms of the charter only he could initiate legislation; thus the function of the assembly was only to approve or reject it. It appears that a first assembly did meet—the records are not extant—in 1635, but it is obvious that the proprietor did not like what it did, because he ordered the governor to inform the legislature in 1638 that all previously adopted laws were void. Cecilius added that he would consider a new body of laws, to be accepted or rejected in toto by him. Thus at the very beginning the question arose as to what extent the freemen could originate laws and how far they might alter laws transmitted by the proprietor. Cecilius denied that the freemen had any rights of this sort, and he upheld that view in theory and in part in practice for many years.[25]

Although it was unnecessary to call an assembly every year, fourteen of them did convene prior to 1660. Attendance at these meetings might have been large to the point of inefficiency, because all freemen were eligible to sit, in addition to representatives from the hundreds and counties. As a matter of fact, however, not more than fourteen to twenty persons were present on the average, including the governor and councillors. A total of only sixteen men, for example, appeared at the 1648 assembly session. Two years later the nine Protestants in a fourteen-man house constituted a majority.

[24] For the judicial role of the governor and council, see Carroll T. Bond and Richard B. Morris, *Proceedings of the Maryland Court of Appeals, 1695–1729* (Washington, D.C., 1933), pp. xvii *et seq.*

[25] M. P. Andrews, *Founding of Maryland*, pp. 75–93, offers a thorough analysis of these earliest legislative sessions. Bernard C. Steiner traces the development of the assembly in *Beginnings of Maryland*, pp. 353–465; *Maryland During the English Civil War* (2 vols., Baltimore, 1906–7), I, 151–271; and *Maryland Under the Commonwealth* (Baltimore, 1911), pp. 9–117.

Proxies often appeared to represent men living at a distance from St. Mary's. Perhaps the reason for this haphazard system of representation can be traced to the limited function of the assembly. In contrast to those of other colonies, the Maryland legislature was at most an advisory body, and the proprietor could, if he chose, ignore whatever it recommended.

There was some early indecision about who had the power to adjourn a legislative meeting once it had convened. The question first came up at the 1638 assembly, which was clearly controlled by a small clique of officeholders and their proxies, although the membership was a medley of provincial leaders summoned by individual writs and freemen summoned by general writ. Replying to an objection, Leonard Calvert declared unequivocally that he alone could adjourn or prorogue the assembly. Unsatisfied with this pronouncement and undoubtedly influenced by the Long Parliament in England, the legislators resolved in 1642 that they could not be adjourned or prorogued except by their own consent. The people's representatives had spoken, but the governor did not choose to heed their resolution.

The assembly followed the parliamentary model in its organization, rules, and use of committees, and its dictum that members be allowed the privileges of Parliament while the house was sitting.[26] On the whole, however, the assembly of 1638 was dominated by the proprietary element. In 1642 the delegates requested that they sit separately in a lower house, but the governor denied their request. They won the right to meet by themselves in 1650, at which time it was enacted that all laws passed by a majority of each house and ordered by the governor should be as binding as if they were assented to personally by the freemen of the province.[27]

Protestants were in the ascendant by 1650, and there was an undercurrent of opposition to the proprietor's absolute authority. There was a feeling, generally shared, that Baltimore would soon lose his charter, because the Puritans had taken control in England. Even in this threatening situation, the proprietor made no concessions to the colonists except to permit the assembly to initiate

[26] W. F. Craven, *Southern Colonies*, pp. 206–208, points out that the Maryland legislators were very conscious of the fact that they were copying the English model in their organization and procedure.

[27] C. M. Andrews, *Colonial Period*, II, 300–301.

legislation. The power of the lower house remained limited throughout these years, but that body was garnering a rich experience in its exercise of parliamentary law and privilege that would stand it in good stead in the future. In 1650 it voted to pass no law that might infringe its members' liberties or their consciences.

William Claiborne continued to be troublesome to Maryland until his death in 1677. Possessing a mixture of admirable and unfortunate qualities, he never failed to be overzealous in upholding Virginia's interests as well as his own. He held many offices in that colony and was frequently a member of its council, and, since he hated Catholicism, his opposition to Maryland was predictable. The focus of his antagonism, however, was Cecilius Calvert's attempts to exercise authority over the plantation on Kent Island. Claiborne obtained a commission to explore the Chesapeake as early as 1621, and he subsequently established a trading post on Kent Island at his own expense and built up traffic with the Indians in that region. While in England in 1630, he secured a commission to trade under the royal signet of Scotland. He then returned to Kent Island with a stock of wares, set up a permanent post there with himself as company factor, and developed it so rapidly that within five years he had a going settlement with a fort, storehouses, dwellings, mills, and a cadre of artisans, laborers, and servants. The venture was not without its difficulties and misfortunes, however, including a fire in the fall of 1631, the failure of additional supplies to arrive, and unhappy relations with his partners in England.[28]

From the start Cecilius Calvert promised Claiborne full liberty of trade, provided he acknowledged that Kent Island was part of Maryland and agreed to hold his lands from him as feudal lord. Claiborne refused, because he did not wish to hold from a Catholic suzerain and also because he continued to support Virginia's claims, even though they had already been rejected abroad. When the rumor got about in 1635 that Claiborne was stirring up the Indians against Maryland, the Catholic colony seized one of his vessels for trading in its waters without permission. Baltimore's pinnaces and Claiborne's vessels engaged during the next year in a series of miniature sea fights, and Claiborne managed to continue trading in

28 Claiborne and his varied activities are described in excellent detail in M. P. Andrews, *Founding of Maryland*, pp. 94–112.

Maryland. At the end of that time, however, the new company factor, George Evelyn, turned against him, seized the island, and persuaded Governor Calvert to come to his defense, placing Claiborne in a state of temporary checkmate. In March, 1638, the Maryland assembly passed a bill of attainder against Claiborne calling for the forfeiture of his properties to the lord proprietor. Although the charges against Claiborne were well grounded, the bill of attainder, in Charles M. Andrews' opinion, was unjust. Claiborne asked the home government for redress, but the Committee on Foreign Plantations held in 1638 that Kent Island belonged to Lord Baltimore and that no trade could take place without his license.[29]

The quarrel with Claiborne pointed up Maryland's insecurity as a colony, while its absolute government and feudal land tenures seemed ill suited to the New World. In the light of events in England, the religious experiment of settling Catholics and Protestants together was premature. The Long Parliament met in England in 1640, the civil war erupted in 1642, and Charles I was beheaded in 1649. A Puritan minority hostile to prerogative government and at sword's point with Roman Catholicism thus gained control and held it for a number of years. This was a difficult period for Baltimore, who was involved in land disputes from 1642 to 1650 and who was forbidden to leave England. He nearly lost his charter at the hands of Parliament in 1647, but by a combination of skill and tenacity he succeeded in warding off that worst of all possible blows.[30]

Meanwhile conditions in the colony went from bad to worse. An Indian war threatened, and Claiborne remained troublesome. Additional difficulty of a new sort was provided by Richard Ingle, a swashbuckler and an ardent Protestant, who now began a career of incendiarism and robbery.[31] Leonard Calvert crossed the Atlantic to consult his brother in England. Claiborne, returning from England and committed to the cause of Parliament, retook Kent Island

---

[29] C. M. Andrews, *Colonial Period*, II, 302–307.

[30] See W. F. Craven, *Southern Colonies*, Chap. VI, for a discussion of Maryland during the English civil war.

[31] Steiner, *Maryland During the English Civil War*, pp. 48–55, describes Ingle's violent career in Maryland, which featured repeated acts of plunder and which came close to constituting piracy.

by force. Ingle, posing as an enemy of prerogative and angered at his arrest by Giles Brent, acting governor, for treasonable words against the king, captured St. Mary's. For two years during this rebellion there was no settled government, and the colony was in an uproar. Leonard survived only with the help of Governor Berkeley of Virginia. Ingle actually went to England, charged the proprietor with enmity to the government of the Commonwealth, and accused the Catholics in the province of being tyrannous recusants. After many hearings the Council of State found that Ingle lacked evidence to prove his charges and dismissed his plea. Without doubt Maryland went through an exceptionally bad time between 1635 and 1660. Discord was general, and rumormongering so rife that a bill was proposed in the assembly to punish anyone purveying false news. If there was a single underlying cause of Maryland's unrest, it was the religious issue.[32]

Cecilius, Lord Baltimore, fashioned the Act Concerning Religion, the most famous document in Maryland history, in 1649, a year when civil liberty was in particular jeopardy in England and when the dangers confronting Catholics were manifest.[33] The Puritans and their political allies executed Charles I in 1649 and then began sequestration of land belonging both to royalists and to papists. At the same time they were placing men faithful to the king under bonds of removal and restraint and were threatening them with imprisonment. Baltimore had prevailed over Claiborne and Ingle, but attacks against him in England continued, and he realized that the Long Parliament would not condone toleration for people of his faith. He therefore turned to the notion of freedom of conscience or, as he phrased it in his act, "conscience in matters of religion." Baltimore's enemies, as he knew, had sought annulment of the Maryland charter on the ground that the colony was a hotbed of popery. To meet this charge, he stated in his act that anyone professing belief in Jesus Christ would be free from any sort of molestation and that severe punishment would be dealt out to anyone attempting to harass a man because of his religious convictions. The proprietor had the double objective of aiding his cause in

---

[32] *Maryland Archives*, I, 307–310.
[33] *Ibid.*, I, 244–247. First printed at the end of John Langford's *A Just and Clear Refutation* . . . (London, 1655).

England and 'drawing to the colony those who could find no peace elsewhere.[34]

When the assembly, dominated by Protestants and particularly by Puritans, passed this act in April, 1649, it excluded all those outside the Trinitarian fold.[35] This provision was, of course, not in accordance with Baltimore's thinking, and its harshness reflected the spirit of a law adopted by the Long Parliament in May, 1648. The act as the assembly amended it went no further than to give, as a matter of expedience and necessity, formal expression to the toleration of one religious body to another, an expression that had already found place in the instructions that Cecilius Calvert issued to his brother Leonard in 1633. It was also contained in the oath required in 1648 of the first Protestant governor, William Stone, which stipulated that no person believing in Jesus Christ and, in particular, no Roman Catholic should be molested.[36]

The Protestants were a numerical majority, but the Catholics, though gradually losing relatively in numbers, still held all the offices. Furthermore, they were better organized, and they had the support of the proprietor, the governor, and his council. The non-Catholic element gained strength suddenly in 1648 when at least four hundred and possibly as many as six hundred Puritans led by Richard Bennett left Nansemond County and the James River region of Virginia and migrated to Maryland, where they could enjoy religious liberty. Accepting an invitation from Governor Stone, they settled near the mouth of the Severn and founded Providence, now called Annapolis.[37] Here they dwelt as a self-governing community, advancing rapidly in influence. In 1650 they sent seven burgesses to the assembly, one of whom, James Cox, was elected speaker.

While Lord Baltimore sought to preserve peace with the Commonwealth government and maintain neutrality in the colony, he recognized that growing Protestant strength was undermining Catholic security, and was concerned about the need for great caution.

[34] For a comprehensive analysis of the Act Concerning Religion, see M. P. Andrews, *Founding of Maryland*, pp. 143–172.

[35] Baltimore accepted the act in August, 1650.

[36] C. M. Andrews, *Colonial Period*, II, 310–312.

[37] See also Babette Levy, "Puritanism in the Southern and Island Colonies," American Antiquarian Society *Proceedings*, LXX, Pt. I (1960), 132–134.

He consequently became the ally of Protestants in containing the ambitions of the Jesuits, who promoted the colony so zealously that they seemed likely to hurt rather than help the members of their faith. He was determined to keep them from extending the canon law of Rome to the colony, out of fear that this could lead to the gaining of temporal or civil authority by the Jesuit fathers. Above all, Cecilius wanted nothing there that looked in any way like an established church. He took action as early as 1641, when he issued a new set of conditions governing settlement. As part of this ruling, he declared void all previous land acquisitions by Jesuits from Indians, whether by gift or by purchase, and he made effective in Maryland the statute of mortmain, which in England forbade the giving of land to societies or corporations. Father Andrew White, head of the Jesuit mission in Maryland, was determined that the Society of Jesus should acquire land as an essential to spiritual independence. He referred the question to Father Henry More, father provincial in England, who in turn referred it to Rome. The eventual answer was an order to Maryland Jesuits to forgo their attempt.[38] The outcome of this controversy established a tradition still in force today, since a Maryland law prohibits the acquisition of land for religious use unless by act of the legislature. The law also bars any priest or clergyman from sitting in the general assembly.

By 1650 Maryland's Catholics and Protestants seemed equally powerful, but the odds actually favored the latter. The proprietor still had possession of the province, and the oath of fidelity acknowledging his authority protected his prerogatives. Although Catholics were now greatly in the minority, they enjoyed complete toleration. They in fact had as much liberty of action as anyone else, justifying a later comment that Maryland was the only colony where Roman Catholics were entitled to "the rights of man." There had, however, been an important recent shift in political control, working to the disadvantage of Catholics. Whereas in 1648 the governor, council, and assembly were all identified with that faith, only two years later the governor, at least half the council, and the majority of the assembly were Protestants.

Paradoxically, Baltimore had opened Maryland's doors to Puritans

---

[38] Hall (ed.), *Narratives of Early Maryland*, pp. 113–144, contains relevant extracts from annual reports written during this period by the Jesuits in England.

to counteract Jesuit influence, and he was about to go down to defeat at their hands. Working to the benefit of the Puritans was the edict issued by the Commonwealth Council of State which reduced Bermuda, Antigua, Barbados, and Virginia to subjection. Without Baltimore's knowledge, Acting Governor Greene added to the danger in November, 1649, by recklessly proclaiming Charles II as his father's rightful heir. Through the use of influence and by means of his Act Concerning Religion, Baltimore had been trying to keep the name of Maryland out of the Prohibitory Act of 1650, but the phrase "all the plantations within the bay of Chesapiak" appeared in the final draft. As we have seen in connection with Virginia, two of the Commonwealth's commissioners were Richard Bennett, the Puritan leader of Providence, Maryland, and William Claiborne of Kent Island. The two of them went to Maryland, dismissed Governor Stone and his council, and appointed a new council amenable to their control.[39] Claiborne had waited a long time for revenge, but now he had his victory.[40]

So vociferous were the complaints of the people of Maryland about the unseating of the administration that the commissioners found it necessary to announce that Governor Stone and his secretary had been left out of the government through a misunderstanding. Both men then resumed office on condition that all writs be issued in the name of the Commonwealth. Bennett and others pushed hard for a decision from the Council of State in London that would join Maryland and Virginia in a single jurisdiction to be ruled by Puritans. A group including a number of London merchants came to Baltimore's aid at this point and presented the proprietor's position in a pamphlet entitled "Lord Baltimore's Case."[41] The Council of State considered the whole matter and referred it to the judgment of Parliament. Before a decision could be made, however, the Rump Parliament disbanded, and Cromwell became master of England. The Barebones, or Little, Parliament of 1653 was in no position to take action. Sensing his opportunity, Cecilius Calvert moved quickly.

[39] Stone was a Puritan from the Eastern Shore of Virginia who came to Maryland with other Puritan emigrants early in 1649.

[40] Stone's administration is treated at greater length in Steiner, *Maryland Under the Commonwealth*, pp. 65–72. See also Herbert L. Osgood, *The American Colonies in the Seventeenth Century* (3 vols., New York, 1904–7), III, 126–127.

[41] Reprinted in Hall (ed.), *Narratives of Early Maryland*, pp. 167–180.

Writing Governor Stone that the province was not lost, he urged him to repudiate all obligations to the commissioners, to reconstruct the membership of the council, and to exact a new oath of fidelity to the proprietary. Thus the undaunted proprietor defied the commissioners and required every tenant to take the same oath of fidelity as the lord of a manor.[42]

Meanwhile at Providence the Puritans had built a citadel of strength remote from St. Mary's, the seat of government. At first they held aloof from the conflicts of civil life, but then, electing members to the assembly, their leaders began to work toward a political system on the model of the Commonwealth of Massachusetts Bay and the Commonwealth of England. The Puritan Commonwealth of Maryland about which they dreamed would be a combination of the colonies of Maryland and Virginia. Convinced that Calvert was about to lose his charter at the hands of Parliament, they opposed the resumption by Governor Stone of the proprietary prerogatives. In January and March, 1654, in two petitions, they protested the oath of fidelity because of its reference to Calvert as absolute proprietor and because it conflicted with their loyalty as subjects of the Commonwealth government. The remonstrants were abetted by the commissioners, who advised them to resist any pretense of power emanating from Lord Baltimore's agents. These protests revealed a deep-seated hostility toward the Roman Catholic religion in spite of all Baltimore's carefully thought-out safeguards.

Bennett and Claiborne, who were in Virginia when they learned of Stone's counteractions and of the protests of the disaffected areas, returned to Maryland. They first upbraided Stone for his resumption of authority, and when they received from him "onely opprobrious answers and uncivill language" in reply to their charges of treason to the Commonwealth, they dismissed him and appointed another Puritan, William Fuller, as governor. Inasmuch as no assembly had met since 1651, they directed Fuller to call one, but with the proviso that no man who had borne arms against Parliament or who professed the Roman Catholic religion be allowed to vote or serve as deputy. These harsh measures opened the door to Puritan power. When the assembly gathered on October 20, 1654, it repudiated

---

[42] See W. F. Craven, *Southern Colonies*, Chap. VIII, for further treatment of Maryland from 1652 to 1660.

the authority of the proprietor. The members quickly repealed the Act Concerning Religion and adopted another that was borrowed from the Cromwellian Instrument of Government. This abrasive law declared that none professing Catholicism could be protected and that freedom to worship God should not be extended to the adherents of popery. The Maryland Puritans had now emulated the intolerant example of their coreligionists in England.[43]

Governor Stone, who refused to yield to Fuller, took matters tactlessly into his own hands. He enforced the proprietor's authority and demanded bluntly that the Puritans take the oath of fidelity. The inhabitants of the southern counties, St. Mary's and Calvert, complied, but those of Ann Arundel and Kent to the north refused to take the oath or recognize Stone as governor. In March, 1655, "a civil war" took place between the northern and southern sections. Opposing contingents led by Stone and Fuller met in combat on the shore of the Severn River. The winning Puritans condemned ten of Stone's followers to death and actually executed four. They plundered the Jesuit religious houses and forced the priests to flee into Virginia, where they lived in a state of misery. The Puritans then imposed heavy fines on their foes and confiscated much of their property. They continued in full control of the province for three years.[44]

The commissioners were still not satisfied and would not be as long as Baltimore was able to hold onto his charter. The proprietor complained to Cromwell in January, 1656, that his adversaries had grossly infringed his jurisdiction in Maryland. Richard Bennett thereupon went to England to present the Puritan claims, accompanied by Samuel Mathews, Jr., substituting for Claiborne, whose duties as secretary of Virginia made it imprudent for him to leave America. Bennett and Mathews delivered a petition to the protector and presented arguments against Calvert and his patent. Cromwell referred the two petitions and the supporting documents to the Committee of Trade and then to the Council of State. The latter body directed both parties to submit their proposals for a settlement. Realizing finally that they could not destroy the charter, Bennett and Mathews expressed themselves satisfied with Baltimore's

43 Osgood, *American Colonies*, III, 130–131; Steiner, *Maryland Under the Commonwealth*, pp. 72–84.

44 C. M. Andrews, *Colonial Period*, II, 310–320.

counterproposals. When the matter became bogged down again in the Committee on Foreign Affairs, Edward Digges, governor of Virginia, disturbed at the prospect of a ruinous delay, took a hand as a friendly intermediary.

The contesting parties reached a final agreement in November, 1657. The terms of the agreement became known in Maryland the following February, and the local authorities took immediate steps to put them into force. Lord Baltimore saved both his patent and his province. He resumed full control of the government, and the inhabitants had to take the oath of fidelity. The proprietor, in turn, promised to forget the past, to make land available to all, and to permit any who wished to remove from the province to do so without penalty. He reaffirmed the Act Concerning Religion and stated that all professing belief in Jesus Christ should enjoy freedom of conscience. Lord Baltimore and Mathews signed the articles of agreement, and Digges and four others acted as witnesses.

Some time before the agreement was reached, Baltimore felt confident enough of ultimate victory to appoint Josias Fendall governor in William Stone's place. Fendall, who assumed office in February, 1657, had taken part in the "battle of the Severn" and had been imprisoned the following October by the Puritan justices of the provincial court for disturbing the public peace. Selected partly because of his record of loyalty to Baltimore, Fendall turned out to be a lukewarm supporter of the proprietor and an open enemy of proprietary prerogatives.[45]

Fendall's antics began with "a kind of pygmy rebellion" in 1660. The new assembly convened in February and, after three weeks of inactivity, addressed a paper to the council which declared that the assembly was the sole legislative body of the province, even without participation on the part of the governor and his councillors. This action paralleled the move made by the Rump Parliament in 1649 to govern without the king and House of Lords. The Maryland council reacted strongly and unfavorably to the pronouncement from the lower house, whereupon Fendall, in association with Thomas Gerrard and Nicholas Utie, a pair of representatives, repudiated his commission from Cecilius Calvert

---

[45] The curious Fendall administration receives detailed treatment in Steiner, *Maryland Under the Commonwealth*, pp. 106–116.

and accepted one from the assembly. Calvert understandably branded this unexpected tactic an act of mutiny and sedition.

Fendall's public career ended abruptly after the Stuarts returned to the throne in May, 1660. The new king, Charles II, addressed a personal letter to Fendall on July 12, instructing him to assist Lord Baltimore in the restoration of his jurisdiction and his rights under the charter. The proprietor immediately revoked Fendall's commission and in his place appointed his half brother, Philip Calvert, who at that time was serving as secretary of the province. Fendall appeared before Philip Calvert in November and submitted himself to the proprietor. The new governor confiscated his goods, released him under bond, and ordered him banished. Later Fendall was pardoned, and his estates were returned to him, but he was forbidden ever to hold office again.

Charles II did not penalize either Maryland or Virginia for supporting the Commonwealth regime. Just before the Restoration, Virginia's council, on behalf of an adjourned assembly, elected its former governor, Sir William Berkeley, as acting governor. The king confirmed his election in due time and expressed satisfaction with that colony's loyalty. In spite of the fact that Puritans had held control of Maryland from 1655 to 1658, the monarch was equally disinclined to seek reprisals there, either. He appreciated Lord Baltimore's unswerving loyalty, and he consequently upheld the proprietor's authority, but he made no attempt to punish the people who had worked so hard and so long to rid themselves of control by the Calvert family. The consideration shown these two colonies contrasted sharply with the treatment dealt out to Massachusetts, which had embraced the Commonwealth with general and obvious enthusiasm. King Charles had the sense to recognize that such pro-Commonwealth moves as were made in the southern provinces resulted from political necessity or the acts of factions and did not express a universal antagonism toward the Stuarts or the institution of monarchy.[46]

[46] C. M. Andrews, *Colonial Period*, II, 274–379, gives the best account of early Maryland. Two earlier histories containing valuable materials are Bozman, *The History of Maryland . . .* , and Newton D. Mereness, *Maryland as a Proprietary Province* (New York, 1901). For further sources, see Elizabeth Baer, *Seventeenth-Century Maryland: A Bibliography* (Baltimore, 1949).

CHAPTER 5

New Plymouth

VIRGINIA and Bermuda, the two earliest English settlements in the New World, owed their establishment to the efforts of profit-minded investors. The Calverts, in founding Maryland, gave some thought to the possibility of gain, but they also strove to create a haven where religious toleration would prevail. No such objective governed the actions of the Pilgrims, who planted a colony of their own farther to the north in 1620, because to them religious toleration was anathema. The Pilgrims, the most closely knit group in the entire history of American colonization, lacked the influence in high places that characterized the men responsible for Virginia, Bermuda, and Maryland, but they overcame this difficulty and many others and succeeded though sheer determination.

William Bradford, the narrator of the history of Plymouth Colony, writing of the early Separatists, states: "The truth is their condition for the most part, was for some time very low and hard. It was with them, as it should be related, would hardly be believed. And no marvel. For many of them had laid long in irons and then were banished into Newfoundland, where they were abused, and at last came into the Low countries, and wanting money, trades, friends or acquaintances, and languages to help themselves, how could it be otherwise."[1] Their first leader was Francis Johnson, a

---

[1] Alexander Young, *Chronicles of the Pilgrim Fathers of the Colony of Plymouth* . . . (Boston, 1844), pp. 440–441.

remarkable man although no Brewster, Robinson, or Bradford. His activities spanned a long period of persecution from 1592 to 1613 when, on his death in Emden, plans were under way to settle the Pilgrims in America.

The crown was more concerned about what to do with the stubborn Separatists than it was about disposing of the Catholics or Presbyterians. The Separatists were the real radicals, who, considering themselves wholly independent of the state in matters of religion, felt impelled to resist the state's intervention in religious affairs. Even at this early date some of these extremists avoided governmental control by journeying temporarily to Middleburg in the Netherlands. The harsh measures initiated by Archbishop Whitgift early in 1592 resulted in the imprisonment of many, including Francis Johnson and his congregation of fifty-six. The war against Spain led to a hardening of the unfavorable attitude toward Separatists, and publication of the Presbyterian Marprelate tracts attacking the Anglican Church reinforced the feeling against religious dissidents of all kinds. The authorities also regarded sectaries as social radicals who were inclined to be subversive toward the established system of property and who were deluded by concepts of a utopian society. Neither officialdom nor the public sympathized with the doctrine of "the gathered church," by which was meant a community of believers bound together into a self-sufficient religious and social unit. The stern Act of 1593 called for imprisonment, banishment, and even death for anyone persisting in this obnoxious course of action after the first offense. Sir Walter Raleigh, addressing the House of Commons, expressed concern about the families of the exiles who would be left behind in England. Lord Burghley also opposed exile, but pressure was brought to bear on him to ship offenders off to Ireland or America. Francis Johnson, speaking from prison, pleaded for toleration at home or, if that were not possible, at least toleration in the British dominions. Henry Ainsworth, the Separatist leader in Holland, stated, "We are but strangers and pilgrims, warring against many and mighty adversaries," and from that time on the Separatists thought of themselves as pilgrims.

Men were speculating about the possibility of colonization, and Burghley became interested because the Spanish war had revealed the need for increased supplies of naval stores, which might be obtained along the northern coast of the American continent. There were other resources available there, too, including fish, fish oil, fur, and the walrus oil so valuable in soapmaking. The Bretons and Basques were sailing in those waters and making frequent landings, but Burghley came to the conclusion that small colonizing groups could actually live there the year around, engaging in agriculture during the summers. Some men in high places suggested that the Separatists could provide the manpower for this project.

The Separatists were incapable of organizing such an enterprise on their own, but there were businessmen willing to give backing in the hope of economic gain. Merchant adventurers decided in 1597 to attempt a settlement on the Magdalen Islands, strategically situated at the mouth of the St. Lawrence, where fish, walrus oil, and foreign prizes seemed equally accessible. A number of merchants and Separatists formed a voluntary company, not unlike the syndicate which underwrote the Pilgrims in 1620. Francis Johnson petitioned the Privy Council for permission to take four Separatists on a pilot expedition to the Magdalens, and that body gave assent in March, 1597, with the proviso that the Separatists take an oath as loyal subjects and agree not to return to England. The enterprise ended in disaster after the two small ships became separated from each other, with one of them being stripped by the French Basques. Charles Leigh, the commander, brought the Separatists back to the Isle of Wight, whence they hastened to Amsterdam to avoid arrest. The merchant adventurers found consolation in a cargo of oil and fish brought into the Thames by Leigh, but it was clear that any settlement in the area of the Magdalens would entail bloodshed.

The "First Pilgrims"—David Quinn's phrase—were premature. The Separatists lacked unity and quarreled among themselves all through their adventure. The Magdalen Islands were too inhospitable for the proposed task, and enemies lurked everywhere in that area. Even in Holland there was much dissension among the Separatists. To be successful, an expedition would need the sort of cohesion supplied by the Leiden church in 1620.[2]

2 David B. Quinn, "The First Pilgrims," *William and Mary Quarterly*, XXIII (July, 1966), 359–390.

Refusing to wait for a reformation of the Church of England, the Separatists proceeded to set up congregations outside the accepted order. The first such group of which a record survives was that organized by Robert Browne in 1580 in Norwich. The Separatists, or Brownists as they were frequently called thereafter, had entirely unrelated congregations. Each church was autonomous, adopting its own covenant, electing its own officers, and restricting its own membership. Not only the government and the Church of England but the Puritans looked on this arrangement with great distaste at the time, but the Pilgrims and even the early Massachusetts Puritans adopted this Independent form of organization rather than the Presbyterian structure with its regional governing bodies.[3]

In the English village of Scrooby in Nottinghamshire a group of dissenters came to the conclusion that the time to establish the true Biblical polity was now, "without tarying for anie." Scrooby lay in the manor of the Archbishop of York, and the leader of these dissenters was William Brewster, known as Elder Brewster, who was a bailiff on the manor. Unlike most of his followers, Brewster was not an illiterate, for he had attended Cambridge University from 1580 to 1582. By 1607 this little congregation, which had adherents in nearby York and Lincoln, had grown to nearly one hundred persons. Other leaders were William Bradford, son of an affluent farmer of nearby Austerfield, and John Robinson, a nonconforming graduate of Cambridge, who became their minister. Since the Separatists were an unpopular minority in Scrooby, they were persecuted by their neighbors, and in November, 1607, they were subjected to investigation by the Ecclesiastical Commission of York.[4]

Greatly disturbed by the specter of persecution, the Pilgrims decided to seek refuge in Holland and to live together there as convenanting Christians. Acting on this first major decision, they migrated to Leiden in 1608 and found employment in that city as weavers, carders, bakers, and assistants in merchandising. In time many of them were admitted as citizens of the city, but they had

---

[3] Perry Miller, *Orthodoxy in Massachusetts, 1630–1650: A Genetic Study* (Cambridge, Mass., 1933), gives a lucid analysis of the similarities of Separatist and non-Separatist Congregationalism and the differences between them.

[4] George D. Langdon, Jr., *Pilgrim Colony: A History of New Plymouth, 1620–1691* (New Haven, Conn., 1966), pp. 4–8.

little concern for worldly status, being primarily interested in their salvation and their obligations to God. In 1611 they were able to purchase a common house and grounds, which brought them closer together.[5]

While the Pilgrims were living in Leiden, memorable events were transpiring in America. We do not know how much they learned about the founding of Jamestown and of subsequent developments, but their educated leaders must have heard about those exciting developments either from letters received from England or through conversations with learned men at the University of Leiden. In time the group living there became dissatisfied, and although one cannot pinpoint a specific reason, a number can be suggested.[6] One source of discontent was the fact that they were barred from membership in the guilds of Leiden. In addition, they felt themselves cut off from home, with their children growing up alien in habit and speech and in an environment where the Sabbath was neglected. Cotton Mather states in the *Magnalia* that the Pilgrims had tried for ten years to remedy the Dutch laxity with respect to observance of the Sabbath. Their main concern, however, as Mather adds and as William Bradford himself testified, was that their posterity "would be in danger to degenerate and be corrupted."[7] The leaders began to discuss the problem among themselves and, with prayer and fasting, sought the will of God. The Hispano-Dutch twelve-year truce was due to expire in March, 1621, opening the possibility of renewal of a religious war that portended nothing but savagery and inhumanity. Leaving Holland for the New World introduced the danger of shipwreck, capture on the high seas, or privation after arrival. Although by 1619 they knew that hundreds had crossed the Atlantic safely to Bermuda and Virginia, when they made the ultimate decision only a fraction of the Leiden group volunteered to make the transatlantic journey.

Many difficulties lay before the Pilgrims; they had no money,

---

5 William Bradford, *Of Plymouth Plantation, 1620–1647*, ed. Samuel Eliot Morison (New York, 1967), pp. 11–22, is, of course, the classic description of the years in Holland.

6 *Ibid.*, pp. 23–27. See also Thomas W. Perry, "New Plymouth and Old England: A Suggestion," *William and Mary Quarterly*, XVIII (Apr., 1961), 251–265, which argues that continuing loyalty to England was one of the reasons for the decision to remove to America.

7 Bradford, *Of Plymouth Plantation*, p. 35.

supplies, or transportation, no land patent, and no friends at court, and they had not even settled on a destination. Then they learned that the Virginia Company planned to create particular plantations, granting the undertakers of these enterprises special privileges with respect to Indian trade, fishing rights, and indentured servants.[8] On the assurance that they could live as a distinct body under their own head and under their own local ordinances, subject only to the laws and government of Virginia, and also assured that the king would guarantee them religious freedom, indispensable in an Anglican colony, they fearfully began negotiations. They did not wish to live outside the king's dominions, since, unlike the later Puritans, they were always willing to acknowledge his sovereignty. For this reason they eventually turned down proposals to remove to Middleburg or some other Dutch city, or to become the first colonists in New Netherland. Instead, it was a group of Walloons who accepted a Dutch offer in 1624 after rejecting one from Virginia, becoming thereby the first settlers in New Amsterdam.

During the years between 1617 and 1620 John Robinson, William Brewster, and several other leaders sounded out their English connections about the proposed migration. Two members of the Leiden church journeyed to England with a letter to Sir Edwin Sandys asking his cooperation and assistance, correctly surmising that Sir Edwin would receive the representatives of his brother's former tenant at Scrooby.[9] Sandys requested the Archbishop of Canterbury to permit the Separatists to go to Virginia, but he was refused on the ground that by their doctrines they asserted a liberty of worship that was unacceptable. The Leiden envoys, Robert Cushman and Deacon John Carver, then obtained a hearing before the Council of Virginia in London and attempted to clear themselves of the charge of disloyalty by submitting seven articles drawn up by Robinson and Brewster.[10]

Although the archbishop would have nothing to do with these

[8] See pp. 36, 39.
[9] Sir Samuel Sandys, brother of Sir Edwin, was the lessee of Scrooby Manor and had therefore been landlord to Brewster.
[10] Charles M. Andrews, *The Colonial Period of American History* (4 vols., New Haven, Conn., 1934–38), I, 256–264, and Herbert L. Osgood, *The American Colonies in the Seventeenth Century* (3 vols., New York, 1904–7), I, 105–109, give detailed descriptions of the Pilgrims' difficult and extended negotiations. Both versions necessarily draw heavily on Bradford, *Of Plymouth Plantation*, pp. 28–46.

articles, Sandys and the council accepted them, and the Virginia Company then approved the Pilgrims' plan to migrate and lent them £300, which was later repaid. In addition, the company was willing to authorize the Pilgrims to undertake the rearing of "infidel children," for which purpose the sum of £500 had been donated. When the secretary of state petitioned King James to allow these Separatists liberty of conscience, he refused but promised not to molest them. This compromise disappointed the leaders in Leiden, but they concluded that they could make some adjustment with the Virginia Company. Accordingly, in the winter of 1617–18 they sent envoys to England again and gave them letters to Sandys and others in which they tried to restate their position more clearly, attempting to resolve doubts that had been voiced earlier by the Privy Council.

Dissension inside the company resulted in a temporary delay in the issuance of all licenses for particular plantations, and during this period the Leiden Separatists kept in close communication with those in London so that the two groups might act together. The quarrel in the company finally resolved itself in the defeat of Sir Thomas Smythe and his replacement as treasurer by Sandys, and the would-be migrants then renewed their petition for a patent, acting this time through John Wyncop, a minister who had been tutor in the family of the third earl of Lincoln and who himself wished to join the party going to America. The final negotiations began in May, 1618, but the company did not give approval for a particular plantation until thirteen months later. It may be assumed that this patent was similar to documents granted later to others, such as those given to the Southampton Associates or the Peirce Associates. Land was allotted, and the associates were permitted, after naming a leader, to draw up ordinances for the local welfare, but it was the practice of the company to make specific land assignments only after colonists arrived in Virginia. Had the Pilgrims gone there, settling presumably in the Jamestown area, they would have been subject to the authority of the governor and council, and they would have been obliged to pay whatever taxes and impositions the Virginia Assembly levied. On the other hand, if the holders of the Wyncop patent had settled at some distant point such as the Hudson, they would have been beyond the control of either the government of Virginia or the Virginia Company in London.

The Wyncop patent reached Holland, where it was examined and discussed, but another development made it inadvisable to attempt to use it. Brewster and a man named Thomas Brewer printed a pamphlet in 1619 which denounced King James's attempt to force episcopacy on the Scottish Church. This publication drew unfavorable official attention to Brewster, who found it necessary to go into hiding, and for some time his friends on both sides of the Channel did their best to keep him out of sight. Under the circumstances, it seemed best not to use the patent which he had helped to obtain.

In February, 1620, the Dutch invited the Separatists to settle in New Netherland, but Robinson rejected the offer, partly because even more tempting possibilities were being suggested by an Englishman named Thomas Weston. This affluent London ironmonger was treasurer and leader of a group of merchant adventurers, one of whom was John Peirce, brother of Abraham Peirce, the Virginia cape merchant.[11] Weston was anxious to establish a particular plantation under the Virginia Company, and using the name John Peirce and Associates, he obtained a patent for land in Virginia. After consulting the London Separatists, he went to Leiden to interest the Separatists there in his project. Meeting with Robinson and others, he urged them to disregard the Dutch offer, to ignore the Wyncop patent, and to join his venture, in the assurance that he and his associates would look after the business and financial side of the enterprise. Since the Pilgrims were destitute of funds, Weston's offer came as a great boon, and in July, 1620, the Leiden group accepted his proposal that they provide the labor while he arranged financial backing. Many of them sold their property in Leiden and put their money into a common stock for the purchase of provisions and other supplies.[12]

[11] The head merchant or resident factor in a trading post.

[12] Historians have generally agreed that Weston's motives were anything but philanthropic. James Truslow Adams, *The Founding of New England* (Boston, 1949), p. 93, suggests that the man was driven entirely by a desire to make money, and Samuel Eliot Morison describes him as "eager to reap quick profits from the new world, and not very scrupulous as to means," in Bradford, *Of Plymouth Plantation*, p. 37 n. Ruth A. McIntyre, *Debts, Hopeful and Desperate: Financing the Plymouth Colony* (Plymouth, Mass., 1963), provides an orderly explanation of the Pilgrims' involved relationship with Weston and the men who later took his place.

There was still some uncertainty about where the Pilgrims should settle. Many of them had reservations about moving into an Anglican colony, and the Peirce Associates felt that the Virginia Company tended toward instability because of its constant internal bickering. It was Weston who suggested that they abandon the Peirce patent and try to obtain a grant in "northern Virginia" from the Council for New England, which was about to be created as nominal successor to the moribund Plymouth Company of London. He maintained that fishing there would be more lucrative than anything the James River country had to offer, and his argument was bolstered by the favorable attention New England was receiving at this time through the writing of Captain John Smith. Weston and his business-minded associates regarded trade privileges as an essential for existence. The majority in Leiden, too, were enthusiastic about the northern fishing prospects, and everyone realized that the Council for New England, despite opposition by the Virginia Company, was soon to receive a fishing monopoly in New England waters. Weston therefore initiated negotiations with the Council for New England, but that organization's charter, which was expected to pass the seals in the summer of 1620, was delayed until June, 1621. In the meantime the worried and desperate Pilgrims decided to leave under the Peirce patent that they already held. At this stage they appeared willing to go to Virginia and establish themselves under the government of that province, intending, however, to exercise as much autonomy as might prove to be possible.

Captain John Smith is our authority for the information that Weston and his associates, a mixture of gentlemen, merchants, and craftsmen, were seventy in number. Unlike participants in similar enterprises, the men who were going to America would be neither tenants nor servants, but would stand on equal terms with those in England as partners. There were three classifications of associates: merchant adventurers, each of whom contributed one or more shares at £10 a share to the common stock; merchant planters, each of whom intended to go to America and each of whom contributed £10 in money or supplies, which together with his labor would entitle him to two shares; and those, mainly Pilgrims, who could contribute only their labor, for which they received credit for only one share. Weston's company was a joint-stock organization, unincorporated, in which every man would share the profits according to his investment. As in the case of the Virginia and Bermuda ventures, both capital and profit were to be held intact for seven years, after which they would be divided proportionately, the capital to include land, houses, goods, chattels, and domestic animals. One estimate has it that £1,200 was paid in and that by 1624 the expenditures had risen to £7,500.[13]

This "common-fund-and-deferred-profit system" was not without precedent, but the plan of having part of the adventurers go to America was. If this company had been incorporated like the Virginia Companies of London and Plymouth, the Bermuda Company, and others later, such a division might not have been permitted, but the managers of an unincorporated company could do as they pleased, and in this enterprise each group had its own organization.[14] The London adventurers had a president and a treasurer and held regular court meetings, for Weston and his associates had been conducting their business in this way long before the Pilgrims entered the picture. The second group, the colonists who were risking their lives in the venture, chose a governor before sailing and thus became a self-governing plantation in which the English adventurers had no right to interfere. This ingenious organization not only consisted of a business and a religious group, but each was quasi-independent, for though the London merchants might give the Pilgrims advice, the latter were free to ignore it. Even the servants and apprentices were independent of the merchants' control, for they received their meat, drink, and apparel out of the colony's common stock.

Trouble soon developed over the agreement that Weston and the merchants had made with Robert Cushman, representing the Pilgrims. The leaders in Leiden believed that Cushman should never have agreed to let the merchants retain a half-ownership of the land and houses after the seven-year term expired, and they objected to the last-minute omission of a clause which would have allowed each planter to work two days every week in his own interest. The men in Leiden said that they had not authorized Cushman to change the intent of the contract and that he had done so without their knowledge, but Weston refused to consider

---

[13] Andrews, *Colonial Period*, I, 264–266, gives detailed information about Weston's organization.
[14] *Ibid.*, p. 265 n.

modifications at such a late date, and Cushman, though much disturbed at these reflections on his reliability, proceeded with the arrangements. For their part, the Pilgrims had already purchased a ship for crossing the North Sea, and they decided that they would have to go ahead. In all this the merchants felt that they were simply acting as businessmen engaged upon an enterprise so speculative that every possible safeguard had to be taken, and they were fully aware that the Pilgrims' only visible assets were their labor and the fruits thereof.

The Pilgrims had arranged for passage from Holland to England by purchasing the *Speedwell* with some of the funds accumulated through sale of their possessions. It was intended that the *Speedwell* should then proceed to America to be used there in trading activities. The majority of the transatlantic passengers, however, were to cross on the larger *Mayflower* which Weston had chartered for that purpose. Of the 238 members of the Leiden church, only thirty-odd decided to migrate, and these Pilgrims left Delfshaven on July 22, 1620, arriving at Southampton at the end of the month. There they met the *Mayflower*, which was carrying Carver, Cushman, and other London Separatists who had elected to join the colonizing party and also approximately eighty passengers enlisted by the merchants, most of the latter being laborers hired by Weston, who were not Separatists.[15]

The little fleet sailed on August 5, but a stop had to be made at Dartmouth to repair the *Speedwell*. At sea again and ten days out, the *Speedwell* sprang such a bad leak that the ships put back to Plymouth. A decision was made there that the *Speedwell* was unsafe and must be abandoned and that the *Mayflower*, taking aboard as many as possible, would have to go on alone. Twenty of Weston's hired laborers begged off at this point, and when the *Mayflower* sailed out of Plymouth on September 16, she carried 101 passengers, thirty-five from Leiden and sixty-six from London and Southampton.[16] There were nine indentured servants and five adult men who had signed on in one capacity or another, and the rest of the pas-

[15] Our knowledge of the departure from Holland and the migration to America derives from Bradford, *Of Plymouth Plantation*, pp. 47–63.

[16] Samuel Eliot Morison, *By Land and by Sea* (New York, 1966), p. 239, has shown that many of the passengers from London and Southampton were closely related to the families migrating from Leiden and that the entire group was consequently more homogeneous than the bare statistics would indicate.

sengers have been identified as fifty-six adults and thirty-one children, including some sent by the merchant adventurers. Forty-eight officers and crew brought the total on board to 149 people. Miles Standish came as a soldier, and John Alden, who became a Separatist later, came as a cooper.

At 180 tons the *Mayflower* was a small ship, and she was chunky, broad of beam, and slow. The vessel was double-decked and square-rigged, and there was a high structure at the stern. The passengers' quarters were between decks, and the only cargo on this voyage was the settlers' effects and provisions, which included chickens and swine but no cattle. Christopher Jones, a competent Harwich man of fifty, was captain, and the *Mayflower* also carried four mates and a boatswain, several cooks and several gunners, and a supercargo. One of the Pilgrims, Samuel Fuller, was a doctor, and there was a ship's surgeon, who returned to England after this voyage. The Massachusetts Bay Company later reckoned that a 200-ton ship should carry no more than 120 persons, and on this basis the *Mayflower* was overcrowded. There was considerable suffering caused by insufficiency of provisions, but only three crewmen and one passenger died, a lower mortality rate than might have been expected. The voyage actually took its toll the following winter, when general debility carried off half the passengers and half the crew, many of whom succumbed to scurvy.

After a relatively short voyage of sixty-five days, the *Mayflower* sighted Cape Cod, which Captain Jones must have recognized from existing accounts.[17] The question has often been raised as to whether the specific destination was the James, the Hudson, or New England. The Leiden congregation first reached a decision "to live as a distinct body under the government of Virginia," which meant that they intended to take up a particular plantation there. As early as 1619 they held such a patent in the name of John Wyncop, but the Pilgrims were not then ready to make use of it. Weston had, moreover, advised them to wait for the reorganization of the Virginia Company of Plymouth, soon renamed the Council for New England, under the aegis of Sir Ferdinando Gorges, but Gorges' intended charter was held up because the Virginia Company protested the granting of a fisheries monopoly. When the Pilgrims sailed, they carried not the Wyncop patent, which had expired, but a second patent for a particular plantation issued in the name of John Peirce, a friend of Weston's. This latter patent was to remain valid only if settlement was made south of 41 degrees north. Thus, although they preferred New England, the Pilgrims felt that they had to locate as far south as the Hudson River, where they could tap the fur trade and enjoy proximity to New England waters, at the same time staying far enough from Virginia to avoid interference. For these reasons, the Hudson River was their destination, but they had to change their plans, because tremendous waves prevented Captain Jones from rounding Cape Cod.[18]

When the Pilgrims made a landfall at Cape Cod on November 9, they had to face the fact that the Peirce patent would not apply there. Hence, they could not claim the right to local self-government, which was one of the provisions of that patent. Because, in spite of this lack of authority, they were determined to assume full authority over the settlement that was soon to become Plymouth, the Pilgrim members of the company entered into a compact by the terms of which they arranged to manage their own affairs.[19] In taking this action, they were also motivated by fear of the "strangers," by which they meant the non-Separatists aboard, who might have caused trouble unless brought under prompt control.[20]

The Pilgrims remained in Cape Cod Bay for a month, using the *Mayflower* as a base for exploration, and then the ship moved into Plymouth harbor in December after a scouting party discovered the advantages of that location.[21] The passengers disembarked, selected

[18] This view is accepted by Langdon, *Pilgrim Colony*, p. 2, and Samuel Eliot Morison in Bradford, *Of Plymouth Plantation*, p. 60 n., but some authorities disagree. Bradford Smith, *Bradford of Plymouth* (Philadelphia, 1951), pp. 108–109, contends that the Pilgrims always had New England as their destination, and Andrews, *Colonial Period*, I, 133, takes the position that they could not have intended to settle as far from Virginia as the Hudson River or even as far north as the Delaware area.

[19] The Mayflower Compact is discussed in greater detail on pp. 120–122. The description of the signing of this famous document will be found in Bradford, *Of Plymouth Plantation*, pp. 75–76.

[20] Samuel Eliot Morison, "The *Mayflower's* Destination and the Pilgrim Fathers' Patents," Colonial Society of Massachusetts *Transactions*, XXXVIII (1959), 387–413.

[21] Darrett B. Rutman, "The Pilgrims and Their Harbor," *William and Mary Quarterly*, XVII (Apr., 1960), 164–182, claims that the Pilgrims apparently had no knowledge of Plymouth harbor until they came upon it during their period of exploration. For the original description of these events, see Bradford, *Of Plymouth Plantation*, pp. 64–72.

a site for settlement, and laid out their village in a field where Indians had formerly cultivated corn. The colonists promptly erected a building for common use, and the heads of families began putting up houses, each with a garden plot, along both sides of a road running up from the harbor. The first winter was not severe, and aside from the sickness arising from the voyage the settlers managed to pull through. They had feared trouble with the Indians, but the natives proved to be no menace, because they had been greatly reduced in numbers and vitality by an epidemic during the previous two years.[22]

Plymouth grew slowly, from 124 in 1624 to 300 in 1630, to 579 in 1637, and to 3,000 in 1660.[23] Half a dozen ships followed the route of the *Mayflower* during those years, bringing settlers to replace those who had perished. Before long a second street crossed the original one at right angles, lined with homes and courtyards compactly arranged. The governor's house was in the center of town, and a square stockade stood in front of it, containing mortars which commanded the streets in all directions. On the hill overlooking the village was a fortress-like structure upon whose sturdy plank roof were six cannons capable of discharging five-pound iron balls. The inhabitants used the interior of this building for their religious services on Sundays and holidays.[24]

Some of the settlers had come from rural areas, while others had urban backgrounds, but they were all simple folk.[25] Those who had been living in Holland came originally from the midland counties of England, but their long residence in Leiden had forced them to give up farming and to learn to support themselves by means of crafts. The rest of the original Plymouth settlers were from

[22] The Pilgrims were reasonable in their dealings with the natives and enjoyed unusually good relations with them. See David Bushnell, "The Treatment of the Indians in Plymouth Colony," *New England Quarterly*, XXVI (June, 1953), 193–218, and Alden T. Vaughan, *New England Frontier: Puritans and Indians, 1620–1675*, particularly pp. 64–92.

[23] Various sources, especially John Demos, "Notes on Life in Plymouth Colony," *William and Mary Quarterly*, XXII (Apr., 1965), 264–286.

[24] Contemporary descriptions of the town will be found in Sydney V. James, Jr. (ed.), *Three Visitors to Early Plymouth: Letters About the Pilgrim Settlement in New England During Its First Seven Years by John Pory, Emmanuel Altham, and Isaack de Rasieres* (Plymouth, Mass., 1963).

[25] Morison, *By Land and by Sea*, p. 236, states that only William Brewster, John Carver, and Edward Winslow were classed as gentlemen.

London and Middlesex, including a large percentage of non-Separatists who had been added to the colonizing party by Weston. Only a few of the *Mayflower* passengers were called "mister" or "mistress," the larger number going by the less exalted titles of "goodman" and "goodwife." Brewster was the only member of the Leiden group who had any financial experience. The leaders who emerged, with the exception of Winslow, Carver, and Allerton (who was not in sympathy with the Separatists) came from London, as did Miles Standish, who had been a soldier in Holland.

The Separatists who came on the *Mayflower* were men of little or no education, and those who followed for the next nine years were of the same type. Only a score of university men came to Plymouth during its first forty years, and of these only three, all ministers, settled there permanently. Plymouth itself was without a minister from 1624 to 1628 and from 1654 to 1669. During the first fifty years there was no public school, and no boy from Plymouth Colony reached Harvard College. It was thought both in England and in America that the Brownists abhorred education and believed that ignorance was the key to heaven. Like most such generalizations, this was an exaggeration, because Brewster on his death in 1643 left four hundred volumes, and Bradford left eighty. Of seventy inventories of wills examined, only a dozen failed to mention printed works of some sort, usually Bibles, catechisms, and religious tracts, although the people of Plymouth were not as theologically minded as those of Massachusetts Bay.

The Pilgrims formed the homogeneous element in the colony, since they organized themselves into a primitive, covenanted church. They stood apart because of their preoccupation with the maintenance of their religious faith, and they avoided anyone not of their persuasion. Inasmuch as they admitted none but their own membership to their services, the others, who constituted a majority, were without any church. In 1624, during a period when the Separatists lacked a minister, a disagreeable clash broke out between the Pilgrims and non-Pilgrims. Brewster as elder had been directing church activities, but he was not a clergyman and therefore could not administer the sacraments. The civil authorities were performing marriages, but baptism was being omitted, since nobody in the colony was qualified to conduct that important ceremony. It was at this time that the Reverend John Lyford, a clergyman of the

Church of England, arrived, having been sent over by the merchant adventurers, possibly in response to the complaints of the majority. The newcomer incurred Bradford's wrath by baptizing children, serving communion, and conducting religious services according to the Book of Common Prayer, and he was shortly ejected from the colony on charges grounded on hearsay and a secret examination of the minister's correspondence. Lyford led a blameless life, and this regrettable episode cast no credit on the Pilgrims.[26]

The Lyford affair dramatized the Separatist dread of having an Anglican church established in their midst and their obsessive fear of all threats to their chosen beliefs and way of life. The Pilgrims thought that anyone acting against their convenanted interest was committing a sin, and they were constantly on the alert to detect infringements of their code of conduct. They complained that the younger men on board the *Mayflower* during the original voyage were unruly, and they decided that others coming over in 1623 "were so bad, as they were faine to be at charge to send them home again next year."[27] The Pilgrims saw misconduct everywhere and interpreted evil so liberally that the term included men addicted to sports as well as men who stole. They found John Billington guilty of murder and executed him, raising the question of the colony's right to pass a sentence of death. Even though they managed to get rid of some vexatious people, the Pilgrims could not remain completely isolated from the rest of the world, and their attempts to supervise conduct and belief could not turn Plymouth into an earthly paradise.[28] Eventually they quarreled with the merchant adventurers, who had made the undertaking possible, when the Londoners exercised their right to offer advice. The Pilgrims accused the merchants of trying to destroy their religious exclusiveness, whereas actually they were interested in the colony

26 All modern interpretations of the Lyford affair are based on Bradford's account in *Of Plymouth Plantation*, pp. 147–169. Not everyone finds Lyford blameless. Adams, *Founding of New England*, pp. 106–107, for example, describes him as "a canting hypocritical clergyman." Langdon, *Pilgrim Colony*, pp. 20–24, provides a thoughtful analysis, concluding that the minister became the center of opposition to Bradford's leadership, that the discontent was economic rather than religious in nature, and that Lyford's conduct made his banishment justifiable.

27 Bradford, *Of Plymouth Plantation*, p. 127.
28 Adams, *Founding of New England*, p. 111.

only as a business concern. There being no way to reconcile the major objectives of the two parties, the only eventual solution was for one of them to withdraw from the uneasy relationship.

Because the Pilgrims settled in New England instead of Virginia, their Peirce patent was valueless. Through the aid of John Peirce and a sympathetic London goldsmith named James Sherley, treasurer of the merchant adventurers, who had an application pending with the Council for New England, the merchants obtained a second Peirce patent dated June 1, 1621. By the terms of this instrument, the council formed the merchants and the Pilgrims into a joint-stock company for the promotion of a plantation in New England, and it vested title to the land jointly in the two groups. This patent, which determined the legal status of Plymouth until 1630, specified no exact boundaries but was an order for certain amounts of land—100 acres for each person transported and 1,500 acres for the public use—to be taken up in any place not yet inhabited. Thus the grantor, the Council for New England, followed the example of the Virginia Company in allocating land to groups; but, unlike the Virginia Company, it never established a general government, and its operation proved to be largely ineffective. Its particular plantations were too widely scattered, and it could not cope with the huge Puritan migration to Massachusets Bay that began in 1629.[29]

The merchant adventurers and their Plymouth partners held their land at a yearly quitrent of two shillings per hundred acres, and the privileges they enjoyed were similar to those prevailing in particular plantations in Virginia. There were some deviations from Virginia practice, however, such as the fact that the Pilgrims had to set up their own government and that the settlers were actual associates in the enterprise rather than tenants and servants. Both sets of partners, those of London and of Plymouth, were legally tenants of the Council for New England, but their relationship did not remain long untroubled. The London merchants broke with Weston by 1622 and bought out his share of the stock. At the same time, men interested solely in profits were also withdrawing, and the adventurers were splitting into factions. The French captured the company's ship, and this loss and other difficulties caused the leadership to become disheartened. On April 20, 1622, Peirce gave up

[29] Andrews, *Colonial Period*, I, 279–280.

his patent, rendering it null and void, and obtained in its place a deed poll, also issued by the Council for New England, which transformed his tenancy into a seigniory. Had this patent been allowed to remain in force, Peirce would have held the land in free and common socage of the king, and the Pilgrims would have stood to him as they had stood formerly to the council, and the monarch could then have treated the Pilgrims as his tenants. To prevent this, the merchant adventurers, led by Sherley, successfully brought pressure on Peirce to resign his patent to them for a valuable consideration. Peirce sued in chancery but died before the case was settled, and the 1621 patent was thus restored.[30]

The necessity for survival caused the Plymouth colonists to give their first attention to agriculture, but their financial obligations to the merchant adventurers made it necessary that they develop some sort of export commodity. They accordingly began fishing and trading with the Indians, and they also experimented with salt-making and boatbuilding. In spite of these efforts, the merchant adventurers developed very little confidence in their American partners' business ability. Furthermore, some of them disliked the Separatists' extreme religious views, which the Anglican Church condemned, and there was a feeling that if the settlers spent less time in disputation, they would have more time left for productive work. Money was going out, and none was coming in, and when hope for a successful commercial fishery collapsed, the company refused to send any more supplies.[31]

The colonists, who were thereby left to shift for themselves, had not, however, been idle, and they continued to seek ways to improve their situation. To enable each man to raise provisions for his family, the authorities made the garden allotments permanent in 1624. Under the communal system of land ownership, as Governor Bradford remarked, the person who carefully nurtured a plot one year would lose the benefit of it the next. Another step toward private ownership came in 1632, when lots for pasture and meadow on the edge of town were distributed among the settlers.[32]

Having been forsaken by their English associates, the Plymouth

30 *Ibid.*, pp. 280–283, and Osgood, *American Colonies*, I, 115.
31 Andrews, *Colonial Period*, I, 279, 283–284, and Langdon, *Pilgrim Colony*, pp. 27–28.
32 Andrews, *Colonial Period*, I, 284.

settlers henceforth exercised complete control over the destiny of the venture, which in form had become a joint-stock company. All adult males in the colony were eligible to join and share in the stock, and fifty-three Plymouth residents, known as the "Old Comers," joined five London merchant adventurers in the new partnership, dividing the assets and liabilities among the several shareholders. Land and livestock formed the collateral for debts, and a share of the assets was evaluated at twenty acres plus one-sixth of a cow and a third of a goat. Each shareholder was to make a contribution of three bushels of corn per year or six pounds of tobacco, until such time as the indebtedness could be paid off. Because the settlers had no money, Governor Bradford and the other leading men formed a partnership to manage the trade of the colony during the period of indebtedness, after which trade would be returned to the shareholders. Eight men in the colony, including Bradford, Standish, Allerton, Brewster, and Alden, and four shareholders in England held themselves responsible for the debt of the colony, an arrangement scheduled to last six years. The participating Englishmen represented a small minority among the merchants who were in sympathy with the Separatists.[33]

The men who guaranteed the debt hoped to make a profit by trading with the Indians for fur and fish and by the sale of surplus corn. The eight who lived in Plymouth received exclusive use of the three company boats and control of the stock of beads, hatchets, knives, corn, skins, and furs. They opened up trade with the Indians of Buzzard's Bay, the Dutch at New Amsterdam, and the coastal tribes as far north as the Kennebec and Penobscot rivers, and in 1632 Edward Winslow, another member of the group, journeyed to the Connecticut Valley. To prevent the settlers about the Piscataqua from monopolizing the Kennebec trade, Winslow arranged for the erection near the present site of Augusta, Maine, of a trading house suitable for both summer and winter operation. This Kennebec concession proved very lucrative and enabled the underwriters to go a long way in the payment of the debt. A second post was established on the Penobscot by obtaining through Isaac

---

[33] *Ibid.*, pp. 285–286; Langdon, *Pilgrim Colony*, pp. 30–32; Osgood, *American Colonies*, I, 116–118. See also Bradford, *Of Plymouth Plantation*, pp. 194–196, for the original account.

Allerton the license of one Edward Ashley, who had violated his privilege there by trading with the Indians for firearms and ammunition.[34]

This commercial activity yielded substantial supplies of beaver, corn, wampum, and lumber, part of which could be reserved for shipment overseas to liquidate the debt. Allerton went to England in 1627 and again in 1628 to find markets and to obtain supplies. He seems to have been unduly careless in his business dealings on these trips, because he borrowed money at ruinously high rates of interest and ran up large debts with his English factors. The underwriters made an accounting in 1631, and when they discovered that their debt had risen from £600 to £5,000, they became suspicious of Allerton and two of the English underwriters. Bradford accused Allerton of fraud and secured his dismissal as business agent for the underwriting group.[35] Once Allerton was out of the way, the trade and finances of the colony improved. The founding of the Massachusetts Bay Colony in 1629 stimulated migration into Plymouth, and as more people arrived, the amount of arable and pasture land increased. The underwriters agreed to extend the period of their original guarantee, but in 1639 Bradford and his partners gave warning that they wished to be relieved of their responsibility. A total of £1,200 was still owed to the English factors, and these businessmen, who were not motivated by the high ideals of the Pilgrims, maintained a continuous and merciless pressure on the underwriters. In order to pay off the last £400, Edward Winslow and Thomas Prence, the future governor, found it necessary to sell their homes, while Alden and Standish each sold 300 acres of land, and Bradford sold a farm.[36]

The beginning of civil authority in Plymouth dated from the

---

[34] Bradford, *Of Plymouth Plantation*, contains contemporary accounts of the several trading activities. See particularly pp. 192–194, 202–204, 219–222, 245–246, 257–260, 262–264, 275–279, and 280–284. See also Andrews, *Colonial Period*, I, 287–288.

[35] Bradford left ample evidence of his suspicions about Allerton. *Of Plymouth Plantation*, pp. 215–218, 226–234, 237–244, 250–252, and 256.

[36] See Bernard Bailyn, *The New England Merchants in the Seventeenth Century* (Cambridge, Mass., 1955), especially Chap. I and sections of Chap. III, for the early commercial life of Plymouth. Also partially concerned with Plymouth is Arthur H. Buffington, "New England and the Western Fur Trade, 1629–1675," Colonial Society of Massachusetts *Publications*, XVIII (1915–16), 160–192.

famous Mayflower Compact, drafted and signed before disembarkation by the Separatists among the passengers, who wished to allay discontent on the part of the non-Separatists and to assure for themselves the retention of power.[37] The forty-one signers, who included nineteen men from Leiden and sixteen Londoners, thus created the first American settlement based upon a social contract. Only a minority of the passengers were Separatists, but they were unified in purpose and determined to preserve their religious integrity as well as to keep the upper hand politically. The signers promised due obedience to whatever laws were promulgated for the general good. Their patent authorized the Pilgrims to manage their own civic affairs until such time as the company at home provided them with a form of government, and they were exercising this privilege when they drew up the compact, but they should not have done it until the Peirce patent of 1621 had been secured. Practical considerations, however, required immediate action, because some passengers had announced that they would act as they wished, arguing that the existing patent was valid in Virginia but not in New England. The Plymouth settlement was a plantation, not a political state, and even after the issuance of the Peirce patent in 1621 the Pilgrims and their associates had the right only to adopt local ordinances and to administer them through persons elected for that purpose. Sir Ferdinando Gorges envisioned that this would be the first of many such settlements, all functioning under a central government with a governor general at its head, but this plan for New England was never put into effect.

The actual government of Plymouth was extremely simple, since the Separatist element, the only organized group, was knit together in a sacred covenant which nobody in good conscience dared break. The Pilgrims chose their governors as they chose their ministers, by vote of the whole body of qualified persons. Deacon John Carver was probably the governor-designate by common consent while the Pilgrims were at sea, for he had been entrusted with the preparations for the departure, and he was governor until his death in April, 1621. William Bradford succeeded him

[37] Adams, *Founding of New England*, p. 98, stresses that the Mayflower Compact was not intended to be the constitution for a new type of government but was, rather, "a perfectly simple extension of the ordinary form of church covenant."

and was reelected annually, with the exception of five years, until 1656. There were five assistants after 1624 and seven starting in 1633, these officials also being elected annually by the freemen, with the resultant governmental structure consisting of the governor and his assistants, or councillors. The freemen met only when the governor decided that important matters required their attention.[38] Although he frequently expressed a wish to be relieved of his heavy responsibility, Bradford in essence was the government. He was not arbitrary, but there were occasions when he did not hesitate to enforce his will.[39]

After 1626 the colony and the corporation were the same, and Plymouth took on the form of a charter colony, a situation that was true in fact but not in law. The Pilgrims were never able to obtain a charter from the crown, although they expended much money on the project from 1629 until 1691. Once they came close, for a concerted effort in 1629–30 failed only because the English government was unwilling to forgo the customary fees, which the Pilgrims could not raise. The right of self-government rested, then, on the Mayflower Compact and the Peirce patent of 1621, later confirmed by the patent obtained by Allerton for Bradford and his associates from the Council for New England with the aid of Gorges and Warwick. This patent, the Old Charter, was issued on January 13, 1630. It added no powers of government, but for the first time the boundaries of the colony were defined.[40] It also confirmed the title to the lands around the Kennebec and the liberty to fish and trade there.

Bradford retained possession of the charter until 1641, when with the consent of the other undertakers he turned it over to the

[38] Detailed descriptions of the civic organization will be found in Langdon, *Pilgrim Colony*, pp. 93–98, and Osgood, *American Colonies*, I, 290–295.

[39] See Smith, *Bradford of Plymouth*, for additional information about the famous governor. Morison includes a brief but interesting sketch in his edition of Bradford, *Of Plymouth Colony*, pp. xxiii–xxvii.

[40] Plymouth and Massachusetts agreed on a boundary in 1640 that began at a point on the bay just south of Cohasset and ran southwesterly and westerly for more than forty miles to the Blackstone River. The western boundary remained in dispute for decades. The Rhode Island Charter of 1663 carelessly described the boundary as three miles to the east of the northeastern parts of Narragansett Bay, then along the Seekonk River to Pawtucket Falls. The various claims were not settled until 1746. See Bradford, *Of Plymouth Colony*, pp. 428–430, and below, pp. 228–229.

freemen of the corporation of New Plymouth, thus giving the Pilgrims the feeling that they were proprietors of both soil and jurisdiction, although the Old Charter gave them no new legal status. Their title to govern themselves actually rested on usage alone—the fact that, without protest from England for sixty-five years, until 1686, they were allowed to regulate and control their own affairs. Without a link with the crown, Plymouth was not really a colony at all, even though the king from time to time sent over letters in his name expressing satisfaction with it and making promises, never fulfilled, of assistance. The general court regarded such communications as a qualified recognition, but inasmuch as Plymouth ceased to be a political entity in 1691, before England had worked out its colonial policy, its status was never really determined. Charles M. Andrews classifies Plymouth as a de facto corporate colony.[41]

With the steady growth of Plymouth, whose population reached one thousand by 1640, the original inhabitants and newcomers spread out toward the north, east, and west, founding Duxbury and Scituate in 1636, Sandwich in 1638, Yarmouth in 1639, and Taunton a year later. Apparently Bradford had not contemplated that other hamlets would spring up in the wilderness and that, despite his concern, they would establish their own churches. The decentralizing pattern of settlement demanded a new constitution, and in 1636 the Pilgrims adopted the Great Fundamentals, a set of laws consisting of nine paragraphs promulgated in the name of the associates of the colony of New Plymouth.[42] The closing paragraph asserted that the laws set forth were essential to their just rights and liberties, and as such "they shall and ought to be inviolably preserved." The freemen in their yearly meetings at Plymouth were to elect the governor, deputy governor, and assistants. Laws were to be enacted by a general court or assembly made up of two representatives from each town chosen by the freemen, sitting with the governor and his assistants as a single house. Plymouth was thereby patterning itself on its younger but larger neighbor, the Massachusetts Bay Colony. The existence of Plymouth

---

41 *Colonial Period*, I, 296 n.
42 William Bradford, *History of Plymouth Plantation 1620–1647*, ed. Worthington C. Ford (2 vols., Boston, 1912), II, 237–241. The laws of New Plymouth were first published by Samuel Green of Boston in 1672.

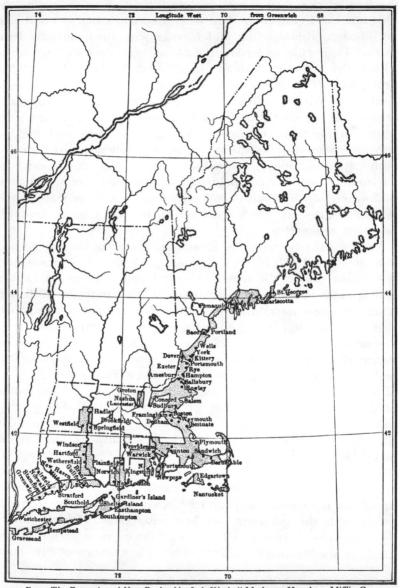

From *The Expansion of New England* by Lois Kimball Mathews, Houghton Mifflin Company

NEW ENGLAND SETTLEMENT, 1660

as a colony received recognition by its neighbors in 1643, when it was invited to become one of the four members of the New England Confederation. When Plymouth accepted the invitation, it was acting as if it were a duly constituted charter colony, which, of course, it was not. Its status was not noticed by the crown until 1660 and then only because of the adoption of imperial legislation affecting all the colonies. Up until that time and even later, Plymouth managed to conduct itself as if it were a legally valid colony, while cautious about taking steps to clarify its status, so long as it was not challenged, it remained unharmed, but only so long.

Historians have failed to agree about the extent of democracy in early Plymouth. George Bancroft praised the Mayflower Compact as "the birth of constitutional liberty in America," but a more recent writer, George Willison, considers the compact as an instrument designed to maintain the status quo, at the same time denying that democracy prospered in Plymouth. Samuel Eliot Morison takes an even stronger stand, concluding that New Plymouth never even pretended to be democratic, buttressing his argument by pointing out that from 1627 to 1639 only the Old Comers had the power to grant land and that as late as 1643 hardly a third of the adult males voted. Whatever conditions actually existed initially, it has been contended that as the seventeenth century wore on, the trend in Plymouth "seems to have been away from rather than toward political democracy."[43]

It seems undeniable that a good deal of democracy was present at the start. The Mayflower Compact having established civil government, the settlers met once a year as a general court to elect the governor and, at first, his one assistant. All voted, since they were all stockholders in an enterprise in which everything, including labor, was the common property of the company. Voting was not restricted to church members, as was to be the case later in Massachusetts. A limitation of the franchise did appear in 1623, when newcomers who had paid their own way to Plymouth were

---

43 On this controversial subject, see George Willison, *Saints and Strangers* (New York, 1945), pp. 317–319; Morison, "Pilgrim Fathers," pp. 367–379; and the reasoned view of George D. Langdon, Jr., "The Franchise and Political Democracy in Plymouth Colony," *William and Mary Quarterly*, XX (Oct., 1963), 513–526.

denied the vote and were barred from trading with the Indians because they were not members of the company. When these newer settlers, who were called "particulars," joined with the others in paying the company debt in 1627, however, they probably received the voting privilege.

After the outlying hamlets were settled, it became desirable to define citizenship, clarifying precisely who could vote and who could hold office, but Plymouth, unlike Massachusetts, never did spell out the qualifications for freemanship. Until 1658 a man needed only to testify to the true worship of God and agree not to oppose the laws. No proof of regeneracy was required, as it was in Massachusetts, and some men not members of the church did in fact become freemen. The right to vote was, however, denied to people opposed to a trained clergy, such as the Quakers. Inasmuch as Plymouth lacked large agricultural estates, there were few servants, and their status was never a problem.

Certainly before 1658 the majority of adult males were freemen, and therefore Bancroft's claim does not seem too wide of the mark. There were, for example, eighty-six taxpayers in Plymouth and Duxbury in 1633, fifty-four of whom were then listed as freemen and another fourteen who achieved that status later. As was true in Massachusetts, some men were negligent about their duties as citizens, and fines were imposed for nonattendance at the general court. With the spread of settlements and the consequent difficulty in getting to meetings of the court, the representative system was introduced in 1638, but every voter was still required to come to the election court in June. Finally, the authorities fined anyone ten shillings who did not vote at all.

Under the representative system, any adult male, freeman or not, could vote for deputies to the general court, but these elected representatives had to be freemen, and only freemen could hold other offices or vote in the annual election court. It is clear that the great majority of men could vote for representation and that no property qualification was required. Only after the perennial governor, William Bradford, died in 1659 and was succeeded by Thomas Prence did Plymouth begin to tighten its qualifications. It was during this period that Quakers began their systematic assault on the churches and that Massachusetts orthodoxy was enjoying its maximum influence throughout New England. Plymouth disenfranchised the Quakers, and a new law stipulated that, in order to qualify as a deputy, a man had to favor suppression of that sect. New residents now had to wait one year before casting a vote in the general court, and nonfreemen were specifically denied the right to vote for deputies. Plymouth later began to impose property qualifications for voting, and the opportunity to share in political life became even more restricted. Bradford had understood how much the new colony needed the support of the whole community, but his successors lacked his breadth of vision.

The old belief that Plymouth, from 1620 to 1660, was an endogenous society has recently been challenged.[44] Bradford and the other leaders did, it is true, seek to limit dispersion, and when, for example, there was a distribution of land, the general court attempted to exact a promise that the owners of new property would continue to reside in Plymouth. Later, in 1640, the court criticized the new towns for permitting settlement without asking questions, and it directed the elders of the several towns to require certificates from the communities whence the newcomers came and testimony regarding their religious and moral reliability.

Yet Plymouth Colony grew steadily though not spectacularly even from the very beginning. There were eight towns in 1646 and twenty-one in 1691, not including many smaller hamlets.[45] Not only were there new settlements, but individuals moved about frequently from house to house and from one community to another. Land titles changed rapidly, and families were broken by death and reorganized by new marriages at an astonishing rate. With a growing population, especially after the founding of the Massachusetts Bay Colony in 1629, the demand for cattle, corn, and other produce proved greater than Plymouth village could meet. But more alluring to the colonists was the prospect of expanding land ownership in a virgin province, especially after Plymouth's boundaries were set. Eventually Plymouth was drawn into the great vortex of commercial Boston, with its voracious demands for grain and other products for export.[46]

---

44 Demos, "Notes on Life in Plymouth Colony," p. 264.

45 Langdon, *Plymouth Colony*, pp. 38–57, gives an excellent description of the geographical growth of the colony.

46 For Boston's expanding hinterland, see Darrett B. Rutman, "Governor Winthrop's Garden Crop . . . ," *William and Mary Quarterly*, XX (July, 1963),

Young and old, rich and poor, and men with and without families all moved freely about New England, and the land grants in Plymouth Colony attest to this mobility. A large percentage of the original settlers in all the early towns quickly dispersed. The early wills reveal that many men owned plots in several towns, and wealth was conceived of in terms of land, which was plentiful, whereas currency was scarce.

The immigration into Plymouth Colony was of modest proportions, but the people living there increased mightily, and in spite of high infant mortality, the average family produced seven or eight children who reached maturity. Health standards, compared with those in Virginia, were high. The oldest group comprised the superannuated women. Marriage was regulated, with the parents' consent required by law. The custom of the marriage portion was prevalent, not in accordance with any set formula, but with the intention of establishing homes for the young people. During the early years of the colony, the scarcity of women caused many men to marry late, but the ratio between the sexes soon equalized. In the frequent second marriages, care was taken to protect the rights of the children. It was the general practice to "put out" stepchildren under a system which proved humane and which was universally accepted. When the child was bound out, he was entitled to learn a trade, and he had to be given instruction in reading and writing. Since one in three parents married twice, between a third and a half of all the children grew up in households other than their own. As was also true in the other Puritan colonies, life among the Pilgrims, despite the severity of the laws, was anything but bleak and oppressive.[47]

Recent research has demonstrated the extent to which relationships within the family and life patterns of individuals differed from those prevailing today. Childhood was a period of relative tranquility, although a certain amount of repression was involved, and the process of growing up was much more gradual than it is today. The modern emphasis on adolescence was then unknown,

---

especially pp. 407 ff. The same author's *Husbandmen of Plymouth: Farms and Villages in the Old Colony, 1620–1692* (Boston, 1968), describes the process of expansion, with emphasis on the fact that the life of Plymouth always revolved around farming.

47 Demos, "Life in Plymouth Colony," pp. 264–286.

because the Plymouth colonists considered that the critical changes occurred much earlier, at the ages of six or seven. The many children in a typical family, spread out fairly evenly over a period of many years, tended to blur the distance between generations. There is little evidence of an unusual degree of family tension in spite of the lack of privacy in the small homes of the early settlers, suggesting to the investigator that there may have been an unconscious restraint on the expression of hostile impulses against the members of one's own household. Old age, like adulthood, came on gradually rather than abruptly. The more important public offices were awarded only to men who had passed forty years of age, and nobody thought of retiring either from those offices or from private employment until forced to do so by actual physical infirmity.[48]

The motivation for the planting of Plymouth differed entirely from that of earlier colonial efforts. The Pilgrims were not hardened adventurers but were simply a small band of inexperienced men and women anxious to eschew all worldliness. They were not seeking riches, and they hoped for nothing more than a means of livelihood. Their main purpose in life was to attain to the Kingdom of Heaven, and while working to earn this reward, they endeavored to lead exemplary Christian lives. Their responsibility as they saw it was to God. They believed that God was directing their course and that, in consequence, they could disregard all ecclesiastical traditions and practices. Art, music, and literature had for them nothing to do with the world to come, and they likewise found no profit in the doctrines of election, predestination, or freedom of the will. Except for their religious sincerity, the Pilgrims never rose above the level of daily toil.

Actually, the Pilgrim's outlook was more liberal than that of the Massachusetts Puritan, who did not look charitably on human frailties and who often ascribed to the work of a Satan-infested mind acts that were either pathological or harmless. The Pilgrim and Puritan nevertheless had much in common, both regarding ease and pleasure as obstacles on the path to heaven and both exhibiting a compulsion to master the sinful temptations of a world

---

[48] John Demos, *A Little Commonwealth: Family Life in Plymouth Colony* (New York, 1970), pp. 46–50, 67–69, 134–150, and 174–176.

doomed to destruction. Backward as the Pilgrim may have been
with respect to cultural achievement, he has exercised a considerable influence on subsequent generations, by the unusual example
he set of moral righteousness.[49]

[49] For a general account, see Andrews, *Colonial Period*, I, 279–299. Wesley
Frank Craven, *The Legend of the Founding Fathers* (New York, 1956), explains
the effect the Pilgrim legend has had on subsequent American history.

CHAPTER 6

The Northern Fringe

FISHERMEN had plied their ships toward the shores of Newfoundland, Nova Scotia, Maine, and Massachusetts from remote times, and among them were Portuguese, Spanish and French Basques, Bretons, Normans, and Englishmen from the West Country. Cod, mackerel, and herring, carried in boats of hardly more than sixty tons burden, reached the markets of France, Spain, and the Mediterranean ports to supply the Lenten season demand. Walrus oil, too, was a valuable commodity because it was used in soapmaking. When Humphrey Gilbert landed at St. John's harbor in eastern Newfoundland in 1583 and took possession, he was well aware that what he was establishing there was a rendezvous for English fishermen. These fishermen found it convenient to use the shores for drying and salting, but once they prepared their catch, they returned to Europe with it. Since only a few spent the winters in America, there was no permanent colonization, despite occasional abortive efforts such as that of Captain Leigh at Magdalen Islands in 1597.[1]

Through the years before 1620 a series of fishing stations grew up along these northern coasts, particularly in Maine. When the Pilgrims settled Plymouth, they hoped to enter the fishing industry

---

[1] Henry S. Burrage, *The Beginnings of Colonial Maine, 1602–1658* (Portland, Maine, 1914), pp. 1–16; Daniel W. Prowse, *History of Newfoundland* (London, 1895), pp. 15–50; and David B. Quinn, "The First Pilgrims," *William and Mary Quarterly*, 3d. ser., XXIII (July, 1966), 371–384 *passim*.

to earn money with which to pay off their debts, but they lacked the necessary knowledge, and their experiment failed. The American fishing frontier extended from Cape Cod to Labrador and constituted big business in the seventeenth century, far exceeding the fur trade in value.[2] At the very beginning of the century men like Captain John Smith and Martin Pring were advocating not only a full English participation in fishing but its association with all plans of settlement.

Bristol, England's great West Country port, was deeply interested in all Atlantic voyages, but especially in those that might affect her thriving herring trade. Richard Hakluyt was connected with Bristol Cathedral. John Popham was an erstwhile recorder of the city, and Ferdinando Gorges owned a house near Bristol. Men of the explorer breed were active in the Merchant Adventurers, the strong commercial underwriting association there.[3] This group assisted both Pring and Popham in making early voyages to the north Atlantic shore, and in 1609 when Gorges' venture was thrown open to the public, he persuaded some of them to subscribe to the stock of the Virginia Company of Plymouth. The Bristol merchants were also familiar with Newfoundland because of the early endeavors of Humphrey Gilbert and George Peckham. They believed that "God had reserved Newfoundland for us Britons, as the next land beyond Ireland, and not above nine or ten dayes saile from thence."[4] With influence at court, they were determined to play a role in American enterprises.

The Bristol merchants applied to the king in 1610 for a charter to form a company similar to the London and Plymouth companies. With the support of Sir Francis Bacon and other government officials, John Guy, an able young Merchant Adventurer, secured a charter for the Company of the Adventurers and Planters of the City of London and Bristol for the Colony of Plantation in Newfoundland. Twelve of the forty-eight patentees associated in this enterprise were members of the Merchant Adventurers of Bristol.

---

[2] An excellent description of how the fishing stations operated and how the catch was shipped to Europe will be found in Ralph G. Lounsbury, *The British Fishery at Newfoundland, 1634–1763* (New Haven, Conn., 1934), pp. 55–64.

[3] Gillian T. Cell, "The Newfoundland Company," *William and Mary Quarterly,* XXII (Oct., 1965), 611–626, discusses the membership of this organization.

[4] Sir William Vaughan, *The Golden Fleece* . . . (London, 1626), pp. 5–6.

The charter created the usual joint-stock company with a treasurer, council, and general court, holding its land as of the manor of East Greenwich, with a trade monopoly except for fishing. The treasurer, John Slany, and the councillors were all Londoners and were vested with full power to govern such colonies as they might establish. In important particulars this charter was similar to the Virginia charter of 1609 and the Bermuda charter of 1615.[5]

John Guy, who was enthusiastic about establishing a colony in Newfoundland, marshaled an expedition of three ships and went out as governor. Thirty-nine persons were aboard, including members of his own family, and they went supplied with seeds, domestic animals, and equipment. The vessels, leaving in July, 1610, made a fine voyage of only twenty-three days before landing at Cupers Cove in Conception Bay. Thanks to mild weather and the aid of fishermen there, they survived the winter with the loss of only four lives. They managed to build a storehouse, a dwelling house, a fort, and other appurtenances and also found time to construct a twelve-ton boat and six small fishing boats. Unfortunately, the second winter was severe. Not only did pirates threaten the settlers, but provisions froze, cattle died, and scurvy appeared. In 1615 the company sent out as governor John Mason, a thirty-year-old ship captain and adventurer, and he remained in charge for the next six years. Captain Mason explored the island, made a map, and wrote *A Briefe Discourse*, which was printed at Edinburgh in 1620.[6] Guy's settlement was the first to weather a winter in Newfoundland, and it proved that the island would support permanent habitation.[7]

Guy's apparent success led to other endeavors. A group of London and Bristol citizens purchased from the London and Bristol Company a large tract north of Cupers Cove, a part of the peninsula between Conception Bay and Trinity Bay, and established a colony at Bristol's Hope in 1617 with Harbour Grace as its center. Though little of the colony's history is known, it appears that it

[5] Lounsbury, *Fishery at Newfoundland*, p. 36.

[6] *A Briefe Discourse of New-Foundland, with the Situation, Temperature, and Commodities Thereof, Inciting our Nation to Goe Forward in that Hopefull Plantation Begunne.*

[7] The most detailed description of this colonizing attempt will be found in Prowse, *Newfoundland*, pp. 93–109.

served as a fishing settlement, and it existed as late as 1640. In 1640 the promoters consummated plans to send over 180 additional persons whose function would be to supply the fishing fleet with such provisions as grain and livestock. The promoters had already announced their intention of maintaining a fishing fleet throughout the year, using Bristol's Hope as their base. Sir William Vaughan, a picturesque eccentric, excited by what was going on in Bristol, purchased from the London and Bristol patentees that part of their grant extending southward from Guy's colony to Trepassy. In 1618 he sent two groups of men and women to settle plantations, which he named Cambrioe Colches and Golden Grove. Vaughan went out in 1622 and while there composed two works, *Cambrensium Cariola*[8] and *The Golden Fleece,* the latter the first original literary effort written by a resident of the English settlements. The "golden fleece" of Newfoundland, he boasted, was destined to halt the decay of trade believed to be taking place in western Europe. He also urged the settlers and fishermen to reconcile their differences, to the advantage of both factions.[9]

Vaughan's effort was noteworthy also because of its association with Captain Richard Whitbourne, sometimes called the "Captain John Smith of the North." Like Smith, Whitbourne had an adventurous career of forty years' duration. He was with Sir Humphrey Gilbert when the latter took possession of Newfoundland in the name of the queen, and he served against the Spanish Armada. Whitbourne took charge of one of Vaughan's colonies in 1617 and later gave an account of Newfoundland and the fishing industry in *A Discourse and Discovery of New-foundland,*[10] valuable for its information and not devoid of literary merit. Another Newfoundland land purchase by Vaughan caused his bankruptcy and ultimately forced the sale of portions of his frigid domain to two former friends at Oxford who had become famous personages, Lord Cary, Viscount of Falkland, and Sir George Calvert. Greatly interested in America, Falkland opened a land office in London, but nothing came of the project. He then sent over a carelessly selected

---

8 (London, 1625). A photostatic edition was published by the Massachusetts Historical Society (Boston, 1926).

9 See Lounsbury, *Fishery at Newfoundland,* pp. 46–47, 88.

10 (London, 1620).

group of colonists, whose abilities were unsuited to the task at hand, and the undertaking failed without leaving a trace.

Calvert tried to establish a real settlement in Newfoundland in the face of opposition by the West Country fishing interests. Between 1620 and 1622 he sent over a large number of men and women to start a colony in the northern reaches of Vaughan's patent, where he had purchased land. At his London office his agent promised prospective immigrants transportation and security at Ferryland, his settlement south of St. John's that he equipped with houses, a fort, and a saltworks, together with prepared garden plots. The settlers there, responding to his encouragement, made an effort to raise tobacco, but the climate made success impossible.[11]

Misled by Edward Wynne, his governor who sent him optimistic accounts of his progress, Calvert went to the considerable expense of obtaining a royal charter for his holdings in 1623. He then gave the name Avalon to his greatly enlarged domain, which he held *in capite* by knight service.[12] Calvert was absolute lord of this county palatine, with the right to promulgate laws, in an emergency, without the consent of the freeholders. He failed to obtain a fishing monopoly, because the government wanted all English subjects to enjoy the right to fish there and also to be able to salt and dry fish on the shores of Avalon. Although there was a small hamlet at St. John's devoted exclusively to fishing activity, only Ferryland gave promise of becoming a permanent settlement. Suspicious that his governor, Wynne, and Captain Powell, were not up to the job, Sir George went there himself in 1627 and 1628. After experiencing the severe weather at first hand, he informed the king that he wished to transfer his efforts to a warmer climate. He announced his intention of moving to Virginia with Ferryland's forty residents and turning Ferryland over to men involved in the fishing industry. In October, 1628, Calvert, who by then had become Lord Baltimore, made his notable visit to Virginia, thus taking the first step toward the founding of Maryland.[13] His first colonizing venture had lasted

11 Calvert's activities in Newfoundland are described in detail in Bernard C. Steiner, "The First Lord Baltimore and His Colonial Projects," *American Historical Association Report* (1905), I, 109–122.

12 Held from the king on condition of rendering a service, formerly military.

13 See pp. 52, 76–78.

longer than any other in Newfoundland, because he had the backing of a royal charter and because he contributed superior management.

Charles I, assuming that all the Newfoundland patentees had abandoned their rights there, regranted the island in 1637 to Sir David Kirke, one of the brothers who took Quebec in 1629, and to others. Kirke himself went out as governor in 1638 with a hundred men and settled in Ferryland. Later the courts decided that the Calverts had been illegally stripped of their property, and in 1662 the Kirkes were ordered to give up Avalon. The Calvert family made one final attempt to re-establish the colony but gave up in 1674 and withdrew the governor. Ferryland remained thereafter for the use of and in charge of fishermen, as did all other Newfoundland settlements.[14]

The various Newfoundland colonies withered away, leaving hardly a trace, yet they were part and parcel of the contemporary zeal for colonization. Several causes contributed to the failure: inexperience of the entrepreneurs, unfavorable climate, and relatively barren soil. The most important negative factor, however, was the unceasing opposition of the commercial interests of the West Country, Devon and Somerset particularly, who wanted no colonies in the fishing grounds. They feared the interference of local colonial governments, just as they dreaded every patent application that asked for monopoly of local fisheries. At the same time they pushed continuously for a charter guaranteeing them a monopoly and full protection of what they considered their ancient rights and privileges. In 1634 Charles I promulgated the Western Charter, giving these men the guarantees they requested. The essential features of this charter were later embodied in an act passed by Parliament in 1699.[15]

A land mass similar in size to Newfoundland lay just to the south of it between the St. Lawrence and the Atlantic, comprising what became Nova Scotia and New Brunswick. The imaginative Scotsman Sir William Alexander was one of Vaughan's friends, and their conversations, recorded in *The Golden Fleece,* led them to

[14] See Henry J. Berkley, "Lord Baltimore's Contest with Sir David Kirke over Avalon," *Maryland Historical Magazine*, XII (June, 1917), 107–114; also Louis D. Scisco, "Kirke's Memorial on Newfoundland," *Canadian Historical Review*, VII (Mar., 1926), pp. 46–51.

[15] Charles M. Andrews, *The Colonial Period of American History* (4 vols., New Haven, Conn., 1934–38), I, 300–313.

the belief that there should be a New Scotland in the New World. Aware that the land between Newfoundland and New England had gone unnoticed except for several unsuccessful attempts by the French to gain a foothold at Port Royal, Alexander approached King James, himself a Scot, who lent an approving ear. At a hint from the king, the Scottish Privy Council granted Alexander the territory named Nova Scotia in September, 1621, to be held by him under James as king of Scotland. Word went to Ferdinando Gorges, president of the Council for New England, to release this part of his patent to Alexander. This truly princely domain was held by a charter unlike that issued to any other proprietor in America. A Scottish document, it bore the marks of feudal and tenurial law that were outmoded even in England. Written in medieval Latin, this instrument might have served for a proprietary in Scotland in the twelfth century, and has been described by a leading authority as a masterpiece of legal pedantry.[16]

In 1622 Alexander purchased a ship in London, and at Kirkcudbright, Scotland, he took aboard provisions, equipment, and a reluctant group of prospective settlers. The vessel did not reach Newfoundland until the middle of September, too late in the season to proceed farther. The immigrants spent the winter at St. John's among the fishermen, and there all efforts terminated, leaving Alexander to absorb the heavy financial losses. Still optimistic, Alexander in 1624 issued his *Encouragement to Colonies*, an unrealistic promotional document that elicited no support.[17] He then turned to King James, who suggested the creation and sale of a number of baronetcies, a scheme that had persuaded many Englishmen to settle confiscated land in Ireland and had yielded the king £225,000. Each Nova Scotia baronet would pay a thousand marks[18] and furnish six men and provisions for two years, and he would receive land and his title in exchange. This scheme had successfully led Englishmen to Ireland, but the prudent Scottish gentry failed to respond.[19] Furthermore, both the Scottish Convention of Estates

---

16 *Ibid.*, p. 315. The English text of the charter is reprinted in Sir Edmund F. Slafter, *Sir William Alexander and American Colonization* (Boston, 1873), pp. 127–148.

17 (London, 1624). Reprinted in Slafter, *Sir William Alexander,* pp. 149–216.

18 An English or Scottish mark was a silver coin worth 13s. 4d.

19 Alexander averaged fewer than eight customers per year over a fourteen-year period. Slafter, *Sir William Alexander,* pp. 233–237.

and the English House of Commons protested that the creation of these titles would dilute the nobility.

Alexander persisted in his colonizing efforts, with varying but generally unsatisfactory results. He gathered ships, supplies, and colonists for another expedition in 1627, but he had his usual bad luck, and it never got off. Two years later, in collaboration with his son William, Lord Alexander, he managed to land seventy-odd men and two women at Port Royal (later Annapolis) in the Bay of Fundy, where they found a few Frenchmen, the residue of a group that had moved to the southeast. This small success resulted from an agreement with a company of merchant adventurers organized in 1628 to develop trade with Canada and led by Jervas Kirke, William Berkeley, and Lord Charlton. Alexander's patent preempted one of their objectives, and so they offered him undisturbed possession of Acadia in exchange for trading rights on the St. Lawrence, at the same time according him membership in their company.[20] Under this arrangement Alexander was able to get his colonists aboard a six-ship fleet which the company was sending to Canada to trade, and he was thus successful in founding a settlement at Port Royal. Several other significant events occurred at just about the time Alexander's followers reached their destination: Captain David Kirke captured Quebec, Baltimore decided to leave Ferryland for some warmer climate, and a group of Puritans obtained a charter incorporating the Massachusetts Bay Company.

That the Port Royal settlement ultimately failed may be ascribed to the fact that Sir William Alexander's venture became a pawn in international power politics. Cardinal Richelieu had encouraged the formation of the United Companies and the Company of New France to open up trade in Canada and extend France's influence but they could not work toward these objectives as long as France and England remained at war. He was willing to restore peace, but the price he demanded was the return of Acadia and Quebec. Richelieu knew that the English treasury sorely needed the 400,000 crowns still due on the queen's dowry, and so he was able to get what he wanted in return for what England needed. By the Treaty

[20] Acadia was originally an ill-defined coastal strip extending from 40 to 48 degrees north, but it was gradually delimited to the present Nova Scotia and the adjoining shorelands.

of Susa in 1629 Charles and Louis made peace, and by the Treaty of St. Germain-en-Laye in 1632 they agreed to the restoration to France of all English plantations in Canada. Despite the crown's interest in Sir William Alexander, Port Royal had to be abandoned, and the vision of a new Scotland in America, for the time, disappeared. The unfortunate Alexander was created Earl of Stirling in 1631 as compensation for his losses.[21] King Charles suffered a drop in popularity in England, because his capitulation to Richelieu was the first retrogression in colonial policy since the accession of Elizabeth. The Treaty of St. Germain fastened a hold of France on the soil of America that was not loosened for one hundred and thirty years.[22]

Sir Ferdinando Gorges was by far the most important Englishman interested in northern colonization.[23] He had invested large sums of money in voyages of exploration and colonization from 1608 to 1620, but these early efforts failed. In 1619, for example, he sent Captain Thomas Dermer to fish in New England waters—the last enterprise of the old Virginia Company of Plymouth—but nothing came of it. Meanwhile Virginia and Bermuda throbbed with activity, while Guy and Mason seemed to be making giant strides in the north. Gorges' rival, the Virginia Company of London, was outdistancing him, and there was even the possibility that he would lose his charter by default. His New England Company had been inactive since 1606, except for the initiative of individual members who underwrote fishing expeditions. The time had come to put new life into the Virginia Company of Plymouth, lest it wither. There was a precedent for change, because the Virginia Company of London had been reorganized twice, in 1609 and again in 1612.

Acting on his own rather than in concert with the London

21 For more information about Alexander's Port Royal venture, see George P. Insh, *Scottish Colonial Schemes, 1620–1686* (Glasgow, 1922), pp. 40–90. Slafter, *Sir William Alexander*, pp. 1–117, tells the same story with emphasis on the Earl of Stirling.

22 Andrews, *Colonial Period*, I, 313–319.

23 The standard work on Gorges is James P. Baxter, *Sir Ferdinando Gorges and His Province of Maine* (3 vols., Boston, 1890). The more recent Richard A. Preston, *Gorges of Plymouth Fort: A Life of Sir Ferdinando Gorges* (Toronto, 1953), argues that Gorges was less reactionary and impractical than Baxter makes him seem. See also Andrews, *Colonial Period*, I, 320–343.

merchants, Gorges decided to obtain a new charter embodying his ideas of what a model company should be. He wanted no generality, quarter courts of shareholders, or "democraticall" procedure. Nor did he want stockholders or a system of votes by the majority of voices. He would eschew a commercial organization or mere elaboration of a commercial company. As a member of the landed class, Gorges was preoccupied less with the hope of gain from fisheries and trading than with the advantages accruing from the ownership of land. Like Baltimore and other proprietors, he wished to reproduce in America the manorial and tenurial system of his native England. He would refashion the Virginia Company of Plymouth along proprietary lines, dispensing with a merchant interest and drawing from the nobility and landed class. In March, 1620, he petitioned the king and received an enlargement of the Plymouth Company patent. There seemed to be no objection, since the matter went from the king to the Privy Council, which instructed the solicitor general to prepare the draft of a charter undoubtedly inspired by Gorges himself. The grant of the new document did not take place until November, the delay being caused by the clause extending exclusive fishing privileges in northern waters. This arrangement aroused instant opposition, and the Virginia Company of London and the West Country fishing interests fought it for years. A debate on the subject in Parliament delayed actual delivery of the charter until 1621.

The revised patent created the Council for New England, and it incorporated a group of forty men, none of them merchants. They were a notable collection of officials and courtiers, many of whom were never active in company affairs. When funds were needed at a later date, merchants such as William Erves, Christopher Levett, and Abraham Jennings, all of Plymouth, were admitted. The council elected its own president and other officials, and it also had the power to fill all vacancies in its membership, provided the number did not exceed forty. The council became the sole owner of a huge domain extending from the fortieth to the forty-eighth parallel of north latitude from sea to sea, an area extending roughly from Philadelphia to the St. Lawrence. As in other instances during these early times, this patent disregarded the London and Bristol Company's right to the region north of 45 degrees north, just as that organization's charter had disregarded the title of the old Plymouth

2. James I (1566-1625), engraving by George Glover

(Huntington Library and Art Gallery)

3. Charles I (1600-1649), painted by Daniel Mytens

(National Portrait Gallery, London)

4. Sir Thomas Smythe (1588?-1625), engraving by Simon Van de Passe

(Huntington Library and Art Gallery)

5. Sir Walter Raleigh (1552?-1618), painted by Nicholas Hilliard

(National Portrait Gallery, London)

6. Sir Edwin Sandys (1561-1629)

(Huntington Library and Art Gallery)

7. Captain John Smith (15
1631), engraving by Simon V
de Passe

(Huntington Library and
Gallery)

8. Pocahontas (Matoaka) (1595-
1617), engraving by Simon Van
de Passe

(Huntington Library and Art Gallery)

9. Oliver Cromwell (1599-1658), painted by Robert Walker

(National Portrait Gallery, London)

o. Sir William Berkeley (1606-677), painted by Sir Peter Lely

By kind permission of the Trustees f the late Randal Thomas Iowbray, eighth Earl of Berkeley)

11. Virginia Indian Chief, from a drawing by
John White, 1585

(Smithsonian Institution, Bureau of
American Ethnology)

12. Indian Fishing
Drawing by John White, 1585

(Library of Congress)

13. Indian Dance, drawing by John White, 1585
(Smithsonian Institution, Bureau of American Ethnology)

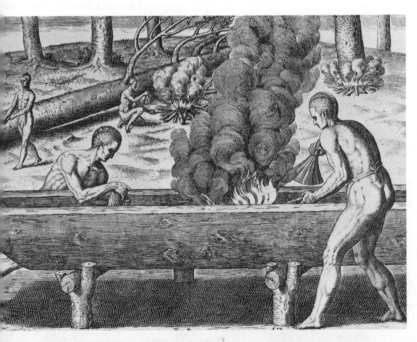

14. Indian Dugout Canoe, from Hariot's *Virginia*

15.   Replica of the *Discovery*
(Virginia Chamber of Commerce)

16.   Replica of the *Susan Co*
(Virginia Chamber of Comme

17. George Calvert, Lord Baltimore (1580?-1632), painted by Daniel Mytens

(Maryland Historical Society)

18. Cecil Calvert, Lord Baltimore (1606-1675), engraved by Abraham Blooteling

(Huntington Library and Art Gallery)

1. *Inpri: His Lo[pp] requires his said Governor and Commissioners th,[t] in their voyage to Mary Land they be very carefull to preserve unity and peace amongst all the passengers on Shipp-Board, and that they suffer no scandall nor offence to be given to any of the Protestants, whereby any just complaint may heerafter be made, by them, in Virginia or in England, and that for that end, they cause all Acts of Romane Catholique Religion to be done as privately as may be, and that they instruct all the Roman Catholiques to be silent upon all occasions of discourse, concerning matters of Religion; and that the said Governor and Commissioners treat the Protestants w'th as much mildness and favor as Justice will permitt. And this to be observed at Land as well as at Sea.*

19.   Lord Baltimore's famous injunction from his Instructions of 1633

(Maryland Historical Society)

20. William Claiborne
(1587?-1677?)

(Maryland Historical Society)

A
RELATION
OF
Maryland;

Together,

VVith ⎰ A Map of the Countrey,
The Conditions of Plantation,
His Majesties Charter to the
Lord *Baltemore*, translated
into English.

These Bookes are to bee had, at Master *William Pexsley* Esq; his house, on the back-side of *Drury-Lane*, neere the *Cock-pit* Playhouse; or in his absence, at Master *Iohn Morgans* house in high *Holbourne*, over against the *Dolphin*, *London*.

September the 8. *Anno Dom.* 1635.

21. *A Relation of Maryland*, 1635

(Huntington Library)

22. John Winthrop (1588-1649)
(Massachusetts Art Commission)

23. Sir Richard Saltonstall
(1610?-1694)

(Massachusetts Historical
Society)

24. Sir Harry Vane (1613-1662)
(Massachusetts Art Commission)

25. Reverend John Wheelwright
(1592-1679)

(Massachusetts Art Commission)

THE

BLOVDY TENENT,
of PERSECUTION, for caufe of
CONSCIENCE, difcuffed, in
A Conference betweene
TRVTH and PEACE.

WHO,

In all tender Affection, prefent to the High
Court of Parliament, (as the Refult of
their Difcourfe) thefe, (amongft other
Paffages) of higheft confideration.

Printed in the Year 1644.

26. Roger Williams, *The Bloody Tenent*, London, 1608

THE
BOOK OF THE GENERAL
LAUUES AND LIBERTYES
CONCERNING THE INHABITANTS OF THE MASSACHUSETS
COLLECTED OUT OF THE RECORDS OF THE GENERAL COURT
FOR THE SEVERAL YEARS WHEREIN THEY WERE MADE
AND ESTABLISHED,

And now revised by the same Court and difpofed into an Alphabetical order
and publifh't by the same Authoritie in the General Court
held at Bofton the fourteenth of the
first month Anno
1647.

Whosoever therfore refiftheth the power, refiftheth the ordinance of God:
and they that refift receiv to themfelves damnation. Romans 13. 2.

CAMBRIDGE.
Printed according to order of the GENERAL COURT.
1648.

And are to be folde at the fhop of Hezekiah Vfher
in Bofton.

27. *The Laws and Liberties of Massachusetts*, 1648

28. John Winthrop Jr.
(1606-1676)

(Massachusetts Historical Society)

29. Reverend John Davenport
(1597-1670)

(Yale University Art Gallery)

30. Peter Stuyvesant (1592-1672), engraving by Thomas Gimbrede

(Huntington Library and Art Gallery)

31. William Pynchon (1590-1662)

(Essex Institute Collection)

Company. The crown lawyers and chancery officials obviously paid little attention to prior grants.

The powers and privileges of the New England Council were considerable. It held its huge domain by free and common socage as of the manor of East Greenwich, and it could divide it as it chose. It could make subgrants, create plantations, and endow them with local governments. It intended to set up a central government with a governor having martial powers like those enjoyed by lords lieutenant of English counties, but it was slow to carry out this part of the program. The council possessed full civil and criminal power in the region it controlled, and its particular plantations were exempt from subsidies and customs for seven years and from duties exported to England for twenty-one years, except for the traditional 5 per cent customs. In many respects the provisions followed precedents set in the Virginia Company charter of 1609, but the new corporation was unique in several ways. It had no governor, for instance, no quarter courts, generality, or stock subscription, and it was a closed self-perpetuating body, a hybrid in that it was partly incorporated and partly feudal. Moreover, it was what Gorges himself wanted: a state more feudal than the palatine of Durham and containing lesser feudal states. Since the Statute of Quia Emptores was not waived as in other feudal grants, subfeudinated land was not held of the council, but of the king.[24] Only this limitation prevented Gorges from wielding absolute power.[25]

The council's charter contained the injunction that no one might frequent or trade within the territory granted, and this restriction provoked an extended controversy. The clause by implication gave a fishing monopoly in coastal waters from the fortieth to the forty-eighth parallel because fishing was impossible without access to the land. Inasmuch as the Virginia Company had formerly enjoyed this monopoly, that organization made its resentment felt in Parliament. It petitioned the king to abrogate the privilege, arguing that under the charter of 1606 each of the two companies was free of the other and thus free to fish in the other's waters, since the sea was as free as the air. The king promised that if anything prejudicial to the

---

24 Strangely, the Statute of Quia Emptores was waived in a number of colonial grants. It was this statute of Edward I that greatly strengthened the crown and permitted those not so restrained to sell their lands at their pleasure.

25 For an analysis of the charter, see Andrews, *Colonial Period*, I, 322–325.

Virginia Company were found in Gorges' charter, and had been obtained without his knowledge, it would be removed. The Privy Council conducted a number of hearings on the subject and finally decided that the Council for New England was entitled to whatever the king had granted. Gorges' enemies continued the dispute in the House of Commons, where they charged him with securing a monopoly contrary to the laws and privileges of the people. They annually introduced a bill in behalf of free fishing and kept the battle going in that arena until 1628, when Parliament ceased to meet. A larger conflict between the fishery and proprietary interests in Newfoundland followed, and it did not end until Charles I gave the Western Adventurers their charter in 1634. Gorges, however, never did profit from his monopoly. In the charter of 1639 confirming his title to the "Province of Maine," a clause was inserted withholding the exclusive fishing privilege and granting all the king's subjects the right to salt fish and dry their nets on the shore.

The fishing industry was never of primary interest to the Council for New England, because it visualized itself essentially as a gigantic land company distributing great tracts among vassals and tenants who would engage ships and plant settlers. The council's function would be to organize, govern, and apportion territory, and indeed its main activity for fifteen years did prove to be the making of land grants. In his *Briefe Relation,* Gorges disclosed that he or some other appointee would administer the territory after the manner of local governments in England, but with feudal overtones.[26] He would be assisted by a council, the usual officials, and an assembly made up of delegates from the local units and summoned by the governor and council for the purpose of making laws. The local divisions would consist of counties, baronies, and hundreds, and the heads of counties and baronies would be allowed to subdivide their territories into fiefs and manors with courts leet and baron for local jurisdiction. It was expected that there would be cities, each of which would provide a delegate to the assembly.

Gorges soon learned that he would need capital, despite the support of "gentlemen of honour and blood." He turned to his neighbors, the merchants of Bristol, Exeter, Plymouth, Dartmouth, and

26 *A Briefe Relation of the Discovery and Plantation of New England* (London, 1627). Reprinted in Baxter, *Sir Ferdinando Gorges,* I, 203–240.

Barnstable, and urged them to join in developing trade and fishing and in the advancement of settlement. This group was shrewd enough to see that Gorges' schemes were impractical, and they were cool about turning over capital to him. They disliked most of all the idea of forming a joint-stock company whose articles required that authority be vested only in the council itself. Even the price of a license, £13 6s. 8d., seemed very high. In January, 1623, Gorges sent letters, with the king's consent, to the lords lieutenant of Somerset, Devon, and Cornwall and to the corporations of Bristol and Exeter urging them to participate in the settlement of New England. Only the town of Dorchester, inspired by the Reverend John White (of whom more later), was moved to undertake a settlement of its own. Gorges' efforts and plans always seemed chimerical to other people, but he could never comprehend why feudal and manorial practices were unsuitable in the New World.[27]

Gorges' princely domain was uninhabited except for the small band of Pilgrims at Plymouth and the tiny groups of fishermen scattered from Cape Ann to the Penobscot in Maine. The island of Monhegan, twenty miles off Penobscot Bay, was the hub of a long-established, thriving fishing industry which the Pilgrims soon learned they could not duplicate. To the southwest were a few Dutchmen at Manhattan, and beyond the Penobscot was French Acadia, soon to be the scene of William Alexander's expedition. In none of these places did the epidemic-ridden Indians offer any trouble.

The next attempts at colonization were directed toward Massachusetts. The first group to arrive there after the Pilgrims were men sent by the same Thomas Weston who had helped the Pilgrims obtain their patent. Without any authorization, Weston transported about fifty "rude and lusty fellows" to Plymouth in June, 1622. After receiving reluctant aid from the Pilgrims, they moved to Wessagussett, now Weymouth, on southern Massachusetts Bay. Although purportedly concerned with fishing and trading, the Weston men frittered away their time building a fort, and by the winter's end the colony had completely dispersed. The next try was made by a Captain Wollaston, who settled, accompanied by

27 James F. Baldwin, in a book review, *New England Quarterly*, V (June, 1932), 352–357.

three or four men of quality and many servants, at Passonagessit, today a part of Quincy to the west of Weymouth. Mount Wollaston, too, was a failure, and Captain Wollaston soon removed most of his followers to Virginia.[28]

The better-remembered Thomas Morton arrived as early as Wollaston or shortly thereafter, bringing thirty servants and provisions. He was a gentleman and a lawyer trained at Clifford's Inn and hardly the pagan he was supposed to have been.[29] It appears that he secured patents to locate in Massachusetts Bay, and his will revealed that he held land on the Kennebec. This cynical and enigmatic man is alleged to have persuaded his servants to settle down at Quincy after Wollaston departed by plying them with strong drink and promising to free them from their indentures and to make them partners in the undertaking. They turned the plantation into a place of revels, greatly shocking the Pilgrims only twenty-five miles away. Governor Bradford asserted that Morton maintained a school of atheism or worse and that he made a practice of drinking up the profits of the Indian trade. Their dancing about a Maypole, which the Pilgrims considered an idol, added to the scandalous impression Morton's company was making. Morton's jolly crew made matters even worse by changing the name of Mount Wollaston to Merry Mount. Sober Plymouth and this carefree community made impossible neighbors, and eventually there was bound to be some sort of open discord between them.

Meanwhile Gorges and his council issued five patents of record in 1622 and 1623 and possibly others that are unknown. The Marianna grant for Cape Ann and the adjoining territory went in March, 1622, to Captain John Mason. The same Mason and Gorges himself received the province of Maine in August. In 1629 the two men divided that territory, which included the seacoast between the Merrimac and the Kennebec.[30] A third grant made in October, 1622, awarded a 6,000-acre tract and an island at the mouth of the Piscataqua to a group led by David Thomson, who tried to settle

28 Andrews, *Colonial Period*, I, 329–332.

29 *Ibid.*, p. 332 and 332, n. 2.

30 The 1662 grant to Mason and Gorges, which made the first written use of the name Maine, is reprinted in Baxter, *Sir Ferdinando Gorges*, II, 123–148. For the early history of the area, see Burrage, *Beginnings of Colonial Maine*, pp. 1–299. Mason and his part of the 1629 division, which became New Hampshire, are the subjects of Charles W. Tuttle, *Captain John Mason, Founder of New Hampshire* (Boston, 1887).

the area in 1623 with the help of three Plymouth merchants. The fourth grant went to Robert Gorges, Ferdinando's son, in December, 1622. The fifth grant of 6,000 acres was given in May, 1623, to Christopher Levett, a councillor and later governor general of New England. He proposed to erect a settlement named York with the aid of a company of Yorkshiremen, but he missed being the founder of York, because he built his own house at Casco Bay.[31] These grants, the main business of the council, reveal the feudal outlook of Gorges. Only the Statute of Quia Emptores, which Gorges could not avoid having in his patent, prevented him from holding these fiefs himself instead of directly from the king "in free and common socage and not in capite or knights service." Had the council succeeded in obtaining the abrogation of Quia Emptores as applied to its charter, the transformation of a feudal proprietary would have been complete.

The Council for New England was authorized to plant colonies of its own as well as to sublet fiefs to others, and the ambitious Gorges never lost sight of the former objective. Whereas distributing land in the form of fiefs and particular plantations would have yielded some revenue, colonizing cost money, and the council, which was not a joint-stock concern, had no funds except those contributed by its members. In the hope of solving this problem, Gorges admitted additional "gentlemen of honour and blood" and also six West Country merchants with money to invest. With a larger council to call upon, he then issued to his son Robert, recently returned from the Venetian wars, a proprietary named Massachustack, located on the upper side of Massachusetts Bay and extending ten miles inland from the shore. Sir Ferdinando regarded this patent, which was issued December, 1622, as his principal domain. He arranged for the appointment of Robert as governor general of all New England and gave him as councillors Captain Francis West, later governor of Virginia; Christopher Levett, who was planning a settlement of his own farther north; William Bradford, governor of Plymouth Colony; and others to be appointed later. Robert Gorges spent the winter of 1622–23 preparing for what he expected to be the orderly colonization of New England.[32]

[31] See James P. Baxter, *Christopher Levett, of York, the Pioneer Colonist in Casco Bay* (Portland, Me., 1893).
[32] Herbert L. Osgood, *The American Colonies in the Seventeenth Century* (3 vols., New York, 1904–7), I, 119–121.

In order to persuade council members that they would obtain some tangible benefit from participating, Sir Ferdinando set about distributing territory among them. He first allocated an area, which was to have been called New Albion, to the Duke of Lenox, Sir George Calvert, and the Earl of Arundel. This transaction, which was never actually consummated, was to have involved a tract fifty miles long, extending from Pemaquid to the mouth of the Saco, and thirty miles into the interior. A second division was made in June, 1623, in the presence of the king himself. This public ceremony, which made use of Captain John Smith's map, was staged to disarm members of Parliament who objected to monopolies and to advertise the fact that the participants did receive tangible rewards. English landowners were suffering losses of income at home, and they were anxious to secure compensation in the form of large estates in the New World. This division, like the New Albion scheme, turned out to be illusory, because no patents ever appeared confirming the grants made at this time.

Having satisfied the querulous council members, Sir Ferdinando dispatched a large expedition led by his son Robert, with the object of creating a great principality in America. Although the elder Gorges had not succeeded in obtaining help from any of the Gloucester, Devon, or Somerset towns, this was the most elaborate expedition to set forth to New England thus far. The prospective settlers included women and children, and care was taken to transport mechanics, farmers, and traders. There were six "gentlemen" and two clergymen, William Morrell and William Blaxton. The members of the council had backed Sir Ferdinando to the limit.

It never occurred to anyone that this plantation could fail, but mistakes were made from the beginning. Instead of proceeding directly to Robert Gorges' own grant at Massachustack, the whole company in September, 1623, settled in Wessagussett, which had been abandoned six months previously. Young Gorges attempted with little success to assert his authority over the fishermen around Plymouth and in the Piscataqua region of lower Maine. He had to cope with a New England winter at Wessagussett, and disasters resulted from a fire and from insufficient provisions and inadequate housing. Robert Gorges was a soldier, and he had looked forward to staging raids on Spanish shipping. When, instead, he found himself involved in an unexciting struggle for survival on the frontier, he became bored. The Reverend William Morrell experienced disappointment of another sort, because he began to realize that there was no immediate likelihood of organizing a great church in New England. The soldier went home to England in the spring of 1624, and the clergyman followed him a year later. Gorges' departure was the signal for a general dispersal. Some of the settlers went to Virginia, and others established homes where they could.[33]

The collapse of Gorges' strenuous effort left New England much as it had been before. Aside from Plymouth Colony and the fishermen, there were only about fifty settlers in 1625, scattered from Natascot (now Hull) and Wessagussett to the mouth of the Piscataqua. We know relatively little about them except that they lived by farming, fishing, and trading. They were a restless brood, except the Pilgrim group, who forsook England primarily because they were dissatisfied. Those who did not like the wilderness returned. Those who remained were rugged individualists who left little trace in history.[34] Yet the Massachusetts Bay Colony owed much to them, for they were the pathfinders. They plied the coasts as fishermen, ventured inland to trade with the Indians, and as true adventurers searched the ocean all the way from Cape Cod to the mouth of the St. Lawrence.

A word remains to be said about Canada during this period. London and Bristol merchants made an unsuccessful effort in 1610 to start a settlement in Newfoundland, as has been mentioned. The next burst of activity came in 1628, when promoters organized the Company of Adventurers to trade on the St. Lawrence River. War had been declared between England and France, and these men hoped to absorb the beaver-skin trade and gain control over all merchandise coming in and out of Canada. In 1629 Lewis, Thomas, and David Kirke, the sons of Jervas Kirke, and other Englishmen and Scots captured Quebec, thus achieving the first conquest of Canada.[35] The two French trading ventures recently

---

[33] Henry S. Burage, *Gorges and the Grant of the Province of Maine, 1622* (Portland, Me., 1923), pp. 26–28. See also the same author's *Beginnings of Colonial Maine* (Portland, 1914), pp. 156–157.

[34] Except the energetic, anti-Puritan Samuel Maverick.

[35] The Kirkes, who originally spelled their name Kertk, were French Huguenots who settled in London about 1618. Berkley, "Lord Baltimore's Contest," p. 107.

formed under the stimulus of Richelieu, the United Companies and the Company of Adventurers, became necessarily inactive. The English firm pursued its interests with such vigor that it antagonized not only the French merchants whose goods it seized but also the Exeter fishermen with whose profitable operations it interfered. One of the associates in this English venture, incidentally, was William Berkeley, who withdrew in 1641 in order to accept the governorship of Virginia.[36]

Charles I found it expedient to make peace with France in order to collect the dower money promised when he married Henrietta Maria, the French king's daughter, and the end of the war brought the activities of the Kirkes to a sudden close. The English king acquiesced in French claims to the ownership of Canada based on Champlain's voyages between 1606 and 1608, reserving only certain rights of trade, and these agreements were formally incorporated in the Treaty of St. Germain-en-Laye in 1632. As part of the reserved rights, King Louis gave the Company of Adventurers a patent for sole trade on the St. Lawrence, the Gulf of Canada, and adjacent places for thirty-one years. Charles then double-crossed the French in 1636 by authorizing the promoters of the English company to take possession of the entire region. The confused state of affairs existing in England by then, however, made any such bold course of action next to impossible. David Kirke, knighted for his past efforts, became governor of Newfoundland, an area exempt from the treaty, but in that capacity he turned out to be autocratic and rapacious. He seized Avalon from Lord Baltimore, who brought suit against him, and the dispute ended with Kirke's imprisonment in England after his retirement. Kirke, the first conqueror of Canada, died in 1654, and in the years that followed the French, not the English, dominated Canada.

[36] *Ibid.*, pp. 108–111, describes the Kirkes' naval and military exploits against the French.

CHAPTER 7

The Genesis of Massachusetts

SHORTLY before the Pilgrims secured their illegal patent for fishing grounds around Cape Ann, a group of Dorchester merchants obtained a patent from the Council for New England giving them similar rights in the same area. One hundred nineteen residents of Dorchester, Shrewsbury, and Exeter, including fifty-five gentlemen and twenty members of the clergy, thereupon organized a company to stimulate and exploit popular interest in a fishing venture. The Reverend John White of Dorchester, the driving force in the enterprise, urged an attempt at establishing a permanent village, arguing that it would reduce overhead expenses and that it would also give the settlers time to hunt and trade with the Indians during the off-season.[1] A settlement of this type could, moreover, become a center of religious activity, to the great benefit of the isolated, unruly folk living in inlets all the way from Maine to Cape Cod.

The Dorchester Company, the most important such organization to be founded since the London and Bristol Company in 1610, tried persistently through four long years to establish a foothold at Cape Ann. The *Fellowship*, fifty tons, disembarked a preliminary group of fourteen men in 1623 and went back a year later, accom-

---

[1] Frances Rosé-Troup, *John White, the Patriarch of Dorchester (Dorset) and the Founder of Massachusetts, 1578–1648* (New York, 1930), is a full-length treatment of this influential man. For a briefer account see Samuel Eliot Morison, *Builders of the Bay Colony* (Boston, 1964), pp. 21–50.

panied by a hundred-ton vessel, carrying additional settlers. Delay prevented a fishing catch, and so the voyage lost money, but thirty-two men remained there, and White and his friends continued to be optimistic. They borrowed another £1,000 and sent out three more ships in 1625, but with no better results than before. The company then put Cape Ann under the charge of Roger Conant, brother of one of its members, who had migrated to the Plymouth Colony and then separated from that community. Soon after Conant assumed his new duties, he had to ward off Miles Standish, sent to take possession of a fishing wharf to which Plymouth laid claim. Conant persuaded the Pilgrims to shift their endeavor to the Kennebec, leaving fifty Dorchester men in full control. Other difficulties proved harder to resolve, particularly the facts that Cape Ann was impractically remote from fishing waters and that her fishermen refused to convert themselves into farmers. Conant finally led a remnant of thirty men, women, and children to Naumkeag (later Salem), twenty miles south of Cape Ann, where they settled and became known in time as the Old Planters.[2]

The Reverend John White was convinced that the time had passed when internal reform could save the Church of England, and he tenaciously refused to abandon his idea of spreading the gospel by establishing a settlement. When Roger Conant wrote in 1625 that Naumkeag was an ideal place for a Christian settlement, White directed him to hold his settlers together while he tried to get a patent and prepare an expedition. Conant and his group struggled through the harsh winter of 1626–27 in a few huts, while White and the West Country Puritans were successfully recruiting adherents both in London and among the East Anglia Puritans. A series of meetings in London paved the way toward organization of another New England company to take over the abandoned Dorchester enterprise. In spite of this encouraging progress, Conant was destined for another dreary winter at Naumkeag before a patent was obtained.

Because the Council for New England would be receptive only if men of family and affluence sponsored a particular patent, White set out to enlist the help of men of that stature. He found collabor-

2 Herbert L. Osgood, *The American Colonies in the Seventeenth Century* (3 vols., New York, 1904–7), I, 128–131, gives a good description of the Cape Ann venture.

ators among Devon friends and also obtained the assistance of three working members: John Humfry, former treasurer of the Dorchester Company; Simon Whetcome, wealthy London clothmaker, originally from Dorset and later an assistant of the Massachusetts Bay Company; and John Endecott, recommended by the London merchants. Since Gorges was in Plymouth during 1627 and 1628, the applicants for the patent presumably did business with Warwick, president of the council, in London. This grant apparently was merely a reassignment by Warwick, with the consent of his associates, of a grant made to him in 1622. On March 28, 1628, the Council for New England issued a patent to the New England Company, including in it all lands "from ocean to ocean" from three miles north of the Merrimack to three miles south of the Charles. Those who drew up the new document understood so little about New England geography that they infringed the 1622 grant to Robert Gorges and included half of Plymouth Colony and all land previously assigned to Mason and Gorges in New Hampshire and Maine.

The New England Company was a voluntary, unincorporated joint-stock organization with funds of approximately £3,000, the amount deemed necessary at that time to finance a plantation. Only six of the ninety members had previously been involved in the Dorchester Company, but the management of the new enterprise prudently and promptly made peace with what remained of the predecessor firm. When the adventurers met in London to plan an expedition, the distinguished men who attended included the Reverend John White; Mathew Cradock, wealthy merchant and promoter; Sir Richard Saltonstall, nephew of the lord mayor and a manor lord; Hugh Peter, a Puritan minister; John Humfry; Richard Bellingham; and John Endecott.[3] While not all Puritans, these men shared a desire to give their settlement a strong religious tone and to make it a haven for English Puritans.

On June 20, 1628, John Endecott sailed from Weymouth, England, accompanied by forty followers in the *Abigail*, a vessel of 120 tons. Inasmuch as the company was unincorporated, it could not appoint Endecott governor, but it named him chief in command

[3] Among biographical accounts of these leaders may be mentioned Raymond P. Stearns, *The Strenuous Puritan: Hugh Peter, 1598–1660* (Urbana, Ill., 1954), and Lawrence S. Mayo, *John Endecott: A Biography* (Cambridge, Mass., 1956).

to succeed Roger Conant, who had served well and had been successful in everything except business ventures. Endecott was stern, unyielding, and wholly prejudiced against the Church of England. Ignoring the Old Planters, he devoted himself to preparations for receiving the settlers the company would send over. He paid attention to the present inhabitants only to the extent of accepting literally the company's injunction to rescue them from the woeful state they were in and to induce them to lead lives beyond reproach. The Pilgrims had succeeded in packing Thomas Morton off to England, ostensibly to curtail the revelries at Merry Mount but actually to rid themselves of a shrewd rival in the Indian trade. When Endecott learned of Merry Mount, he completed its downfall by driving out Morton's followers and renaming it Mount Dagon, "the place of idolatry."[4]

Patent difficulties had gradually caused trouble for the New England Company. The Council for New England granted land northeast of Massachusetts Bay to Robert Gorges in 1623, and by this time some of his tenants and servants had settled there. Robert transferred his rights to his brother John, who in turn conveyed portions of the property to others. When their father, Sir Ferdinando, made his grant to the New England Company, he included reservations in favor of Robert's grant which were not recorded. In the hope of finding a way out of this dilemma, the company determined to bypass the elder Gorges and the Council for New England and to deal directly with the king, inducing him, if possible, to give them a charter of incorporation for both land and government. If the company succeeded in this move, it would be completely free of the council and on a par with other incorporated companies created for trade and plantations. Their plan worked, and on March 4, 1629, the king approved a charter transforming the New England Company into the Massachusetts Bay Company.[5]

Enemies of the Massachusetts Bay Colony later contended that the charter was obtained surreptitiously and without the knowledge

<hr>

[4] Charles Francis Adams, *Three Episodes of Massachusetts History* (2 vols., rev. ed., New York, 1965), I, 162–182, 194–208, tells the full story of Morton's troubles with the Massachusetts Bay Colony.

[5] See Frances Rosé-Troup, *The Massachusetts Bay Company and Its Predecessors* (New York, 1930).

of the New England council. In truth, considering how disturbed the times were, the council could hardly have acted as a whole body. The war with France did not end until November, 1629, which meant that Sir Ferdinando Gorges as governor of the fort at Plymouth, Captain John Mason as treasurer of the navy, and others were too much engaged to take part. Furthermore, many of the council members had lost interest. At the same time, the powerful Earl of Warwick, an opponent of Gorges, and Viscount Dorchester, a principal secretary of state, both brought great influence to bear on behalf of the Puritans. John White,[6] who had gained experience aiding the Pilgrims, and Richard Bellingham of Boston, England, and later a governor of Massachusetts, were active in making the legal arrangements, and they received help from Lord Saye and Sele and from Nathaniel Rich. The financial backing, substantial because the process was costly, came from London merchants such as Mathew Cradock and from members of the country gentry. Cradock, an enthusiastic participant who stated that the charter was obtained "with great cost, by the favor of personages of note, and much labor," later received shabby treatment from John Winthrop and the magistrates of Massachusetts Bay, because they did not sympathize with anyone who retained an affection for the mother church.

One effect of the granting of the Massachusetts charter was to take away a large part of the territory given to the Council for New England, an injustice but certainly one not without precedent. The petitioners probably argued that the council was moribund and that when Robert Gorges' unsuccessful efforts came to an end, the charter had in effect lapsed. They stressed the likelihood that New England would revert to a fisheries coast unless some positive course of action were undertaken. What nobody could anticipate at the time was that the Council for New England would soon revive to some extent and that it might conceivably have solved its own problems without outside interference.

The Massachusetts charter, which was essentially similar to that of a trading company, created a twenty-six-man corporation and gave it extensive land with definite boundaries.[7] The Governor and

[6] A well-known counselor-at-law, not the Dorchester minister.
[7] Summarized in William MacDonald, *Documentary Source Book of American History* (New York, 1943), pp. 22–26.

Company of the Massachusetts Bay in Newe-England, as the document described the new organization, differed from the council in that it had the right to rule and administer the territory it owned. Men like the Reverend John White and John Humfry, part of the small band that had tried so desperately to promote a settlement at Cape Ann in 1624, were now members of a rich and powerful corporation. Its governing body consisted of a governor, deputy governor, and eighteen assistants (councillors) who were to be elected by the membership of the company. The entire membership was to meet as a court four times a year to elect officers, admit new members, and adopt ordinances for the welfare of the company. The Massachusetts Bay Company charter was peppered with conventional Puritan expressions of piety, but it was obviously modeled on the Virginia charter of 1612, and there is reason to believe that it was drawn up by John White, the eminent counselor-at-law. The instrument devoted great attention to all matters relating to administration of the colony and to the liberties and immunities of Englishmen. The document evidenced a will to establish a religious community and a determination to ward off Gorges and anyone else who wished to establish a proprietary form of government.

There were about 110 investors in the Bay Company. Inasmuch as religious motivation was so strong, the influence of the mercantile members was not as great as in the predecessor New England Company. There were many shades of Puritanism, but not many representatives of the extreme left or right. A few men, like John and Samuel Browne, remained staunch adherents of the Church of England and deplored the early Separatist tendencies that arose in the colony. Most of the investors were conforming members of the Church of England whose desire was still to reform the church from within, but they were at one with the nonconformists from East Anglia in their desire to advance the cause of Christ. The strongest advocates of Christian zeal were Saltonstall, Emmanuel Downing, Thomas Dudley, Endecott, Bellingham, Simon Bradstreet, William Pynchon, and Ward.

Because of its mixed motivation, the Bay Company was from the first both a corporation dedicated to the pursuit of trade and a refuge for men of a particular religious outlook, and this duality of purpose introduced a question about how the organization should be controlled. Trading companies, even those operating colonies in such faraway places as Virginia and Bermuda, had all of their essential power centralized in England. The crown intended that this should also be true in the case of the new company, and it would not have made a grant to petitioners requesting any other arrangement. Puritans considering migration to Massachusetts were uneasy about English control, however, because the new charter did not limit membership in the company to men sympathetic with their religious views. If forces antagonistic to Puritanism gained a voice in the firm, residents of the proposed colony might find themselves in serious trouble. The belief formed slowly that membership should be restricted and that, furthermore, the charter itself should be transferred physically to America. Actual power would follow the charter, and the end result of such a revolutionary move would be to shake off the control of the organization in London and even to ignore the authority of the crown. Men drawn to this plan acknowledged the existence of the king, but they were prepared to deny his jurisdiction over them. They thus went far beyond the Pilgrims, who rejected the Established Church but who never questioned the authority of the Council for New England or the higher authority of the monarch.

The formal organization of the Massachusetts Bay Company took place on March 23, 1629, with an officialdom consisting of Mathew Cradock as governor, Thomas Goffe as deputy governor, eleven assistants, a secretary, and a treasurer. These men, who met periodically in London with the general court, addressed themselves from the first to preparations for the founding of a large colony. They rented ships and purchased provisions, arms, and merchandise considered suitable for the Indian trade. Anticipating the need for men with a variety of skills, they appointed a minister, a schoolteacher, and a surgeon, and they employed artisans, craftsmen, and laborers and drew up contracts with indentured servants. Looking ahead to the time of actual settlement, they planned how to divide up and distribute land, and they even arranged for books, including the Book of Common Prayer, to be sent to the colony.[8]

By pursuing its objective vigorously, the company was able to

---

[8] Charles M. Andrews, *The Colonial Period of American History* (4 vols., New Haven, Conn., 1934–38), I, 344–374.

begin colonization early in 1629. The first ship it dispatched was
the *George,* carrying official instructions and a cargo of cattle. The
Talbot and *Lyon's Whelp* followed several weeks later, and the
Four Sisters and *Mayflower* departed from the Thames three weeks
after that. This was the best-equipped expedition that had ever
sailed for New England, and the passengers suffered little during
the voyage. There was not much illness and no scurvy, and because
departure took place in the mild season, the weather was relatively
good. Endecott, who met the ships at Cape Ann and escorted them
to Salem, had by then become governor of the settlement, having
been formally elected to that honor on April 30, 1629, by a meeting
of the company officials in England. The sudden arrival of several
hundred newcomers overtaxed existing accommodations, and a
number of families had to seek out neighboring sites along the bay.
The influx of people caused a modest building boom in Salem
itself, and both the old and the new settlers turned their attention
to making boards and barrel staves, tilling the soil, and planting
corn. A new rule forbade the raising of tobacco, which the Old
Planters had engaged in, because many of the company's leaders
frowned on its use.

The new arrivals organized a church at Salem with the Reverend
Samuel Skelton, a divine silenced for his nonconformity in Lincolnshire, as minister, assisted by the Reverend Francis Higginson of
Leicestershire, also silenced, who received the title of teacher. The
parishioners pledged themselves to "walk together" in the ways of
God, "according as he is pleased to reveal himself unto us in his
blessed word of truth."[9] While they did not acknowledge themselves
to be Separatists like the Pilgrims at Plymouth, they adopted a
similar church organization and became in fact if not yet in name
nonseparating Congregationalists. It was once believed that John
Endecott forced his ministers to shape the Salem church on the
Pilgrim model after Dr. Samuel Fuller of Plymouth told Endecott
how ecclesiastical matters were arranged in his town. In recent
years, however, Perry Miller has argued convincingly that men
sympathetic to Congregationalism were in control of the Massachusetts Bay colony and had previously agreed to adopt in Salem the

[9] Quoted in Williston Walker, *The Creeds and Platforms of Congregationalism*
(Boston, 1960), p. 116.

two essential features of Congregational polity: restriction of church membership to the proved elect and the autonomy of individual congregations. It is therefore now generally believed that Endecott had instructions to set up a church on this basis in Salem long before he had his famous interview with the visiting physician.[10] Not everyone in Salem entered into membership; many, including most of the Old Planters, preferred the Church of England. There were also "libertines" in the settlement who espoused no church, and these Endecott was instructed to punish.

The Puritans and Pilgrims differed in attitude toward the Church of England. There were similarities in their outlooks: both groups rejected the Book of Common Prayer and the validity of ordination. They also both adhered to Calvinism, particularly the doctrine of predestination, and the form and polity of the primitive Christian church intrigued them equally. Their differences centered in the fact that the Puritans continued to recognize the Church of England in all things spiritual while insisting on looking to the Bible as their inspired guide, whereas the Pilgrims erected a church without a bishop. The Puritans in America actually hoped to build a reformed but not a separate church, and they fervently believed that such an institution would come to the rescue of the mother church when it became "ecclipsed in parte, darkened or persecuted." The Puritans were already moderate Separatists, however, and their proposal to found a model church in New England was bound to result in an independent plan. As was true in Bermuda, Massachusetts Bay's first ministers rejected the formalities of the Church of England. The long distance from home and from bishops accelerated the change. The First Church of Salem became an independent, self-governing body whose members were joined together for the worship of God. This congregation served as a model not for a reformed Church of England but for the "New England Way,"

---

[10] For a statement of Miller's position, see *Orthodoxy in Massachusetts, 1630–1650: A Genetic Study* (Cambridge, Mass., 1933), pp. 127–129. Raymond P. Stearns, *Congregationalism in the Dutch Netherlands* (Chicago, 1940), demonstrates that there were nonseparating Puritans before 1630 who were disposed toward Congregationalism. Not everyone has accepted Miller's argument completely. Larzer Ziff refutes him in "The Salem Puritans in the 'Free Aire of a New World,'" *Huntington Library Quarterly*, XX (Aug., 1957), 373–384, but he modifies his position somewhat in his subsequent *The Career of John Cotton: Puritanism and the American Experience* (Princeton, N.J., 1962).

a compromise between extreme Separatism and a national church.[11]

The company in London was not pleased by the trend toward Separatism in Massachusetts, and John Humfry wrote John Winthrop in December, 1630, that the settlement must not continue to drift in that direction. What bothered the company was the probable unfavorable influence on public opinion and especially the reaction of those who had invested large sums. Governor Endecott aggravated the touchy situation by sending two of his assistants, John and Samuel Browne, back to England when he discovered that they were trying to maintain the service of the Church of England. The company itself was divided between merchants like Cradock, Goffe, and Venn, who adhered to the Reverend John White's moderate Puritanism, and a group of more extreme men. The company warned Endecott to be more careful, lest the authorities investigate, and he undoubtedly would have come under official censure if affairs in England had not been falling into disorder. The king's foreign policy had produced disaster, the Protestants of Europe seemed on the verge of destruction, and Parliament, after two tempestuous years, had been dissolved. The Star Chamber and the Court of High Commission were seeking out and punishing opponents of the established religious policy. As part of this activity, the government had embarked on a program of silencing Puritan ministers or depriving them of their benefices, and Puritan publications ran a great risk of being banned or burned. Many Puritans thought of emigrating, and the situation was particularly acute in Middlesex and East Anglia, where opposition to the crown was stiffening.

Puritanism was strongest, both numerically and in point of leadership, in the region known as East Anglia, the area from the Thames to the Wash, which consisted of the counties of Norfolk, Suffolk, Essex, and southern Lincolnshire. Theophilus, Earl of Lincoln, the chief Puritan peer, lived at Sempringham in Lincolnshire, and Thomas Dudley, whose daughter later married Governor Simon Bradstreet, was a manager of the Lincoln properties. The earl's wife was a daughter of Lord Saye and Sele, another Puritan nobleman, and the latter's sister became the third wife of John Humfry in 1630. John Winthrop lived at Groton in Suffolk, and his sister married Emmanuel Downing, father of the famous Sir George Downing.[12] After attending Cambridge University, Winthrop became an attorney in London, where he was magistrate in the Court of Wards and Liveries, which had to do with the king's tenants. Although he was not a subscriber to the Massachusetts Bay Company stock, Winthrop as a Puritan was aware of what was going on in London. Like others of his persuasion, he was discouraged by the outlook for England, and everywhere he looked he saw corruption, bad treatment of the nonconforming clergy, and growing Arminian influence in high places. Arminianism, which included belief in the free agency and responsibility of man and disbelief in the absolute sovereignty of God in man's affairs, was the archenemy of Calvinism. Winthrop feared the spread of this system of thought, and he consequently became convinced that God's wrath would descend on the nation. Impending calamity, then, was a factor that drove many Puritans to consider emigration. "General Observations for the Plantation of New England," a manuscript treatise written by the Reverend John White and distributed in 1629, publicized this view and stimulated discussion among the leading Puritans.[13] The belief grew that God had selected New England as a chosen land.

Circumstances at this time caused John Winthrop to become increasingly involved in Puritan affairs. Deeply discouraged by the burden of heavy debt and responsibility for a large family, he returned to Groton in 1629, and there his troubles multiplied. Two severe illnesses and an infected hand interfered with the conduct

12 John Winthrop, who was so vital to the early development of Massachusetts, has naturally received considerable attention from historians. Edmund S. Morgan, *The Puritan Dilemma: The Story of John Winthrop* (Boston, 1958), is an excellent full-length portrait. Shorter biographies include Morison, *Builders of the Bay Colony*, pp. 51–104, and Albert Bushnall Hart, "John Winthrop, Commonwealth Builder (1588–1649)," in *Commonwealth History of Massachusetts, Colony, Province and State*, ed. by Albert Bushnell Hart (5 vols., New York, 1927–30), I, 159–190. Darrett B. Rutman, *Winthrop's Boston: Portrait of a Puritan Town, 1630–1649* (Chapel Hill, N.C., 1965), is an analysis of early Boston in terms of Winthrop's expectations. Richard S. Dunn, *Puritans and Yankees: The Winthrop Dynasty of New England, 1630–1717* (Princeton, N.J., 1962), is devoted to Winthrop and his immediate descendants.

13 Attributed by some to John Winthrop. The several drafts and a careful discussion are in Allyn B. Forbes (ed.), *Winthrop Papers* (5 vols., Boston, 1929–47), II, 106–127.

of his business affairs, and, turning to religion for succor, he became
more active in Puritan discussions and attempts to formulate plans
In July, 1629, Winthrop and Emmanuel Downing visited Sempring
ham for a lengthy meeting with Isaac Johnson and the Earl o
Lincoln. They then shared the fruits of their cogitations with such
Bay Company officials as White, Cradock, Saltonstall, and Humfry
Cradock on his own responsibility came up with the bold proposa
to transfer the government of the colony to the people who actually
lived in it, giving them sufficient control so that the company could
not thereafter interfere in the plantation's affair. The men engaged
in these secret debates considered this idea carefully and finally
developed and adopted an even more revolutionary scheme, which
involved moving the company and the very charter itself to New
England.

On August 26, 1629, twelve men, including Saltonstall, Dudley
Humfry, Winthrop, and Pynchon, met at Cambridge and agreed
to transport themselves and their families to New England, pro
vided that they received by legal transfer the whole governance
together with the charter prior to September 30. The Cambridge
agreement went far beyond Cradock's proposal, but the Puritan
leaders feared a possible future hostile majority among the stockholders. Such an antagonistic combination could defeat the whole
purpose of the plantation and allow God's purpose to be thwarted.
The conspirators, for such they had become, could prevent this
calamity simply by taking the company and the charter to America,
thus swallowing up the company in the colony. They insisted, as
a second condition, that the transfer be legal, because they wanted
no embarrassing questions raised in high quarters. Such an act
would be without precedent, involving as it did the complete transformation of an English trading company. The Puritans considered
engaging a skillful lawyer, but they never did, because they were
anxious for absolute secrecy, without which the whole plan might
collapse.

A special meeting of the company considered the Cambridge
agreement on August 28, 1629, choosing one committee to defend
it while another presented the strongest case against. Saltonstall
and Johnson, who had signed the agreement, and John Venn, a
merchant tailor of London, were called upon to act as defenders.
President Cradock was discreetly absent, but Saltonstall, Johnson,

and Humfry were all on hand. Only 27 out of a general court of 125 attended, but seven of them were signers of the Cambridge agreement, and many of the remainder were well-known Puritans, John Davenport among them. The motion to transfer the company and the charter passed easily, giving the sponsors of the Cambridge agreement a great victory, but the question of legality remained unanswered. Cradock and Goffe retired from office on October 20, and Winthrop and Humfry were elected president and deputy president in their places. The membership was now committed to the plan of erecting a Puritan state in New England, to be a separate, self-governing community free from dependence on authority in England and free to exercise for itself all the powers vested in the charter. The seat of the Massachusetts Bay Company was henceforth in New England, and John Winthrop and his associates were to build the new state. Inasmuch as the charter did not provide or authorize any constitution, the leaders, in developing civil government in the colony, were acting *ultra vires*.[14]

During the winter of 1629–30 the Puritan undertakers assembled a great fleet headed by the *Arbella,* and on March 29, 1630, the first seven ships left Southampton. The Reverend John Cotton, the renowned Puritan divine, journeyed down from Boston to preach the farewell sermon to this first contingent. The *Arbella,* carrying Winthrop and the charter, sailed directly west and sighted the coast of Maine, off York, on June 10, and by July 2 the other six vessels had all arrived either at Salem or at Charlestown. Meanwhile another seven ships left England at the end of April, carrying more passengers as well as horses and livestock and so much freight that some of the animals had to be thrown overboard. This second group reached New England at various dates up to July 6. Before the end of the year seventeen vessels in all left England bound for Salem, Charlestown, Dorchester, Natascot (Hull), and Plymouth—a feat not equaled until the Quaker migration to Pennsylvania in 1682–83. The thousand passengers who came on those ships and other Puritan groups that went to Bermuda and the West Indies were the vanguard of a spectacular English migration to the New World.[15]

14 Andrews, *Colonial Period,* I, 375–393.
15 C. F. Adams, *Three Episodes of Massachusetts History,* I, 209–239, gives a full description of the Winthrop fleet of 1630 and its arrival in Massachusetts.

The Great Puritan Migration, as historians call it, was the larges
and most important of all movements overseas by English people
in colonial times.[16] It included non-Puritans as well as Puritans
but the latter led it and gave it its special tone.[17] Men of wealth
and education, of middle-class origins, with some awareness of
politics, these Puritans were a hardheaded and dogmatic lot. Tena
cious of purpose, they regarded themselves as chosen by God to
create a purer church and a City of God in the wilderness. The
success of the Bay Colony rested not alone upon its possession of a
charter but upon the high character of its leaders and the uni
formity of its religious teaching and polity.

Not satisfied with Salem, the Puritan leaders sought a new site
to the south. Endecott had already chosen Charlestown and had
built a house there among a sprinkling of settlers. But the new
comers who arrived in 1630 could not agree on that location, and
so they crossed over to Shawmut (which became Boston), pushed
on to Mystic (later Medford), and found their way to Roxbury and
Dorchester.[18] Dispersion was inevitable, because the water supply
at Charlestown was by no means adequate. Two hundred people
died during the first year, many from fever and scurvy. Without
drugs, Dr. Fuller was helpless. A hundred immigrants returned to
England because of fear of famine. At one time men back in Eng
land were convinced that the colony could not survive.

[16] For a discussion of the motivation of these migrants, see Nellis M. Crouse,
"Causes of the Great Migration, 1630–1640," New England Quarterly, V (Jan.,
1932), 3–36.

[17] There has been some dispute about the role of Puritanism in the Great
Migration. James Truslow Adams, The Founding of New England (Boston,
1949), p. 121, points out that no more than one in five of the migrants to
Massachusetts "was sufficiently in sympathy with the religious ideas there
prevalent to become a church member, though disfranchised for not doing
so," and he maintains that the reasons for migrating were essentially secular.
Morison, Builders of the Bay Colony, pp. 379–386, challenges this view, arguing
that the migrants were predominately Puritans who supported their leaders'
religious purposes enthusiastically.

[18] Rutman, Winthrop's Boston, pp. 23–40, describes the selection of the
several town sites and the founding of Boston. As Roy H. Agaki, The Town
Proprietors of the New England Colonies: A Study of the Development, Organization, Activities, and Controversies, 1620–1670 (Philadelphia, 1924, republished
Gloucester, Mass., 1963), pp. 15–16, points out, the original settlers in these
towns were at first mere squatters, with no legal land titles until they made
purchases from the Indians or received grants from the colonial government.

In spite of the confusion incident to migration, the colonists organized their government promptly. Following a last meeting at Southampton, they held their first general court on the *Arbella* just before they sailed, electing Thomas Dudley deputy governor to replace John Humfry, who stayed behind in England. The next meeting of the governor and his assistants, held at Charlestown in August, 1630, provided for a minister, a surgeon, and a beadle to wait upon the governor. In order to get trade started, it was decided to erect within the company a subordinate body of men, some in England and some in America, who would have a monopoly over the transporting and sale of goods. At the end of seven years, this group would endeavor to return to the subscribers the amounts they had invested, an arrangement resembling the one involving the eight men at Plymouth who managed the joint stock of trading goods there during the earliest years. The joint-stock assets of Massachusetts remained in England as a trading fund quite distinct from the common stock, which consisted of assets in the colony, such as land, buildings, and livestock.

The trading company dwindled, and there is no record of it after 1638. The associates living in England were Cradock, Goffe, Humfry, and two others, while Saltonstall, Winthrop, Revell, Dudley, and Johnson managed affairs in America. Winthrop and Dudley were the only representatives still in America by 1634, so that from that time on activity centered in London. The company proper, which had become the corporate government in New England, had nothing to do with this trading venture and assumed no responsibility for its debts. The business operations turned out to be so feeble that little is known about them. The trading company hoped to purchase furs from the Indians and sell commodities furnished by the settlers, paying dividends to the subscribers from the profits. The Puritan undertaking originally had the aspect of a trading company with a charter, but by 1638 it had become a self-governing corporation in America whose main purpose was to erect a Puritan state.[19]

The reactivation of the almost forgotten Council for New England now posed an unexpected problem for the colony. During the planning of the Massachusetts Bay settlement, the leaders of

[19] Andrews, *Colonial Period*, I, 393–399.

the council had been preoccupied with public affairs and particularly with the French war. By 1630 five of them were dead, and only two members were still active and available: Sir Ferdinando Gorges himself and the Earl of Warwick. Gorges was most anxious to block the Puritan scheme, but his military duties still held him at Plymouth. Warwick, in London, kept the council alive, but he scarcely served any of Gorges' purposes, because his sympathies were with the Puritans. At this time Warwick was in fact the entire council, and it seems certain that it held no meetings. It can be said in Warwick's defense that northern colonization was of little interest to anyone during the years immediately preceding 1629. No grant of record was issued between May, 1623, and November, 1629. The last grant was that of the supposed patent to the New England Company, which could hardly have been made legally.[20]

When the fighting with France and Spain ended, Gorges was finally free to reactivate the council. Between November, 1629, and July, 1632, the council proceeded to make twenty grants, all of which, except the Bradford patent of January, 1630, were issued in the interest of Gorges and his friends for land north of the Merrimack River.[21] Because of the secrecy of the Puritans, Gorges actually did not learn the facts of the Bay Company's charter until the summer of 1632. The Council for New England then demanded that the patent of March, 1628, be brought in for inspection, only to learn that it had gone to New England. Humfry, Cradock, and Saltonstall were called upon for an explanation. Warwick, who had until then continued as president, ceased attending meetings when an order issued in November, 1632, required that all existing patents be called in for examination and confirmation. Warwick's departure put Gorges in complete control, and he enlarged the council to his liking, eventually drawing in Captain John Mason as vice-president. Gorges hoped to send commissioners to New England to reconcile all differences, and he also hoped to obtain a new charter from the king giving him large proprietary powers like those Lord Baltimore had just obtained for Maryland.[22]

The Massachusetts Bay Charter was the chief obstacle to the

20 *Ibid.*, pp. 400–402.
21 James P. Baxter, *Sir Ferdinando Gorges and His Province of Maine* (3 vols., Boston, 1890), I, 154–156, gives detailed information about the grants.
22 Andrews, *Colonial Period*, I, 402–405.

creation of a feudal proprietary by Gorges. Consequently, although he bore the Puritans no enmity, Gorges wanted to get their charter annulled, and he was pleased to get the cooperation of several men who were anxious to hurt Massachusetts in any way they could. The first of these dissidents to make himself available was the notorious Thomas Morton, who left England to return to Massachusetts in the summer of 1629, and who, even before Winthrop arrived, resumed his former life with great gusto. The meeting of the Court of Assistants at Boston in August, 1630, voted to try Morton and punish him. After condemning him to sit in the stocks, the officials had his house burned down, and then they returned him to England on the first available ship. The shrewd and influential Morton thereupon aligned himself with Gorges. During the summer of 1629, the overzealous Endecott also sent the Brownes back to England, incurring the displeasure of Mathew Cradock and other members of the old company. Since there were still many Church of England adherents in the colony, the company in Massachusetts continued on its course. The servants on Cradock's plantation, for example, were considered an unruly lot who spoke "wickedly and boldly against the government and the governor."[23] The local authorities put Philip Ratcliffe, one of this group, under arrest, and then fined him forty shillings, ordered him whipped, and had his ears cut off. Ratcliffe returned to England, understandably eager for revenge. Sir Christopher Gardiner, a picturesque character who had turned from Catholicism to Protestantism, paid New England a visit, claiming that he had forsaken the world, although in fact his trip was probably prompted by a matrimonial scandal at home. Impressed by his title and his airs, the Puritans dealt with him very cautiously. Suspecting that he was a spy for Gorges, they ordered him banished but then did not dare to execute the sentence. Gardiner returned to England voluntarily and made a report that was hostile to the colony.[24]

Five men—Gorges, Mason, Morton, Ratcliffe, and Gardiner—plotted to have the Bay Company charter expunged. The well-informed Gardiner drafted a statement of conditions in New England, which in its final form reached the Privy Council in December,

23 *Ibid.*, p. 407.
24 Baxter, *Sir Ferdinando Gorges*, I, 158.

1632. A committee made up of twelve members and two principal secretaries of state undertook an investigation of the allegations, interviewing Cradock and Saltonstall as representatives of the colony and also drawing unfavorable testimony from Gorges, Gardiner, Morton, and Ratcliffe. The committee rendered its report on January 19, 1633, indicating that Massachusetts did not lack defenders. Captain Thomas Wiggin wrote a letter describing Winthrop as a discreet and sober man, ruling with mildness and justice. He repudiated the "false rumors" that were current and described Morton, Gardiner, and Ratcliffe as "discontented and scandalous characters." Edward Winslow, in jail for being a Separatist, condemned the same men and indicated that it would be a great mistake to sacrifice the colony. Emmanuel Downing wrote Secretary Coke demanding that "these lewd and scandalous persons" be punished and that the colony receive the encouragement it deserved. On the basis of the evidence collected by Sir John Coke, the committee recommended that Massachusetts should be upheld as beneficial to the kingdom. The Privy Council adopted this report and asked the king to maintain the privileges of the colony. It added that Massachusetts Bay might develop into a useful supplier of much-needed naval stores.[25]

A favorable opinion by the Privy Council did not end the matter, because the legal status of the colony had not yet been determined. In May the investigating committee was directed to continue its activities under the chairmanship of William Laud, newly appointed Archbishop of Canterbury, who was, of course, hostile to the Puritans. Early in 1634 the Privy Council detained all vessels going to New England until instructions could be prepared. Masters were to see that all persons bound for New England took the oaths of supremacy and allegiance and attended services on board according to the Book of Common Prayer. At the same time these official inquiries and acts brought into the open the whole question of emigration and its relation to national policy. Many predicted injury to the nation in the departure from England of hundreds of men and women of substance. Archbishop Laud opposed emigration on the ground that it tended to increase nonconformity.

[25] See *Ibid.*, pp. 159–161, for the details of Gorges' plot and the resulting investigation.

Others believed the movement deleterious because it deprived England of gentry, artisans, and laborers, and they argued that it would drain off her supplies of gold and silver.

In April, 1634, the Privy Council issued a commission under the Great Seal to those who had composed the second committee plus one new member, Sir William Alexander, Earl of Stirling. This newly created board, known as the Laud Commission for Regulating Plantations, received extraordinary powers in colonial matters, and it was, in fact, the forerunner of the Lords of Trade and Plantations (1675–96). The Privy Council practically abdicated its authority over the plantations; the Laud Commission was empowered to govern and legislate, to safeguard things ecclesiastical, to remove officeholders, to hear complaints and grievances, and to frame new laws. The commission could order any usurper in the colonies to return to England, and it could also examine all charters and patents, revoking any found to have been obtained surreptitiously or any injurious to the crown. This degree of control over the colony was exactly what Gorges and Morton wanted, but they had prejudiced their case by failing to make their accusations stick. Aside from awarding Kent Island to Baltimore, however, the commission kept its attention concentrated on New England.[26]

When Winthrop learned that the Laud Commission had been appointed, he became convinced that its purpose was to destroy the Massachusetts charter and install Gorges as governor. Now definitely off the Council for New England, Warwick supported Winthrop and expressed his sympathy by offering to help him as best as he could. Nonetheless, the colony was thrown into a state of agitation.[27] John Endecott foolishly cut the red cross out of the royal ensign at Salem, alleging that the pope had given the cross to the king. There were other manifestations by Puritan leaders smacking of defiance of both church and state. An alarmed Winthrop named an advisory committee which denounced Endecott's

[26] *Ibid.*, p. 164, analyzes the commission's powers. See also Andrews, *Colonial Period*, I, 410–414.

[27] Later on, when Warwick better understood New England intolerance, his sympathies changed. After 1643, for example, he headed a royal commission that showed dissatisfaction with the colony, upheld religious liberty, supported Samuel Gorton in his struggle with the Massachusetts authorities, and granted a patent to Rhode Island.

act as rash and likely to be construed as an act of rebellion, and forbade Endecott from holding public office for one year. The sentence might have been much more severe had not the committee believed that Endecott committed his act "out of tenderness of conscience and not of any evil intent." This, as Charles M. Andrews wrote, was the "Puritan way of saying that he let his religious convictions get the better of his discretion."[28] Concern about the future became even greater when Winthrop was shown a letter written by Thomas Morton to the effect that the king and council were incensed against the colony and that Laud had labeled Cradock and Humfry as knaves. Morton indicated that there would soon be a governor general of Massachusetts Bay appointed by the crown, and that he would accompany him to haunt his former tormenters.

When John Humfry arrived in the colony in June, 1634, and warned its leaders of the seriousness of the situation, the general court undertook various measures of defense. It fortified strategic positions around Boston, organized armed bands, instituted compulsory military drill, and appointed a war council that included Winthrop, Endecott, and Humfry. These preparations continued over the next two years, but there was no concurrent effort to eliminate actions apt to be frowned on abroad. The general court omitted the crosses in the company colors, laying the colony open to a charge of treason. The only place it permitted the king's flag to fly was on Castle Island, because that was the king's fort and because the flag was recognizable from the sea. Whatever the cost, Massachusetts seemed determined to avoid any recognition of the king's authority. The Reverend George Burdett, former minister at Agamenticus in Maine, an Antinomian and a questionable character, wrote Archbishop Laud in 1638 that the Puritan government intended to resist any measures that would strip them of their self-appointed privileges. He added that the Puritans were a menace to all their neighbors.

Sir Ferdinando Gorges was now determined to get rid of the Council for New England and to do away with its charter, but at the same time he wanted to retain possession of the council's territories. Accordingly, he divided its holdings into eight parts, as-

28 Andrews, *Colonial Period*, I, 415.

signing some to members of the council and the remainder to influential noblemen who might aid Gorges. The beneficiaries were Arundel, Lenox, Hamilton, Carlisle, Stirling, Lord Edward Gorges, Captain John Mason, and, of course, Sir Ferdinando himself. Under the new arrangements the grantees were to hold their land directly from the king by knight service, but Sir Ferdinando's deed was the only one ever actually confirmed by the crown. In June, 1635, the council formally surrendered the old charter to the king, at the same time excoriating the Massachusetts Bay Company for surreptitiously obtaining a grant impinging upon the council's lands, for assuming political independence, for punishing objectors, and for making themselves masters of the country. It asked the king to confirm all grants that the Council for New England had made and to establish a general government for New England. Gorges, now seventy, offered his services and solicited the opportunity of suppressing the Massachusetts Bay Colony's government.[29]

At the moment things did not appear hopeless for Sir Ferdinando. Though the king would not confirm his patents or create a new government, Gorges had the good will of Laud and the Privy Council. The English authorities disliked the Puritan attempt to assert independence and to reject the Established Church. In May, 1635, on the basis of the Laud Commission's report, Sir John Banks, the attorney general, received instructions to call in the Massachusetts Bay patent. When it became known that this document was not in England, Banks was directed to file charges against the company and to obtain a writ of quo warranto against the governor and his assistants. Ironically, Gorges himself was the man selected to serve the writ upon the company in America, and Thomas Morton received the appointment to prosecute the suit before the Court of King's Bench. Final judgment was rendered for the king in May, 1637. The attorney general then undertook to regain the charter and transmit it to the (Laud) Commission for Foreign Plantations. Morton, an able lawyer, had conducted his case against the New England Company with consummate skill. The king accepted the surrender of the charter of the Council for New England on July

29 Henry S. Burrage, *The Beginnings of Colonial Maine, 1602–1658* (Portland, Me., 1914), pp. 281–289, gives an illuminating account of Gorges' machinations during this period.

23 and, assuming that the charter of Massachusetts Bay was as good as defunct, issued a declaration that the king was taking over the government of Massachusetts and appointing Gorges governor.[30]

The outlook for the Bay Colony was not, however, as bad as it appeared to be. As much as he might wish to control events, Laud could exercise no more than a nominal influence over Massachusetts Bay. More important, the king, because of the political situation, was in no position to aid Gorges financially, and money was needed if anything was to be accomplished, Gorges and his friends being by then practically bankrupt. Even the ship that Gorges and Mason had built in 1635 with which to serve the quo warranto broke up when it was launched. In the same year Mason died, and by that time Gorges had become very feeble. Gorges' last opportunity slipped away and with it the last serious threat to the Bay Colony.

It was now up to the home authorities. In April, 1638, the Laud Committee sent Winthrop a letter, commanding him to return the charter by the first ship; otherwise the king would immediately take over the whole plantation. The Privy Council put into force a regulation forbidding ships' captains to transport any passengers without a license. Because the king had his hands full with the Scottish revolt, Winthrop felt safe in refusing to return the charter, and in his letter of explanation he stated his reasons sincerely and convincingly. The Privy Council declared itself satisfied with this reply, but it reiterated its demand of the charter and threatened penalties in case of refusal. It diminished the force of this order by instructing the government of the colony to continue until a new charter could be procured, and all activity in this connection ended with the approach of the English civil war. Massachusetts Bay emerged, for the time, unscathed. No governor general appeared until 1684, when Sir Edmund Andros was appointed governor of the Dominion of New England.

In 1639, at the age of seventy-four, Gorges obtained confirmation of his share of New England lands in the form of a charter for the "Province of Maine." He became, at long last, proprietor and absolute lord of a huge territory whose bounds included half of New Hampshire, one-eighth of Vermont, and three-eighths of Maine. At the time there were a few settlers on the southern tip of Maine

[30] Baxter, *Sir Ferdinando Gorges*, I, 171–189.

between the Piscataqua and Casco Bay—at Kittery, Richmond Island, and Saco—and at fishing stations at Monhegan, Pemaquid, and Damariscove. Gorges was especially interested in a small farming village, Agamenticus, also on the southern tip, which he planned to make his capital. In 1640, his cousin, Thomas Gorges, went over as deputy governor and established orderly government. In April, 1641, he set up Agamenticus as a borough, making provision for a mayor, aldermen, a recorder, and other officers. Governor Gorges then proceeded to lay out a cathedral town there called Gorgeana (later York), organized on the plan of the city of Bristol. The proprietor himself envisaged an episcopal see along the Maine coast populated by immigrants from his own West Country. Sir Ferdinando, who never realized the impracticability of what he was attempting to do in America, died in 1647 at the age of eighty-two. The Maine provincial court sat periodically under successive deputy governors, Thomas Gorges, Richard Vines, and Henry Jocelyn, until its demise in 1649.[31]

Deserted by their leaders because of the disorders in England, the inhabitants of Maine set up an ad hoc government in July, 1649, pending the turn of events in England. This minuscule government, with Edward Godfrey as elected governor, administered the towns of Kittery and York until 1652. Holding meetings at those two places, the Maine General Court enacted laws and orders and imposed penalties upon a somewhat unruly body of subjects. The people selected the governor, magistrates, and deputies by popular vote, and they introduced trial by jury and a measure of religious freedom. Little Maine stood with Maryland in the matter of religious moderation. The even smaller "Province of Lygonia" (or Laconia), extending from Casco Bay to Cape Porpoise, separated itself from Maine from 1646 until 1652, electing its own deputy president, general court, and officers.[32]

Maine attracted a different type of settler than Plymouth or Massachusetts. These men from the West Country of England, scattered along the coast from the Piscataqua to Casco Bay, were seamen and adventurers who cared nothing about religious dogma or

---

[31] Burrage, *Beginnings of Colonial Maine*, pp. 289–324. See also C. T. Libby (ed.), *Province and Court Records of Maine, 1636–1668*, I (Portland, 1928).

[32] *Ibid.*, pp. 356–369. See also Baxter, *Sir Ferdinando Gorges*, I, 189–190, for Lygonia.

church reform. The enterprisers themselves were of the landed gentry, loyalist in sympathy and adherents of the Established Church. Their settlers were sturdy, coarse, hard-drinking, and profane, indifferent churchgoers, and impatient of strict enforcement of law and order. In the years after 1652, when Massachusetts took control of Maine, the records of the York county court attest amply to the difficulties of regulating drinking, prohibiting swearing, enforcing attendance at worship, and punishing contempt of the public authority. It proved impossible to maintain Puritan morals and conduct. There were no schools, and except for a few Bibles, there were no books in evidence. Because the "Province of Maine," created by the "social compact" of 1649, was without royal authorization, its general court made an attempt in 1651 to obtain confirmation of its assumed privileges from the Parliament of the Commonwealth government in England. Before anything was accomplished toward this objective, however, Massachusetts, attracted by the timber and the salt marshes, seized the entire region. This action was consistent with the fixed policy of the Bay Colony, which was to push back boundaries on all sides to avoid proximity with troublesome neighbors. Edward Godfrey, the last deputy governor, returned to England and was thrown into prison for debt at the age of seventy-five. The Puritans had pursued Gorges even "beyond the grave" when they took over the last remnant of his territory in the north.[33]

Massachusetts Bay in thirty years not only succeeded in extending its boundaries to the Kennebec but, beginning as an incorporated company in the city of London, it became by degrees "a full-fledged, quasi-independent, self-governing community."[34] The Puritans counted obstacles as of no moment. They believed it was their religious duty to frustrate all enemies, to eradicate all hostile opinions, and to push their way of life to distant frontiers. The transfer of a trading company charter to America and the use of it to erect an independent state necessarily resulted in the straining of the terms of the charter. In addition, purposes and events brought a

[33] Libby (ed.), *Maine Province and Court Records*, I, *passim;* Burrage, *Beginnings of Colonial Maine*, pp. 370–382.
[34] Andrews, *Colonial Period*, I, 430.

concentration of control in the colony that violated certain of the charter's provisions. Examples of this are Winthrop's retaining office for a span of eighteen months instead of a year and his failure to convene quarterly courts in which the generality were present. Moreover, this trading company charter was never designed to care for the governance of an unwieldy population and, very soon, a whole cluster of settlements.

John Winthrop was no democrat; he was certain, to paraphrase his famous statement, that God had made some rich and some poor, some high in power, others in mean estate, and that it was the duty of the chosen people to rule.[35] Puritan theory acknowledged the divine authority of the magistrate and the necessity of obeying him. But the charter indicated some measure of popular participation, with four meetings of the court annually, at which "freemen" would be present. Freemen, then, must somehow be created, since the only freemen then in Massachusetts were the members of the court of assistants, who were also called the magistrates. An invitation therefore went out to all who wished to be freemen to submit their names. Of the one hundred who responded, most had been residents before Winthrop's arrival. In this period when the very existence of the colony was at stake, no qualification for membership was imposed. Many, especially at Salem and Dorchester, were Church of England adherents; others had little sympathy with the Puritans. But by May, 1631, after the organization of churches in several towns, the Puritans felt more secure and, at the general court held that month, they resolved that no man should be made a freeman unless he was a member of one of the Puritan churches. An oath of allegiance was required of freemen, not to the king, but to the government of the Commonwealth of Massachusetts. This was an infringement of the charter, but those in control feared that a broader suffrage might result in great injury. "In case worldly men should prove the major part, as soon they might do, they

---

[35] Rutman, *Winthop's Boston, passim*, but particularly pp. 21–22, skillfully develops the thesis that Winthrop in the broadest sense was a utopian, a dreamer of heaven on earth. He was doomed to failure in part because in America the acquisitive instincts of the English settlers came to the surface, overwhelming Winthrop's communal ideal. See also Morgan, *Puritan Dilemma*, an illuminating study of Winthrop's thought.

would as readily set over us magistrates like themselves such as might . . . turn the edge of all authority and laws against the church and the members thereof."[36]

With the suffrage thus restricted, the government now rested on a religious base. Although the Reverend John White wrote in 1630 that three of every four adhered to the Anglican Church, the turn toward nonconformity and Congregationalism in succeeding years was rapid. The population stabilized into three groups: first, the freemen, always a minority in every town, who alone voted for the governor, magistrates, and deputies; second, those who were neither freemen nor church members but who took the oath of allegiance; and third, those who were legally in the colony but not of it. The second was the largest group; the third, comprising many indentured servants and apprentices, the least important. Winthrop stood in dread of a tyranny of the masses and was never convinced that "the people" were to be trusted. The arrangements made in October, 1630, specified that the freemen should elect the assistants, but that the assistants alone should choose the governor and the deputy governor, who, with the assistants, should make the laws and execute them. These stipulations violated the charter, which reserved the election and the lawmaking functions to the generality of the members. In 1631 the court decided that a majority of the assistants might hold court even though the charter required a quorum of seven. Winthrop and the leaders of the colony had shifted to the principle that they might change the charter whenever necessity required.

The continuous straining of a trading company charter to satisfy the necessities of a self-governing community met with opposition in the colony as well as in England. A group at Watertown claimed in 1632 that the charter bestowed no right to tax. Winthrop explained that the body that levied the tax, the court of assistants, was like a parliament, inasmuch as the freemen chose the assistants, and he added that the freemen had the right to ask questions at the annual meetings of the court of elections. The Watertown

---

[36] Quoted in Thomas Hutchinson, *The History of the Province of Massachusetts Bay*, ed. Lawrence S. Mayo (3 vols., rev. ed., Cambridge, Mass., 1936), I, 26. In *Puritan Dilemma*, Chap. VII, Morgan argues that the governor's belief in the role of the covenant in religion and politics prompted him to extend the suffrage.

protest may have influenced an order of the general court in May to the effect that the whole body of freemen assembled in court should choose the governor and assistants, provided that they selected the governor from among the assistants. At the same time, the general court considered the matter of taxation and decided to appoint sixteen men, two from each settlement, to advise with the governor and the assistants "about raising a publique stock." In 1634, in response, the general court voted that it had the right to raise money and impose taxes. Although this committee of townsmen was not as yet a representative body, it was the first time the towns participated in dealing with an important issue. The trading corporation was slowly moving toward a self-governing plantation.

The freemen, however, had not yet gained all the rights and privileges granted them by the charter. Though they had won the right to help elect the governor, and, in the general court, to participate in matters of taxation, they were not yet permitted to take part in the legislative or executive business or to come together, as the charter required, four times a year to make laws. The governor and the assistants had made all the laws, distributed land, raised revenue, and punished offenders. Winthrop's arbitrary conduct drew criticism, and his retention of power in his own hands was notorious. After acrimonious discussions, the freemen in May, 1634, won a notable victory. Orders were adopted declaring that only the general court had authority to raise money and dispose of land. Another important ordinance specified that the freemen in each town should choose two or three deputies to represent them in three of the four meetings of the general court. The fourth meeting, in May, was the court of election, in which freemen or their proxies must be represented directly. This new arrangement was far from democracy, there being only several hundred freemen among 4,000 inhabitants, but the original tight-knit oligarchy had given way to the extent of becoming rule by a privileged class.[37] Despite John Cotton's election sermon, the freemen turned Winthrop out in 1634 and elected Thomas Dudley as governor. For the first time the written ballot was used. Winthrop returned to

[37] For accurate estimates of Massachusetts' population growth, 1630–60, see Rutman, *Winthrop's Boston*, pp. 178–180. By 1638 the population rose to 10,000 without any appreciable rise in freemanship.

office in 1637, but the freemen had amply demonstrated their power.[38]

The next notable change took place in 1644, when the general court separated into two branches. The deputies had been aroused for some time because no action could be taken unless a majority of both deputies and magistrates voted favorably. Thus the magistrates could negate the decisions of the deputies, who greatly outnumbered them. The deputies strongly resented this "negative vote," but Winthrop argued that it would be dangerous to the general welfare if the magistrates gave up this power. The government, "if it were taken away, would become," he insisted, "a mere democracy."[39] The deputies, supported by three younger magistrates, Richard Saltonstall, Richard Bellingham, and Simon Bradstreet, finally triumphed. Henceforth the magistrates would sit by themselves and the deputies by themselves in the general court, and the two groups would formally communicate with one another. When both houses reached agreement, the measure would pass. This decision marked another step in the development of the commonwealth form of government.[40]

From the start the clergy played a conspicuous role in settling affairs of a purely secular character, and the ministers' election sermons through the years dealt with political issues. Time and time again the people turned to the teaching elders (ministers and teachers) for advice and recommendations. Yet Massachusetts was not a theocracy, as it has frequently been called. A man could not be a civil magistrate and a ruling elder at the same time. Actually, the influence of the clergy was entirely unofficial and without the sanction of law. These men never did more than offer opinions and recommendations, either unasked or upon request. On the other hand, the magistrates were regarded as "the nursing fathers" of the churches, and there was no important religious or churchly issue that did not call for their intervention. For example, they exercised jurisdiction over all offenses involving idolatry, blasphemy, and the breaking of the Sabbath; they inquired into the fitness of the clergy; they examined quarrels in the churches; they took the lead in locating ministers; and they sought out heresy and acted as the

[38] Osgood, *American Colonies*, I, 153–156.
[39] Andrews, *Colonial Period*, I, 451, quoting Winthrop.
[40] Osgood, *American Colonies*, I, 157–158.

judges who delivered the sentences for that offense. But the magistrates, though they might ask the elders for their opinions, sat as the secular court which reproved, fined, imprisoned, or banished malefactors. In 1646, the general court itself drafted a moral code dealing with blasphemy and similar offenses, as well as with such heresies as denying the immortality of the soul and the resurrection of the body. Guilty persons, after suffering the censure of the church, would first be reproved by the court and after a second offense fined five pounds or forced to stand on the block, labeled "a wanton gospeller." The general court in 1647 ordered the clergy to draw up a confession of faith and a plan of church government. Conversely, the church of Boston took upon itself the drawing up of a code of commercial ethics for use in business. The functions of church and state were in many respects interchangeable.[41]

By the early forties the colony was a self-governing state based upon the assent of a small body of freemen. The colony gave recognition to the king but denied his right to interfere. The Puritans were consistently determined to resist the authority of any government in England, whether that of Charles I, the Council of State under the Commonwealth, or the king in council after the Restoration in 1660. They would, above all, protect the Kingdom of Christ that they had established on earth. They would not have anyone disallow their laws. They were in effect struggling for religious freedom. To the Puritans, religion and government were inextricably interlocked, and there was no such thing as separation of state and church. Each element in their public life strengthened the other—the clergy acting as advisers in lay matters, the magistrates issuing orders for the maintenance of the true faith. In church polity the Massachusetts Puritans, by now Congregationalists, stood between Separatism and Presbyterianism; in government they sought the middle ground between self-appointed tyranny and popular confusion.[42]

[41] Perry Miller discusses the relations between church and government in *Orthodoxy in Massachusetts*. See Chaps. VI, "The New England Way," and VII, "The Supreme Power Politicke."

[42] Osgood, *American Colonies*, I, 167–199, analyzes the early Massachusetts government with admirable thoroughness, and the same author discusses the ideology on which the government was based in "The Political Ideas of the Puritans," *Political Science Quarterly*, VI (Mar., 1891), 1–28, and (June, 1891), 201–231.

CHAPTER 8

The Commonwealth
of Massachusetts

MASSACHUSETTS, like Virginia, was a maturing colony during the years between 1640 and 1660. The struggle for survival was behind it, and there was little danger of interference from an England deeply involved in an internecine struggle. The colony no longer had to cope with agglomerations of immigrants from England. The representatives of the people, the deputies, had already made their power felt vis-à-vis the magistrates, first by the elimination of the "negative vote" and then by the separation into two houses. The much-sought publication of the laws of the colony followed soon, and participation in town government was extended. These measures would solve other discontents. The religious controversies of the thirties and the dilemma of the church would result ultimately in a broader-based church with more precise goals. Finally, by 1649 the colony had completely recovered from the depression of 1640, and a period of great agricultural and commercial prosperity ensued. By 1652 Massachusetts had become a de facto commonwealth, performing all the functions of a sovereign state and extending its borders into Maine and New Hampshire.

In spite of the victory of the deputies in gaining the right to meet as a separate body, the Bay Colony magistrates had shown themselves anything but supine in their effort to maintain power. In 1635 they had proclaimed their right to sit as a standing council with full executive powers while the general court was not in session. The elders supported the magistrates, but the deputies were opposed. The struggle continued, with the deputies for a time yielding to the pressure of the magistrates and the clergy. The deputies then made new demands of privileges heretofore enjoyed only by the magistrates. A modus operandi was arrived at only when it was agreed to formulate and make public a body of laws that would protect the people from any arbitrary decisions on the part of the magistrates.[1]

Sentences imposed by the magistrates were actually mild compared with those in England, there being only twelve capital offenses compared with thirty-one in England. Moreover, the general court adopted a legal device termed remission that permitted the colony to retain the form of law while continually making lenient exceptions. A convicted man acknowledging his offense fully and declaring his intention to reform stood a good chance of having his sentence remitted in part or in whole. This act of atonement, for such it had to be, satisfied the Puritan tenet that a restored conscience was a necessity. Thus, from 1631 to 1641, a full half of all sentences were remitted. Governor Winthrop is credited with this policy, adopted because the colony was short not only of money with which to pay fines but also of men to perform labor and defend against possible Indian onslaughts. There were remarkably few hangings, and in whippings the number of strokes rarely reached the nominal total of thirty-nine, while stocks took the place of branding. Because of the scarcity of money, more than half the fines were remitted. Prisoners served only short terms, and private bondage was common. The occasional harsh sentence aroused public disapproval, but there was little feeling that the laws were too severe. What bothered the people in general was the conviction that there was discrimination in the way the law was applied. Gentlemen and men of property were rarely whipped, and drunken masters were only occasionally punished, but poor people and servants enjoyed no such immunity.[2] The common people became convinced that

[1] Perry Miller, *Orthodoxy in Massachusetts, 1630–1650: A Genetic Study* (Cambridge, Mass., 1933), contains the best discussion of the extensive debate between the magistrates and the deputies regarding their relative powers.

[2] While it is true that servants were penalized for misbehavior, the Massachusetts laws went beyond common-law precedents in the matter of protecting them against maltreatment by their masters. See Richard B. Morris, "Massachusetts and the Common Law: The Declaration of 1646," *American Historical Review*, XXXI (Apr., 1926), 443–445.

a published law code would give them more equal protection, and so they demanded that the rules be written down for all to see.[3]

Drafting a legal code proved to be a long-drawn-out process. The deputies were so insistent that something had to be done to put the laws into written form that the magistrates asked John Cotton to undertake the task in 1636. He submitted a draft of what he considered acceptable, but it was not adopted. Then, in 1639, he and Nathaniel Ward of Ipswich, formerly an attorney, worked together to produce the "Body of Liberties," which was approved by the general court and in effect for three years.[4] Because the deputies felt that this code left too much power in the hands of a few men, it was never published, and the deputies continued their agitation for something better. A revised code was prepared in 1647, at which time the general court asked for additional study and purchased English law books to aid in the task. *The Book of General Lawes and Libertyes* was printed in 1648, but of the six hundred copies printed only one is extant.[5] Because the general court wished to make alterations, all copies were called in and destroyed three years later. Although the *Lawes and Libertyes* was ostensibly a blend of Mosaic law and the law of the colony, the common law of England proved the dominant influence, and this code later became a model for those of New Haven and Connecticut. The rights and privileges of the inhabitants were now made public, and the printed law could therefore be pleaded against arbitrary judgments.[6]

It was accepted for a long time by historians that Massachusetts was undemocratic, with a few hundred freemen monopolizing all

[3] Jules Zanger, "Crime and Punishment in Early Massachusetts," *William and Mary Quarterly,* XXII (July, 1965), 471–477, stresses not only the great leniency of Massachusetts law but the partial way in which it was administered.

[4] The Cotton draft code of 1636 was published in London in 1641 under the misleading title *An Abstract of the Lawes of New England, as they are now established.* For parallels with the Body of Liberties see Richard B. Morris, *Studies in the History of American Law* (New York, 1930), p. 29 n. Samuel Eliot Morison, *Builders of the Bay Colony* (Boston, 1964), pp. 217–243, gives a sketch of Ward.

[5] It is at the Huntington Library and Art Gallery. See illustration.

[6] George L. Haskins, *Law and Authority in Early Massachusetts: A Study in Tradition and Design* (New York, 1960), is an outstanding study of the development of the Massachusetts legal system; Andrews, *Colonial Period,* I 454–459; II, 156.

political rights, but that view had been challenged in recent years. Samuel Eliot Morison made an early effort to revise the prevailing opinion, pointing out the extent of democratization after 1652, when church membership had declined sharply. Clifford Shipton has added to the force of this argument by insisting that even in the preceding period four-fifths of the adult males had the right to vote, at least in town meetings. Contemporary opinion on the subject was divided. Thomas Lechford, a severe critic of the Bay Colony, claimed in 1640 that three-fourths of the adult males were outside the church and hence ineligible to vote, but John Cotton contended that the majority were really church members. Edward Winslow maintained that many men did not become freeholders simply because they did not want the responsibilities attached to freemanship. As for the general court itself, it steadfastly denied that there were any large divisions among the people regarding the franchise, and it consistently urged all eligible men to become freemen.

After examining conditions in specific towns, a recent investigator, B. Katherine Brown, concludes that substantial democracy did exist. Three-quarters of the adult males in Cambridge were church members in full communion and were thus eligible for freemanship. Moreover, many of those who were not church members were in sympathy with the existing political moves. It is true that only between 50 per cent and 80 per cent of the churchmen became freemen, but this is explained by the fact that some were shirkers while others were apathetic. Brown finds no political oligarchy in Cambridge, there being no large estate owners and few economic extremes, among either voters or officeholders. Both groups were of "the middling orders of society." Selectmen and constables, on the whole, served but one or two annual terms. In a similar study of Dedham, Brown finds much the same pattern. If these communities were typical, and there seems no reason to believe otherwise, the great majority of adult males in Massachusetts could participate in annual elections and exercise the right of petition, and the town records were open to all.[7]

[7] B. Katherine Brown, "Puritan Democracy: A Case Study," *Mississippi Valley Historical Review*, L (Dec., 1963), 377–396, and "Puritan Democracy in Dedham, Massachusetts: Another Case Study," *William and Mary Quarterly*, XXIV (July, 1967), 378–396. See also her "Freemanship in Puritan Massachusetts," *American*

If in fact discontent with the government, both provincial and local, was at a minimum, this happy condition did not come about until the authorities made some adjustments in the original rules governing political participation. Nonfreemen who had taken the oath could vote for minor militia officers and could even hold those offices themselves, but they objected to being otherwise excluded from public life. The general court partially obliged them in 1647, ruling that nonfreemen twenty-four years of age or older who had taken the oath of fidelity might henceforth serve on juries and vote for selectmen, who were the local officials administering town governments and setting tax rates. The next year the general court went a step further, providing that any man, whether freeman or nonfreeman, could attend any court or town meeting and introduce any necessary motion, provided it was done properly. The officials did impose a property qualification of £20 on all voters in 1658, but in 1664 the provincial franchise was thrown open to all Englishmen twenty-four years of age who had rateables of £10 and who were orthodox in religion. These qualifications spread to Plymouth Colony.[8]

Town government followed English precedent, except that a board of selectmen took the place of a select vestry. These selectmen derived their powers from the town meeting, which had been given authority by the general court to regulate local matters. The towns (the resident freemen acting collectively) gained the right in 1635 to make local bylaws or ordinances, dispose of land, and elect local officers, such as constables and surveyors of highways. The town meeting assembled only a few times during a year for

---

Historical Review, LIX (July, 1954), 865–883. "Puritan Democracy in Dedham," 377–378 for above opinions on Massachusetts as a democracy.

[8] Richard C. Simmons, "Freemanship in Early Massachusetts: Some Suggestions and a Case Study," *William and Mary Quarterly,* XIX (July, 1962), 422–428, finds that in Watertown there was a marked but not an absolute correlation between wealth in land on one hand and freemanship and office-holding on the other. In "Godliness, Property, and the Franchise in Puritan Massachusetts: An Interpretation," *The Journal of American History,* LV (Dec., 1968), 495–511, the same author argues that Massachusetts church members wanted to maintain political control but that they did not have this end in view when they widened or narrowed the franchise. Stephen Foster, "The Massachusetts Franchise in the Seventeenth Century," *William and Mary Quarterly,* XXIV (Oct., 1967), 611–623, warns that it is difficult to determine exactly how many men did actually vote.

election purposes, to remunerate the minister and the schoolmaster, and to make minor adjustments in the ordinances. The freemen trusted their selectmen, who met monthly or more often, "to prepare and ripen answers," and so the town meeting existed largely as a passive veto power. The selectmen prepared the agenda for the town meeting, promulgated the ordinances, assessed taxes due from each resident, and cared for the town's indebtedness. In some towns, such as Dedham, the selectmen assumed important social control functions, such as care of the poor, support of the idle, and examination of the school. Since on the whole the people trusted the selectmen, who were prominent and highly respected citizens, these officials served by annual election for many years. It is true that the town meeting rarely made use of its latent strength, but the selectmen never lost sight of the fact that they derived their authority from the larger group, and after 1680 there was a gradual shift of power back to the town meeting.[9]

Thus, before 1652, when Massachusetts declared itself an independent commonwealth, all men who had taken the oath of fidelity possessed some share in the government, at least locally. All had full rights before the law and were protected in their persons and property. The leaders of the colony felt that they had successfully molded an independent political structure. A decade later there were those both in England and in America who regarded the Commonwealth of Massachusetts as presumptuous and questioned its loyalty to the crown. Captain Thomas Breedon, for example, told the Privy Council in 1661 that Massachusetts looked upon itself as a free state without any dependence on England or the crown. He questioned the colony's loyalty because its rulers had failed to proclaim Charles II king and did not take the oath of allegiance to him—"instead they forced an oath of fidelity to themselves and the government."[10]

---

[9] Kenneth A. Lockridge and Alan Kreider, "The Evolution of Massachusetts Town Government, 1640–1740," *William and Mary Quarterly*, XXIII (Oct., 1966), 549–574, and John F. Sly, *Town Government in Massachusetts, 1620–1930* (Hamden, Conn., 1967). For a description of how towns were first organized and land was divided among the settlers, see Thomas J. Wertenbaker, *The Puritan Oligarchy* (New York, 1947), pp. 42–57.

[10] Charles M. Andrews, *The Colonial Period of American History* (4 vols., New Haven, Conn., 1934–38), I, 461n. Breedon, later governor of Acadia, was a Boston merchant loyal to the crown.

Massachusetts' relations with the Indians were amicable during the period before 1660, except for the Pequot War of 1637.[11] The Pequots, "destroyers of men," were Mohegans who had swept across Connecticut and had settled on the coast west of the Narragansett Indians, beyond the borders of Massachusetts. They were cruel neighbors who exacted tribute from the local tribes. After they murdered John Stone and his trading party and later slew John Oldham on Block Island, Governor Winthrop sent a force against them. The next year, in the spring of 1637, the Pequots raided Connecticut, killing thirty people at Wethersfield. Connecticut then joined in the war against the tribe, and a vigorous campaign by the colonists destroyed the Indian fort at Mystic and with it five hundred Pequot men, women, and children.[12]

Alden T. Vaughan, a student of the Pequot War, apportions the blame more heavily upon the Pequots than upon the Puritans. The Puritans always recognized the Indians' title to land and, with the exception of the Pequot War, obtained it through orderly purchase and transfer. But these Indians were blatantly provocative and were hated by the neighboring tribes. John Endecott, Winthrop's commander, was, it is true, harsh in his dealings with the Pequots, and Winthrop was criticized by other New England colonies. Massachusetts did send a military force beyond its own boundaries, but at the time there was nobody else in a position to act. Although extermination of the Pequot tribe opened settlement in southern New England, Vaughan concludes that the factor of land hunger was not an issue. The Connecticut Valley offered ample room for everyone, and even the neighboring Indians were not alarmed at the white man's settlements. There was no repetition of Indian troubles until King Philip's War of 1675–76.[13]

The ideal of the Puritan churches of Massachusetts, which soon emerged as the New England Way, was to approximate the pure

11 William Kellaway, *The New England Company, 1649–1776: Missionary Society to the American Indians* (New York, 1961), gives an account of the efforts that were made to convert the Indians to Christianity.

12 Alden T. Vaughan, *New England Frontier: Puritans and Indians, 1620–1675* (Boston, 1965), describes the war and the events leading up to it. For a briefer version, see Howard Bradstreet, *The Story of the Pequot War Retold* (New Haven, Conn., 1933).

13 Alden T. Vaughan, "Pequots and Puritans: The Causes of the War of 1637," *William and Mary Quarterly*, XXI (Apr., 1964), 256–269.

church to the extent humanly possible. The Donatist view was that on earth there could be a group of worshipers constituting a church without spot or wrinkle, but the more worldly St. Augustine envisaged two: an invisible church that included only those destined for salvation and a visible church that would receive many not destined for salvation, including even some sinners. Such a church would labor to maintain purity by instruction, admonition, expulsion, and imposition of penance. Sects like the Anabaptists were not satisfied with this degree of compromise, and they excoriated the Puritans, who took the middle view, for not believing in perfect purity.

The Puritans, for their part, criticized the Anglican Church for its ignorance and neglect, exposing its errors and labeling its clergy as incompetent. Since the bishops would not expel the wicked, Puritans insisted that the individual churches had to accept that responsibility. A true church to them was a group of believers "gathered out of the world," who would elect their own officers and rid the congregation of the wicked. Neither Queen Elizabeth nor King James would undertake reform. The Separatists broke away and formed their own churches, but the Puritans held back for reasons of loyalty and because they did not believe that they could equate a visible church with the invisible, which was confined to those predestined for salavation. Nevertheless, the action taken by the Separatists forced the Puritans to rethink their ideas.

The Separatists, like the Puritans, believed that a church could not be formed by governmental compulsion but only by the free consent of the good. A national church was not, in their judgment, a gathering of true believers. Moreover, if a church could not discipline or expel wayward members, it was no church at all. A Separatist "gathered church" was beholden to no hierarchy and imposed no tithing. Its worship was spontaneous, with election and ordination in the hands of the congregation, and with freedom to question the minister. Above all, the Separatist faith required an understanding and belief in the Christian doctrine, coupled with exemplary behavior.

The Separatists held that "saving grace" was necessary for entrance into the invisible church but admitted that it was not within everyone's grasp, for it lay in the heart where only God

could discern it. A demonstration of saving grace, developed later
by the Massachusetts Bay Puritans, was not a Separatist requirement. The visible church could not and should not examine into
the hearts of its members. Children were accepted as members on
a provisional basis and were admitted to the Lord's Supper as soon
as they were old enough to examine themselves. They then made a
profession of faith, gave assent to the covenant, and became members. Outsiders were similarly admitted. Thus the Separatists occupied themselves with good works and good behavior, but their
leaders believed it beyond human capacity to probe further.[14]

John Cotton, teacher of the Boston Church, began to be concerned with "saving faith" in 1633, arguing that the church covenant on any other basis was a covenant of works only.[15] Other
ministers accepted the doctrine by 1635, and it spread throughout
Massachusetts Bay and into Connecticut and New Haven. This was
the beginning of the New England Way, and its genesis had a
long history. A whole morphology of conversion developed wherein
each individual could check his present condition by a set of
recognizable signs. The Puritans ventured where the Separatists
held back, for the latter did not believe that individual men could
discover their prospects for salvation. As Protestants, the Puritans
believed in predestination: one did not know whether or not one
was predestined to salvation, but rigid self-examination could reveal
clues. Justification—the imputation of Christ's righteousness to
man—depended on faith, not works, and sanctification—the improvement of man's behavior in obedience to God—was the product
of justification. Sanctification would not in itself guarantee salvation, but it could be a sign that one was saved. Thus the ministers
set their listeners to detecting signs of a saving faith. William
Perkins, a famous English divine, and his associates developed a
morphology of saving faith in progressive steps and concluded that
without saving faith—knowledge, conviction, faith, combat, and
true, imperfect assurance—there was no hope of salvation.

14 Edmund S. Morgan, *Visible Saints: The History of a Puritan Idea* (New
York, 1963), pp. 1–73. See also the writings of Perry Miller, *Orthodoxy in Massachusetts,* and *Errand into the Wilderness* (Cambridge, Mass., 1956).
15 Emery Battis, *Saints and Sectaries: Anne Hutchinson and the Antinomian
Controversy in the Massachusetts Bay Colony* (Chapel Hill, N.C., 1962), pp.
28–35, analyzes John Cotton's theological thought.

John Cotton and his disciples decided that evidence of grace in the heart—saving faith—was necessary for church membership. They associated it with the sacrament of communion and decided that only those possessing saving grace were fit to participate in communion. The routine they developed required a candidate for membership to have a personal interview with an elder. If the applicant demonstrated satisfactory knowledge of the doctrine and if he gave adequate evidence of his religious experience, he then had to subject himself to inquiry by the whole congregation. Candidates whose brief narrations convinced the congregation that God's saving grace was within them would then be tendered the convenant by the ruling elder. This pattern became universal, and the general court gave it official approval in 1636, adopting a law confining freemanship to those who had passed the new tests.

The demand for signs of saving grace gave the New England churches their unique character. In order to found a church, at least seven men, each satisfied with the others' knowledge of the doctrine, good behavior, and experience with saving faith, would interview the neighboring ministers and even the magistrates. If they received approval of their application, they could then subscribe to the covenant and elect a minister or a teacher, ruling elders, and deacons. As qualified candidates appeared, the congregation could elect additional members.[16]

There was some opposition to adoption of the New England Way. It is thought that John Winthrop's failure to be reelected governor and Roger Williams' banishment from Salem were connected with their lukewarm attitudes. Thomas Hooker of Connecticut thought the tests too strict and the strides to achieve an invisible church on earth too great. The Reverend Thomas Worsham, who led a congregation from Dorchester to Windsor in 1635, sided with Hooker, and Connecticut never did make church membership a condition of freemanship. However, the founder of New Haven, John Davenport, accepted the morphology of saving faith wholly, and church membership became a requirement for freemanship in the New Haven Colony. Roger Williams, the founder of Rhode Island, insisted as long as he stayed in Massachusetts on

16 Wertenbaker, *Puritan Oligarchy*, pp. 58–68, gives additional information about the organizing and operation of New England Puritan churches.

a greater degree of purity than did other ministers, but he was an extremist on all subjects. He and Anne Hutchinson, who led the largest group of emigrants to Rhode Island, demanded the severest tests, and the volatile Williams, who was forever changing his religious opinions, finally attained perhaps the ultimate in strictness when he decided that only he and his wife together could constitute a true church.

The Massachusetts Puritans made a supreme effort to reduce the gap between God and man, and the colony stood as the farthest outpost in its striving toward ecclesiastical holiness. It disclaimed as sacrilegious those who, like Roger Williams and Anne Hutchinson, insisted on making huge jumps, but the New England Puritans hoped to make themselves as pure as humans could. They thought they were succeeding, but as Edmund S. Morgan remarks, "the world has many ways of defeating those who try to stand too far from it."[17]

The Bay Colony contained twenty-three churches in 1645. Each church chose its own pastor, who preached, and its teacher, who instructed in matters of doctrine. These two men, whose duties were virtually indistinguishable, were called teaching elders. The ruling elders, who also knew their theology well, ordered meetings, visited, and saw that the faithful maintained godliness. The deacons looked after the finances of the church and its charities. The congregation elected the pastor, who was then ordained by the leaders. The services consisted of psalms and hymns, prayers, and the holding of communion. There were also lecture days during the week to supplement the Sabbath service. The admission of a new member was a solemn event. Delinquents received summary treatment: they were first admonished, then censured by vote of the entire church. If these measures proved ineffective, they were excommunicated, and when this occurred, the pastor, in the name of Jesus Christ, delivered the sinning member over to Satan—a fearful sentence.[18]

When differences of opinion occurred, discussion was arranged for; if this failed, the clergy and even the magistrates came in to

[17] *Visible Saints,* pp. 73–112. Another stimulating discussion of New England religious attitudes is Alan Simpson, *Puritanism in Old and New England* (Chicago, 1955).

[18] Ola Elizabeth Winslow, *Meetinghouse Hill, 1630–1783* (New York, 1952), describes religion in New England at the community level, stressing the way in which the meetinghouse helped establish and maintain the patterns of conformity.

act as peacemakers. When on occasion an individual church could not eradicate the corrupt opinion and suspicious practice in its midst, the Puritans appealed to the magistrates, "the nursing fathers amongst us," who would convene an assembly of elders. The contending factions then stated their positions, the elders declared their opinion, and anyone else could express his view without fear of reprisal. Debate continued until all were satisfied. Should the offending church remain recalcitrant, fellowship was withdrawn. The Cambridge Platform of 1648 first brought together the rules governing the management and disciplining of churches. Polity rather than doctrine was of maximum interest during this period.[19]

The relatively small number of church members formed the ruling element, and they were determined to keep the faith pure even if it meant purging the colony of undesirables. Some of the people offensive to them opposed the government, some lacked respect for the magistrates, and others were immoral in the eyes of Puritans because they inveighed against the clergy. Religious groups such as the Anabaptists, Familists, and rigid Separatists who had infiltrated the colony were more serious and more dangerous, and those of them who remained obstinate were banished. Jesuits, an even greater menace, were debarred from entering the colony. Of the greatest concern of all were the "Remonstrants," those Puritans who took exception to some of the cherished tenets of the Puritan creed, and the most important of these were Roger Williams, Anne Hutchinson, and Dr. Robert Child. The result of controversies with these three, which lasted from 1635 to 1660 and concluded with the harsh treatment accorded the Quakers, was a victory for the orthodox party, and a rigid and schismless Puritanism was established that lasted for nearly a century.[20]

Born of an upper-middle-class family in London, Roger Williams

[19] The literature on the theory and practice of Puritanism is, of course, enormous. The essay "The Puritan Way of Life" in Perry Miller and Thomas H. Johnson (eds.), *The Puritans* (2 vols., rev. ed., New York, 1963), I, 1–63, is particularly illuminating. Perry Miller, *The New England Mind: The Seventeenth Century* (Cambridge, Mass., 1954), pp. 365–491, gives a detailed analysis of covenant theology and the Puritans' peculiar outlook. James Truslow Adams, *The Founding of New England* (Boston, 1949), pp. 64–85, is an interpretation by a scholar unfriendly to Puritanism. See also Daniel J. Boorstin, *The Americans: The Colonial Experience* (New York, 1958), 3–31.

[20] Andrews, *Colonial Period*, I, 462–470. In connection with the topic of misbehavior, see Emil Oberholzer, Jr., *Delinquent Saints: Disciplinary Action in the Early Congregational Churches of Massachusetts* (New York, 1956).

was graduated from Pembroke College, Cambridge, in 1627, and became a chaplain in Essex. He married Mary Barnard in 1629, and a year later they arrived in Massachusetts, where he accepted appointment as assistant at the church in Salem. Williams became acting pastor there and then, in 1635, pastor. At the age of thirty-three he had become known as a man of integrity and good intentions but also as excitable and impulsive, qualities destined to get him repeatedly into trouble. Very soon he sponsored an extreme form of Separatism in church polity and held to his views with all the zeal of youth. Although he was of course a church member, Williams never became a freeman, and he thus stood somewhat apart from those responsible for the government and the preservation of the orthodox faith. As a nonfreeman, his views were not restrained by the oath of fidelity to the commonwealth. He upheld religious liberty but not as an advocate of religious toleration. He also denied the validity of the Massachusetts charter, a sore point in a colony that lived in dread of interference from England. The young minister outraged the authorities by arguing that the power of magistrates extended only to the bodies, worldly goods, and outward state of man, but not to offenses against the first four commandments. [21]

The town of Salem requested an assignment of land from the general court in 1635 and received a refusal, probably because Williams had been ordained there in spite of protests by a number of churches. Williams, with the consent of his church, sent letters of admonition to the other Massachusetts congregations, accusing the magistrates of "sundry heinous offenses." He then informed his own church that unless it agreed to separate from other churches, he would separate from it. Salem declined to follow its impetuous minister to that extreme, so Williams then refused to attend the church assembly or to have religious communion with his congregation. He started a meeting in his own house, where he carried Separatism to extreme lengths. Accepting Williams' challenge, the general court ordered the Salem deputies in September, 1635, to force the freemen of the town to apologize or otherwise give satisfaction for the letters Williams had sent with their approval. On October 9 it ordered Williams to leave Massachusetts and not return

[21] Biographies of Roger Williams are listed in footnote 2 on page 211.

without the permission of the court. Thus banished from civil jurisdiction, Williams voluntarily withdrew from the church.[22]

Williams was an individualistic intellectual who plowed a lonely furrow. In Massachusetts he accepted the church with its emphasis on a good moral life, its religious tenets, and its discerning of God's saving grace. He held dearly the ideal of a pure church restricted to saints only. He insisted, however, that the Massachusetts churches must disavow the Church of England, because it was an impure church refusing to repent of its sins. His ideal of a pure church led him to repudiate the Massachusetts churches and finally even his own church at Salem. Once in Rhode Island, his view of church membership narrowed further, leading to the ultimate absurdity that there could be no true church at all. He believed, too, that the pope was antichrist and that there was no way to restore the true church until antichrist was destroyed. Until Christ returned and appointed his ministers, there could be no church. All of his contemporaries disagreed with him.[23] They argued that the church was not wholly extinct under the pope and that even the English church did maintain an existence, shabby though it was, as a visible church. They denied that the minister had to trace his commission directly to Christ. They rested the validity of the existing churches on the continuity of the church, however precarious, throughout the reign of antichrist. Williams could never discover any way to restore the true church and concluded, "There could be no church of Christ in the existing state of the world."

The state was linked to Williams' thinking about the church, and his reasoning pointed toward a daring concept of government. Inasmuch as God acted upon men and not men upon God, it was blasphemous to believe that the Puritans could make God a party to a convenant simply by saying that they were doing so. Government, he held, was good in that it protected lives and property, but

22 Edmund S. Morgan, *The Puritan Dilemma: The Story of John Winthrop* (Boston, 1958), pp. 115–132, gives an account of these events.

23 The chief spokesman for the orthodox position was John Cotton, and his controversy with Roger Williams is discussed in Larzer Ziff, *The Career of John Cotton: Puritanism and the American Experience* (Princeton, N.J., 1962), pp. 85–90, 212–216, 251. On this same subject see also the probing comparison of their theological theories in Jesper Rosenmeier, "The Teacher and the Witness: John Cotton and Roger Williams," *William and Mary Quarterly*, XXV (July, 1968), 408–431.

it should not pretend to bring God into the process. This assertion was revolutionary and disturbing, since John Winthrop had announced to all that God had ratified His covenant with the Massachusetts colonists by selecting them as a special people and bringing them safely to the New World. But if God were not a party to such an agreement, as Williams contended, no people could enforce His religion, because God did not condone force. A state church that enforced Christianity was in fact a contradiction in terms. Williams' opponents naturally charged that by depriving the government of its divine mission, he was undermining its authority. He replied that his was the conservative position, theirs the radical one. He persisted in arguing that government was an instrument of civilization and that without it men would revert to barbarism and wickedness. It was in religious matters only, he said, that government had absolutely no authority.

Williams' arguments are deceptive, not because of their substance, but by virtue of their relentless rationality. He would support a government attacked by Indians, but he was unwilling to support one when it was the attacker. He rejected the Puritan claim that theirs was a holy cause, that they were God's people, and that their armies were the armies of God. Reason is constructive, writes Edmund S. Morgan, but also subversive. If it supports government in one instance, it may undermine it in the next. So, Morgan concludes, Williams' claim to conservatism breaks down; his "rationality," even couched in his obscure, involved, and awkward prose, remains thrilling, noble, and seditious. John Winthrop and Perry Miller were both right in considering him a dangerous man.[24]

The years 1635–37 were turbulent: England was threatening to recall the charter; important men like the Reverend Thomas Hooker, Reverend Samuel Stone, Reverend John Davenport, and William Pynchon were dissatisfied and were leaving the colony; and there was the problem posed by Roger Williams and his disturbing ideas. Complaints were reaching England about the persecuting spirit in the colony; in the colony itself, the deputies were striving for more power from the magistrates. There was also the Pequot War, and there were threats from the French. To its leaders the young colony seemed beset by dangers, and its religious life appeared to be in

[24] Edmund S. Morgan, "Miller's Williams," *New England Quarterly*, XXXVIII (Dec., 1965), 513–523.

jeopardy. Greatest among all the difficulties was the Antinomian controversy.

In 1634 the amazing Anne Hutchinson and her husband and children arrived in the colony.[25] Young Harry Vane came in 1635, and the next year Anne's brother-in-law, the Reverend John Wheelwright, brought his family. All of them became members of the Boston church, of which John Wilson was the pastor and John Cotton the teacher. Soon Mrs. Hutchinson, who had been a member of John Cotton's former church in Lincolnshire, began to stir up trouble. She possessed a dominating personality and a gift of disputation. She proceeded, like Roger Williams, to gather small groups in her own home and then announce her unflattering findings regarding the church, where before long she made herself an unwelcome member. The Antinomians were those, in New England, who refused to accept the requirements of the New England Way or to conform to its practices to attain salvation. They denied that outward concurrence unaccompanied by a truly devout inner life was a sufficient test of true religion. They questioned whether churchgoing, obedience (as defined by the Puritan leaders), and good works (characterized by John Cotton as secret prayer, family exercises, reverence toward ministers, glorification of the Sabbath, attendance at sermons, diligence in calling, and honesty in dealing) were necessary duties of a Christian.

Mrs. Hutchinson was a "perfectionist," believing that the Holy Spirit dwells in every man, and she denied the need of any evidence of sanctification other than the realization of Christ in oneself, conscientiously and exhilaratingly felt. For her this indwelling of Christ was far more important than the outward manifestation of good works. One was not a Christian by works, but by virtue of the Spirit prevailing within one. This was the "inner light" of the mystics, the Quakers, and other evangelical sects from time immemorial.

The magistrates resented Mrs. Hutchinson's attacks on the existing system and the support she received from Wheelwright and from Vane, who was elected governor in 1636. At this time John Cotton was pushing the doctrine of saving faith. The magistrates were

---

[25] Battis, *Saints and Sectaries,* is a recent biography of Mrs. Hutchinson containing a dramatic account of her conflict with the Massachusetts authorities, with significant psychological insights.

especially angered by the easy road to salvation offered by the Antinomians. This doctrine seemed to destroy the obligation to lead a
moral life or to be bound by the law of the Scriptures, by written
covenants, or by the teaching of the clergy. Moreover, the Antinomians would not accept proofs taken from the Bible as valid.
To them religion was not a matter of demonstration but of pure
faith. Justification and sanctification came not from works but
from faith in Christ alone. All this was also anathema to the Puritan
theologians. At first they tried to convince the followers of the
covenant of grace of the error of their ways. John Cotton, whose
preaching had always had a marked influence on Mrs. Hutchinson,
was partly in agreement with her, but finally, after much soul-
searching, he turned against her. But Wheelwright, Vane, and a
large group in Boston stood by Mrs. Hutchinson when the controversy reached its height in 1637.[26]

The Antinomians and Mrs. Hutchinson sponsored the Reverend
John Wheelwright as assistant pastor of the Boston church, hoping
to use him as a wedge for the reform movement. This attempt failed,
and Wheelwright withdrew to the church at Braintree. He spoke at
the Boston church by invitation in January, 1637, and used the
occasion to denounce those who espoused the covenant of works.
The alarmed magistrates decided to bring Wheelwright to trial for
sedition, or, as they put it, for "kindling" the people. Some forty
members of the Boston church then petitioned the magistrates to
confine themselves to secular matters and not to interfere with the
consciences of men, and they also asked the authorities to throw open
the trial to the public. The general court, supported by the clergy
of the colony, at first refused these requests, but the anticlerical
party, which opposed such highhanded methods, won the day, and
the trial was made public.

The general court found Wheelwright guilty of sedition and contempt of authority, but because not all the members agreed with this

[26] Bernard Bailyn, *New England Merchants in the Seventeenth Century* (Cambridge, Mass., 1955), pp. 39–44, points out the extent to which Mrs. Hutchinson
drew her strength from merchants, who, the author argues, fought Puritanism
from the start and were ready to accept Antinomianism as part of their protest
against restrictions. Battis, *Saints and Sectaries*, pp. 258–271, describes the core
group of her supporters as thirty-eight men, mostly church members and freemen
living in Boston, including a high percentage of merchants, skilled craftsmen,
and professional men.

verdict, sentence was deferred. Governor Vane, who had led Wheelwright's defense, then prepared himself for a second round. He was due to come up for reelection by the general court in May, and the campaigning became so virulent that a decision was made to move the meeting of the court to Newtown (Cambridge) to avert a public uprising. When the meeting convened, the court first considered whether or not to take up a petition in Wheelwright's behalf before proceeding with the election. This move had Vane's support, and when Winthrop as leader of the opposition succeeded in blocking it, the final outcome of the election was presaged. The removal to Newtown, away from the influence of the Boston freemen, had proved the decisive factor, and the Antinomians were roundly beaten. The defeated Vane left the colony in August, 1637, a disillusioned young man, and his departure left Wheelwright without his chief supporter and protector.

The victors called a synod in September to settle the Antinomian controversy, and twenty-five ministers met at Newtown with all magistrates. The participating clergymen included Hooker and Stone from Connecticut and also Davenport, who had recently arrived from England. The group stayed in session twenty-four days and brought to light and condemned eighty-two errors, although not unanimously. The meeting produced no statesmanlike body of doctrine, and its only end result was the creation of long-lasting climate of bitterness. Winthrop glossed over the situation and piously spoke of "the Lord having been graciously present and all matters having been carried on so peaceably and concluded so comfortably in all love."[27] His suggestion that such conferences be renewed went unheeded. Wheelwright, unsilenced, had to be banished. Anne Hutchinson, whose weekly meetings of sixty women the synod condemned as disorderly, continued to denounce the clergy. John Cotton, under pressure, returned to the ranks of the orthodox. But popular opposition continued, and the orthodox leaders, fearing that the general court elected in May would not prove amenable, dissolved it in gross violation of the charter and ordered a new election. The orthodox party triumphed and then, from its new position of strength, purged William Aspinwall and John Coggeshall, two popular Boston deputies. Coggeshall was disenfranchised and

[27] Quoted in Andrews, *Colonial Period,* I, 484.

threatened with banishment, and Aspinwall and Wheelwright were actually ejected from the colony.

Anne Hutchinson came to trial in March, 1638, in a Newtown church crowded with spectators. Forty members of the court were present, including Winthrop, and so, too, were many members of the clergy, including John Wilson, Cotton, Thomas Welde, Hugh Peter, John Eliot, and Thomas Shepard. Mrs. Hutchinson's accusers conducted anything but a fair trial, it being an examination in which the inquisitors sought responses that would convict the witness.[28] The field of inquiry was theological, pertaining to matters normally beyond the competence of any legislative body, but in the Bay Colony church purity was regarded as essential to the safety of the state. The preeminence of the clergy appeared to be at stake, for it was alleged that Mrs. Hutchinson had traduced the ministers, denied the soundness of their judgments, and dishonored them publicly. Giving support to opinions contrary to those held by the colony's leaders also seemed to flout authority. In addition, her activities had succeeded in stirring up a good deal of discontent.

The accused woman dealt with her accusers steadily and with moderation, and for a long period she successfully avoided their traps. She demanded that those who testified against her do so under oath, a request that the court summarily rejected. Toward the close in a moment of exaltation, she asserted that what she said was by an immediate revelation—"the mouth of the Lord hath spoken it." This prophetic utterance destroyed her. Even John Cotton, the waverer, thought her deluded, and Thomas Dudley decided that the devil had taken possession of her. She did retain some supporters until the end, because she was a profoundly religious woman. William Coddington denied the equity of the proceedings, and William Colborn, a Boston delegate, held that censure was the only reasonable verdict. The general court, however, condemned her "to be banished out of our jurisdiction as being a woman not fit for our society."[29]

[28] Indeed, Edmund S. Morgan calls it "the least attractive episode in John Winthrop's career." *Puritan Dilemma*, p. 147.

[29] There are a number of accounts of the trial, including Charles Francis Adams, *Three Episodes of Massachusetts History* (2 vols., rev. ed., New York, 1965), I, 363–532, and II, 533–578; Andrews, *Colonial Period*, I, 476-487; Morgan,

The colony had survived two serious attacks, but these contributed to the great constitutional and legal changes, some of which have been alluded to, that took place during the decade. Many of the deputies and a large portion of the inhabitants were restless and refused to be stilled. The elimination of the "negative vote," the separation of the two houses, the demand for a broader franchise, the persistent efforts to draw up and publish the laws, and the pressure to minimize the influence of the clergy were all related to the general dissatisfaction. The next controversy, that involving Dr. Robert Child and the Remonstrants, was, like the others, partly political and partly religious, concerning as it did both the colony's political independence and the issue of religious toleration. For four years in England, from 1643 to 1647, the Presbyterians controlled Parliament, until purged by the Independents. During this period of ascendancy, the Presbyterians abolished episcopacy, introduced the Westminister Catechism, and set up an ecclesiastical form of government after the Presbyterian plan. In New England the trend was in the opposite direction, because the New England Way was close to the method espoused by the Independents. The Presbyterians had no official standing in Massachusetts, but they now determined to make themselves heard.

When the ministers at Newbury set up innovations based on Presbyterian practices in 1643, a Puritan assembly ordered them to stop, on the ground that Parliament might attempt to impose Presbyterianism on the colony. The Reverend Peter Hobart, in a dispute over a militia election in 1645, charged that the government was exceeding its powers and violating the charter, which he held was no more than that of a corporation in England. This led to a counter-charge that Hobart was managing church affairs without consulting his congregation, "being of a Presbyterial spirit." Then in May, 1646, Dr. Robert Child and the Remonstrants presented a petition to the general court that attempted to nullify the charter and reduce the colony to absolute dependence on the Presbyterian Parlia-

Puritan Dilemma, pp. 134–154; and Richard B. Morris, *Fair Trial: Fourteen Who Stood Accused, From Anne Hutchinson to Alger Hiss* (New York, 1952), pp. 3–32. See also, James F. Maclear, "'The Heart of New England Rent': The Mystical Element in Early Puritan History," *Mississippi Valley Historical Review*, XLII(Mar., 1956), 621–652, which analyzes the reasons why the colony would not permit nonconformity.

ment. Child, a young man with a medical degree from Padua, came to New England in 1641, returned to England, then came back in October, 1645. He knew what had happened in England, was an ardent Presbyterian, and soon became a man of influence in Boston. He persuaded six well-known men to join him in signing his petition. This remonstrance declared that conditions were bad, that the people were discontented, and that the only solution was to change the administration of affairs to conform to English models and to permit the Presbyterian system in the churches. Unless their demands were met, the Remonstrants threatened to appeal to Parliament.[30]

The growing discontent alarmed the General Court, which endeavored to meet the charges of arbitrary government by broadening the franchise in 1647, by completing the revision of the laws a year later, by tax reform, and by other measures. The court, however, reacted unfavorably to the action taken by Child and his friends, seeing them as conspirators seeking to overthrow the government, establish a state Presbyterian system, and make the Commonwealth dependent upon the English government. The court haled the signers, only two of whom were Presbyterians, before it, found them guilty, and fined them.[31] Three magistrates, Richard Bellingham, Richard Saltonstall, and Simon Bradstreet, and five deputies opposed the verdict. When an appeal was rejected, the Remonstrants tried to carry it to England, but their ship was searched before departure, and two petitions and other subversive material were found. One of the petitions demanded liberty of conscience and the appointment of a governor general. The other one also requested a royal governor and in addition pleaded for settled churches according to the Presbyterian system. Another document asked whether the charter had been violated and whether the Puritan leaders were guilty of treason to the crown. The Massachusetts authorities seized Child, bound him over to the next court, and fined him the enormous sum of £200 in 1647. Four of the other signers were also fined, while the fifth escaped to England. Edward Winslow was hastily dispatched to

---

[30] See George Lyman Kittredge, "Dr. Robert Child the Remonstrant," *Massachusetts Colonial Society Publications*, XXI (1919), 1–146, and Morris, "Massachusetts and the Common Law," pp. 443–453. Biographical information about Child will be found in Morison, *Builders of the Bay Colony*, pp. 244–268.

[31] Bailyn, *New England Merchants*, pp. 105–111, finds that Massachusetts merchants gave Child his backing.

England to anticipate any damaging action, because a copy of the petitions had been sent by another ship. The commissioners wisely decided not to encourage appeals from the colony, and so Massachusetts survived its current dangers, emerging so strong that it was not seriously threatened again until 1684.

In their quest for holiness through the medium of the doctrine of saving grace, the New England churches were, even before 1650, withdrawing from the world. Their anxiety over this one aspect of their religion caused them to neglect another of the great duties of a Christian church—spreading the gospel and offering all men the means of salvation. Admittedly, many sinners arrived during the Great Migration, and even more people came who were visibly good but lacked the experience of saving grace. In abdicating Christian responsibility toward these newcomers, the Puritans left to the state the task of disciplining those whom they excluded. They not only designed their churches for the saved, but they forbade the establishment of rival churches. Outsiders and their families could not receive baptism or the Lord's Supper. Except for Thomas Hooker of Connecticut and John Eliot, who undertook conversion of the Indians, the church was interested only in those who had already attained saving grace, yet paradoxically, a 1646 Massachusetts law required everyone to attend the preaching of sermons.

By 1640 the church had to recognize the problem created by members' children. God required their baptism, but granting them membership at that time would imply a presumption of saving faith in every child. This solution would have been comforting, but unfortunately no Christian could argue that saving grace was hereditary. The Cambridge Platform wrestled with this problem but ended by taking an evasive position, arguing that each church had to work out its own arrangements. One could not become a member of a congregation until he gave evidence of saving grace, which was not an easy accomplishment, and only then was he admitted to the sacrament. But if a person did not experience saving grace, and many did not, should he be expelled? This step was unspeakable. Thus by the 1650's adherence to the doctrine of saving faith was causing a sharp decline in church membership, to the point where soon the majority of the population would be unbaptized. This prospect was truly alarming to all serious Puritans.

At a meeting of ministers in 1657 and at a called assembly, or synod, in 1662, new efforts were made to solve the ecclesiastical dilemma, and the famous Halfway Covenant was adopted, dealing with the limited question of members' children. In seven propositions it was agreed that the churches were responsible for children; that they should baptize them, although not admitting them to Holy Communion without further qualifications; and that those baptized in the church could continue partial membership without saving grace, providing they led lives free from scandal, professed the doctrine of Christianity, and voluntarily submitted to God and His Church ("owning the Covenant"). These concessions were made to accommodate the well-meaning but wayward offspring of the faithful. Adults could continue in the church, retaining the status they had enjoyed as children. Since they were not accepted as full members, however, they could not participate in the Lord's Supper, nor could they vote in church affairs. They gained two privileges as halfway members: baptism for their children and the benefits of church discipline. Skeptics dubbed this solution the Halfway Covenant. Supporters rationalized by arguing that baptism was not as exclusive a sacrament as the Lord's Supper, which they were sure they had to protect. The Reverend Richard Mather argued that this "watching over" would produce the desired results. Another interested observer, John Davenport of New Haven, was not convinced.

Edmund S. Morgan contends that the Halfway Covenant was not a sign of decline or a betrayal of standards, but was in fact an honest attempt to rescue the concept of a church of visible saints from problems created by the advent of second-generation children. Its adoption, however, marks the end of the period when, by the tests of saving faith, the Massachusetts Puritans pushed the New England Way to its outermost limits. The Halfway Covenant enabled the Puritans to keep within the church a multitude that might otherwise have deserted it. The compromise demonstrated a willingness to think a little more about the need to gather new members and a little less about those already gathered. It was in part a recognition of the church's evangelical function. During the generation after 1660, the ramparts of the saints weakened badly, but that is another story.[32]

[32] Morgan, *Visible Saints*, pp. 112–138.

The Bay Colony's period of most rapid growth was from 1630 to 1642. Seventeen ships brought 1,500 people in 1630; there were 6,000 settlers by 1636; and by 1642 the total was possibly as high as 15,000. Several historians have estimated the population in 1665 at 25,000.[33] Many of the troubles that arose before the end of the Great Migration in 1642 resulted from problems relating to the necessity of absorbing so many settlers in such a brief time. A long lull in immigration began in 1642. Reform efforts by the Long Parliament in England made some men more willing to stay on there, while others went into the army once the civil war started. The war itself prevented laborers from leaving, and the colony's unsavory reputation for persecution discouraged persons of all classes. This break in the intercourse with England severely depressed prices. Men could not meet their obligations and fell into debt, and foreign commodities became expensive, with the result that the general court saw fit to regulate both prices and wages. Exports dwindled, and many men lost confidence. Some pushed into the interior; others left for Virginia, Barbados, and New Amsterdam, while many returned to England.[34] It was a period of considerable movement from one place to another, but in the final analysis neither Massachusetts nor the other New England settlements lost any considerable number of people.

The colonists located their earliest settlements at likely points along the shore of Massachusetts Bay or at short distances inland. There were eleven communities by 1631: Weymouth, Natascot (now Hull), Salem, Charlestown, Boston, Dorchester, Medford, Newtown (now Cambridge), Roxbury, Watertown and Saugus (now Lynn). Twenty-one settlements were in existence in 1642 and thirty-three in 1647, Dedham being the farthest town inland. These plantations, as they were called, were not at first incorporated, but in 1636 the privileges of township status were carefully defined. Before that time, the only act of incorporation consisted in entering the name of the community in the assessment lists. After 1643 each established

---

[33] Darrett B. Rutman, *Winthrop's Boston: Portrait of a Puritan Town, 1630–1649* (Chapel Hill, N.C., 1965), pp. 178–180; and W. F. Craven, *Colonies in Transition,* pp. 15–16.

[34] William L. Sachse, "The Migration of New Englanders to England, 1640–1660," *American Historical Review,* LIII (Jan., 1948), 251–278, describes the flow of people back across the Atlantic during these years.

town was entitled to send one or more deputies to the general court. Population was largely concentrated on or near the seacoast, so that Boston, Charlestown, Dorchester, Roxbury, Watertown, and Newtown in 1644 contained half the population and half the wealth of the colony.[35]

There were five distinguishable social classes in Massachusetts: a few individuals of high rank; a limited number of representatives of the English squirearchy, referred to in the records as "mister"; law-abiding farmers of yeoman rank and skilled tradesmen, both groups generally called "goodmen"; tenants, inferior in position and education; and indentured servants, a coarse and quarrelsome element demonstrating little interest in Puritan theology.[36] Here and there could be found an Irishman, a Jew, or a Negro from Guinea, Providence Island, or the West Indies.[37] The great majority of the inhabitants were of the middle or lower-middle class.

Edmund S. Morgan emphasizes the overwhelming importance of the Puritan family to the ordering of society, and he argues that there was a basic distrust of the family as a socializing agent. Instead of regarding apprenticeship as a rational method of training artisans, he suggests the Puritans placed their children in other households "because they did not trust themselves with their own children," being "afraid of spoiling them by too great affection." Where fathers would indulge, a neighbor would discipline. He discerns a weakness

[35] Andrews, *Colonial Period*, I, 496–500. William Haller, Jr., *The Puritan Frontier: Town-Planting in New England: Colonial Development, 1630–1660* (New York, 1951), provides information on the origins and growth of the earliest settlements.

[36] Lawrence W. Towner, " 'A Fondness for Freedom': Servant Protest in Puritan Society," *William and Mary Quarterly*, XIX (Apr., 1962), 201–219, for a discussion of the servants' antisocial behavior. An analysis of the social structure of the colony will be found in G. Andrews Moriarty, "Social and Geographic Origins of the Founders of Massachusetts," in Albert Bushnell Hart (ed.), *Commonwealth History of Massachusetts, Colony, Province, and State* (5 vols., New York, 1927–30), I, 49–65.

[37] Robert C. Twombly and Robert H. Moore, "Black Puritan: The Negro in Seventeenth-Century Massachusetts," *William and Mary Quarterly*, XXIV (Apr., 1967), 224–242, finds Negroes in the colony as early as 1633 and states that while they received impartial justice, they hovered on the fringes of full participation in social and economic life. Lorenzo J. Greene, *The Negro in Colonial New England, 1620–1776* (New York, 1942), p. 316, estimates that even at the end of the seventeenth century there were probably fewer than a thousand Negroes in New England, most of them in Massachusetts.

in Puritan society in "family tribalism," a selfish preoccupation with the family.[38] David J. Rothman, looking to the Puritans' English and European backgrounds, questions this thesis, pointing out that by the seventeenth century parents abroad preferred to keep their children at home, and that with the decline of apprenticeship the schools stepped in to fill the gap. But apprenticeship was a common way of life throughout New England, particularly, as in the Plymouth Colony, where numerous double and even triple marriages required the placing of firstborn children outside the current family unit.[39]

Among the few gentry were Winthrop himself, lord of Groton Manor; Sir Richard Saltonstall, nephew of a lord mayor of London; Lady Arbella Johnson, sister of the Earl of Lincoln; and Lady Deborah Moody, eventually excommunicated, who became a famous resident of Long Island. The more numerous lesser gentry, some of whom were well connected, included Thomas Gorges, Richard Bellingham, and John Haynes, a governor of Massachusetts and later of Connecticut. The settlers originated in nearly all the English counties, with the largest group from Suffolk in East Anglia, a center of Puritan influence. A surprisingly large number retained property connections in England, freeholds and tenancies, and as time wore on communication with England was reinforced through English merchants and creditors. Massachusetts was in closer touch with the homeland than any other colony, regardless of its desire to keep the political ties as tenuous as possible.

A relatively large number of university men lived in Massachusetts, possibly as many as one hundred. The great majority were, of course, products of Oxford and Cambridge, particularly the latter, since it lay nearer the Puritan centers and afforded a more congenial environment than the Laudian-dominated Oxford. The Cambridge men included Cotton, Hooker, Bradstreet, Nathaniel Ward, Thomas Shepard, Samuel Stone, and John Harvard, and the learning

---

[38] Edmund S. Morgan, *The Puritan Family: Religion and Domestic Relations in Seventeenth Century New England* (New York, 1966), *passim*. An interesting study of family structure in one specific community is Philip J. Greven, Jr., "Family Structure in Seventeenth-Century Andover, Massachusetts," *William and Mary Quarterly*, XXIII (Apr., 1966), 234–256.

[39] David J. Rothman, "A Note on the Study of the Colonial Family," *William and Mary Quarterly*, XXIII (Oct., 1966), 627–634.

possessed by these men, characteristically, was chiefly theological. The Puritan mind, with its intricacies and niceties of doctrine, was a world of its own. It was through the outpouring of theological tracts that some English culture reached the Bay Colony and acted as a cultural stimulus there. Hezekiah Usher kept a bookshop in Boston as early as 1645. A schoolmaster was employed in that town in 1635, and Roxbury, Dorchester, and other communities soon built schools that were supported by public funds. The date of the founding of Harvard was 1636, and three years later a printing press began pouring forth sermons, psalmbooks, and almanacs. A public library was established in Boston Town House in 1657.[40]

Even in this period before the founding of the Royal Society, men in New England as well as Old England were demonstrating the first stirrings of curiosity, feeble to be sure, about the phenomena of nature and the nature of man. Older Puritans, however, firmly held that all that went right or wrong in human affairs was God's will. The God of the Old Testament, they believed, did not hesitate to punish the wayward; moreover, the devil had his tricks, too. The possibilities for objective inquiry were limited in that sort of environment, but the general court permitted Harvard medical students to anatomize the body of a malefactor once every four years, and it set up a quarantine in the harbor in order to prevent epidemics. It warned physicians and midwives in 1649 that they must adopt standard procedures in making deliveries.[41] Nevertheless, credulity reigned, and even John Winthrop accepted the tale that a calf born at Ipswich had three mouths, three noses, and six eyes. Several women who had denied "inherent righteousness," such as Mary Dyer and Mrs. Hutchinson, were cruelly alleged to have given birth to monsters.[42]

[40] Samuel Eliot Morison, The Intellectual Life of Colonial New England (New York, 1956), pp. 27–152, describes education, printing, bookselling, and libraries. The same author furnishes a rich fund of information about higher education in The Founding of Harvard College (Cambridge, Mass., 1935), and Harvard College in the Seventeenth Century (2 vols., Cambridge, Mass., 1936). Bernard Bailyn, Education in the Forming of American Society (Chapel Hill, N.C., 1960), offers some theories on the early role of education, to which some rebuttal is offered in Rothman, "A Note on the Study of the Colonial Family," pp. 627–634.

[41] Morison, Intellectual Life of Colonial New England, pp. 241–276.

[42] Battis, Saints and Sectaries, gives credence to the belief that Anne Hutchinson gave birth to a malformed fetus.

"The natural world," states Charles M. Andrews, "was viewed with the eyes and understanding of a child."[43] Eclipses, comets, and meteors were danger portents, the phases of the moon were factors to be reckoned with, and the signs of the zodiac were held to influence man's future. Earthquakes expressed God's displeasure. One must wait until after 1660 for the scientific attitudes of John Winthrop, Jr., and Increase Mather. "That anything could happen in the physical universe uncontrolled by God was incomprehensible to the Puritan mind."[44] With strict laws against entertainment, plays and players and the like, something very human was left out of Puritan life.

The waning of migration after 1642 relieved certain social and economic pressures, because there was finally time for adjustment and a proper physical distribution of settlers. Especially held in check was the influence of men of strong will that disturbed the peace of the community. More time became available for the organization of communities after the English model. Houses and home lots, with the church and later the schoolhouse in the center, were provided for. The surrounding arable lands were divided into fields and strips with hedged enclosures, largely used for pasture and meadow. The holdings allotted by some towns depended on the size of the family; by others, on the value of ratable income, on the size of the home lots, or on a combination of these factors. The chief object was to give each man a fair share of what the town possessed. Sometimes, when the holdings were of the same size, the assignments were determined by lot. As the town land became exhausted, problems arose over allotments to newcomers and servants.[45] As early as 1635, Boston ruled against setting aside any more land for arrivals unlikely to qualify as church members, and landowners received instructions not to sell any part of their property to men of this type.[46] Every colonial settlement, in and out of Massachusetts, concerned itself with a variety of local problems, such as the care of fences, the building and maintenance of high-

[43] *Colonial Period,* I, 509.
[44] *Ibid.*
[45] Wertenbaker, *Puritan Oligarchy,* pp. 43–57, explains how towns were organized and land was distributed.
[46] Land distribution in Boston is described in detail in Rutman, *Winthrop's Boston,* pp. 68–97.

ways, and the oversight of livestock, especially stray hogs and cattle. Despite the religious controversies, the great majority of men were deeply involved in the acquisition of a home and land and the making of a living.[47]

Massachusetts enjoyed prosperity at first, then fell into an economic slump, and finally revived by developing new types of trade.[48] The Great Migration, which reached its peak in 1638, created the original boom. Arriving immigrants purchased land, equipment, and produce, and the cash they brought enabled merchants to import English wares, especially cloth, apparel, utensils, and tools. The migration played itself out by 1640, and the colony then experienced a widespread depression. As the market for agricultural surpluses fell, prices and even land values plummeted, until Massachusetts lay virtually prostrate.[49] The subsequent commercial revival was almost accidental. Merchants sending wood products, such as clapboards, to Spain, the Canaries, and the Madeiras discovered there in 1642 a great demand for cheap wheat. This trade became substantial by 1647, and ultimately it expanded to include the shipment of wood products, grains, salted beef, and fish. As the West Indies turned to growing sugar to the exclusion of everything else, trade also developed with the Caribbean Islands. Wherever Massachusetts shipped, English merchants were there before them. Bills of credit, needed to purchase English goods, emanated from London; consequently Massachusetts was drawn into the British network of trade.[50] Boston proved a convenient port of call for provisioning both English and foreign ships, and this activity grew to major proportions by 1649.[51]

As the villages and towns became more settled, industrial and commercial activity began. Watermills, windmills, and sawmills

[47] Sumner S. Powell, *Puritan Village: The Formation of a New England Town* (Middletown, Conn., 1963), describes the formation of the Massachusetts town of Sudbury.

[48] The fur trade had an early importance, but it proved to be less satisfactory than had been expected, and it faded fast. Arthur H. Buffington, "New England and the Western Fur Trade, 1629–1675," *Colonial Society of Massachusetts Publications*, XVIII (1915–16), 161–162; Bailyn, *New England Merchants*, pp. 23–32.

[49] Bailyn, *New England Merchants*, pp. 45–49.

[50] *Ibid.*, pp. 82–86; William B. Weeden, *Economic and Social History of New England, 1620–1789* (2 vols., Boston, 1890), I, 117–129.

[51] Darrett B. Rutman, "Governor Winthrop's Garden Crop: The Significance of Agriculture in the Early Commerce of Massachusetts," *William and Mary Quarterly*, XX (July, 1963), 396–415.

soon appeared, as did retail and craft shops. The shops were located at first in private homes and then in buildings erected for the purpose. There were ship carpenters in the colony from the beginning, and John Winthrop's 30-ton vessel was built for the coastal trade as early as 1631. Builders in Salem constructed a 300-ton ship in 1641, and the next year another ship made its maiden voyage to the Canaries. By 1640, shipbuilding and commerce became the leading enterprises in Boston, Charlestown, and Salem. Ships ranging in size from 12 tons to 400 tons sailed the coastal and ocean waters, bringing new wealth to their towns. Wharves, jetties, seawalls, and ferries were common by 1650, and prosperity was general throughout the colony. Emphasis on shipping was not an unmixed blessing, however, because the emergence of a large seafaring element often vexed the souls of the Puritan fathers.

By 1660 New England ships were trading regularly to distant lands. Coastwise vessels went to the Maine settlements and Ferryland in Newfoundland to the north and to New Haven, New Netherland, and Virginia to the south. Oceangoing vessels called at the leading ports of England, Ireland, Holland, France, Portugal, Spain, Italy, and occasionally at the Barbary States and Guinea (for elephant ivory, gold, and a few Negroes). Wine was imported from the Wine Islands of Madeira and the Canaries. The most important overseas trade was with the West Indies, chiefly Barbados, but also Antigua, Nevis, and St. Kitts. This trade was reciprocally highly lucrative for decades, with Massachusetts exporting fish, beef, and grain in exchange for sugar and rum.[52] Many ships calling from port to port did a thriving huckstering business at sea. In addition to importing, Boston became a great distributing center for English goods, especially those destined for the Massachusetts and Connecticut towns. Cotton, sugar, and indigo came from the West Indies and wine from the Canaries and Madeira. France, Spain, and Portugal furnished oil, soap, wines, raisins, lemons, and other fruit, and also a good deal of salt. From England came a great variety of apparel and household goods, a large proportion of which originated in western European lands.[53]

---

[52] A good description of the fishing industry will be found in Weeden, *Economic and Social History*, I, 132–142.

[53] Bailyn, *New England Merchants*, pp. 32–39, and Carl Bridenbaugh, *Cities in the Wilderness* (New York, 1964), pp. 3–139, describe the rise of Boston as a commercial center.

The Boston merchants were energetic, efficient, and foresighted, and they arranged for many salutary regulations governing even the smallest details of business. For example, in 1657 Boston voted that no one except an admitted inhabitant might open a shop or engage in manufacturing, and in 1660 it added the provision that no one might do these things unless he was twenty-one and had served a seven-year apprenticeship. The merchants thus hoped to protect the quality of their trade and commerce.

Barter, commercial paper, and cash all played a part in transacting business outside Massachusetts.[54] Tobacco was exchanged for sugar, for example. Debts were the rule in commerce everywhere, and powers of attorney for collection were freely used from colony to colony. Interest was at 8 per cent per annum. Bills of exchange and promises to pay were common, but cash and barter were even more popular. The settlers brought some hard money from England, but they also made use of Spanish, Portuguese, French, and Dutch coins. Because of the difficulty resulting from the shortage of coin and from clipping, sweating, and counterfeiting, the general court in 1652 voted to establish a mint and to limit legal money to its own coins. Increasing trade also demanded that this step be taken. Silver plate, silver bullion, and silver coins went thereafter for smelting to the mint house of John Hull, who converted them into pine-tree shillings, sixpences, threepences, and twopences.[55] From 1660 onward, Massachusetts became the dominant influence in New England, the center of its trade, and the leader of resistance to the commercial policies of the home government.[56]

The agricultural hinterland responded to the challenge, growing grain and raising cattle which went to Boston, from which point these products were exported. Four of every twenty acres produced crops for the Boston market. Highways were kept open, and Long Island Sound became a great waterway to the hinterland as far as Fairfield, near the New Netherland border, and extending into the

---

[54] As did wampum, whose use is discussed in Weeden, *Economic and Social History*, I, 32–46.

[55] For the story of John Hull and his pine-tree shillings, see Morison, *Builders of the Bay Colony*, pp. 135–182.

[56] Andrews, *Colonial Period*, I, pp. 512–519, for discussion of Boston's commercial activities.

Connecticut River towns, Narragansett Bay, and the Thames. As Boston became more and more dependent on produce from the rural areas, it became known as "Boston in New England." The great Boston fortunes were being laid down in the fifties and sixties. "Here was a new formula for prosperity to replace that which had failed in the 1640's: farmers to produce, merchants to deal in their products, and ships to carry to faraway markets." As a recent scholar sees it, "The paradox posed by historians looking at agriculture and commerce separately disappears."[57]

[57] Rutman, "Governor Winthrop's Garden Crop," pp. 396–415.

CHAPTER 9

Rhode Island

D URING the crowded years from 1630 to 1640, more settlers came to Massachusetts Bay than the colony could absorb. Among so many, it was inevitable that some could not adjust either to the wilderness environment or to the type of political and religious regime imposed by the Puritans. There were many strong-minded and opinionated individualists among the settlers. Even the Puritan leaders disagreed among themselves, Harry Vane and John Winthrop holding different ideas about how the Common-wealth should be organized, and Winthrop, Thomas Dudley, and John Haynes differing about how it should be governed. John Winthrop believed that Dr. Robert Child and the Remonstrants were the most subversive element in the colony and that John Wheelwright was more dangerous than Roger Williams, whom from time to time he advised. John Humfry, William Pynchon, and William Vassall, all signers of the Cambridge agreement of 1629, fell out with Winthrop and the other leaders and eventually left Massachusetts. Pynchon moved to Springfield in 1636 and later criticized the Puritan oligarchy severely in a book which, allegedly for its errors, the general court ordered burned on the Boston Common in 1650.[1] A number remained who steadily opposed the reigning magistrates, but despite this opposition two-thirds remained loyal to the Commonwealth government. It is estimated that by

[1] William Pynchon, *The Meritorious Price of our Redemption, Justification, & c., Cleering it from Some Common Errors, etc.* (London, 1650).

1641 sixty-five Puritan ministers came from England to add strength to the Puritan hierarchy, and the deference paid them made them resentful of opposition. The great majority of the settlers shunned the frontier and remained close to the coast, the bays, and the rivers. Even Dedham and Concord, farthest west, were accessible to streams. Nevertheless, there were always venturesome men, of whom little is known, who explored the waterways and who followed the Indian paths overland.

The founding of new colonies in New England stemmed principally from the overflow of population from Massachusetts. There were a few exceptions, like Milford and Guilford in Connecticut, which were settled by emigrants from England. A large number of those leaving Massachusetts departed either because they were unhappy there or because they were driven out. There is no parallel to this in American colonization, with the possible exception of the small Puritan groups that forsook Virginia for Maryland.

The most famous of the unwilling migrants was Roger Williams, who was "allowed to escape" from Salem in January, 1636.[2] John Winthrop himself advised Williams that there was land free of any patents in the Narragansett Bay country. Leaving Salem, Williams wintered among the Indians and endeavored to establish peace among them. He purchased land from a chief, Massasoit, on the Seekonk River. He was accompanied by Thomas Angell, a relative, and at Seekonk five other émigrés joined them. Governor Edward Winslow warned them that they were trespassing on Plymouth Colony territory, so they moved by canoe to the Great Salt River, an estuary of Narragansett Bay, and settled there on the eastern side, founding a plantation later known as Providence. Whether Williams wished to establish an Indian mission there, or a trading post, or a plantation, we do not know. Nevertheless, when

[2] Williams, as is to be expected, has been the subject of many biographies. Three durable versions of his life which today seem somewhat too uncritical are Vernon L. Parrington, *Main Currents in American Thought: The Colonial Mind, 1620–1800* (New York, 1927); James E. Ernst, *Roger Williams, New England Firebrand* (New York, 1932); and Samuel Brockunier, *The Irrepressible Democrat: Roger Williams* (New York, 1940). More recent works include the well-regarded Ola E. Winslow, *Master Roger Williams: A Biography* (New York, 1957), and Cyclone Covey, *The Gentle Radical: A Biography of Roger Williams* (New York, 1966). Two stimulating analyses of Williams' political and theological thought are Perry Miller, *Roger Williams: His Contribution to the American Tradition* (Indianapolis, 1953), and Edmund S. Morgan, *Roger Williams: The Church and the State* (New York, 1967).

other displaced settlers and their families drifted in, Williams constructed simple shelters along the river. In this disorderly-appearing settlement every head of family received a five-acre home lot and a six-acre field. Williams purchased the land from the Indians out of his meager resources and eventually recouped £30. Like everything else in Rhode Island, the vagueness and inaccuracy of these early grants led to bitter controversy.

Named in appreciation of God's mercy, Providence, unlike Newport, which was founded three years later, prospered very slowly. Its resources were agricultural rather than commercial, and its chief activities by 1641 were the raising of corn, tobacco, swine, goats, and cattle, with wool added by 1666. In the long run, tobacco, which was sent to Boston for export before 1650, and sheep became the agricultural staples of Rhode Island. The population increased gradually.[3] The farmers used hoes and other simple tools, for there were no plows, and household furnishings were meager, with no silver, only wood and pewter. There was no gristmill until 1646, and no bridge across the Moshassuc until 1662.[4] In the beginning the heads of families met once a fortnight to act in the common welfare, and later single men were admitted on an equality with the others. Williams drew up a social compact in which the signers promised to subject themselves to the will of the majority until such time as the crown specified otherwise. The second draft specified that such obedience should be "only in civill things," for Williams was determined that the state should not interfere in religious matters. Moreover, in distributing the land purchased from the Indians, he laid down two rules—first, that every man should have an equal share; second, that the colony was "for those who were destitute especially for conscience's sake."[5]

3 Possibly 2,000 in 1660 compared with perhaps 20,000 in Massachusetts. See Evarts B. Greene and Virginia D. Harrington, *American Population before the Federal Census of 1790* (New York, 1932), pp. 13, 62; F. W. Craven, *Colonies in Transition*, pp. 15–16.

4 Herbert L. Osgood, *The American Colonies in the Seventeenth Century* (3 vols., New York, 1904–7), I, 332–341, provides details about the founding of Providence, while William Weeden, *Early Rhode Island: A Social History of the People* (New York, 1910), pp. 28–44, is excellent for the early growth of the community, 1636–47.

5 *Rhode Island Records*, I, 14, 22, and Howard M. Chapin, *Documentary History of Rhode Island* (2 vols., Providence, R.I., 1916–19), I, 32–40.

William Coddington of Boston was one of those implicated in the Hutchinson controversy, and, although never formally banished, he decided to abandon Massachusetts. In April, 1638, he led a band of settlers including Dr. John Clarke, John Coggeshall, William Aspinwall, and William Dyer by boat to Providence, where Mrs. Hutchinson had preceded them in March. Aided by Williams, Coddington purchased the large island of Aquidneck lying between Narragansett Bay and the Sakonnet River. He and the Hutchinsons and others then laid out a settlement on the northern end, first called Pocasset and later named Portsmouth. Coddington became chief magistrate, and it was agreed that no one was to suffer persecution for religious reasons. Coddington, an Antinomian who later became a Quaker, was wealthy, politically sagacious, and urbane, and he worked harmoniously with the dominating and spiritual-minded Anne Hutchinson for a considerable period of time, but this mutually cooperative spirit could not last.[6] When the Hutchinsons welcomed the radical Samuel Gorton, Coddington, who disliked the man's religious eccentricities and disagreed with his views on government, resented it. While Coddington was absent from the settlement in April, 1639, a minority faction revolted and elected William Hutchinson magistrate in his place. Influenced by Gorton's respect for English law, the signers of a new compact declared themselves "to be loyal subjects of King Charles and in his name to erect ourselves into a Civill body politicke and submit ourselves unto his lawes according to matters of Justice." Coddington's compact had acknowledged only the authority of "Jehovah."[7]

Coddington and his loyal followers, joined by others, then moved by boat to the southern tip of Aquidneck and founded Newport on May 1, 1639. With the consent and advice of three elders, Coddington presided over the new plantation as chief magistrate. The religious freedom prevailing at Providence was maintained also at Newport. It was Coddington's ambition to develop a single, self-contained colony on Aquidneck, distinct from that at Providence, and to that end he obtained the appointment of commissioners

---

[6] Emery Battis, *Saints and Sectaries: Anne Hutchinson and the Antinomian Controversy in the Massachusetts Bay Colony* (Chapel Hill, N.C., 1962), pp. 40–44, traces the European origins of Antinomianism, describing it as "a reaction against the doctrine of good works and the idea of human participation in the regenerative process."

[7] *Rhode Island Records*, I, 52.

who would undertake to bring Portsmouth back into the fold. Union had become a possibility, because by this time Gorton and Mrs. Hutchinson were at odds, and in March, 1640, the two towns agreed to consolidate under a common administration. Two men from each community were chosen assistants, serving under Coddington as governor and William Brenton as deputy governor. The new state proclaimed itself a democracy in 1641 and guaranteed religious liberty to all. The next year it ordered "that the Law of the Last Court made concerning the Lib'tie of Conscience in point of Doctrine is perpetuated."[8] Coddington made a vain attempt in 1643 to obtain a patent for Aquidneck from the crown. Perhaps influenced by his failure, Portsmouth voted unanimously in 1648 to dissolve the union and return to an independent status, thus bringing Coddington's little state to an end after nearly a nine-year career.[9]

Samuel Gorton, who allied himself with Anne Hutchinson against Coddington at Portsmouth, had arrived in Boston in 1637 at the height of the Antinomian controversy. He sought liberty of conscience there, then at Plymouth, and finally at Portsmouth, where he remained for three years. He opposed the union of Newport and Portsmouth bitterly, claiming it to be the work of a minority. Moreover, he was continually being haled into court for challenging the constitutional status of the governing authorities. He was finally presented to the grand jury at Portsmouth for refusing to acknowledge the validity of the government, for maligning the magistrates to their faces, and for generally defying the men in office. They sent him to prison and then banished him from Portsmouth. He had denied the jurisdiction of the courts because they were not held under the authority of a crown charter and were not conducted according to the rules of English common law. On his ejection from Portsmouth, he and his restless followers moved on to Providence, where they were refused the status of freemen.

Gorton's entourage then journeyed to Pawtuxet, several miles to the south, where they encountered John Greene, a youth of twenty, who became one of Gorton's chief disciples. All of them looked for-

8 Chapin, *Documentary History of Rhode Island*, I, 106–115 *passim*.
9 Irving Richman, *Rhode Island: Its Making and Its Meaning* (2 vols., New York, 1902), I, 117–151, is a comprehensive account of the founding of Portsmouth and Newport.

ward to establishing a refuge at Pawtuxet, but Benedict and William Arnold, who held the local land grants, declared that they wanted to unite with Massachusetts.[10] Gorton, dreading what might become of him if such an event transpired, purchased land from the Indians a few miles still farther to the south and founded Shawomet, later renamed Warwick. The crafty Arnolds induced the Indian chief to repudiate the sale, whereupon the Massachusetts commissioners moved into Shawomet territory and, after some resistance, seized Gorton and ten of his band. Ultimately the Boston magistrates condemned Gorton and all twenty-five of his followers for holding erroneous opinions and confined them in irons. This action so shocked the Boston populace that it became necessary to release the prisoners. Actually what motivated the Massachusetts authorities as well as their allies, the Arnolds, was the desire to secure territory on Narragansett Bay. Gorton went to England and obtained an order from the Warwick commissioners instructing the Massachusetts magistrates to cease molesting Shawomet. He then returned, and, although the troubles at Shawomet were far from ended, he was able to live there as an honored resident until 1677, when he died in his eighty-sixth year.[11]

Historians have found Gorton a controversial subject, some celebrating his independence and the firmness of his convictions and others deploring him as an intellectually confused troublemaker. It has been argued that his theological ideas were obscure, but they were in fact no more so than those of many Puritan divines. What he stood for primarily was liberty of conscience, and he denied the right of the civil government to interfere with spiritual matters. Gorton nurtured his own ideas, not those of any sect, and he opposed the formalities and perfunctory worship of the churches. He agreed with Mrs. Hutchinson regarding the doctrine of grace before works but disagreed with her in his conception of Christ, because he believed less in emotionalism than in a rational interpretation of the Scriptures based on sound learning. In his view the Trinity amounted to no more than three manifestations of spiritual distinctions in the nature of Christ. Devoted to English

[10] This Benedict Arnold was the ancestor of the American general and traitor.
[11] Osgood, *American Colonies*, I, 345–352, gives a good account of the founding of Warwick.

law, he urged its adoption as the law of New England, despite the importance the clergy attributed to what they thought was the law of God. It followed logically that he repudiated the authority of the civil magistracy, recognizing as he did that its judicial system was not rooted in English common and statute law. Never denying the people the right to self-government, Gorton did demand that this right be in accord with the rights of Englishmen. He considered charters necessary and respected all claims based on patents and deeds.

Incipient Rhode Island embraced four separate settlements—five if briefly independent Pawtuxet is included. These minuscule states of varying political and religious suasion were primitive, since they operated with land held by Indian purchase and upon agreements or compacts as their only legal warrant for exercising governmental authority. Each one, however, recognized the sovereignty of the king and the superior authority of the crown. Providence, Portsmouth, Newport, and Warwick were separate communities, all with strong-minded leaders for whom cooperation and union were painfully difficult. Bitter rivalries existed, for Newport and Warwick had been formed by separation from the others. Providence and Portsmouth generally sided against Newport, because Coddington never stopped trying to erect a separate government for Aquidneck and the neighboring island of Conanicut, which would have enabled him to control Narragansett Bay.

The key figure in the molding of Rhode Island was not the wealthy Coddington, but Roger Williams, the idealist. In his writing subsequent to 1640, Williams concentrated on the problems of government and religion. In his *Bloudy Tenent*, which was burned, he rejected the church as a part of the state, in opposition to the view held in Massachusetts, Connecticut, and New Haven, and he insisted that the church was bound to several civil institutions that the government was bound to protect.[12] He emphasized liberty of conscience and separation of church and state. In civil matters he conceded the powers of magistrates but demanded that the church be free to regulate its own affairs and also be free from interference by magistrates. The latter, in his opinion, had no right to set up any form of church organization or to punish with

[12] *The Bloudy Tenent, of Persecution, for the Cause of Conscience Discussed* . . . (London, 1644), published in July and ordered burned in August.

church censures. Their authority was solely temporal, he maintained, just as that of the church was spiritual. In religious matters Massachusetts had taken the extreme position that no church upholding any form of organization other than Congregationalism had a right to exist there. Richard Mather in 1643 stated categorically that the Puritan discipline was that of Christ, that it was unalterable, and that it was the only lawful one.[13] Williams, who differed, exhibited a far healthier attitude in his pleas for religious tolerance. The world, he stated, was full of admirable people, some not even Christians, who, though they might differ from him, had every right to live and worship in their own way. He stood for absolute equality where liberty of conscience was concerned. Williams was a great polemicist and was engaged throughout his life in theological controversy.

The state, a commonwealth of families, was to Williams a purely civil institution. People who agreed to live together for their common good alone had the power to elect governors and magistrates. He rejected divine right of government as he rejected the divine character of the Massachusetts magistracy. Magistrates derived their power from the people for only so long as the people wished to retain them in office. Williams believed in individual freedom. This was not freedom to do as one wished, but a privilege bestowed upon one as a member of a community in which the individual had his duties as well as his rights. Charles M. Andrews states that this view, which was given form in the Rhode Island Orders of 1647, was published for the first time in the French constitution of 1792.[14] Surrounded by strong-willed individualists, Williams unfortunately had trouble molding Providence and Rhode Island into his model community.

Roger Williams, like John Eliot, was anxious to proselytize the Indians.[15] He strove to maintain peace among the various tribes and between the white man and the Indian. He personally per-

---

[13] *Church Government and Church-Covenant Discussed* (London, 1643); Charles M. Andrews, *The Colonial Period of American History* (4 vols., New Haven, Conn., 1934–38), II, 19n.

[14] Andrews, *Colonial Period*, II, 20–21.

[15] Eliot was a Cambridge-educated preacher whose famous *Primer or Catechism, in the Massachusetts Indian Languages* was published in 1654, and whose New Testament and Old Testament (the first printing of the Bible in North America) were printed in 1661 and 1663. See sketch of Eliot in Samuel Eliot Morison, *Builders of the Bay Colony* (Boston, 1964), pp. 289–319.

suaded the Narragansetts not to ally with the Pequots, thus preventing what would otherwise have been a major Indian war. He received Indians at his home, and he learned their language. Through they proved burdensome to him and though he could condone little of their conduct, he maintained a close relation with the chiefs of southern New England. He urged Eliot, who at the time was attempting to convert the Indians at Natick, not to relinquish his evangelical labors.

The main troubles with which Williams had to contend came not from the Indians but from his friends and neighbors and from the adjoining colonies of Plymouth and Massachusetts. Rhode Island contained many strongly opinionated men: William Harris, Richard Scott, and Gregory Dexter at Providence; the Hutchinsons at Portsmouth until 1643; William Coddington, John Coggeshall, Nicholas Easton, and Dr. John Clarke at Newport; Samuel Gorton, John Greene, and Randall Holden at Warwick; and the Arnolds at Pawtuxet. These individualists, heading separate communities, strove for local independence and their own religious forms. A strong colony was unthinkable without jurisdiction over the islands in Narragansett Bay, and Coddington on Aquidneck was able for fifteen years to prevent any real progress toward union in Rhode Island. Aided by Coggeshall, a former English silk merchant, and Clarke, a physician of great shrewdness, Coddington had worked to build Portsmouth and Newport into a commercial colony supported by trade with Massachusetts, Plymouth, and New Amsterdam. Williams, on the contrary, knew that any development of Rhode Island depended on mutual cooperation. The situation became threatening in 1643, when both Massachusetts and Plymouth were claiming parts of Rhode Island, and the New England Confederation was organized without including or even recognizing the Providence Plantations. Rhode Island applied for membership in 1644, 1648, and 1655 but was turned down every time on the ground that no stable government existed and that Williams' principles were shocking. All this while, Coddington and the Arnolds were courting Massachusetts, the Indians were threatening, and there was doubt about the legality of the Indian deeds upon which all enterprise was based.

In desperation Williams went to England to try to secure a charter for Rhode Island. Although civil war was raging there, he obtained a patent in 1644 through the influence of the Committee on Foreign Plantations, of which the Earl of Warwick was the head and Cromwell, Pym, and Vane were members. It was while in England that he got into the controversy between Presbyterians and Independents and wrote *The Bloudy Tenent*. In some measure this work sowed the seed for the revolution of 1648 and the victory of the Independents, because it urged liberty of conscience, separation of church and state, and the right of the people to elect their governors. Williams returned to New England in September, 1644, with a patent naming and specifically covering Providence, Portsmouth, and Newport.[16] It was not a full-fledged charter, but it granted these towns sufficient authority in civil matters to rule themselves and others who might settle in any part of the region bounded by Massachusetts and Plymouth and extending into the interior for twenty-five miles. The patent was later construed to include Gorton's community at Warwick. The commission thwarted Coddington's scheme for a separate patent for Aquidneck and for the first time gave legal recognition to the Rhode Island settlements. It is noteworthy that Williams, who ten years before had objected to the Massachusetts charter, now sought one himself. The Rhode Island patent was not very specific, for it did not describe the form the government should take but left the colony free to determine the means of carrying forward its own affairs.[17]

The patent was not immediately put into effect, partly because of uncertainty about the outcome of the civil war. If Charles I won, a patent from Parliament might become worthless, but the battle of Naseby in 1645 removed that danger. In May, 1647, a general assembly called at Portsmouth, composed of freemen from the four towns and with John Coggeshall as moderator, met to organize a government and draw up a body of laws. Under the patents, whose terms Williams certainly influenced, a federal system was created in which the towns became parts of a larger community. They retained corporate rights but had neither legal nor political supremacy. The state thus formed inclined toward central control

16 Dated March 14, 1644. *Rhode Island Records*, I, 143–146.
17 Richman, *Rhode Island*, I, 165–196, gives excellent information about how Williams obtained the charter, and Osgood, *American Colonies*, I, 352–362, analyzes that document and the government it created.

and away from the powerful local forces making for decentralization.

The Acts and Orders of 1647 "constitute one of the earliest programs for a government and one of the earliest codes of laws made in America—and the first to embody the precedents set by the laws and statutes of England throughout."[18] The assembly adopted the laws, set up a government to attend to executive, legislative, and judicial business, and drew a line between the authority of the central government and the towns. The officers, consisting of a president, four assistants, a recorder, a treasurer, and a sergeant, were henceforth to be nominated by the towns and chosen by the court of election each May. The first year the assembly consisted of a meeting of all the freemen of the towns who could attend, a quorum of ten from each settlement being empowered to act with full authority in case a majority of the freemen could not be present. This was essentially democratic government, limited only by the fact that freemanship was restricted to landowners, who were greatly in the majority among the settlers.[19] Moreover, voting on all matters concerning the central government was not at large but by towns. Several provisions were designed to help the towns keep a check on the power of the central government: there were frequent elections, the towns could initiate legislation, an undesirable law could be recalled by popular vote, and measures could be referred to the people before a vote was taken. The last stipulation became overcomplicated and was several times revised as a kind of referendum that was retained until 1663.

The assembly met four times a year, rotating among the towns. After the conclusion of legislative activities, it converted itself

18 *Rhode Island Records*, I, 147–208; Andrews, *Colonial Period*, II, 26.
19 Although Roger Williams insisted on government by consent of the governed, Alan Simpson in "How Democratic Was Roger Williams?" *William and Mary Quarterly*, XIII (Jan., 1956), 53–57, considers that he was a religious rather than a political theorist; and although he wanted no state interference with the practice of religion, he was by no means democratic in his other ideas. James Ernst in *The Political Thought of Roger Williams* (Port Washington, N.Y., 1966), deems him an essentially political thinker who sought to found a democratic commonwealth; while Brockunier, *The Irrepressible Democrat*, and Covey, *The Gentle Radical*, see their subject as a fighter for political democracy. Edmund S. Morgan in his perceptive essay, "Miller's Williams," *New England Quarterly*, XXXVIII (Dec., 1965), 513–523, reveals him as applying "relentless rationality" to government and religion in equal measure.

into a judicial body, superseding the former quarter courts introduced at Aquidneck in 1640 during the union of Portsmouth and Newport. The colony instituted a separate trial court in 1655, which met three times a year in each town in succession. This court tried a large variety of cases, but its work was dilatory, because, as was true in other colonies, men chosen for jury duty tried to avoid serving. In spite of increased fines for nonattendance and threats of distraint of the property of delinquent jurors, the jury system was never very efficient. The town trial courts met four times a year for the maintenance of local order, as specified in the town charters. Both the colonial court and the town courts used common law and drew their juries from among the freemen, who were all landholders. Roger Williams, as president of the colonial court from 1655 to 1657, used arbitration between litigants with great success, and when money was involved, he chose arbitrators with a knowledge of accounts.[20]

Williams believed that any system of law should result from continuous growth, and consequently the Acts and Orders of Rhode Island were not completed all at once, and they were regarded as alterable at the will of the assembly. Williams was not a lawyer and had little knowledge of English jurisprudence, but under his guidance the Rhode Island laws, particularly those of 1647, took as their models the laws of England and the statutes of Parliament and not, as was true in the Puritan colonies, the alleged word of God. Gorton, too, probably had a hand in making the code, for he was a firm believer in basing legislation and judicial procedures on English common and statute law and in giving the individual the protection to which he was entitled. He was probably the author of the famous Rhode Island Act of 1652 forbidding Negro slavery, inasmuch as he was then the moderator of the general court and Williams was away in England.[21] Although it was never enforced and although in the eighteenth century Rhode Island contained four thousand Negro slaves, most of them at Newport, this law must stand as the first legislative act of emancipation in the American colonies. The Rhode Island code began with a bill of rights, then recited a large number of capital crimes and

20 Richman, *Rhode Island*, I, 233–266.
21 *Rhode Island Records*, I, 243.

minor offenses. The death penalty was imposed for treason, murder, manslaughter, robbery, burglary, arson, witchcraft, and unnatural sex crimes.[22] During Williams' time there were only two executions and two trials for treason without conviction; there were no trials for witchcraft. The colony contained no prisons until 1656, only stocks and whipping posts. The towns had complete responsibility for care of the poor, and there were no schools during this period, because the inhabitants were preoccupied with defending themselves against Indian threats and in gaining a living. Relatively prosperous Newport voted in 1640 to start a school under the Reverend Robert Lenthal, but it went by default. No town had public education until after 1670, and Rhode Island was devoid of cultural interests.

Coddington was cool toward the unification movement and unfriendly toward the patent of 1644, yet, as one of the assistants from Newport in 1647 and president of the court in 1648, he tried to placate the Aquidneck faction. He maintained negotiations with Massachusetts regarding its possible annexation of Providence and Warwick, and in 1648 he petitioned the New England Confederation for the admission of Aquidneck. The latter plea was rejected unless Aquidneck agreed to become part of Plymouth or Massachusetts. He appeared to be striving underhandedly to effect the overthrow of the patent, yet Williams patiently tried to obtain a reconciliation with him without resorting to England or the neighboring colonies. The general court finally brought charges against Coddington and his friends, laying down the dictum that if Coddington appealed outside the colony, the chief assistant of the town where the president was chosen should act in his stead. When Coddington refused to attend the court, Dr. John Clarke took his place. Coddington left for England in October, 1649, to present his case to the Council of State and to petition for a separate patent for Aquidneck and Conanicut. Surprisingly, his appeal was successful, for in April, 1650, the home government appointed him governor for life with authority to administer the law, raise forces, and appoint councillors nominated by the Newport and Portsmouth freeholders. To all intents and purposes Coddington became the owner and proprietor of the islands. The Council of State inexplicably had thus abrogated and superseded the patent of 1644.

22 *Ibid.*, pp. 156–190.

This patent was, incidentally, made over the protest of Edward Winslow, who claimed Conanicut for Plymouth.

It turned out that a powerful group on Aquidneck was opposed to Coddington's patent, and these men persuaded Dr. Clarke to go to England to have it rescinded. At a meeting of the general court in October, 1651, Providence and Warwick joined the movement and urged Williams to accompany Clarke and, if possible, obtain a renewal of the patent of 1644. Williams was loath to undertake a second long sea voyage but finally acquiesced. To obtain money he sold his trading store at Narragansett, and he and Clarke sailed from Boston in November. In England, with the help of Sir Harry Vane and the good will of Cromwell, he was able to aid Clarke and also to execute his own mission. In October, 1652, the Council of State annulled Coddington's commission because of his intrigues with the Dutch at New Netherland and confirmed the patent of 1644.

Despite the victory of the unionist forces, peace did not come to Rhode Island. Roger Williams did not return from England until 1654, and when he did, he learned that the old prejudices continued: distrust of central government, dislike of any power superior to that of the towns, lack of mutual trust, and unyielding adherence to individualism. The Arnolds of Pawtuxet were still conniving with Massachusetts to bring about the annexation of Warwick, the Coddington faction still refused to unite with the mainland, and in Providence license was still mistaken for liberty. There were individuals still contemptuous of all authority. The New England Confederation, now ten years old, regarded Rhode Island as a corrupting influence and a center of erroneous ideas. From 1651 to 1654 the mainland and the islands were separated, and the general court seated delegates only from Providence and Warwick. Newport and Portsmouth retained complete independence and resisted all efforts to enlist them in a common cause.

Williams, as ever undaunted, vowed to restore the government as it had operated under the patent of 1644 and to bring the four towns under unified control. Commissioners summoned from each of the towns drew up new articles of agreement, and in September, 1654, Williams was elected president of the court.[23] He assumed his responsibilities with great misgiving, being tired, worn out from

23 *Ibid.*, pp. 276–277, 282.

his labors in England, and in poor health. But he rose to the occasion and step by step brought the colony back to the position it had occupied before 1651. He was cheered by a letter, dated March 29, 1655, from Oliver Cromwell, now lord protector, urging him to proceed "according to the tenor of your charter . . . takeing care of the peace and saftie of those plantations; that neither through any intestine commotions or forraigne invasions, there doe arise any detriment or dishonour to the Commonwealth or yourselves, as farr as you by your care and diligence can prevent."[24] Williams was not afraid to take drastic action, threatening ringleaders of recalcitrant or troublesome groups with trial in England and warning lesser offenders that they might be fined or whipped. So successful were these measures that Coddington in March, 1656, freely submitted to Williams' authority in the now united colony. The danger was over. The central government had triumphed, and the law of the colony became the law of the land. Disharmony and enmity tended to disappear. The Pawtuxet men, led by William Arnold and William Carpenter, deserted Massachusetts. Williams reached his greatest heights during these two crucial years. After retiring from the presidency in the summer of 1657, he continued as a commissioner from Providence. With the help of Benedict Arnold, the new president, who surprisingly had become one of his most ardent supporters, Williams continued to exercise control.[25]

No sooner had this semblance of peace and order been established than unfortunate Rhode Island had to face outside dangers that threatened its existence. In 1659 the Atherton Company, which included Major Humphrey Atherton, John Winthrop, Jr., and other influential Massachusetts, Rhode Island, and Connecticut speculators and traders, purchased a large tract of land in the northern part of the Narragansett territory.[26] Williams protested this transaction as unneighborly and un-Christian, since Rhode Island was weak and particularly since the purchase was con-

[24] *Ibid.*, pp. 316–317.

[25] Richman, *Rhode Island*, II, 3–42, covers Coddington's efforts to break away and Williams' eventual triumph.

[26] Richard S. Dunn has written on the role of the Winthrops in New England generally and on the younger John Winthrop's activities in Rhode Island specifically. See "John Winthrop Jr., and the Narragansett Country," *William and Mary Quarterly*, XIII (Jan., 1956), 68–86, and *Puritans and Yankees* (Princeton, N.J., 1961).

summated without the consent of its general court. Even appeals to the New England Confederation brought no response. The Rhode Island assembly had already protested the actions of the confederation for attempting to cut off its trade and to control the price of its commodities.[27]

While the struggle with the Atherton Company was at its height during the summer of 1660, an even greater disaster threatened from England when it became known that Charles II had been restored to the throne. Before any other New England colony took action, the general court of little Rhode Island ordered the king proclaimed with great solemnity in the presence of its deputies, and it later formally beseeched Charles to continue his goodness "to his most faithful though poor and unworthy subjects." The restoration of Charles II rendered doubtful the validity of the charter of 1644, inasmuch as it had been issued by Parliament, which, though acting in the king's name, had not followed proper procedures. Moreover, the patent in Rhode Island had served to enforce principles of government that were in harmony with those of the Commonwealth and the Protectorate.

Dr. John Clarke, a man of honor, tact, and shrewdness, was selected to plead Rhode Island's case with the crown. Born in Sussex in 1609, he had migrated to Boston at the end of 1637. Though in sympathy with Antinomianism, he did not engage in the controversy. He followed Coddington to Portsmouth and then to Newport, of which he was one of the founders. Both a physician and a preacher, he was unusual among New England ministers in being without formal education. He later became pastor of the church at Newport, organized before 1648, and recognized as the first Baptist church in New England. He aided in effecting the union of Portsmouth and Newport in 1640, was a commissioner of the general court in 1647, and twice served as general treasurer, and he ranks with Williams, Gorton, and Coddington as one of the leading men of early Rhode Island. Clarke was influential in shaping legislation during the crucial period from 1647 to 1651. In the latter year, while he was attempting to conduct a private Baptist service in a house at Lynn, the Massachusetts authorities arrested him and took

27 In spite of its age, Elisha R. Potter, *Early History of Narragansett* (Providence, R.I., 1835), remains valuable on the Atherton Company and the struggle for the Narragansett country.

him to Boston, where he was humiliated and fined £20. His companion, the famous preacher Obadiah Holmes, received even crueler treatment, and the incident aroused bitter animosity in Rhode Island.

Clarke and Williams left for England in November, 1651, seeking an annulment of the Coddington commission. Clarke remained there for thirteen years, serving loyally as agent and attorney for the colony, meanwhile eking out a living as preacher and physician. Using great tact, he influenced Cromwell to write a gracious letter, already alluded to, to the colony in 1655. He also obtained powder, shot, and bullets, which were greatly needed, for the Rhode Island towns. When the New England Confederation, angered because Rhode Island welcomed Quakers, threatened to cut off its trade, Clarke intervened in England. The general court expressed its great gratitude to him in 1663 and sent him a gift of £100 current money. When Charles II was restored in 1660, it was of the greatest importance that Rhode Island secure confirmation of its patent in the form of a royal charter. In October the colony authorized Clarke to act in its behalf and undertook to raise £200 for this purpose. Because raising the money was a slow process—it was not entirely paid until 1680—Clarke mortgaged his house and land in Newport so that he could proceed. Williams, thoroughly discouraged, scolded the town of Warwick for its laggardness and accused it of want of loyalty.

It was not until January, 1662, that Dr. Clarke's first petition reached the office of the secretary of state, and in February he followed it with another.[28] The petitions were ordered to be brought before the Privy Council on March 28, but this was not done. The reason for the delay was that John Winthrop, Jr., governernor of Connecticut, was in England to institute proceedings for a charter for his own colony. Winthrop, a unversity man who moved easily in higher political and social circles, was well provided with funds, and his petition was naturally considered first.

Clarke was utterly dismayed when he learned that Winthrop, a good friend of Roger Williams, had requested that the eastern boundary of Connecticut be specified as Narragansett Bay, a demarcation that would have deprived Rhode Island of two-thirds of the

28 *Rhode Island Records*, I, 485–491.

territory it claimed. The Earl of Clarendon, the king's most trusted adviser and a member of the Privy Council, received a petition in May that Clarke had addressed to the king, imploring that Rhode Island's case be considered with Connecticut's "for as much as he [John Winthrop] hath injuriously swallowed up the one half of our Colonie."[29] Winthrop, despite the fact that he had been instructed by Connecticut and the Atherton Company to obtain Narragansett Bay as the eastern boundary, was a man of honor and agreed to submit the matter to arbitration. This action was later repudiated by Connecticut as being in excess of Winthrop's power. An impartial body deliberated carefully, and then made a decision in April, 1663, in favor of Rhode Island, designating the Pawcatuck River as the boundary. This award began a boundary dispute that lasted for sixty years.

Meanwhile, Winthrop assisted Clarke in every way in his power to obtain a charter for Rhode Island, and the charter did in fact finally pass the seals principally because of the confidence that the crown had in John Winthrop, Jr. Issued on July 8, 1663, the Rhode Island charter contained the memorable clause, insisted upon by Williams, that no person could be punished or called into question for any differences of opinion in matters of religion, providing that this liberty was not used for license or for the disturbance of others.[30] Freedom of conscience for colonists was not questioned despite the Act of Uniformity passed in England in 1662. Jamaica, New Jersey, and the Carolinas, as well as Rhode Island, also received this boon.

A great meeting of freemen convened in Newport on November 24 to hear the charter read for the first time by George Baxter, a Boston sea captain to whom Dr. Clarke had entrusted the document. The meeting adopted the charter unanimously, voted to repay Clarke for his personal outlay, and gave thanks to the king. The colony's travail was by no means over, but the granting of the charter dispelled a cloud that had hung over it for nearly thirty years. Rhode Island was now on the same footing as Massachusetts and Connecticut, and it had won a victory over the New England

[29] Quoted in Andrews, *Colonial Period*, II, 44, from "The Clarendon Papers," *Collections of the New-York Historical Society for the Year 1869* (New York, 1870), p. 44.
[30] *Rhode Island Records*, II, 3–21.

Confederation. Moreover, the king's approval of religious freedom rendered Rhode Island's neighbors powerless to interfere in its religious affairs ever again.

Among the signers of the charter were representatives of all factions—Williams, Coddington, Gorton, Greene, Coggeshall, Dexter, Holden, and Dyer. All were now committed to the continuance of the colony as a single corporate unit with a strong central executive and judicial system. Though the type of government described in the charter did not differ essentially from the system that had been in existence since 1647, the new document gave it paramount recognition. The president became governor, a deputy governorship was created, there were ten assistants instead of the previous four, and there was also an eighteen-man assembly, consisting of six representatives from Newport and four from each of the other towns. The assembly had full power to make any laws not contrary to those of England, and it was to sit twice a year, in May and October, or more frequently in case of emergencies. The assembly was also authorized to set up courts of common law, create towns, and inflict penalties and punishments upon delinquents and offenders. The inhabitants of Rhode Island received the right to fish along the New England coast, and they were granted all trade privileges not prohibited by English statutes. They could pass through any other colony without molestation, a privilege that had very real meaning to Roger Williams.[31]

The charter defined the boundaries of the colony, presumably for all time, but nothing could have been further from the truth. The northern boundary was described as the southern boundary of Massachusetts, but because of an erroneous survey, its exact location was not settled finally until 1751. The boundary Rhode Island shared with Plymouth was almost unintelligibly defined as three English miles to the east and northeastern parts of Narragansett Bay and along the east bank of the Seekonk River to Pawtucket Falls, thence northward to the Massachusetts line. There was bad feeling between Rhode Island and Plymouth, because the latter had tried first to annex the whole territory and had then attempted to

[31] The obtaining of the charter and its terms are the subjects of Richman, *Rhode Island,* II, 105–148. The essential parts of the charter will be found in William MacDonald, *Documentary Source Book of American History* (New York, 1943), pp. 66–72.

get Aquidneck. In 1665 a royal commission trying to allay bitterness endeavored to push Rhode Island's eastern border back to the Narragansett Bay shore, but Rhode Island ignored this recommendation and extended its claim eastward to the Taunton River. This impasse continued until Massachusetts acquired Plymouth in 1691 and took its stand on the royal commission's report. It was not until 1746 that a later commission designated a line that is practically the one used today. The effect of this boundary revision was to take Tiverton, Compton, Bristol, and Warren away from Massachusetts and give them to Rhode Island.

The Connecticut boundary line was not settled until 1727 and not surveyed until 1738. The royal commission of 1665 confirmed the line of the Pawcatuck River north to the Massachusetts border. Previously, however, Connecticut had repudiated the Clarke-Winthrop agreement that had established that line, claiming that Winthrop's authority as agent ended the moment he obtained the Connecticut charter. That colony claimed the territory east to Narragansett Bay, insisting that its charter was older than Rhode Island's. This stalemate lasted for years, with those living in the disputed area bearing the burden. After a great deal of wrangling, Connecticut, wearied with the whole business, declared it was willing to leave the settlement to the Privy Council. The Connecticut-Rhode Island line as drawn in 1738 was, to all intents and purposes, the line agreed upon by Winthrop and Clarke back in 1663.[32]

Rhode Island towns, unlike those of Massachusetts and Connecticut, never maintained a searching disciplinary watch over their inhabitants. In the absence of an established church organization, backbiting and slander were common. There were no Sunday ordinances and no regulations imposing church attendance, so the magistrates confined themselves to punishing only violations of the civil law on the Sabbath. A few offenders, both men and women, were whipped, put in stocks, fined, or imprisoned, but their number was not large. In general, punishment for crime was not harsh, and mutilation, such as clipping the ears, was rare. Owing to the influence of Roger Williams, many disputes continued to be settled by arbitration. Because of the unsettled political condition of the

[32] *Ibid.*, pp. 244–272.

colony from the beginning, there was an unusually large amount of grumbling against the government, and protests against interference by magistrates were more frequent than in other New England colonies.

Compared with growing trade centers such as Boston and New Amsterdam, Rhode Island was relatively isolated from commercial contacts before 1660. For the most part her people were denizens of the wilderness. But Newport, led by Coddington and others, refused to accept this situation and sought to establish trade relationships with other areas. Rhode Island was thereafter synonymous for a hundred years with Newport, and the hinterland was neglected save as it furnished surplus products as ships' cargoes.[33] In all the towns wampum, at so many shells per penny, served as the medium of exchange, and it became legal tender for the discharge of taxes and other public obligations. Soon the produce of the colony—corn, sheep, cattle, and tobacco especially—supplemented wampum and eventually replaced it as the medium of exchange. Little if any money was in circulation before 1660, and the efforts of the New England Confederation to boycott Rhode Island's trade stopped the flow of the sorely needed Massachusetts coins. After the charter was granted, coins trickled in from the Bay Colony, and after the capture of Jamaica by the English in 1655 some Spanish silver coins reached Rhode Island. We know little of its commerce during the seventeenth century, but Darrett B. Rutman shows that Rhode Island towns and merchants were brought into Boston's hinterland as early as the late 1640's.[34] Eventually Rhode Island tobacco reached Boston, whence it was reshipped to London. Coddington sent horses to the West Indies in 1656, and it is evident that traffic such as this had been going on for some time. There was no shipbuilding before 1660, and Rhode Island's great commercial future lay after that date.

Roger Williams nurtured ideals of human liberty and religious freedom that Rhode Island through the years not only did not improve upon but was unable to maintain. Williams himself,

---

[33] The best account of Newport during the seventeenth century is in Carl Bridenbaugh, *Cities in the Wilderness* (New York, 1964), pp. 3–139.

[34] "Governor Winthrop's Garden Crop: The Significance of Agriculture in the Early Commerce of Massachusetts," *William and Mary Quarterly*, XX (July, 1963), 396–415.

though he worked unselfishly for harmony and cultivated the spirit of humility, was thwarted by the "sad differences" among the towns. The spirit of noncooperation, especially in dealing with other colonies, outlived the colonial period. Williams ardently upheld government with the consent of the people, although he did not question the restricting of freemanship to those who owned land, a qualification for voting that lasted into the nineteenth century. His most sacred belief, the right of the individual to worship as he pleased, received a setback when Roman Catholics were disfranchised in 1729. It was Williams' cross during his long career that he had to cajole and coerce an unwilling people in every step he undertook. And it was Rhode Island's tragedy that the heritage he bequeathed was so often forgotten or ignored. His transcendent triumph was the unified colony he molded.[35]

[35] See Andrews, *Colonial Period*, II, 1–66, for an excellent account of Rhode Island's early years.

CHAPTER 10

The Beginnings of Connecticut

M ASSACHUSETTS men who disliked the Puritan regime or
who wanted richer soil became the founders of Connecticut,
but natural conditions contributed to the relatively slow development of that area. Few white people ventured into the interior of
the wilderness between Massachusetts and the Hudson before 1632,
and the region was unknown except for a few poorly manned Dutch
trading posts. Dense forests delayed penetration into New England
generally, and even the inhabitants of Massachusetts clung tenaciously to the coasts and the river basins. The settlers lacked equipment to cope with the huge trees and heavy undergrowth, and hence
only a few fur trappers ranged very far inland. These trappers and
the Dutch made it known that a great river flowed into Long Island
Sound, but no English colonists were prompt to recognize the
possibilities of a profitable trade on the Connecticut River. Edward
Winslow, who had returned from England in 1632, was the first
to do so. The opportunity seemed both real and timely, because
he and other Plymouth leaders had been seeking some means of
making money with which to pay off the debt owed by the colony
to London merchants. In 1632, a year before the Dutch came into
the Connecticut Valley, Winslow claimed that he had visited the
future site of Windsor and had briefly occupied the very spot where
Lieutenant William Holmes of Plymouth set up a trading post
the next year.

In July, 1633, the Massachusetts Bay Colony refused the invitation of Winslow and William Bradford of Plymouth to join in a trading expedition to Connecticut. John Oldham, a pioneer of the Indian country, led a four-man scouting trip to the Connecticut River in September, and the group returned with specimens of beaver, black lead, and hemp. The next fall he led another band of eight from Watertown, the Massachusetts settlement where he lived, to Pyquag, the point on the river that later became Wethersfield. There he erected shelters, and from that base he wandered about in quest of furs until Indians killed him on Block Island in April, 1636. Meanwhile, disturbed by the appearance of Englishmen in territory they regarded as theirs, the Dutch, as early as June, 1633, constructed the House of Hope, a redoubt on a small stream near the center of present-day Hartford. In August Winslow, who was then governor of Plymouth, dispatched Lieutenant Holmes to the Connecticut. Sailing past the Dutch post and continuing nine miles farther north, Holmes erected a trading house on the Farmington River that later developed into the village of Windsor.

Massachusetts did not react immediately to this activity, but by 1635 residents of Dorchester, Newtown (Cambridge), Watertown, and Roxbury became interested in reports of excellent land to the west. The pioneer company left Dorchester in June, 1635, seeking new homes in the Connecticut Valley, and others followed in rapid succession. Elder William Brewster's son Jonathan, in charge of the Plymouth trading post at Windsor, welcomed them, though they were a burden to his enterprise. The Dorchester men high-handedly proceeded to settle on lands purchased by Plymouth on the theory that they had a right to any unoccupied land. It took two years and a visit from Governor Thomas Prence of Plymouth to put them straight. All men living there were eventually absorbed into the town of Windsor.

A settlement of a different type was sponsored from England by Sir Richard Saltonstall, who planned to establish a particular plantation on land the Earl of Warwick expected to obtain from the Council for New England but never did. He sent a master carpenter and eighteen indentured servants from London to Boston in June, 1635, and ten days later they embarked for Windsor, where they were coldly received by the Massachusetts men, whom Saltonstall angrily accused of snatching up the best land in anticipation of his expedition's arrival. Meanwhile, a group at Newtown also was planning to settle on the Connecticut but could not do so until its members disposed of their houses and farms. It was not until the end of October that fifty of them made their way through the wilderness to Windsor. Since all the land around Windsor was by then taken up, they moved southward toward the Dutch fort and settled on part of the land that was later included in Hartford. After a palisade was built, twelve of the men started back to Massachusetts and, the winter of 1635–36 being unusually cruel, got there only because Indians assisted them along the route. Later that winter seventy discouraged Windsor settlers struggled to the mouth of the Connecticut, where they were picked up by the *Rebecca,* an icebound vessel trying to make its way up the river.

So far all the Connecticut pioneers were squatters with the exception of Saltonstall, because their only claim to the land they occupied was based on Indian purchase, but more systematic settlement was about to begin.[1] On July 7, 1635, a group of lords and gentlemen who held a deed from the Earl of Warwick authorized John Winthrop, Jr., to lay out land at the mouth of the Connecticut River at what became Saybrook, and he was also to build a fort and erect houses there suitable for adventurers and planters of their class.[2] The sponsors of the expedition, who included Lord Saye and Sele, George Fenwick, Sir Richard Saltonstall, and Sir Arthur Haselrig, supplied Winthrop with men, ammunition, and £2,000. Prompt action was indicated, because the patentees had already held their deed for three years without accomplishing anything. When Winthrop arrived in Boston in October to assess the situation, he demanded that all those already in Connecticut should acknowledge the legal rights of the grantees and submit to him as governor or else leave the country. He stated categorically

[1] Roy H. Agaki, *The Town Proprietors of the New England Colonies: A Study of the Development, Organization, Activities, and Controversies, 1620–1670* (Philadelphia, 1924; republished Gloucester, Mass., 1963), pp. 15–16, comments on the squatter status of the pioneer settlers in Hartford, Wethersfield, and Windsor.

[2] The Warwick patent of 1631 ("The Old Patent") and Winthrop's commission are printed in Benjamin Trumbull, *A Complete History of Connecticut* (2 vols., Hartford, Conn., 1797), I, 526–527; see pp. 528–529 for the articles of agreement. The Warwick patent also appears in Mary Jeanne Anderson Jones, *Congregational Commonwealth: Connecticut, 1636–1662* (Middletown, Conn., 1968), pp. 173–175, and a thorough review of that document and its history will be found in Charles J. Hoadly, *The Warwick Patent* (Hartford, 1902).

that Connecticut lay beyond the jurisdiction of Massachusetts and that settlement there could be made only with the consent of the Warwick grantees. This announcement was a bombshell, because the Massachusetts General Court had recently given permission to its inhabitants to remove to Connecticut, had appointed a constable to serve those who planned to leave, and had provided them with pieces of ordnance. Moreover, the Reverend Thomas Hooker's congregation at Newtown was about ready to take its departure for Connecticut.

Members of the Massachusetts General Court held conferences from October, 1635, to March, 1636, with Thomas Hooker, John Haynes (later a Connecticut governor), Roger Ludlow, and the Reverend Samuel Stone. Hooker and his associates concluded that they had no choice but to recognize Winthrop's claim and accept him as governor of the whole territory. Winthrop's agents agreed to the proposed settlement within the bounds of the Warwick deed; but since they had no authority from the Council for New England to permit the establishment of an independent government within the borders of their grant, they had to find a solution elsewhere. This objective was accomplished when the Massachusetts General Court, acting in behalf of both parties, issued a commission on March 3, 1636, that satisfied everyone—Winthrop, the prospective emigrants, and the court itself.[3] Eight men who were ready to leave Connecticut, including William Pynchon, received authorization to exercise judicial power, to impose military discipline, and to wage war if necessary. Their instructions directed them to convene the inhabitants of the towns (not church members only) and, acting as a court, to proceed to execute their authority. Since half of these eight men were later members of the Connecticut General Court that drew up the Fundamental Orders of 1639, it is not surprising that their concept of government was repeated in the Fundamentals. The caveat "government by the consent of the inhabitants" explains in part why they were leaving Massachusetts.

Now that both Winthrop and the emigrant leaders had gotten what they wished, the westward exodus resumed. John Warham, minister of the Dorchester church, led his congregation to Windsor.

[3] *Records of . . . Massachusetts Bay*, I, 170–171. Jones, *Congregational Commonwealth*, pp. 176–177, reprints the Massachusetts Bay commission.

William Pynchon and his associates built his trading house at Agawam (later Springfield). Several other groups moved, by land and water, from Watertown to Wethersfield. Then finally John White, Samuel Wakeman, and perhaps Hooker's assistant at Newtown, Samuel Stone, joined others already located on the Quinatucquet (Connecticut) River. These last-named men carried with them the Massachusetts commission of 1636, and in April five of the commissioners met as the first general court at Hartford and adopted a number of orders. Thus organized government began in Connecticut two months before the arrival of Thomas Hooker and three years before promulgation of the Fundamental Orders.

The Reverend Thomas Shepard, educated at Cambridge, arrived in Boston in October, 1635, and was installed as Hooker's successor at Newtown.[4] The people who migrated with Shepard took up the houses in the town already vacated or about to be vacated by families going to Connecticut. Hooker and his flock had not yet departed because of the difficulty of moving a whole congregation a hundred or more miles through the wilderness. Meanwhile, with the blessing of John Cotton, Shepard and his associates entered into a covenant and became a church, affording Hooker and his group the opportunity of leaving. But it was not until the end of May, 1636, that Hooker with thirty-five men and their families finally departed. Since the migrants had with them one hundred and sixty cattle, their caravan could make only ten miles a day. It crossed the Connecticut at Windsor and moved slowly toward the House of Hope, now within the bounds of Hartford.[5]

The settlers of Connecticut were enthusiastic Puritans, but their motives for migrating put heavy emphasis on economic and political considerations. There was no intention of establishing a religious colony in any way different from that in Massachusetts, and all the nascent Connecticut churches followed the New England Way. Hooker had no patience with troublemakers like Anne Hutchinson and Roger Williams, nor did any of the other emigrant groups. All of them wanted fertile land in the stream valleys, and they left

[4] For a biography of Shepard, see Samuel Eliot Morison, *Builders of the Bay Colony* (Boston, 1964), pp. 105–134.

[5] Dorothy Deming, *The Settlement of the Connecticut Towns* (New Haven, Conn., 1934), pp. 1–7, describes the preparations for departure from Massachusetts and the migration of 1636.

Massachusetts behind because there was a dearth of such land available. The inhabitants of Newtown turned a deaf ear to the offer of the Massachusetts General Court to find cultivable land for them along the Merrimack, because they knew that such areas abounded in Connecticut. There were also many men who preferred cattle-raising to the hard task of tilling the soil. Another factor leading to emigration was the fear that Massachusetts might lose its charter, and some people criticized Winthrop's administration of the Bay Colony. Then, too, Thomas Hooker and John Haynes, one of Hooker's affluent parishioners, and Roger Ludlow, a trained lawyer, were nourishing their own ideas about how a colony should be governed.[6] Another group of able men, of whom William Pynchon was one, found Massachusetts uncomfortable because of the dominating influence of the magistrates and the rigid controls imposed by the elders. New England contained many strong-willed individualists, each wishing to carve out his own little satrapy. Williams, Coddington, Gorton, Davenport, Hooker, and the younger Winthrop were all men of this type.

Thomas Hooker had personal reasons for wishing to leave Massachusetts, as he was opposed to the prevailing strictness governing admission to church membership and deplored the great division between ministers and people in religious matters. Hooker had in mind the Antinomian controversy and his own controversy with the Reverend John Cotton. In 1635 Cotton taught that faith was built upon Christ, not upon sanctification obtained through good works, and that faith went before works. Hooker resented Cotton's statement that to believe otherwise was "flatt Popery." John Winthrop minimized the bad feeling between the two and denied that Hooker left for such a reason, but Winthrop always played down personal controversies in the Bay Colony. Cotton was a Hutchinson sympathizer at this time, while Hooker opposed her; and though Cotton was more liberal in religious matters, Hooker upheld more progressive views concerning government. Hooker's ideas were not applicable in Massachusetts, because church membership there was a qualification for freemanship, and the magistrates were accepted as "oracles of

6 Biographical data on Ludlow will be found in William A. Beers, "Roger Ludlowe: The Father of Connecticut Jurisprudence," *Magazine of American History*, VIII (Apr., 1882), 264–271; and John M. Taylor, *Roger Ludlow, the Colonial Lawmaker* (New York, 1900).

God." Hooker also sensed a feeling among the Bay Colony leaders that they were anxious to discredit the movement of settlers to Connecticut. As late as 1648, when the New England Confederation commissioners disagreed over the claims of the two colonies, the Connecticut delegates insisted that the emigrants themselves initiated the Commission of 1636, for they were determined to reside no longer in a land for whose spirit and government they had no liking.

Hooker believed that mutual convenanting gave "constitution and being to a visible church." Members so convenanting, according to the New England Way, had a share in the government of the church. What troubled Hooker was the limiting of membership to the "regenerate" only, because he could find no way to discover who was truly regenerate in spirit. He was willing to admit all who were followers of Christ, providing they were freeholders, to participation in government. He also believed that if members convenanting in a church had a share in its government, those subscribing to a social compact should have a share in governing the colony.[7]

The Puritan system in Connecticut was not a democracy as we conceive it. The people chose the church elders and the civic magistrates, but once these officials took office, the people conformed to their will. No one joined the church without the elders' approval; likewise, no one became a freeman without general court approval. A proper voting age was not used as a criterion for determining participation in the franchise. Hooker, however, did seek some form of popular participation for the adult male residents. The Commission of 1636 provided that the "inhabitants" of Connecticut should convene in a court for the execution of such powers as were entrusted to them. This idea was well thought of, but not until Hooker's famous May 31, 1638, sermon was it stated in so many words that "the foundation of authority is laid in the free consent of the people."[8]

[7] George L. Walker, *Thomas Hooker: Preacher, Founder, Democrat* (New York, 1891), is an excellent biography, and the same author's *History of the First Church in Hartford, 1633–1883* (Hartford, Conn., 1884), pp. 118–145, gives a probing analysis of Hooker's writings. Warren S. Archibald, *Thomas Hooker* (New Haven, Conn., 1933), is a briefer but more recent biography. Perry Miller, *Errand into the Wilderness* (New York, 1956), pp. 16–47, is the most balanced interpretation of Hooker. Clinton Rossiter, "Thomas Hooker," *New England Quarterly*, XXV (Dec., 1952), 459–488, sees Hooker as somewhat less orthodox than does Miller.

[8] *Connecticut Historical Collections*, I, (1860), 170–171.

This phrasing is similar to that used by Roger Williams in *The Bloudy Tenent*, and the two men were well acquainted. Plymouth, Connecticut, and Rhode Island, unlike Massachusetts, permitted political participation by at least a part of the people regardless of church membership. There was a modicum of self-government from the beginning in Connecticut in which "admitted inhabitants" and "freemen" had a definite and important share.[9]

Government remained simple in form during the first three years of the colony. The Commission of 1636 gave full power to the eight men named in it to carry out all its instructions. They had among other things the power to summon the inhabitants and obtain their consent, thus placing the government on a broader base than in Massachusetts. The commissioners, however, did not call a general court or assembly but conducted the administration themselves at a court that met from April, 1636, to March, 1637. The commission jurisdiction, then, which lasted a year, was based on the consensus of the inhabitants. No governor was chosen, because John Winthrop, Jr., was recognized as the titular head of the territory, and it was understood that his superiors might replace him if they chose. Only with the drawing up of the Fundamental Orders in 1639, after the lords and gentlemen had withdrawn from the enterprise, was provision made for election of a governor.

An exception was made to government by the commissioners in 1637, an action made necessary by the threat of war with the Pequots. The inhabitants received instructions at that time to convene in their respective towns to elect representatives who would join with the magistrates at a general court at Hartford. The only business of that court was to declare war on the Pequots and to distribute the burden of cost among Windsor, Wethersfield, and Hartford, the only three plantations then existing. Actually, in this instance the magistrates were, with one exception, the original commissioners. The Pequots, as mentioned previously, had come down the Connecticut Valley, pushing the local tribes before them, and had settled down in the area between the lower Thames River and Rhode Island. The immediate cause of the war was the

[9] David H. Fowler, "Connecticut's Freemen: The First Forty Years," *William and Mary Quarterly*, XV (July, 1958), 312–333, concludes that by 1669 the majority of adult males had become freemen where the local conditions were most favorable and that probably most Connecticut men who were not servants could vote as freemen if they wanted to.

murders of Captain John Stone and several companions, of John Oldham, who had a post at Wethersfield, and of three women and six men, also of Wethersfield.[10] Forces led by Captain John Mason, Captain John Underhill, and Lieutenant Robert Seeley brought the war to a successful conclusion in three weeks, and relations with the Indians were relatively peaceful for the next forty years.[11]

The three earliest plantations developed normally during 1637 and 1638, with the householders giving most of their attention to apportioning land, erecting dwellings, and making their living. Although not formally organized as towns until 1639, the inhabitants did meet from time to time to adopt local ordinances and to choose committees to attend the general court. At its first meeting, considered a court of elections in accordance with Massachusetts precedent, committees named the magistrates who had been nominated by each town, and the whole body gave its approval in a formal election.[12] The magistrates sat separately after the general meeting to conduct judicial, financial, and probate business. In other words, the general court transacted affairs before 1639 in much the same manner as it was called upon to do after that date.[13]

Today Springfield is a full five miles inside the Massachusetts line, but in the beginning it was regarded as one of the Connecticut River towns, and William Pynchon and his son-in-law Henry Smith were named as two of the original eight governing commissioners. Because of distance, however, they attended only the first meeting of the general court. During the Indian trouble Springfield was left defenseless, although Pynchon's shallop was requisitioned and the

10 Alden T. Vaughan discusses the causes of the Pequot War in "Pequots and Puritans: The Causes of the War of 1637," *William and Mary Quarterly*, XXI (Apr., 1964), 256–269.

11 A vivid contemporary account of the campaign will be found in John Mason, *A Brief History of the Pequot War . . .* (Boston, 1736). Howard Bradstreet, *The Story of the War with the Pequots, Re-Told* (New Haven, 1933), is a more modern version. For a comprehensive analysis of Indian-Puritan relations, see Alden T. Vaughan, *New England Frontier: Puritans and Indians, 1620–1675* (Boston, 1965), and see pp. 122–154 for a description of the military action against the Pequots.

12 *Colonial Records of Connecticut*, I, 27 ff.

13 See also Charles M. Andrews, "The Beginnings of Connecticut Towns," *Annals of the American Academy of Political and Social Science*, I (Oct., 1890), 165–191, the first of the author's many studies of this subject, and his *The Beginnings of Connecticut, 1632–1662* (New Haven, Conn., 1934).

sum of £86 15s. was assessed against the community, an amount that Pynchon asserted equaled the value of his whole estate. The other plantations claimed that Pynchon refused to furnish the supply of Indian corn he had contracted for in return for a monopoly of the Indian trade up the river, and he in turn complained that the monopoly had been thrust upon him. In April, 1638, the general court fined him forty bushels of corn for his alleged failure to keep his promises. Deeply offended, Pynchon decided to remove his post from Connecticut's jurisdiction.[14] The Connecticut leaders thereupon left Springfield out of consideration when they drew up their new frame of government. Added to this friction was the fact that Hooker and Pynchon got along no better than Hooker and Cotton. Hooker became angry when Pynchon, one of the original commissioners and a leader in the migration, was willing to break away because of what Hooker considered a trifling pretext.

Massachusetts did not admit Springfield's deputies into its general court for ten years, and during that period Springfield had to fend for itself. In 1641 Massachusetts appointed Pynchon chief judge and magistrate of Springfield, the people retaining the right to appeal his decisions to the general court. The next year he became a Massachusetts assistant, and in 1649 Springfield deputies finally appeared in the general court of that colony. After Pynchon left for England temporarily in 1652, his son John presided over this minuscule republic. The town prospered, extending its fur-trading interests, establishing frontier posts at Westfield, Hadley, and Northhampton, and doing business as far away as Albany.[15] William Pynchon survived until 1662.[16]

The Springfield controversy was bound up with two events of major importance in the development of New England, one of which concerned plans to erect some sort of cooperative union among the several colonies. Connecticut proposed the formation of a confederation of Puritan colonies for mutual protection

[14] Andrews, *The Beginnings of Connecticut, 1632–1662*, pp. 32–37, analyzes the factors leading to Springfield's decision to withdraw.

[15] Henry M. Burt (ed.), *First Century of the History of Springfield* (2 vols., Springfield, Mass., 1898), I, 156–158.

[16] Ruth A. McIntyre, *William Pynchon: Merchant and Colonizer* (Springfield, Mass., 1961); and Samuel Eliot Morison, "William Pynchon, the Founder of Springfield," *Massachusetts Historical Society Proceedings*, LXIV (1930–32), 81–107.

against the Indians and Dutch, the distribution of Pequot territory, the extension of the fur trade, and the maintenance of the
common welfare. Discussion began in 1636 and continued for six
years, because there were many obstacles, such as Massachusetts'
support of Pynchon, that colony's claim to Pequot land, boundary
disputes with Connecticut, and the controversy over Connecticut's
right to levy tolls at the mouth of the Connecticut River. The
wonder is that in 1643 an agreement was reached at all, permitting
organization of the New England Confederation. That body underwent subsequent ups and downs, but it managed to remain generally
useful until 1665.[17]

The problem involving Springfield also contributed to the necessity for Connecticut to give its disparate plantation system a constitutional form. Massachusetts had a charter, Plymouth had its
Bradford patent of 1630, and newly founded New Haven soon had
a "Civill Government according to God." But Connecticut had
as yet no formal instrument of government. We are not even sure
that the towns had covenants such as those enjoyed by New Haven,
Milford, and Guilford, which commanded obedience to duly elected
authorities. The lords and gentlemen, always an obstacle, had by
1638 definitely abandoned their enterprise. Hooker, confronted
with Pynchon's desertion, probably concluded that the time was
right to forge the river settlements together in loyalty to a common
government. Then, too, talk of a New England Confederation was
in the air, and if Connecticut aspired to become a member, it must
create a jurisdiction of its own. The Connecticut General Court
accordingly faced the task in 1638 of framing governing principles
for the colony.

An assembly of the plantations met in May, presumably to discuss
a closer union with Massachusetts and Plymouth, and on the last
day of that month Hooker delivered his significant sermon or
address, probably to the members of the general court.[18] It seems

[17] Harry M. Ward, *The United Colonies of New England, 1643–1690* (New
York, 1961), is the most complete study of the New England Confederation.
Herbert L. Osgood, *The American Colonies in the Seventeenth Century* (3 vols.,
New York, 1904–7), I, 392–423, offers briefer comment on the same subject. A
slightly condensed version of the confederation's charter appears in William
MacDonald, *Documentary Source Book of American History* (New York, 1943),
pp. 45–50.

[18] Connecticut Historical Society, *Collections*, I, 20–21.

likely that he was putting into expository form certain principles, already agreed upon, according to which a civil government was to be erected. There was little new in them as far as existing practice in Connecticut was concerned. The chief difference between the principles of Connecticut and the other New England colonies was the question of what was understood by the word "people." Hooker declared that the foundation of all authority lay in the free consent of the people and that the choice of the public magistrates, by God's own allowance, resided in them. If the magistrates were chosen in this manner, the freemen would more likely yield obedience. He stated that those who had the power to choose officers and magistrates also had the authority to set the bounds of their power. Like Roger Williams in *The Bloudy Tenent,* Hooker meant that authority should come from below, not from above. Inspired by Hooker, the court then set to work framing a constitution, but there is little record of how this was accomplished. Charles M. Andrews conjectures that Roger Ludlow, John Haynes, John Steel, and Edward Hopkins had a hand in the process, and that Ludlow, who was a lawyer, shaped the instrument into final form. Its brevity, clarity, and compactness certainly reveal the work of a competent legal mind. The final draft was put to a vote and adopted on January 14, 1639.[19]

The Fundamental Orders consisted of a preamble and eleven orders or laws.[20] The preamble was a covenant binding the three river plantations to be governed in all civil things by these orders. This "combination," as Hooker called it, was simply a confirmation of the established system of government that had been functioning since 1636. From the beginning the institution of government in Connecticut had contained within itself all the essentials of self-rule, free from the limiting influence of any external authority except that of God. The preamble was the civil equivalent of a church covenant, and the covenant idea lay, of course, at the base of all Puritan organization, in both church and state. The eleven orders that followed the preamble, though not differing in substance from the laws of the other New England colonies, did seal together

[19] Charles M. Andrews, *The Colonial Period of American History* (4 vols., New Haven, Conn., 1934–38), II, 102.
[20] Connecticut Historical Society, *Collections,* I, 20–26.

a concise scheme of government. They expressed the essentials of popular rule such as the Connecticut leaders had conceived.

The main govermental features followed the Massachusetts model and were based on the usual trading type of charter. There were to be two general court meetings every year, one in April (later changed to May) for the election and legislative meeting and the other in September for legislative, judicial, and administrative business. For the first time since Winthrop's commission expired in 1636, a governorship was provided for. The man holding that position was to be a member of some approved congregation. He also had to be selected from among the magistrates, and he could hold office for only one year, a set of restrictions that lasted until 1660. To prevent a hasty election, nominations had to be made at the court meeting preceding the election, and the court had the power to add names to those brought in by the deputies. The thesis was that the governor and the magistrates were elected "by a vote of the country."[21]

It should not be assumed that every male received the right to vote and that the majority ruled. The Fundamental Orders made a distinction between an "admitted inhabitant" and a freeman, the former being allowed to vote only in town elections, whereas the latter could vote for colony officers. An admitted inhabitant was a "man of honest conversation" who had taken an oath of fidelity to the Commonwealth. After being properly qualified by his town meeting, he could take part in local affairs, participate in the election of local officials, and vote for deputies to the general court. Massachusetts developed the same practice, except that such people could not vote for deputies. The more privileged freeman was an admitted inhabitant who had been selected for freemanship either by the general court or by one or more magistrates who were authorized by that body to make such nominations. Only after admission to freemanship could an adult male householder offer himself for election as a deputy, vote for higher officials, or himself fill the office of magistrate, and only freemen could attend the court of election. Inasmuch as nonfreemen, women, servants, apprentices, and convicted persons were not allowed to vote, it followed that in Connecticut the words "people" and "inhabitants" had special and

21 Jones, *Congregational Commonwealth*, pp. 178–183, reprints the Fundamental Orders.

different meanings. The admitted inhabitants of a town had to be religious and godly men, not necessarily members of a congregation but men with some estate. They helped manage local affairs and voted for deputies, but the freemen, constituting only a third of the adult males, exercised the actual control over the government of the colony. The Connecticut freemen, unlike those of the Bay Colony and New Haven, determined, however, to rest participation in government on a relatively broad religious base, and they defined their religious requirement in the oath of fidelity required of every man. Anyone who was "Godly" played some part in government.[22]

The Connecticut Fundamentals were less elaborate than those John Cotton drew up for Massachusetts in 1636 or the New Haven Fundamentals of 1639 and 1643, and authority was very concentrated in the general court. This body, men felt, should have most of the executive, judicial, and administrative power, and it could delegate some of it whenever it saw the necessity to do so. The governor could summon the general court, but once it was in session, only its own members could dissolve or prorogue it. The governor, deputy governor, and magistrates constituted a special court during the early years to dispense justice according to the laws or, when the laws were not explicit, to "the Word of God." The general court was the supreme authority, authorized to make and repeal laws, impose taxes, dispose of land to persons and towns, apprehend and punish people for misdemeanors, and adopt measures for the general good. It could not, however, elect magistrates, a privilege reserved for the whole body of freemen.

The plan of government guaranteed freedom of speech in the general court, which was to meet in Hartford, but it did not provide, surprisingly, for election of a speaker or for any rules of parliamentary procedure. The presiding officer, known as the moderator, put matters to a vote, and whenever there was a tie, his vote became the deciding one. Later, to meet what was felt to be a need, the members of the court were required to maintain secrecy. Fearing the rise of a powerful magistracy, the authors of the Fundamentals decreed that should the governor or the majority of his fellow officeholders fail to summon the general court, the freemen could petition the magistrates to do so. If the latter refused, "the admitted

---

[22] On the limited nature of Connecticut democracy, see Miller, *Errand into the Wilderness*.

freemen" of the towns could elect deputies who would meet and conduct the business of the Commonwealth. Actually, no such assembly of freemen-deputies was ever convened. Another device to limit magisterial power was the provision that the deputies could at any time preceding a regular meeting of the court prepare an agenda of matters of public concern. The deputies could also review elections of their own members and exclude any erring member until the general court passed judgment. The authors of the Fundamentals had no intention of restricting the general court's complete control over legislation, and they omitted, perhaps unintentionally, all reference to the authority of the crown. Inasmuch as other Connecticut laws regarded as "fundamental" passed through the legislature from time to time, the Connecticut "Orders" cannot be considered as completely fashioned as those of Carolina in 1669 or West New Jersey in 1677.

Connecticut's system of self-government has been extravagantly admired as "the first written constitution of modern democracy" and "the first fixed formal and established expression for, by and of the people to be governed." Such descriptions are not wholly accurate and should be sedulously guarded against.[23] The Fundamental Orders were not a constitution and had little connection with democracy. If this was government by "the people," it was so only in a limited sense. As a matter of fact, Connecticut copied its system from Massachusetts with only one or two important differences. It must not be forgotten that Plymouth, Massachusetts, Rhode Island, and New Haven were to a degree all self-governing colonies. The argument that Connecticut was more akin to modern democracy does injustice to other colonies such as Virginia (1619), Bermuda (1620), and Barbados (1639). All had representative assemblies, and because participation did not rest on a religious foundation, their systems were more nearly democratic than Connecticut's. What Connecticut did have was complete self-government which was earlier in origin and lasted longer than that of any other colony or state.[24]

The Fundamental Orders underwent frequent additions and

23 Andrews, *Colonial Period*, II, 142–143n.

24 Jones, *Congregational Commonwealth*, pp. 61–98, provides a judicious discussion of the Fundamental Orders and the extent to which self-government existed from the earliest years.

amendments during the twenty-two years after 1639. The general court made five changes on its own, and in only three cases were the freemen called upon for approval. In 1644 the general court ordered that a quorum of these magistrates instead of four was sufficient to constitute a general court, and in 1647 it decreed that the governor (or any deputy governor) and two magistrates could hold a particular (judicial) court. This last alteration was so basic as to constitute what amounted to a twelfth fundamental. A noteworthy innovation in 1661 provided that in an emergency a general court might consist only of the deputies with as many magistrates as the law allowed. One of the three occasions when the freemen gave their approval to a change was in 1654, when they voted that in the absence of the governor and deputy governor, the magistrates could by a majority vote call a regular assembly, choose a moderator, and pass laws. In 1660 the general court altered the law regarding the choosing of a governor so that henceforth the choice was thrown open and not restricted to the magistrates as originally stipulated. The new arrangement applied, of course, only to freemen, who alone elected the governor and the magistrates. Normally the magistrates and deputies acting together in general court sufficed in matters of general legislation, and because that body chose all the freemen, it possessed the ultimate power. Still, matters of the greatest importance could be and were referred to the freemen as the final authority. As the number of freemen increased, their influence grew. Thirty-six were admitted in the year 1654 alone.[25]

The Puritans did not strive consciously for a democratic society; they were more interested in preserving their covenants and in community welfare than they were in individual welfare. Freedom of the individual came under restraint wherever the needs of the community were involved. The towns were covenanted groups as much as were churches. In the distribution of land, in the control of meadows, in the use of timber, in the obligation of the individual to assist in building roads and bridges, and in many other ways the interest of the community came first. Town liberty was placed above individual liberty. The same relationship was true of the Commonwealth government, which was largely divorced from the

25 *Ibid.*, pp. 95–98, describes all changes to the Fundamental Orders made subsequent to 1639.

inhabitants as a whole and which did not regard them as necessary
to its existence. A relatively few men controlled the higher government. The civil organization worked through the towns, not
through the people in them, though it did not hesitate to punish
and penalize the individual who defied the colony, whether the
individual had rights or not. In the political creed of Connecticut,
the essentials of modern democracy—the rights and liberties of
the individual and the sacredness of popular representation and
majority rule—were in an embryo state.[26]

The authors of the Fundamental Orders were specific concerning
the relative importance of deputies and magistrates, with the
former receiving greater power than did their counterparts in
Massachusetts. There was no "negative vote" as there was in the
Bay Colony. The deputies were supreme in the passage of legislation, and the magistrates could not override their will. As time
elapsed, however, suspicion of the magistrates gradually dissipated,
and those officials tended to grow in prestige and dignity. Although
they received no enlargement of political power, they obtained
additional privileges. With the governor and his deputy they
constituted the court of magistrates (quarter court), which dealt
with individuals. This common-law court with a jury was supplanted
in 1664 by county courts and the court of assistants.[27] Furthermore,
the magistrates could incarcerate incorrigibles, swear in juries,
alter damages awarded by a jury, grant divorces, superintend the
disposal of servants, perform the marriage ceremony, choose freemen, tender the oath of fidelity, draft men and supplies for war,
serve as commissioners at New England Confederation meetings,
and discharge similar responsibilities. Thus they eventually attained
a position of superior influence, but they never succumbed to the
notion prevalent in Massachusetts that magistrates were the beneficiaries of divine guidance.

As if to balance the rise of the magistrate, the other partners in
public life, the "admitted inhabitant," the freemen, and the deputy,
all seemed to lose status. There was a feeling in the general court of

[26] Andrews, *Colonial Period*, II, 112–113.
[27] A thorough study of Connecticut law courts and the working of the legal
process there prior to 1662 will be found in Jones, *Congregational Commonwealth*, pp. 99–138.

decreased confidence in the men who elected the deputies and admitted others to a share in local government. Connecticut was growing, and the new men coming in doubtless included many who were unlikely candidates for participation. As was true in other colonies at this time, crime and sinfulness were on the increase, and it was no longer possible to blame all of the difficulty on apprentices and servants, as had been the case in earlier years. Goodmen, "misters," and even esquires were now contributing to the immorality as well as to defiance of law and authority. The court pried deeply into the conduct of the inhabitants, taking cognizance of the use of tobacco, liquor, and playing cards, as well as of travel on the Sabbath, adultery, and divorce. There were more than twenty cases of "familiarity with the devil" before 1663, resulting in ten hangings, some of them in the neighboring and highly orthodox colony of New Haven. Some persons showed disrespect for the clergy, an intolerable situation requiring correction. One preacher was removed from the pulpit by the court, but was not silenced, for saying that persons not in the visible covenant were "dogs and among dogs and in [the] Kingdom of Sathan and at Sathans command." The witchcraft mania was approaching its height.[28]

In an attempt to bar undesirables from any participation in government, the general court took a series of steps designed to correct lax admissions by the towns and resultant disorderliness by freemen at the courts of election. Significantly, the court came to its conclusions and carried out its program without bothering to consult the freemen. In 1646 it decreed that anyone fined or whipped for a scandalous offense should be disfranchised, and in 1657 it ruled that no one might be admitted as a freeman unless the deputies certified that he was "of a peaceable and honest conversation." Like Massachusetts, Connecticut also set up a property qualification, £30, for an "admitted inhabitant," thus restricting the definition of that class. To curb tumult at elections, the court ordered in 1659 that no one possessing a personal estate valued at less than £30 might be admitted as a freeman. Hooker's aspirations had apparently not survived the first two decades of the Fundamental Orders.

[28] Andrews, *Colonial Period*, II, 116–117.

Connecticut could not grow rapidly because development was based largely on the slow process of agricultural expansion. The population, estimated at 800 in 1636, rose to 2,000 in 1642 and 3,200 in 1654 and then reached 6,000 in 1665, after Connecticut absorbed New Haven.[29] The pioneer farmers planted corn and other grains and raised horses, cattle, swine, sheep, and poultry. Their horses were adequate for hauling but were too small to do heavy plowing, a task for which oxen were much preferred. Cattle were an absolute necessity, not only for this purpose but for the food and leather they provided. Garden plots contained small amounts of tobacco, flax, and hemp, while the forest yielded timber, pitch, tar, staves, and headings. In an attempt to facilitate business, the authorities held two fairs a year at Hartford.

Trade with other areas began soon after settlement, but it remained on a relatively small scale during the early years. Pinnaces and sloops were in operation, but they had to be small to get past the bar at the mouth of the Connecticut River. Customs duties were collected at that point as early as 1644, but waterborne trade was confined to the coast between Boston and Manhattan, and there was no real seafaring traffic until 1681. Corn was the biggest export item, but the general court restricted its sale for that purpose out of fear of a shortage. Livestock, grains, and some beaver pelts found their way to Boston, New Amsterdam, Long Island, the Delaware, and eventually to Barbados and the Leeward Islands. The Connecticut towns soon became part of Boston's great commercial hinterland. The river towns, New Haven, and especially Winthrop's New London on the Thames were prominent in this trade by the midforties. Winthrop sent cattle, wheat, corn, rye, and peas, a rich variety matched only by the river towns.[30] Products of the soil formed the medium of exchange, because there was less wampum inland than along the coast. There was no local coinage, but in time various coins drifted in from other places.[31]

[29] Evarts B. Greene and Virginia D. Harrington, *American Population Before the Federal Census of 1790* (New York: 1932), p. 47.

[30] Darett B. Rutman, "Governor Winthrop's Garden Crop: The Significance of Agriculture in the Early Commerce of Massachusetts," *William and Mary Quarterly*, XX (July, 1963), 396–415.

[31] Discussions of the settlement and early growth of the Connecticut towns will be found in Deming, *Settlement of the Connecticut Towns, passim;* and George L. Clark, *A History of Connecticut, Its People and Institutions* (New York, 1914), pp. 4–27.

The colony was not notable for either poverty or riches, and living conditions remained primitive. Connecticut afforded fewer money-making opportunities than most of New England, and the few men of wealth and property—such as William Pynchon, Edward Hopkins, the Eatons of New Haven, Captain Richard Lord, James Lord, John Haynes, and George Wyllys—brought their affluence along with them when they came. Aside from water travel, transportation was practically nonexistent, and travel difficulties prompted the general court to reduce the number of deputies in 1661. The river Indians caused no trouble except for an occasional foray. Wild life abounded, and for years the towns, as in other colonies, paid bounties for wolves and other predatory species that threatened their poultry and livestock. Beaver and other furbearing animals contributed some income, but the Connecticut River is not famous in the annals of the fur trade. The rivers teemed with edible fish, and Long Island Sound furnished those of the saltwater variety. The settlers captured porpoises and whales as early as 1647. Life in Connecticut was not unlike that which the Swedes, Finns, and Dutch pursued on the Delaware River from 1638 to 1660—simple and close to the soil.

All New England Puritans were dismayed by the restoration of Charles II in 1660, but the news particularly disconcerted Connecticut, which had no royal charter and extremely meager legal standing. Its leaders very rightly had no confidence in the Warwick patent, and efforts to secure something more valid had been unsuccessful. Connecticut had joined with New Haven in 1644 in sending an agent, George Fenwick, to London to seek a charter. He was unable to accomplish anything, a fact that might have led his principals to question their titles. With only the slight claim provided by the Warwick deed, Connecticut stood defenseless. The colony also shared an additional danger with the rest of New England, because there was reason to fear that the crown might take over the whole region and put a governor general in charge of it. Connecticut's leaders moved swiftly in 1661 and appointed Governor John Winthrop, Jr., then fifty-five years old, to go to England to obtain a charter.

Winthrop was an ideal man for a diplomatic mission. The son of the illustrious governor of Massachusetts, he was educated at Trinity College, Dublin, and had traveled widely. He was a member of the Inner Temple, and although he had never practiced law, he was well acquainted with the leading men in England, Puritan and otherwise. His career had made him an expert in the problems of colonization. He joined his father in Massachusetts in 1631, then returned briefly to England, where he accepted the offer of an influential group of lords and gentlemen in 1635 to found a settlement at Saybrook at the mouth of the Connecticut. In 1640 he received a grant of land at the mouth of the Thames River from Massachusetts, subject to the prior claims of Connecticut. This grant called his attention to the adjacent Pequot country, where he established the New London plantation under Connecticut auspices to curb the Indians. When the New England Confederation validated Connecticut's claims to the area, that colony appointed Winthrop its local commissioner in 1648 with broad powers. He became a Connecticut freeman in 1651, and after a sojourn in New Haven, he cast his lot with Connecticut in 1657 by accepting its governorship.[32]

With the news of the Restoration, Winthrop called a meeting of the magistrates and deputies, who speedily agreed that at the next general court in March, 1661, they would adopt an address to the king proclaiming themselves his loyal subjects and asking for a confirmation of such privileges and liberties as were necessary for the welfare of the colony. They perfected the address in May and sent copies to influential men in England who might be of help. Among the few Puritan lords they could call upon were the Earl of Manchester, Lord Saye and Sele, and Lord Brooke. In June the general court gave Winthrop his instructions. It allowed him full expenses, together with letters of credit up to £500 to take care of perquisites and gratuities. The court instructed him to obtain a confirmation of the Warwick patent, if it could be found, and to have that instrument replaced by a royal charter with liberties and privileges equal to those of Massachusetts.

Winthrop sailed from New Amsterdam and arrived in London in September, 1661. After putting the petition into more suitable form, he spent his time making friends with persons of influence. Among them were Robert Boyle, a founder of the Royal Society;

---

[32] Robert C. Black III, *The Younger John Winthrop* (New York, 1966), is a recent and solid biography. See also Richard S. Dunn, *Puritans and Yankees: The Winthrop Dynasty of New England, 1630–1717* (Princeton, N.J., 1961), pp. 59–187, and Morison, *Builders of the Bay Colony*, pp. 269–288.

Sir Kenelm Digby, a naval man interested in the old Council for New England; Samuel Hartlib, author of many pamphlets on current affairs; and William Brereton, who sponsored Winthrop for membership in the Royal Society. Saye and Sele was ill at the time, but Manchester gave Winthrop access to Lord Chancellor Clarendon and others at court.

Despite his ability, Winthrop met with some obstacles before he attained his objective. The Puritan cause was not in favor, and the Puritan colonies had many enemies, some of them in America. Samuel Maverick had written Clarendon many letters on the subject, especially asserting that Connecticut and New Haven lacked patents and should be taken over by the crown.[33] Maverick was a leading member of a group that wanted to see a governor general placed over all the New England colonies. Fortunately, Saye and Sele was able to counteract these influences. Winthrop's final petition, presented some time before February 6, 1662, eventually reached the attorney general, who reported it favorably to the king in council. The attorney general's office then cast the charter into proper legal form, and it passed the seals on May 10, 1662. It cost about £600, including Winthrop's expenses, to obtain this document. The colony levied that amount on the towns, commanding them to send wheat and peas to New London until enough was accumulated to reimburse the London merchants who had lent the money.

Because Winthrop did not return to New England at once, two Massachusetts agents brought the charter to Connecticut. A meeting of the New England Confederation was in progress at Hartford when the document arrived there, and Connecticut's representatives submitted it to the commissioners for examination before releasing it to the colony. It was then read to the Connecticut freemen on October 9, 1662.[34]

By its charter Connecticut became a recognized corporate government with authority vested in the governor and freemen. The

---

[33] Maverick also published *A Briefe Description of New England and the Severall Townes Therein* in his effort to persuade Clarendon to supervise the New England colonies more closely. See *New England Historical and Genealogical Register*, XXXIX (Jan. 1885), 34–48.

[34] MacDonald, *Documentary Source Book*, pp. 60–62, reprints the charter, slightly condensed.

people received official status on the one hand, while in turn the sovereign, completely ignored in the Fundamental Orders and the Code of 1650, was given due recognition. The freemen henceforth took an oath of supremacy, and the admitted inhabitants of the towns still had to take the old oath of fidelity. The king's subjects would now enjoy the liberties and immunities of his subjects everywhere. Justice, as before, was to be rendered according to the Word of God and the law of righteousness. All writs ran henceforth in the king's name. With a royal charter, Connecticut was willing to accept English law and authority as long as it retained the power of self-government.

The charter provisions themselves were based on the Fundamental Orders and subsequent laws and practices. Winthrop and the other leaders had determined to allow as few changes as possible, and thus the charter essentially placed a seal of approval on what was already being done in the colony. Although the charter did not contain the word "commonwealth," Connecticut continued with a governor, deputy governor, assistants chosen by the freemen, and two annual general assemblies with two members from each town. Connecticut retained the power to make its own laws providing they were not contrary to the laws of England. It also retained the right to erect courts of justice, full freedom to carry on trade, to admit or reject individuals, to impose fines or imprison offenders, and to convert the heathen. The colony was not, to Winthrop's disappointment, exempt from the payment of customs dues. Land was to be held in free and common socage as of the king's manor of East Greenwich in Kent.[35] Connecticut paid no quitrent, but it was to remit to the king a fifth of all gold and silver found there, the usual optimistic royal reservation. The colony was guaranteed security against aggression or interference within its bounds.

The boundaries established by the charter invited controversy from the start.[36] Warwick, in a grant solicited but never received from the Council for New England, requested in June, 1632, terri-

[35] The Manor East Greenwich served as a model in many colonial charters of a form of tenure unburdened by military service or other bothersome requirements stemming from feudal practices. In essence, the tenant simply paid a money rent for the use of the land.

[36] See Clarence W. Bowen, *The Boundary Disputes of Connecticut* (Boston, 1882).

tory stretching from Narragansett Bay to a point thirty miles to the west along the shore and fifty miles inland. This proposed western boundary would not have reached the mouth of the Connecticut. However, in the deed Warwick issued three weeks earlier to the lords and gentlemen, he granted them a coastal frontage of one hundred twenty miles and a westward delineation "to the South Sea," which he thought to be just beyond the western mountains. When the general court handed its instructions to Winthrop in 1661, it directed him to obtain not only that land but much more. The court's notion of suitable bounds for the new charter involved pushing Connecticut's eastern boundary to Plymouth, thus obliterating all of Rhode Island's claims, and its western boundary to the Delaware—an area, incidentally, in which Connecticut had always been interested. Nor was Connecticut hesitant about absorbing weak and defenseless New Haven. The Duke of York ended Connecticut's southward ambitions in 1664 by annexing New Netherlands and its southern appendages for his personal fief. But apparently England had no idea of destroying the independence of either Rhode Island or New Haven, and, as we have seen, Rhode Island did save itself with Winthrop's help. New Haven, however, with both Winthrop and the crown disclaiming all responsibility, was irretrievably lost to Connecticut.[37]

[37] Andrews, *Colonial Period*, II, 66–143, and Albert E. Van Dusen, *Connecticut* (New York, 1961), pp. 7–74, are the most comprehensive accounts of the earliest period of Connecticut's history.

CHAPTER 11

New Haven

T HE defeat of the Pequot Indians in 1637 led to a closer examination of the shoreline of Long Island Sound by many who were interested in its potential. Except for the fort at Saybrook, this area was occupied up until that time only by such small tribes as the Nehantics, Quinnipiacs, Hammonassetts, and Paugassets. Although these coastal lands were forty miles from the Connecticut River towns, they were easily accessible by water. The Dutch more than once had declared their intention of occupying part of this area, because many river and stream mouths offered sites for harbors, but the only result was their short-lived outpost, the House of Hope, established in 1633 at what shortly became Hartford. The harbors were unquestionably inviting, but the land behind them was not promising for agriculture or even for stock raising.

By 1635 events in England were going badly for all men of Puritan persuasion. The trial of John Hampden was in progress, the Laud Commission was beginning its inquisitions, and the courts of High Commission and Star Chamber were engaging increasingly in repressive activities. The government was issuing writs of ship money, and it had published a writ of quo warranto against the charter of Massachusetts Bay. The alarmed Puritan lords and gentlemen sent over John Winthrop, Jr., to select and prepare a refuge at the mouth of the Connecticut River for themselves and their sympathizers. Members of the nonconforming clergy, too, were restless, and many left for Holland. There were others, however, who determined to venture to distant New England.

The Reverend John Davenport, Oxonian, was pastor for nine years of St. Stephen's Church, which was located in the middle of a prosperous nonconformist neighborhood in London. Because the vestry of this church enjoyed a large measure of independence, the influence of the bishop had been neutralized. Davenport had not, however, given the authorities any trouble, and he was well liked by rich and poor. A number of the leading parishioners interested themselves in the activities of the Massachusetts Bay Company, but because they were urbanites little at home in the manor or the field, few of them were likely to participate in founding an agricultural colony. Davenport himself was an active member of the company. He contributed £50 toward obtaining the charter, and he was close enough to the inner circle so that he was later informed about the decision of the signers of the Cambridge agreement to transfer the company and its charter to America. When Laud learned that Puritans were buying up benefices and appointing sympathetic ministers as incumbents, he decided to put an end to this practice because it threatened the unity of the church. Davenport, who was participating in this subterfuge, then joined the group of nonconformists to which Cotton and Hooker belonged, and he began to believe that reform from within the Church of England was hopeless.[1]

Cotton and Hooker, now fast friends of Davenport, were preparing to migrate to America, and he, too, decided that he would have to leave England. He consequently resigned his pastorate and in mid-November, 1633, removed hurriedly to Holland, where a number of Puritan divines had preceded him. He first assisted the Reverend John Paget, clergyman of the English church at Amsterdam, but the two soon fell out. Recognizing that his chance of being appointed Paget's co-pastor had evaporated, Davenport went to Rotterdam as assistant to the famous Reverend Hugh Peter. It was here that the Puritan lords and gentlemen perfected their scheme to settle Saybrook. Peter himself accepted a post with John

[1] Franklin Bowditch Dexter, "Sketch of the Life and Writings of John Davenport," *Papers of the New Haven Colony Historical Society*, II (1877), 205–238, provides a brief biography. Dorothy Ann Williams, "Some Aspects of the Puritan Movement in London, 1610–1640" (unpublished Ph.D. dissertation, Washington University, 1951), explains Davenport's activities in London. For his relations with Cotton, see Isabel MacBeath Calder, "John Cotton and the New Haven Colony," *New England Quarterly*, III (Jan., 1930), 82–94.

Winthrop, Jr., and Lion Gardiner also left to take service with the Warwick grantees. Davenport remained in Rotterdam as Peter's replacement, but he had reason to believe that he was not safe there. Laud and his henchmen were working to secure Davenport's dismissal, and Sir William Boswell, a hostile English merchant residing in Holland, was instigating an investigation into his activities.[2]

The minister decided in April, 1636, to return to England, and by then he had made up his mind to follow Cotton and Hooker to the New World to escape "the extremities" of Laud, now Archbishop of Canterbury. Disguised as a countryman, he traveled about England seeking old friends and former parishioners who would migrate with him. As the group grew, Davenport shared the responsibility for planning with Theophilus Eaton, who had been his schoolmate when they were boys together in Coventry and who had later become a wealthy London merchant and a member there of St. Stephen's Church. They were assisted by the Reverend Samuel Eaton, brother of Theophilus; Edward Hopkins, Theophilus' son-in-law and a Warwick grantee; David and Thomas Yale, sons of Mrs. Eaton by her earlier marriage; and several other prosperous London merchants.[3]

The St. Stephen's group and their friends chartered the *Hector*, two hundred fifty tons burden, and made ready to leave.[4] The government held up the vessel's departure for a time, but it sailed late in April, 1637, with about two hundred fifty persons aboard and arrived at Boston on June 26. By then Hooker had gone to Connecticut, but Cotton was on hand to welcome Davenport, and the other members of the party found temporary lodgings in the town.

Davenport and his followers apparently gave some consideration to the possibility of settling in Massachusetts, and the general court

[2] Charles M. Andrews, *The Colonial Period of American History* (4 vols., New Haven, Conn., 1934–38), II, 148–149.

[3] *Ibid.*, pp. 149–150. The best review of the life and importance of the colony's earliest civic leader is Simeon Eben Baldwin, "Theophilus Eaton, First Governor of the Colony of New Haven," *Papers of the New Haven Colony Historical Society*, VII (1908), 1–33.

[4] The St. Stephen's men provided the leadership, but they had recruited a number of families from other areas. See Isabel MacBeath Calder, *The New Haven Colony* (New Haven, Conn., 1934), pp. 29–30.

of that colony officially invited them to establish a plantation anywhere they wished within its boundaries. They received specific
offers from Charlestown and from Newbury, whose people wished
to emigrate to Winnacunnet (now Hampton, New Hampshire),
and the Plymouth Colony also made overtures.[5] The mercantile-
minded newcomers refused all these suggestions. They sought a
harbor of their own, and no good one remained unoccupied in
Massachusetts, and they did not want to settle in the interior where
the opportunities for trade would be limited. Moreover, they chose
not to become involved in the Antinomian controversy then pitting
Winthrop against Vane, and they were aware that the king might
at any moment impose a governor general on the Bay Colony.[6]
During the peak of the Hutchinson controversy, it was Davenport
more than anyone else who won Cotton back to orthodoxy, just as
in England Cotton had converted Davenport to nonconformity.
But Davenport would not compete for place among the Massachusetts clergymen, nor did he wish to become involved in the tangled
skein of New England theology. Davenport and Eaton believed
that God had something else in store for them.

Davenport's followers apparently decided that their best course
of action would be to acquire suitable unoccupied territory somewhere outside of Massachusetts, and recent events drew their attention to the northern shore of Long Island Sound. Hugh Peter had
been to Saybrook with George Fenwick and so had some familiarity
with the area. Israel Stoughton and the Massachusetts militia
traveled down the coast in July, 1637, helping John Mason pursue
the remnants of the Pequot tribe, and they formed a good impression of Quinnipiac, the region where New Haven is now located.
Accordingly Theophilus Eaton led a party of exploration out of
Boston on August 30, and he came to the conclusion that Quinnipiac and its harbor would suit their needs.[7] Eaton then went on
back to Massachusetts, leaving seven men to maintain possession

5 Andrews, *Colonial Period*, II, 151–152.

6 Edward Elias Atwater, *History of the Colony of New Haven to Its Absorp-
tion into Connecticut . . .* (Meriden, Conn., 1902), pp. 58–61.

7 Bernard Bailyn, *The New England Merchants in the Seventeenth Century*
(Cambridge, Mass., 1955), p. 29, suggests that three considerations determined the
selection of Quinnipiac: its large harbor, the probability of a local fur supply,
and the proximity of New Amsterdam, which represented a market for agricultural products.

of the land until he could bring the rest of the party to settle a town there in the spring.

Davenport spent a busy winter in Boston, preaching and trying to persuade others to join the enterprise. He was particularly anxious to lure Harry Vane and John Cotton, but the former decided to return to England and the latter, chastened by the Hutchinson affair, elected to remain in Massachusetts.[8] A number of people did join the Quinnipiac venture, however, including the Reverend Peter Prudden, of Hertfordshire, England, who had reached Boston with a party of followers shortly after the *Hector* arrived.[9] Two other volunteers destined to play important roles in the early history of New Haven were Nathaniel Turner, who had been living in Lynn, and Captain George Lamberton, a member of a migratory group led by the Reverend Ezekiel Rogers. Several others of the Rogers party settled in New Haven during 1638, but the majority participated with their minister in the founding of Rowley, Massachusetts.

The enlarged Davenport-Eaton company left Boston late in March, 1638, rounded Cape Cod, passed the fort at Saybrook, and settled on the shore of the spacious harbor at the mouth of the Quinnipiac River. The survivors of the party that had wintered there were living in underground shelters, and although these habitations proved to be very inadequate, the new settlers found it convenient to build more such cellars to provide temporary housing in a short time, and some of them remained in use as late as 1642.[10] A surveyor laid out the town in nine rectangles, eight being destined for residential purposes while the one in the center was reserved for a market place, drill ground, and site for a house of worship. After home lots, fields, and meadows were assigned to the heads of families, the settlers began building houses and barns and planting crops.[11] By 1643 the settlement was beginning to resemble any other plantation.

Like the founders of Connecticut, the New Haven settlers had no

[8] Calder, "John Cotton," pp. 85–86.

[9] Calder, *New Haven Colony*, p. 47.

[10] Atwater, *Colony of New Haven*, pp. 68, 71. The underground shelters were outlawed in 1632 because unmarried young men of uncertain reliability had taken possession of them. *Records of the Colony and Plantation of New Haven, from 1638 to 1649*, ed. C. J. Hoadly (Hartford, Conn., 1857), p. 7.

[11] See Atwater, *Colony of New Haven*, pp. 76–77, 103, for a description of the way in which the town was laid out and the lots were distributed.

royal patent or any other legal authorization entitling them to occupy the king's domain.[12] They might have negotiated for land with Peter or Fenwick, who were agents for the Warwick grantees, but any agreement made with those individuals would have had little significance. Eaton and his associates did make a series of purchases from the local Indians as land was needed, but these transactions did nothing to improve the legality of the settlement. In 1644 the New Haven General Court set about obtaining a royal charter, sending Thomas Gregson, one of its more affluent citizens, to London for that purpose and setting aside £200 for his expenses and other charges. The New Havenites were optimistic, because Roger Williams had just obtained a patent for Rhode Island from the Warwick committee of the Long Parliament, but the ship carrying Gregson was lost at sea. The disappointed settlers then asked George Fenwick to try to get a royal confirmation extending the Warwick grant to cover the new town. It developed that nobody could find the original of the Warwick patent or even a copy, and Fenwick therefore took no action in New Haven's behalf. The Earl of Warwick himself was the chairman of the parliamentary committee, and Sir Harry Vane was a member, yet neither showed any interest in New Haven, although the nobleman had helped Massachusetts, and Vane had given support to Rhode Island. Possibly they were repelled by Davenport's extreme orthodoxy, for which he had already become well known. New Haven tried again in 1653 to improve its situation, asking Edward Winslow of Plymouth to petition the Council of State for a patent to the Delaware region, at that time claimed by the Dutch but actually occupied by the Swedes. The petition was referred to Vane as president, but nothing came of it. The want of a patent remained a great weakness, and even the Dutch referred to New Haven as "a pretended colony."[13]

Lacking the security of a patent or charter, New Haven nevertheless undertook the formation of a civil government. Because Davenport had lived with Cotton during his winter in Boston, it seems certain that he derived much of his thinking on the nature of government from Cotton. His library in New Haven contained

12 They were, from London's point of view, nothing more than squatters. Roy H. Akagi, *The Town Proprietors of the New England Colonies: A Study of the Development, Organization, Activities, and Controversies, 1620–1670* (Philadelphia, 1924; republished Gloucester, Mass., 1963), pp. 15–16.

13 Andrews, *Colonial Period*, II, 154–156.

a copy of "Moses his Judicials," which Cotton had drawn up at the request of the Massachusetts General Court in 1636.[14] This code, inaccurately regarded as based on the Old Testament because of its marginalia, was a proposed outline for the government and law of the Bay Colony. It was actually based on the charter and on the common law of England, but it relied on the Mosaic code for its capital punishments.

The organization of the New Haven government followed the same general pattern as other New England colonies. As was customary, the settlers entered into a solemn covenant on their arrival, but it soon became clear that a more orderly structure was needed.[15] Accordingly, in June, 1639, some seventy free planters gathered in a large barn for the purpose of establishing "such civill order as might be most pleesing unto God." Davenport opened the meeting by discussing what qualifications the colonists should establish for those who might be entrusted with the affairs of government, fortifying his recommendations by reference to both the Old and the New Testaments. With only one dissenting voice his fellow townsmen agreed that all free burgesses (the term they used to describe freemen) must be members of an approved New England church.[16] Following the Cotton code, only church members would have the right to choose magistrates and officials, transact public business, make laws, settle any altercations that might arise, and in general care for the public weal. Having made this decision, the settlers then appointed eleven worthy men who in turn selected seven of their own number, "the seven pillars of the structure," to organize the local church and to become its first members. These seven soon added nine members of other New England churches to their number, electing themselves into a general court to govern the town.[17]

This general court elected a magistrate and four deputy magistrates whose duties were largely judicial. Theophilus Eaton became the original magistrate in 1639 and was reelected every year until

[14] Calder, *New Haven Colony*, pp. 40–44, 106–129.

[15] But Leonard Bacon, "Civil Government in the New Haven Colony," *Papers of the New Haven Colony Historical Society*, I (1865), 12–16, argues that the covenant must have been signed before the departure from Massachusetts.

[16] The one dissenter was the Reverend Samuel Eaton, brother of Theophilus, and a year later he found it convenient to go home to England.

[17] Atwater, *Colony of New Haven*, pp. 94–102.

١is death in 1658. He had little faith in any judgment but his own ١nd those of other magistrates, and he was so reactionary that he ١rought about the rejection of trial by jury. Davenport was the ١astor, Eaton the dictator. Both believed fervently in Davenport's ١ictum, "Power of Civil Rule, by men orderly chosen is God's ١rdinance"; and again, "In regular actings of the creature, God is ١he first Agent; these are not two several and distinct actings, one ١f God, another of the People; but in one and the same action, ١od, by the Peoples suffrages, makes such an one Governour, or ١agistrate, and not another."[18] The system of government adopted ١n 1639 remained in effect until 1643, when physical expansion ١f the colony resulted in elaboration of the political organization.

Many new settlements sprang up along Long Island Sound after ١he Pequot War of 1637. Connecticut promoted the development of ١tratford and Fairfield, and New Haven added to its territory by ١ second Indian purchase in 1638, giving it an area thirteen miles ١ong and ten miles wide. Peter Prudden left New Haven in the fall ١f 1639 and, with the assistance of loyal followers from both Hert-١ordshire, England, and Wethersfield in Connecticut, founded a ١own ten miles to the west, which was later named Milford.[19] Like ١any Puritan clergymen in New England, Prudden wanted a set-tlement of his own. His people agreed to a church covenant, chose their own seven pillars, and then organized their church. They selected five magistrates, provided for town meetings, and distrib-uted town lots and arable meadow lands. They followed the New Haven formula in all essentials except one, which was the matter of limiting participation in government to men who had been accepted into a church. Taking a more relaxed stand on this issue than did the older town, Milford admitted ten men into full citi-zenship who were not covenanted members of any congregation, but four of this number did subsequently join the local congrega-tion.[20]

[18] Quoted from Perry Miller, *Errand into the Wilderness* (Cambridge, Mass., 1956), pp. 149, 150.

[19] Prudden's son Peter became minister in Newark, New Jersey, a community dedicated to preserving New Haven's uncompromising orthodoxy.

[20] Leonard Labaree, *Milford, Connecticut: The Early Development of a Town as Shown in Its Land Records* (New Haven, Conn., 1938), pp. 4–5. See also Andrews, *Colonial Period*, II, 158–159.

Totoket, lying five miles to the east of New Haven, was part of the town's second purchase. The Reverend Samuel Eaton planned to bring followers of his from England to establish a plantation there, and the district was allotted to him for that purpose in 1640. He went home to enlist and organize colonists, but he never returned to America and so his land remained temporarily undeveloped.[21]

The Reverend Henry Whitfield, who had been a friend of Hooker's in Surrey, England, became the founder of Guilford immediately to the east of Totoket. Feeling that his nonconformist views made it necessary for him to leave his homeland, Whitfield obtained permission from George Fenwick to settle on part of the land set aside for the Puritan lords and gentlemen under the Warwick deed. After receiving a grant on Long Island Sound just east of where Madison is now located, he set sail in May, 1639, with a company of friends and parishioners. They adopted a plantation covenant during the passage, purchased their land from the local Indians when they landed, and set up a community which was entirely self-governing for four years. By restricting political privileges to members of their own church, Guilford created the narrowest franchise in all New England. Nonfreemen were, however, allowed to attend town meetings, although they could not vote for officials. In most respects, Guilford followed closely the New Haven model in the management of town affairs.[22]

In 1640 Captain Nathaniel Turner, acting on behalf of a New Haven group, purchased a large tract at Toquams, to the west of Fairfield.[23] That same year certain residents of Wethersfield, headed by the Reverend Richard Denton, a contentious clergyman from Halifax, England, fell into dispute with their neighbors over local church matters, and they decided that they should relocate. Davenport advised them to settle at Toquams and to accept the New Haven system in principle and form and to acknowledge political control by New Haven. Denton and his discontented friends agreed to this plan and in 1641 settled what became known as Stamford. The new town began immediately sending deputies to the New Haven General Court and submitting nominations for local mag-

[21] Henry White, "The New Haven Colony," *Papers of the New Haven Colony Historical Society*, I (1865), 5.

[22] Andrews, *Colonial Period*, II, 160–161.

[23] Vicinity of Stamford.

istrates and constables to the central authorities for approval.[24] Thus the general court assumed jurisdiction over more than one settlement, and New Haven began to grow from an isolated community into a colony.

New Haven made another acquisition in 1640, purchasing Yennicock, a part of northeastern Long Island, from the agent of the Earl of Stirling, to whom the Council for New England had granted Long Island. The Reverend John Youngs settled there with a number of families, who named their town Southold and who, like Stamford, accepted political subordination to New Haven. They followed the "New Haven Way" in all particulars, allowing the parent community the right to appoint their constable until a magistracy should be settled upon the place. New Haven retained this degree of oversight until 1649, when the Youngs' group completed paying for the land and received title to the territory.[25]

The New England Confederation, organized in 1643, accepted New Haven into its membership along with Massachusetts, Plymouth, and Connecticut, recognizing that its control over two other towns made it a political jurisdiction rather than merely an individual settlement. Milford and Guilford, both sympathetic with New Haven's principles, found it desirable to surrender their independence and become parts of the jurisdiction, joining in July and October of 1643, respectively.

New Haven soon added another town to its growing structure. Squatters had been filtering into Totoket, and they were proving to be boisterous as well as unwelcome. New Haven was therefore pleased to be able to sell the area in 1644 to another group of families from Wethersfield, who accepted the tenets of the parent community and became part of its jurisdiction. Other settlers came from Southampton, on Long Island, led by Abraham Pierson, a minister who later achieved fame as the founder of Newark in East Jersey. Totoket became known as Branford, honoring the London suburb of that name. The town grew unusually slowly and had no formally organized church or town government until after 1650.[26]

24 Information about earliest Stamford will be found in Andrews, *Colonial Period*, II, 162; Atwater, *Colony of New Haven*, pp. 174–175, and Albert E. Van Dusen, *Connecticut* (New York, 1961), p. 55.
25 Andrews, *Colonial Period*, II, 163; Atwater, *Colony of New Haven*, pp. 171–172.
26 Elijah C. Baldwin, "Branford Annals," *Papers of the New Haven Colony Historical Society*, III (1882), 249–270.

In the short space of five years New Haven had extended its boundaries from Guilford on the east to Milford on the west. Farther west, beyond the Connecticut towns of Stratford, Fairfield, and Norwalk, it controlled Stamford, to which Greenwich was added in 1650 by agreement with the Dutch.[27] The northern boundary of New Haven never reached more than ten or fifteen miles inland, but there seemed to be opportunity for expansion across the Sound. The Dutch occupied the western portion of Long Island, but from its base in Southold, New Haven increased its sway in the eastern area until it built up some relationship with Southampton, East Hampton, Oyster Bay, and Huntington. New Haven was unsuccessful in maintaining the loyalty of these four towns, however, and they soon slipped away from its control.

The transformation from a single town to a province necessitated an expansion of New Haven's governmental structure. A magistrate, four deputy magistrates, and a general court had sufficed until 1643, the court amounting for all practical purposes to a town meeting. All householders and planters could become members of this organization by taking an oath of fidelity, but they could not vote unless they were church members who had been accepted by the court as free burgesses and who had then taken the freemen's charge. As dependent towns were admitted, a hybrid arrangement was worked out allowing them representation in the general court. Finally, in October, 1643, when Guilford and Milford had joined the jurisdiction, the authorities drew up a "fundamental agreement" providing a more suitable organization. A governor and deputy governor were elected, as well as magistrates for New Haven, Milford, and Stamford, and on October 27 a general court convened, made up of the governor and deputy governor and two deputies each from New Haven, Milford, Guilford, and Stamford. This new body dealt only with provincial affairs, and New Haven henceforth kept separate records relating to purely local matters. This frame of government followed closely that of Massachusetts and owed a particular debt to the Cotton code of 1636.[28]

The New Haven jurisdiction was never more than a loose con-

[27] White, "New Haven Colony," p. 4, explains the circumstances under which Greenwich came under New Haven control.

[28] Bacon, "Civil Government," pp. 21–27, discusses thoroughly the organization of the colony.

federation of towns held together by the general court, which was unicameral and had no speaker. The fundamental body of law was contained in the Code of 1656, which owed much to the thinking of John Cotton, but the court periodically made amendments or additions to it.[29] The laws were read at all town meetings, and all inhabitants were expected to know and obey them. A court of magistrates had responsibility for seeing that justice was done, but appeals from its decisions were presented to the general court. Of all the New England colonies, New Haven alone rejected trial by jury. Although this form of government endured until 1665, when New Haven was annexed to Connecticut, the inhabitants themselves regarded their civil arrangements as temporary, and they always looked forward to some major reorganization of the colony's affairs.

The fact that the founders of New Haven were interested mainly in commercial activities was a persuasive argument for the maximum possible geographical expansion. The colony was hemmed in along the shore by the inland Connecticut towns behind it, however, and Saybrook blocked any move eastward. Most of the newly established English-speaking settlements in eastern Long Island were disinclined to accept New Haven control, and so the ambitious merchants had to look toward the west and south. The Dutch occupied Manhattan and the Hudson River Valley. They had also built Fort Nassau (now Gloucester), farther south on the Delaware, in 1626, but the Swedes had moved into that area in 1638. At the time of the founding of New Haven these two powers, each represented by a government-supported trading company, were bitter rivals, and the Dutch were not able to overcome the Swedish arms in the district until 1655.

In 1640 John Davenport of New Haven, with the approval of the town, formed the Delaware Company to examine the Delaware basin for its potential value as a place for trade and settlement. Captain George Lamberton and Captain Nathaniel Turner led a small expedition there a year later and with the consent of the Swedes took up land on the east side of the river at Salem Creek. They then purchased additional land from the Indians near the

[29] *Records of the Colony or Jurisdiction of New Haven, from May, 1649, to the Union*, ed. C. J. Hoadly (Hartford, Conn., 1858), pp. 567–616.

mouth of the Schuylkill on the west bank. The Dutch intervened at this point, seizing Lamberton and others and imprisoning them temporarily in New Amsterdam before permitting them to go home to New Haven. They also destroyed the trading post that the English had built, and the twenty-odd families who tried to stay on at Varkens Kill (now Salem) endured such hardships that the company withdrew them and abandoned the project in 1643.[30] Lamberton later attempted to resume trade with the Indians in the area, but Governor Johann Printz of New Sweden arrested him and his crew, tried them, and ruled that Lamberton had no right to trade there. When New Haven brought the matter before the New England Confederation, Governor Winthrop wrote to Printz, demanding satisfaction, and amicable relations were restored. Governor Theophilus Eaton and the Delaware Company then obtained a commission from the confederation authorizing Captain Turner to revive the plantation and continue trading on the Delaware.[31]

Efforts were now made to improve trade conditions and to create an atmosphere conducive to geographical expansion. Governor Eaton complained to Governor Peter Stuyvesant because the Dutch assessed duties at New Amsterdam, and he demanded freedom of trade at Manhattan as well as permission for New Haven ships to pass through to the Delaware without Dutch interference. He took this occasion to reassert New Haven's rightful ownership of its Delaware land, but Stuyvesant denied the validity of this claim. The New England Confederation backed Eaton, and New Haven decided to go ahead with its plans. Several New Haven residents made a private effort to organize a colonizing party, and although they gave up when Stuyvesant threatened to use arms against them, many men in New Haven remained anxious to move to a better location. They asked Eaton himself to lead them, but he begged

[30] Arthur H. Buffington, "New England and the Western Fur Trade, 1629–1675," Colonial Society of Massachusetts Publications, XVIII (1915–1916), 169, suggests that this calamity probably increased New Haven's willingness to join the New England Confederation.

[31] Epher Whitaker, "New Haven's Adventure on the Delaware Bay," Papers of the New Haven Colony Historical Society, IV (1888), 209–230, gives a good description of these events, as does Charles H. Levermore, The Republic of New Haven: A History of Municipal Evolution (Baltimore, 1886), pp. 90–93. See also Andrews, Colonial Period, II, 168–169.

off on grounds of poor health. The general court debated the matter in January, 1655, but no action was taken. The authorities made it clear at a town meeting in April that any settlement undertaken on the Delaware would become part of New Haven's jurisdiction. The project had altered by 1654–55 so that settlement rather than trade had become its object, but in the end no action was taken. New Haven did, however, maintain its claim to Delaware land even after it became part of Connecticut.[32]

A number of New Haven settlers were wealthy and experienced merchants, but the drain on their capital during the first fifteen years proved extremely discouraging. The *Hector* expedition was expensive, as was the winter spent in Boston, the land purchased from the Indians, and the first houses that were erected. There were subsequent misfortunes, including £1,000 lost on the first Delaware venture, a ship lost at sea, and an unprofitable attempt to start an ironworks.

The New Haven spokesmen gradually became convinced that the only real solution to their problem would be to drive out the Dutch and thereby gain easy access to the Delaware region. William Hooke wrote to that effect in 1653, stating: "We and our posterity (now almost prepared to swarme forth plenteously) are confined and straitened, the sea lying before us and a rocky rude desert, unfitt for culture and destitute of commodity, behind our backs, all convenient places for accommodations on the sea coast already possessed and planted."[33] New Haven attempted to organize a war against New Netherland in 1653 but had to back down when it could not win the support of Massachusetts, which enjoyed a good trade with the Dutch at New Amsterdam and was therefore, perhaps, unwilling to aid its fellow countrymen.[34] Cromwell tried twice to persuade the New Haven leaders to migrate, once suggesting Ireland as their destination and later recommending Hispaniola or Mexico, both of which he expected to capture from the Spanish. When the English seized Jamaica in 1655, the New Haven settlers refused to consider going there, still arguing that a better course

[32] John E. Pomfret, *The Province of West New Jersey* (Princeton, N.J., 1956), pp. 20–31.

[33] Quoted from Andrews, *Colonial Period*, II, 173.

[34] Henry Taylor Blake, *Chronicles of the New Haven Green, 1638–1862* (New Haven, Conn., 1909), p. 54.

of action would be for Cromwell to drive out the Dutch.[35] Their hope of getting this sort of assistance vanished when England made peace with Holland.

The loss of George Lamberton's "phantom ship" was a particularly severe blow to New Haven's trade aspirations. Built in 1645 for the purpose of opening direct trade with England, this craft was, at eighty tons, the largest constructed at New Haven. A number of the leading figures financed her, including Theophilus Eaton, Stephen Goodyear, Richard Malbon, and Thomas Gregson, and these and other merchants loaded her with cargoes worth £50 to £80 each. The vessel sailed in 1646, carrying Nathaniel Turner and Gregson as well as Lamberton, and it was never heard from.[36] Davenport observed gloomily in 1659 that the colony's inhabitants could not subsist unless they found some way to improve trading, and he insisted again in 1662 that additional shipping was a necessity.

Despite its commercial ambitions, the New Haven Colony never became more than a congeries of rural communities in an area not well adapted for farming, and the life of the great majority of the people was closely linked to the soil.[37] In 1660 New Haven was the largest town, followed by Milford, Guilford, Stamford, Southold, and Branford. The colony did not encourage the expansion of the village system because of the loss of taxes to the mother town and because the influence of the ministry might be weakened.[38] Most of the inhabitants were English, but there were also a few Dutchmen, Scots, Negroes, and Indians. The population was a mixture of freemen or church members, free planters who were not church members, indentured servants, and apprentices. The majority were gainfully employed as merchants, mariners, farmers, artisans, and hired laborers, and, as was true in other New England coastal towns, there was a transient element made up of wanderers from other colonies and seamen, always an unruly lot. The towns kept watch

[35] For a discussion of Cromwell's offers to New Haven, see Atwater, Colony of New Haven, pp. 200–202.

[36] Ibid., p. 208, explains the financing of the voyage.

[37] Splendid crops during the summer of 1638 encouraged the settlers, but no harvest thereafter ever equaled that first one. Sarah Day Woodward, Early New Haven (New Haven, Conn., 1929), p. 21.

[38] Levermore, Republic of New Haven, pp. 107–110.

over the residents and their activities. They regulated the cutting of timber and firewood and the building of highways, bridges, and fences, and they provided protection against fire. They maintained militia companies in each town, which kept themselves in a certain state of preparedness in spite of confusion and disorder every training day.

Industry never developed beyond a primitive level in New Haven. There were gristmills, but sawing was done in a pit. There were tanneries, but many complaints in the records suggest that both the leather and the shoes made from it were of inferior quality. There were bakers, hatters, blacksmiths, coopers, carpenters, ropemakers, wheelwrights, and dish turners, but they performed their services on a small scale, working in their houses or barns or in little shops on their premises. Accusations were leveled at the bakers for selling underweight loaves, and so an assize was included in the Code of 1656. The government also adopted other regulations of a similar nature regulating the size of hogsheads, dry and liquid measures, and measures of weight, in all instances following English precedents. Such finished goods as came into the colony were retailed in private houses and in small shops. The authorities gave approval to a limited number of ordinaries and private houses to retail liquor, but the licensing, as was true in other colonies, was a perplexing matter. There was no manufacturing except for the iron-making in East Haven.[39]

Business, such as there was, was hampered by lack of a medium of exchange. Hard money was scarce, and there is no mention of silver until 1651. Black and white wampum was the sole medium of exchange in the early days, but it deteriorated in quality and hence depreciated greatly in value, and even the general court was unable to stabilize it. As the result, barter and payment in kind became increasingly popular. Corn and other grains, cattle, wool, peas, beef, pork, bread, and even brass and iron passed, at prices fixed by the Boston traders. The people paid rates, taxes, and imposts by resorting to "good current country paye at cuntry price" determined by the local authorities.

The town fathers had enough time left over from their normal

---

[39] Even the ironworks, like so many other ventures in New Haven, resulted in failure. Bailyn, *New England Merchants,* p. 71.

duties so that they could give obsessive attention to what they considered to be the increasing frequency of sin. They had a double interest in drunkenness and sexual misdemeanors, because they maintained that the guilty were responsible to God as well as to the courts. The magistrates probed so thoroughly into these aberrations that the examinations could not, in good taste, be included when the town records were published. Such offenses were bad enough when nonfreemen committed them, but when members of the church were involved, the crimes seemed truly heinous, and the offenders were excommunicated. Although the preservation of peace and righteousness was the immediate purpose of punishment, the ultimate aim of justice was to reform man and avert God's wrath, and so the authorities felt obliged to exercise the greatest vigilance in all matters. They interdicted card playing, dancing, and singing as tending to corrupt youth, but the young and some of their elders nevertheless pursued these activities on the sly. There was some feeling against the use of tobacco, and smoking was not allowed in public. The greatest number of offenders, as was true in other colonies, were indentured servants and seamen. Law enforcement was vigorous, and there was at least one execution for adultery. Banishment, too, was used as a penalty, while ordinary misdemeanors were punished by stocks, whipping, imprisonment, fines, and humiliating penances such as wearing a halter.[40]

Davenport hoped to establish a school and eventually a college, and he endeavored to collect books for the use of the ministers, but in spite of this zeal on his part, the New Haven Colony did not thrive as a center for educational or cultural activity. The town did manage to build a school in 1641 and to employ an instructor from the common funds, but what started out as an ambitious program to teach Latin and English soon dwindled to a course in reading and spelling, and the number of pupils fell to five or six. A proposal was made in 1659 to erect a central school, with feeder

---

[40] Leonard Bacon, a defender of New Haven, admits that great stress was laid on administration of the laws, but he points out that the community was scrupulously just toward the Indians and that it avoided what he calls "frivolous or extravagant legislation," in which category he places sumptuary laws, witchcraft trials, and the persecution of Quakers. *Thirteen Historical Discourses* (New York, 1839), pp. 92–96.

schools in every village, but the colony lacked the resources to execute so extensive an undertaking, and the best it could do was to create a single "Colony School" offering instruction in Latin, Greek, and Hebrew. Even this limited accomplishment was possible only because of a bequest from Edward Hopkins, who left his entire estate in New England and £500 from his estate in England for the purpose of founding the Hopkins grammar schools in New Haven, Hadley, and Hartford. Davenport did not live to see the founding of the college, which dates from 1701 and was named for Elihu Yale. There was talk in 1664 of building a library to house the many books belonging to the town, but no action was taken. New Haven boasted a meetinghouse fifty feet square with a tower, a turret, and a casement window. Hastily built in 1640, it soon showed signs of decay and required frequent repairs, but it was not replaced by a more substantial structure until 1670. All public notices were posted on the meetinghouse door, as in England, and the town drummer in the marketplace summoned the inhabitants to meetings on lecture days, days of humiliation and thanksgiving, and on the Sabbath.

Until 1660 the government of New Haven accorded closely with Puritan ideas of faith and polity, but there were some rumblings of discontent in the colony. About 1653 some of the inhabitants of Stamford, Southold, and Milford demanded an extension of the suffrage, the adoption of English law, and the right of appeal to England. The most verbal of the discontented colonists was Robert Bassett of Stamford, who took the position at a town meeting there that he would obey no authority save that which came out of England, and he incited others to join him in a protest that the New Haven jurisdiction was tyrannical. From time to time the general court summoned such recalcitrant individuals before it and charged them with disturbing the peace in their respective towns and with disloyalty to the colony. All of them were severely reprimanded, heavily fined, and put under bond to answer in court to the magistrates, but they were released once they submitted and acknowledged their transgressions. The general court insisted that all inhabitants bind themselves by oaths of fidelity, and it required the deputies from the several towns to take a special oath promising to do justice in all cases and to use their best skill and knowledge according to the laws of the colony. By these means the leaders hoped to secure the colony against disaffection, and to an extent they succeeded. But financial conditions did not improve, efforts to expand into Long Island failed, and the hope of establishing a commercial center on the Delaware receded. By 1660 New Haven was economically weak and legally insecure, and thus poorly prepared to meet the crisis that arose.[41]

When the Reverend John Davenport heard in 1660 that Charles II had become king, he refused to believe the news, and both he and his neighbors were slow to understand the peril in which the Restoration had placed them. Hugh Peter and Sir Harry Vane, two of Davenport's old friends and supporters, were executed by the new monarch. Sir Isaac Pennington and Owen Roe, other close associates, were imprisoned in the Tower of London and died there, and the Reverend William Hooke, Davenport's associate in the New Haven church before his return to England, had to run for his life. Many regicides and their sympathizers fled, some of them finding their way to America. The new regime in England sent agents across the Atlantic to track down these men and arrest them, and the Puritan colonies had to make the difficult decision either to repudiate their friends or to disobey the royal command. Massachusetts hastened to condemn those who assisted in the execution of Charles I and ordered the seizure of two men who were then in that colony. These two regicides fled to New Haven, where Davenport indicated that he would give them asylum. Although the royal agents warned the colony that it would do itself injury, the towns of both New Haven and Milford harbored the fugitives for a period of time.[42]

The New Haven Colony did, however, finally proclaim the new king in a public ceremony, as did Massachusetts and Rhode Island, whereas Connecticut and Plymouth merely acknowledged him. Recognizing that it had many enemies in England, Massachusetts felt called upon to send two agents to London bearing an address

[41] Rollin G. Osterweis, *Three Centuries of New Haven, 1638–1938* (New Haven, Conn., 1953), p. 60.

[42] The experiences of the regicides who came to New Haven are described in Franklin Bowditch Dexter, "Memoranda Respecting Edward Whalley and William Goffe," *Papers of the New Haven Colony Historical Society*, II (1877), 117–146.

couched in unctuous humility, and Connecticut delegated John Winthrop, Jr., to make a diplomatic journey on its behalf. New Haven was too poor to bear such an expense, and so its governor, William Leete, offered to share expenses with Massachusetts if that colony would represent New Haven's interests in England. When Massachusetts showed no interest in such an arrangement, Leete asked Connecticut to have Winthrop speak for New Haven abroad and obtain patents for both colonies. Unfortunately for New Haven, Winthrop had already sailed for England.[43]

Connecticut directed Winthrop to seek a grant of territory extending from the Massachusetts-Plymouth border to the Delaware. Thus Connecticut ignored the claims of both New Haven and Rhode Island, and its instructions to its agent did not, in fact, contain any mention of New Haven, a fellow member in the New England Confederation. It would seem as if Connecticut had made up its mind to emulate Massachusetts, not only in obtaining like privileges and liberties, but in extending its jurisdiction.[44]

New Haven's case seemed hopeless, and news of the Restoration brought forth the malcontents once again. One prominent dissenter, whose views were echoed, spoke against the government, denied the magistrates' authority, and refused to obey any laws not emanating from England. Other men ranted against the limitations of the suffrage and demanded the wider privileges enjoyed by Connecticut citizens. In October, 1662, a month after Connecticut received its charter, Southold asked to be taken under the jurisdiction of that colony. A number of Guilford inhabitants followed suit, and the entire populations of Stamford and Greenwich went over to Connecticut, which immediately appointed constables for those towns. Elsewhere men refused to accept office because of the uncertainty of the future. The New Haven General Court, confronted by disorder, could only apprehend disturbers and bring them before the magistrates as violators of the peace. By the end of 1662, New Haven's jurisdiction had shrunk greatly, with only New Haven, Branford, and Milford remaining, and the latter broke away in 1664. Only Branford stayed loyal to the end, but in all the towns there were groups that continued to adhere to the New Haven Way. The government and its leaders steadfastly refused "to breake

[43] Andrews, *Colonial Period*, II, 186.
[44] *Ibid.*

or conclude anything that may have tendencie to change of the present government."[45]

Connecticut delivered an ultimatum to New Haven in October, 1662, demanding a union of the two colonies, but the contest lasted until the arrival of the royal commissioners in July, 1664. During the interim Connecticut based its adamant stand on its new charter, and New Haven, inspired by Davenport and Leete, was equally firm in opposing annexation. New Haven appealed to the king, but Winthrop, who was not unfriendly toward New Haven, opposed submitting the appeal, because he feared it would cause trouble in the Rhode Island case. He wrote Deputy Governor John Mason deprecating the course that Connecticut was pursuing, but Mason ignored his plea. Once the charter passed the seals, Connecticut regarded Winthrop's work as done and therefore ignored his counsels. New Haven brought its plight before the New England Confederation in 1663, charging that Connecticut's interference with New Haven towns constituted a violation of the rules of the confederation. New Haven obtained support for its position, and the meeting at Hartford voted that encroachment upon New Haven's jurisdiction should cease. Thus encouraged, New Haven wrote Connecticut asking that she desist, but instead of answering the letter Connecticut demanded that New Haven submit to the terms of her charter forthwith.[46]

In October, 1663, the New Haven General Court decided on another appeal to the king, and in January, 1664, it arranged to have Davenport and the Reverend Nicholas Street draw up a statement of the colony's position.[47] "New Haven's Case Stated," the review they wrote of the entire situation from the beginning of the colony, made a number of assertions, among which was the claim that Winthrop, before leaving for England, had written a friend that he had no intention of extending the bounds of the Connecticut patent to include New Haven. For this reason, it was alleged, New Haven made no effort to obtain a patent of its own, and if that actually was the case, it becomes clear that the English authorities did not realize that they were encroaching on New Haven when

[45] *Records of the Colony or Jurisdiction of New Haven*, p. 453.
[46] Andrews, *Colonial Period*, II, 188–189.
[47] Street was teacher in the New Haven church and later succeeded Davenport as minister.

they gave the charter to Connecticut. It is no wonder that Davenport and Street charged Connecticut with breach of faith, and Connecticut's self-righteous and unfair reply did nothing to improve matters.[48]

Two events occurring before the end of 1664; the royal grant of a huge proprietorship on March 12 to the Duke of York and the subsequent dispatch of four royal commissioners to New England, combined to bring the whole controversy to an end.[49] The king vested his brother, the duke, with various territories extending from Maine to the Delaware, and one effect of the gift was to obliterate New Haven and deprive Connecticut of half its territory.[50] Conditions in the government departments in London must have been in a state of confusion to countenance such a grant. The royal commissioners went to America for a dual purpose: to conquer New Netherland and to report on the New England colonies with a view toward their reorganization.

The arrival of the commissioners sent a chill through New England. Massachusetts sent word to Connecticut and New Haven to settle their dispute. Connecticut responded by summarily sending agents to New Haven to demand submission. That beleaguered colony procrastinated, but it was too late to consider removing to the Delaware, because the duke had granted all of New Jersey to his friends and former associates, Lord John Berkeley and Sir George Carteret. The thought of remaining within the duke's jurisdiction being more offensive than a forced union with Connecticut, New Haven yielded in December, 1664, and the formal act of submission was passed a month later.[51]

[48] "New Haven's Case Stated" is reproduced in Atwater, *Colony of New Haven*, pp. 565–580.

[49] *Records of the Colony or Jurisdiction of New Haven*, pp. 517–537.

[50] Connecticut's western boundary (ten miles east of the Hudson) was restored in 1667 by Governor Richard Nicolls of New York.

[51] The best book on the New Haven Colony is Calder, *New Haven Colony*, and excellent briefer accounts will be found in Andrews, *Colonial Period*, II, 144–194, and Osterweis, *Three Centuries of New Haven*, pp. 1–64. Also useful are Atwater, *Colony of New Haven*; Charles M. Andrews, *The Rise and Fall of the New Haven Colony* (New Haven, Conn., 1936); and Ernest H. Baldwin, "Why New Haven Is Not a State of the Union," *Papers of the New Haven Colony Historical Society*, VII (1908), 161–187.

CHAPTER 12

New Netherland, New Sweden, and New York

THE Dutch ignored England's claims to all the land between Newfoundland and Florida, in the same way that the English ignored the papal bulls of demarcation dividing the newly discovered territories in the world between Spain and Portugal.[1] Although the Netherlands based its pretensions on the activities of the Greenland Company in 1598, there was no Dutch exploration in North America until the voyage of Henry Hudson in 1609. Even that trip was fortuitous, inasmuch as the powerful Amsterdam Chamber of Commerce of the Dutch East India Company employed Hudson, an Englishman, to sail to the Arctic, where he had gone twice before, to discover a passage via the northeast to the Orient.[2] Hudson set out in the *Half Moon* in April, 1609, for the Russian island of Novaya Zemlya, about 81 degrees north. Arriving there a month later and finding the seas icebound, he turned westward to the Chesapeake but did not visit his countrymen at Jamestown, since he did not wish the English to learn of his presence. He then began to explore the coast to the north.

[1] Readers seeking background on Holland during this period of national vigor and expansion should consult the third and fourth volumes of Petrus A. Blok, *A History of the People of the Netherlands* (5 vols., New York, 1898–1912).

[2] Henry C. Murphy, *Henry Hudson in Holland* (The Hague, 1859), is an excellent study of the motives, purposes, and character of the men who projected the voyage and of Hudson's own designs.

Hudson entered the as yet unnamed Delaware Bay on August 26, 1609, but soon decided that those shoal-like waters could be no part of any northwest passage. He thereupon sailed to Manhattan, arriving there on September 12. Although New York Bay had been visited before, it was on the basis of Hudson's voyage that the Netherlands laid claim to all American territory between Cape Cod and Delaware Bay. After examining the mouth of the Hudson River, the explorer recrossed the Atlantic and anchored at Dartmouth in his native England. He was allowed to forward to the Dutch East India Company only a summary report and a copy of his journal, and the English refused to let him make another voyage for his Dutch employers. His fourth journey, undertaken under English auspices, ended in 1611 when his mutinous crew set him adrift in a small boat in Hudson's Bay while he was still searching for the passage.[3]

Private merchants maintained Dutch interest in the New World for more than a decade after Hudson's third voyage. Three enterprising Amsterdam and Hoorn businessmen secured a three-year trading monopoly in 1614 covering the ill-defined region lying between New France and Virginia, and they formed the United Netherland Company, which was a loosely formed association rather than the more conventional joint-stock company. During the firm's brief existence, it undertook only four voyages, but these demonstrated, if nothing else, the great potential value of the Hudson River fur trade. The voyages did, however, also increase geographical knowledge about what soon became known as New Netherland. Ships' captains, among them Hendrick Christaensen, Adriaen Block and Cornelis May, explored estuaries up and down the coast searching for furs. Block sailed as far as Cape Cod, and the name Block Island is a testimonial of this voyage. Captain May was the most persistent of these explorers, reconnoitering the coast as early as 1613 and sailing up the Delaware in 1620. His name is perpetuated in Cape May, while Cape Henlopen, on the opposite shore, was

<hr/>

[3] Contemporary accounts of Hudson's third voyage by Meteren, Juet, and De Laet are printed in J. Franklin Jameson (ed.), *Narratives of New Netherland, 1609–1664* (New York, 1909). Llewelyn Powys, *Henry Hudson* (New York, 1928), is the best biography, although Edgar Mayhew Bacon, *Henry Hudson: His Times and His Voyages* (New York, 1907), still retains some usefulness. Lawrence J. Burpee, "The Fate of Henry Hudson," *Canadian Historical Review*, XXI (Dec., 1940), 401–406, summarizes the known facts about the explorer's death.

named by him for a Dutch village. Delaware Bay was called Nieuw Port May by the Dutch but soon afterward received its permanent name in honor of the Virginia governor, Lord De la Warr.[4]

In 1617 the United Netherland Company was denied a renewal of its privileges, the States General, with an eye to national policy, having determined to create something larger and more effective. The expiration of the truce between the Netherlands and Spain in 1621 gave the signal for a general attack upon Spain in the New World. The Dutch West India Company, dreamed of since 1592 by William Usselinx, the remarkable Flemish émigré in Amsterdam, and now chartered in time of war, was intended to constitute an offensive agency in regions where the Dutch East India Company was not active.[5] Although incorporated in June, 1621, the new organization did not commence operations for two years. It received an exclusive right to trade, govern, and colonize unoccupied land from Newfoundland to the Strait of Magellan and on the west coast of Africa from the Tropic of Cancer to the Cape of Good Hope. Its American operations were principally along the coasts of Surinam and Brazil, on certain Caribbean islands, and from Cape Cod to Cape Henlopen. There was no specific mention of New Netherland in the charter. The company organization was complex, but power was concentrated in the Board of Nineteen which sat at Amsterdam. The largest block of delegates represented the Amsterdam Chamber of Commerce, whose members supplied more than 40 per cent of the capital. Until New Netherland passed to England in 1664, the Amsterdam Chamber virtually ruled the province, acting through the Board of Nineteen.

The company devoted its main energies to preparations for the conquest of Brazil, but it did send thirty families, most of whom were Walloon refugees, to America on the *Nieu Nederlandt* in the spring of 1624. The majority of these homeseekers, the first real

[4] For descriptions of Dutch activities during this period, particularly their exploratory visits, see Adrian J. Barnouw, "Dutch Background of New Netherland," in Alexander C. Flick (ed.), *History of the State of New York* (10 vols., New York, 1933–37, reprinted as 10 vols. in 5, Port Washington, N.Y., 1962), I, 177–214; also Mrs. Schuyler Van Rennselaer, *History of the City of New York in the Seventeenth Century* (2 vols., New York, 1909), I, 20–27.

[5] See J. Franklin Jameson, "William Usselinx, Founder of the Dutch and Swedish West India Companies," American Historical Society *Papers* (1887), I, Pt. 3, 1–220.

New Netherland colonists, settled at Fort Orange (now on the west side of Albany) on the Hudson, but others under the direction of May settled on Burlington Island, New Jersey.[6] Fort Nassau on the Delaware, just opposite the present Philadelphia, was also established in 1626. There were no dwellings at Manhattan until the coming of Peter Minuit in that year, and Long Island was not settled until ten years later. Soon after his arrival, Director Minuit relocated all his colonists at Manhattan, thus reversing the previous policy of distributing settlers to the several outlying posts. By 1628 there were 270 persons at New Amsterdam on Manhattan Island, while at Fort Orange only traders, fourteen in number, were permitted to remain.[7] On the South River (now the Delaware) a single trading vessel replaced Fort Nassau. The ugliness manifested by the natives when the Dutch interfered in an Indian quarrel revealed just how untenable these little outposts really were. Building the New Netherland population proved to be a slow process, because conditions in Holland did not favor any large exodus of people. The company endeavored to recruit emigrants, but industry and commerce were prospering in the homeland, and few were willing to go. At the same time there were always dissatisfied or disillusioned settlers who wished for nothing better than to return to Holland.[8]

The Dutch West India Company was a poor instrument with which to fashion a colony worthy of Dutch enterprise, but its powers and privileges were not challenged until the last years of its existence. The directors and stockholders, as in all business ventures, wanted a return on the invested capital. Farming was neglected in the quest for furs, and food was always difficult to obtain. The company regarded the farmer as nothing more than an investment. It leased land to the settlers and advanced them such necessities as livestock, wagons, and plows, but these loans were entered on the books as debits to be repaid with interest. No settler held title to a single foot of land, nor until 1647 could any person trade on his own account, these privileges being reserved to

[6] Clinton A. Weslager, *Dutch Explorers, Traders and Settlers in the Delaware Valley, 1609–1664* (Philadelphia, 1961), pp. 63–81, 121–126.

[7] Victor Hugo Palsits, "The Founding of New Amsterdam in 1626," American Antiquarian Society *Proceedings*, XXXIV (Apr., 1924), 39–65, is excellent.

[8] Pieter Geyl, *The Netherlands in the Seventeenth Century* (2 vols., New York, 1961–64), gives a classic account of conditions in Holland during this period.

the company. Yet, as the company itself came to realize, settlers were necessary, if for no other reason than to defend the feeble establishment against the sheer weight of the English to the east and, after 1638, the threat of the Swedes on the Delaware.[9]

There was considerable early activity at Manhattan Island but not at first any real settlement. Cornelis May served as managing director of New Netherland until November, 1624, when he returned to Holland. In April, 1625, the company sent out three vessels and a "yacht" carrying livestock, farming implements, and six "completely equipped" families numbering forty-five persons. The little fleet landed the livestock at Nut (now Governor's) Island, where there was a small fort, and from that point they were soon transported up the Hudson. William Verhulst, a supercargo on the voyage, became the second managing director upon his arrival. One of the councillors appointed to serve with him was Peter Minuit, who shortly embarked on a round trip home and back. Cryn Frederickson, an engineer, came with orders to stake out a large blockhouse at a place near the entrance to the river, an instruction foreshadowing the founding of New Amsterdam. In May, 1626, the *Sea-Mew,* carrying Minuit and additional immigrants, reached Manhattan. During the summer and autumn, the settlers built thirty log cabins thatched with reed, principally on the west side of Manhattan above the fort. In addition there was a windmill for sawing lumber, one for grinding corn, and a stone business building. Verhulst managed so badly that in the fall he was ordered back to Holland, and the local councillors chose Peter Minuit to take his place. Minuit, the first to bear the title of director general, acting under instructions sent to Verhulst, immediately purchased Manhattan Island from the Indians for sixty guilders (approximately $24) in trading goods such as knives, beads, and trinkets. He then named the settlement New Amsterdam.[10]

New Amsterdam was weak and remained weak for a number of reasons. The territory itself was far from compact, and the nature of the economy resulted in the establishment of a series of trading posts: on the Hudson at Fort Orange, Esopus (now Kingston), and

[9] Van Rensselaer, *City of New York,* I, 100–119, gives a vivid description of the company's bad colonization policies.
[10] *Ibid.,* I, 68–99.

Manhattan; on the Delaware at Fort Nassau and Fort Casimir below it; and on the Connecticut at Fort Hope (now Hartford). All of them were widely separated and incapable of defense. Several of the posts lay within disputed territory and brought the company into conflict with the English in New England and on Long Island and with the Swedes and Marylanders on the Delaware. It should be recalled, too, that the Dutch West India Company held a patent for territory without definite boundaries such as were granted by the crown to each English colony.

The heart of New Netherland was New Amsterdam. The posts on the Delaware and the Connecticut yielded no profit to the enterprise; in fact, the only economic successes were Fort Orange, a center that dealt in beaver, otter, muskrat, and deerskins; and Esopus, halfway between Fort Orange and Manhattan, where sixty Dutch families combined in trading and agriculture. But these forts were open to Indian attack and had to be protected constantly. New Amsterdam, flanked by villages and farms on Long Island and Staten Island, along the Harlem, and on the Jersey shore, was the only settlement of a permanent nature. Unlike a New England town, where everyone was grouped around a church and a green, the Dutch in New Amsterdam were clustered about the fort, whose vicinity was protected by a palisade and a canal. Beyond were the farms and plantations, perhaps fifty in number, which were located on sparse soil on the eastern and western ends of Manhattan.[11] The Manhattan population increased from 300 in 1630 to 1,500 in 1664, the year of the English conquest. At that time, the total population of New Netherland was less than 5,000, while the population of New England had risen to nearly five times that number.[12]

New Netherland, then, grew slowly. Land was acquired, in some instances by the director general, in others by private individuals.

[11] Maud Wilder Goodwin, *Dutch and English on the Hudson: A Chronicle of Colonial New York* (New Haven, Conn., 1919), pp. 23–31, describes the early settlement at Manhattan.

[12] On population, see Evarts B. Greene and Virginia D. Harrington, *American Population Before the Federal Census of 1790* (New York, 1932), pp. 9, 88–89; Charles M. Andrews, *The Colonial Period of American History* (4 vols., New Haven, Conn., 1934–38), III, 79 n.; and Jameson (ed.), *Narratives of New Netherland*, p. 363. W. F. Craven, *Colonies in Transition*, p. 15, estimates about 25,000 for New England.

In the course of time "the five Dutch towns"—Breuckelen (now Brooklyn), Boswyck (Bushwick), Ameersfort (Flatlands), Midout (Flatbush), and New Utrecht—developed, as did Flushing and Gravesend (Lady Moody's settlement on Long Island). Farther eastward, other English villages appeared—Heemstede (Hempstead), Rustdorp (Jamaica), Oyster Bay, Huntington, and Setauket.[13] On Manhattan, to the north, New Harlem grew up, and Eastdorp lay beyond the Harlem River. Farms and hamlets sprang up across the North River in Pavonia (Bergen). The posts on the New Jersey frontier lands were in constant danger, lying defenseless before the Indians. Most of them were at best liabilities, seeking protection with every alarm.[14] On Long Island, just before the English conquest, the notorious Colonel John Scott instigated revolts among the English population. Connecticut connived with him at first, but Scott later took off on his own, forming a loose confederation of Hempstead, Gravesend, Flushing, Middelburg, Jamaica, and Oyster Bay in opposition to the Dutch. His ambitions to rule were thwarted by the grant of New Netherland to the Duke of York in 1664.[15] Through the years the Amsterdam Board of Nineteen adhered to its policy of developing trade but not agriculture. This arrangement worked well enough in other areas exploited by the Dutch West India Company, but it was hardly suitable for New Netherland, where there was no great prospect for trade. Colonists and farmers were granted credit most reluctantly, for the board believed that they would eventually try to usurp the fur trade. The local government at New Amsterdam did nothing to alleviate the settlers' difficulties, because the officials from the director on down were all busy making their own fortunes. The company enjoyed a trade monopoly until 1647, and New Amsterdam maintained a monopoly of the staple.[16] Heavy import and export duties caused

[13] Southold for a time was under the jurisdiction of New Haven, and Southampton maintained its independence until it joined Connecticut. Benjamin F. Thompson, *History of Long Island from Its Discovery and Settlement to the Present Time,* ed. Charles J. Werner (3d ed. rev., 3 vols., Port Washington, N.Y., 1962), I, 1–183, covers the Dutch period on Long Island.

[14] John E. Pomfret, *The Province of East Jersey, 1609–1702: The Rebellious Proprietary* (Princeton, N.J., 1962), pp. 9–17.

[15] Lillian T. Mowrer, *The Indomitable John Scott: Citizen of Long Island* (New York, 1960), is a revisionist interpretation.

[16] In a staple port, it was illegal to export certain goods unless they were brought there to be rated and charged with duty.

hardship among the residents, who were already burdened with heavy local taxes. After 1657 nobody could trade with New Netherland without a license. Community spirit such as existed in the New England towns was completely lacking.[17]

Kiliaen Van Rensselaer, Amsterdam jeweler and an influential company director, opposed the whole system in New Netherland, and he became the principal advocate of large-scale agricultural subcolonies called patroonships. He visualized New Netherland as a great supplier of grain, cattle, and other provisions for the West Indies, in which situation Dutch vessels returning from Holland could limit their cargoes to primary goods only. This point of view put Van Rensselaer at odds with the type of company director who sought personal profit by supplying the colony with provisions and equipment. Taking a broad view, he argued that if it granted large privileges to entrepreneurs who would develop the country, the company would shortly be relieved of any expenses in connection with the colony. He and his supporters drew up a plan for self-sufficient agricultural settlements, the Charter of Freedoms and Exemptions, which the Chamber of Nineteen adopted and the States General itself approved in June, 1629. The patroonship envisoned therein was to be a miniature feudal state, a perpetual fief, with the patroon possessing the rights and jurisdictions common to the province of Gelderland in Holland. Usually two or more men combined to establish a patroonship, but the one with the major share was the patroon. Thus in the case of Van Rensselaer himself, he was recognized as the dominant partner in the ownership of Rensselaerswyck, since he held two of the five shares, while Albert Contraets, Samuel Godyn, and Samuel Bloomaert held but one share each. Even though Van Rensselaer helped draw up the Charter of Freedoms and Exemptions, he thought it too restrictive, especially the provision that the patroon had to recognize the staple privilege of New Amsterdam.[18]

[17] A. Everett Peterson, "Population and Industry," in Flick (ed.), *State of New York*, I, 323–346, discusses the economy of New Netherland and its shortcomings.

[18] Samuel G. Nissenson, *The Patroon's Domain* (New York, 1937), examines the system with particular reference to Rensselaerswyck and concludes that the patroons were mainly motivated by a desire to break in on the company's fur trade monopoly. On the subject of the patroonships, see also Clarence W. Rife, "Land Tenure in New Netherland," in *Essays in Colonial History Presented to Charles McLean Andrews* (New York, 1931).

Five patroonships were established, but of them all only Rensselaerswyck was a success. The others were abandoned, were transferred to the company, or became ordinary landed estates. Kiliaen Van Rensselaer continued to reside in Amsterdam but managed his holdings through an agent (*commis*) and an under-agent (*schout*). Through his agents he expanded his landed possessions on the upper Hudson both up and down the river, eventually surrounding the company's fort. The hamlet of Beverwyck flourished and eventually became Albany. Van Rensselaer was most industrious and enterprising, sending over cargoes of livestock and implements that included everything his farmers needed. Equally important, he transported farmers, indentured servants, and laborers at his own expense. By 1646 there were about one hundred men, including staff, farmers, and laborers. Van Rensselaer had his troubles: with farmers over their leases and the payment of tithes, with his officials over extravagance and neglect, with commanders at Fort Orange about the fur trade, and with the company about the use of its ships. Contrary to his commands, his settlers hunted and trapped, whereas he wanted them to barter with the Indians for merchandise and food. He became exasperated, too, because of the poachers hunting his territory. Personally, he got nothing except trouble for his pioneering in New Netherland.

From the start New Netherland contained a strange assortment of economic groups, national origins, and religions. In addition to the settlers at Rensselaerswyck, there were petty officials scattered throughout the colony, "free men" who had come at their own expense and who had been allocated land by the company, the mechanics and tradesmen of New Amsterdam, and the considerable class of indentured servants. One found there not only Dutch and Walloons but English, French, Portuguese, and, after 1655, Swedes and Finns. There were many Indians and Negroes, a small number of them slaves and a few Jews.[19] The official church was Dutch

[19] See Edgar J. McManus, *A History of Negro Slavery in New York* (Syracuse, N.Y., 1966). The early arrival of Negroes in the colony is demonstrated by a deposition relating to their use in the construction of Fort Amsterdam, completed in 1635, which is reprinted in Edmund B. O'Callaghan and Berthold Fernow (eds.), *Documents Relative to the Colonial History of the State of New York* (15 vols., Albany, N.Y., 1853–1887), XIV, 18. Another work bearing on this subject is Edmund B. O'Callaghan, *Voyagers of the Slavers St. John and Arms of Amsterdam, 1659, 1663* (Albany, N.Y., 1867).

Reformed, which was one of the Calvinist sects, but the colony harbored many Lutherans and English Puritans and a number of Quakers and Anabaptists. The Calvinists, contrary to the liberalism prevailing in Holland, were so intolerant of the Lutherans and other faiths that in 1663 the company rebuked Director Stuyvesant.[20]

New Netherland was unfortunate in the chief executives assigned to it by the company. Peter Minuit (1626–32) was an able man who returned to America in 1638 as director of the New Sweden Company, but his successors gave little satisfaction. Bastiaen Jansen Krol, a temporary appointee (March, 1632–April, 1633), was succeeded by Wouter Van Twiller (1633–38), a nephew of Van Rensselaer's, who was charged with indolence, drunkenness, and hostility toward religion. Even his uncle reprimanded him. Just when the company had completed its conquest of Brazil (1635) and increased its stock by one-third and was planning to reduce its monopoly and increase the population of New Netherland, it sent out William Kieft as the new director. He proved a most unfortunate choice, becoming notorious for his uncontrolled temper, rapacity, and drunkenness. He and his secretary, Van Tienhoven, were responsible for the series of Indian wars that put an end to any hope of building up New Netherland. Relations with the Indians had always been precarious, and there were frequent killings. In 1643 Kieft, partly for revenge and partly to exact tribute, began a disastrous war which lasted until 1645. The Indians were well supplied with guns and ammunition in spite of continuing efforts to keep European weapons out of their hands, and they destroyed crops and farms, killed many settlers, and drove everyone back onto Manhattan. Only after the entire strength of New Netherland was thrown against them did they sue for peace.[21] For three years the province

20 Maud W. Goodwin, *Dutch and English on the Hudson,* (New Haven, 1919), pp. 83–93, describes New Netherland's churches and their organization and services. For the position of the Jews under Stuyvesant, see Samuel Oppenheim, "The Early History of the Jews of New York, 1654–1664," American Jewish Historical Society, *Publications,* XVIII (1909), pp. 4–5; Richard B. Morris, "Civil Liberties and the Jewish Tradition in America," *loc. cit.,* XLVI, No. 1 (1956), pp. 25–29.

21 The principal Indian wars of New Netherland were Kieft's wars, 1643–45; the New Amsterdam outbreak, 1655; and the Esopus wars of 1659–60 and 1663–64. Anne Hutchinson was murdered at Eastchester during the first war. The first six chapters of Allen W. Trelease, *Indian Affairs in Colonial New York: The Seventeenth Century* (Ithaca, N.Y., 1960), deal with the Dutch period.

lay prostrate, engulfed in a feeling of hopelessness and despair. Indeed, many settlers and their families returned to Holland. Kieft also left but lost his life on the way home when his ship foundered off the coast of Wales.

Much criticism of the directors came from the colony itself. David de Vries as early as 1633, referring to Van Twiller, said that the company appointed men who had never before commanded and fools who knew nothing except how to drink. In 1642 he added that men were sent whether or not they were fit and that most of them returned home having accomplished nothing of importance. This bitter disdain of successive governors continued in New Netherland until the end. Actually, New Amsterdam was not noted as a peaceable community; rather, it was always marked by drinking, rowdyism, and hopeless quarreling.

New Netherland developed no tradition of self-government, and in time the lack of it became a real grievance. Until 1641 the directors governed with the help of one or more advisers chosen by themselves or by the company. With the approach of serious Indian troubles in that year, Kieft sought the cooperation of the heads of families on Manhattan and chose twelve of them to advise him. The Twelve, as they were called, counseled delay; but as the situation worsened they, under Kieft's badgering, agreed to reprisals. Having obtained what he wanted, he did not call on them again. In 1643, when conditions had become even more dangerous, he again saw fit to solicit advice. A Committee of Eight, composed of farmers and townsmen, refused to be manipulated and insisted that they should have a part in the conduct of the Indian war and in civil matters. Their unprecedented direct appeals to the company finally led to Kieft's recall in 1647.[22]

The company had failed to prosper, to the point where its very solvency was threatened, and in their dilemma the directors sought a more capable governor. They believed that they had found such a man when they selected Peter Stuyvesant, who had been governor of Curaçao, where he lost a leg in a military engagement with the Portuguese. He had governed with ability, displaying some of the traits of a proconsul. His injury prompted his return to Holland,

22 Van Rensselaer, City of New York, I, 172–208.

but by 1647 he was ready to embark upon his new appointment as director general of New Netherland.[23]

Stuyvesant discovered on his arrival that there was a need for new taxation to help effect recovery, and so he had to call an election. Eighteen persons were chosen, and that body selected a Committee of Nine, consisting of three merchants, two burghers, and four farmers, to advise upon and promote the general welfare. They met with the governor and his council in an advisory capacity. Stuyvesant was inclined to go along with them so long as they agreed with him, but this did not prevent them from appealing over his head to the company. The Nine actually sent two representatives to Holland to make their protests, and the governor found it necessary to send Secretary Van Tienhoven to present evidence in his defense. The company granted certain concessions to the inhabitants; but Stuyvesant, dedicated to the restoration of prosperity, would not brook any infringement of his executive authority. Charles M. Andrews reminds us that Stuyvesant's violent outbursts of temper and language tended to conceal his considerable administrative qualities.[24]

The Committee of Nine was an advance toward public participation, but in spite of the fact that the burghers won a modicum of control over local affairs, the gulf separating the governor and the leading burghers continued until the English conquest. Though the Nine hoped that the States General would change the status of New Netherland from dependent trading company to colony, this was never done. The best that New Netherland could hope for was self-administration and self-taxation comparable to that existing in the Dutch cities. It is unlikely that assemblies with law-making and money-appropriating powers, such as existed in the English colonies in the eighteenth century, would ever have developed.

The situation of New Netherland was in the last analysis hopeless. Discounting the many charges and countercharges, there were subversive and weakening influences that were fundamental.

[23] Henry H. Kessler and Eugene Rachlis, *Peter Stuyvesant and His New York* (New York, 1959), is an interesting account which has largely superseded Bayard Tuckerman, *Peter Stuyvesant, Director-General for the West India Company in New Netherland* (New York, 1898).

[24] Andrews, *Colonial Period*, III, 88, 91.

There was no unity in this mélange of languages, religions, and mixed types of local government. Throughout the province there was a wide gulf between the minority, interested in personal profits, and the majority, who were bona fide settlers. Even at Rensselaerswyck there was perpetual strife among the patroon managers, the commander at Fort Orange, and the director general himself. There was also a marked disparity between the merchants and the burghers in New Amsterdam, who favored trade rather than populous settlement, and the majority, who were simple folk. Nor did the company have a good record despite its claims. It was the tool of the merchant group, with an indifferent attitude toward the colony's needs. After 1645 its finances became involved, and after 1654 it was in effect bankrupt because it lost Brazil, its best market, and concurrently its trade with Guinea fell off. The directors, vested with too much authority, were inconsiderate of the settlers' needs. For two decades before the conquest, the burghers fought autocratic and unpopular administrators. They were convinced that greed was the motive underlying company policy, that taxes were levied without consideration of ability to pay, that money left the province never to return, that trade restrictions encouraged monopoly and smuggling, and that the directors in Holland were oblivious to the safety of the people. They pointed to the lack of all public improvements and of all public spirit.[25]

During its brief existence, New Netherland was harassed not only by the Indians but by both the English and the Swedes. In March, 1638, the *Key of Calmar* and the *Griffin*, flying the Swedish ensign, dropped anchor just above Cape Henlopen in Delaware Bay.[26] This was a colonizing expedition under the command of Peter Minuit, former director of New Netherland, who had been employed by the newly formed Swedish West India Company. The ships moved up the Delaware to Christina Creek and up that body of water until they reached high ground. There Minuit purchased land and erected Fort Christina. Trade with the Indians began, and Minuit took home beaver and other furs worth 15,400 Dutch

[25] Harold C. Syrett, "Private Enterprise in New Amsterdam," *William and Mary Quarterly*, XI (Oct., 1954), 536–550, shows that the company sought to minimize economic restrictions.

[26] Albert C. Myers (ed.), *Narratives of Pennsylvania, West New Jersey, and the Delaware, 1630-1707* (New York, 1912), pp. 53–89, and Jameson (ed.), *Narratives of New Netherland*, pp. 292–354, especially pp. 312–320.

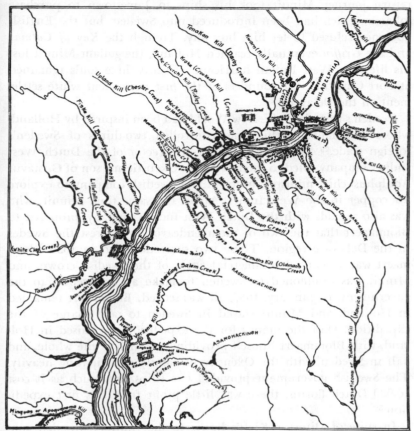

From *Swedish Settlements on the Delaware* by Amandus Johnson
SWEDISH SETTLEMENT ON THE DELAWARE

florins.[27] Meanwhile he proceeded to explore the Delaware, where Peter May challenged him at Fort Nassau. Director Kieft, as soon as he heard of the expedition, ordered Commander Jan Jansen, then in New Amsterdam, to investigate the matter on his return to Fort Nassau. He warned Minuit that the whole South River (Delaware) was Dutch and had been for many years. Kieft's position was clear, but his force at Fort Nassau was too small to act. On his

[27] Amandus Johnson, writing in 1911 in *The Swedish Settlements on the Delaware: Their History and Relation to the Indians, Dutch, and English, 1638–1664* (2 vols., New York, 1911), valued the Dutch florin (guilder, gulden) at $2.25.

return journey Minuit took his ships to Jamestown to purchase tobacco, which had been introduced into Sweden, but the English governor refused to let him buy any. Though the *Key of Calmar* and the *Griffin* eventually reached Holland, the gallant Minuit lost his life in a West Indian hurricane. Twenty-three souls remained at Fort Christina, the founders of the first permanent white settlement on the Delaware.[28]

Sweden's foray into the New World had been inspired by Holland, whose merchants at this time controlled two-thirds of Sweden's foreign trade.[29] Samuel Blommaert, a director of the Dutch West India Company, tried to interest Johan Oxenstierna, son of Gustavus Adolphus' chief minister, in forming a Swedish company to explore for copper in the West Indies. About the same time Minuit, who was also at odds with the Dutch West India Company, proposed to Blommaert that the two of them endeavor to interest the Swedes in the Delaware region. These two succeeded, and in 1636 Blommaert was appointed commercial agent of the Swedish crown, and Minuit was summoned to Sweden to make an oral report to the government. In January, 1637, all was settled; Blommaert remained in Holland, and Minuit stayed in Sweden to take charge of the expedition. Half the money for the expedition was raised in Holland, with Blommaert himself providing a fourth of the whole, and half in Sweden, with the Oxenstierna family participating heavily. The Swedish government provided two ships. Inasmuch as it cost 46,000 Dutch florins, there was little profit from this first expedition.[30]

In spite of Director Kieft's hopes to the contrary, Sweden continued to send out expeditions. The Swedish entrepreneurs were apparently more enthusiastic than the Dutch, for many of them redeemed their subscriptions at a time when the Dutch hesitated to continue. The Swedish people, on the other hand, demonstrated no greater desire to settle in the New World than did the in-

[28] Christopher Ward, *New Sweden on the Delaware* (Philadelphia, 1938), p. 38, characterizes it as a trading post but not a true colony.

[29] Johnson, *Swedish Settlements*, is a definitive work and also contains much material on Dutch and English activities.

[30] Christopher Ward, *The Dutch and Swedes on the Delaware, 1609–64* (Philadelphia, 1930), pp. 67–86, gives an account of these episodes.

habitants of Holland. The second expedition left in 1640, at which time the Dutch subscribers, who had already lost 18,000 florins, withdrew from the enterprise, though Blommaert continued in the service of the Swedish crown. Peter Ridder succeeded Minuit as governor, and this expedition carried additional settlers and two preachers to the Delaware. Ridder was energetic and also somewhat of an expansionist. He purchased land from the Indians extending from the Falls of the Delaware (where Trenton now stands) to Cape Henlopen, and on the New Jersey side from Narraticons Kill (Raccoon Creek) to Cape May. The *Key of Calmar* departed Fort Christina in May, 1641, carrying a valuable cargo of furs.[31]

Beginning in 1640 the English also impinged upon the southern part of New Netherland. Governor Theophilus Eaton of New Haven, George Lamberton, Nathaniel Turner, and others formed the loosely organized Delaware Company, planning to purchase and develop lands on the Delaware. They had instructions to investigate, without interfering with the Dutch or the Swedes, the possibilities of opening up an area to which in time the entire New Haven Colony might move permanently, the feeling being that New Haven was being hemmed in on all sides and was cut off entirely from the Indian trade. The next year Turner and Lamberton paid the local Indian chiefs £30 for land on Salem Creek (Varkens Kill) in southern New Jersey and for the area between Chester Creek and the Schuylkill in Pennsylvania. Governor Ridder protested bitterly, stating that he had purchased this territory himself for the Swedes. Turner and Lamberton ignored him and proceeded to build a blockhouse along Salem Creek and brought in twenty-odd settlers. With the approval of the New Haven General Court, Robert Coxwell led an expedition to the Schuylkill in the spring of 1642. Both the Dutch and the Swedes warned him not to cross over from the Salem district. When he did, they made prisoners of his party and sent all of them to New Amsterdam except Lamberton, who escaped. Since Ridder had instructions not to fight the Dutch and since Jansen at Fort Nassau lacked the strength to displace the Swedes, the two nations tolerated

[31] Ward, *Dutch and Swedes on the Delaware*, pp. 87–94, describes these events in detail.

each other temporarily and were able to act in concert whenever the English put in an appearance.[32]

Meanwhile Sweden continued its attempts to expand its foothold in America. A third expedition brought only thirty-five colonists, many of them Finns who were regarded as undesirable citizens because of a tendency toward petty lawlessness.[33] The returning ships took back few furs. The Swedish government assumed direct control over the colony in 1642 and made a new but not too successful effort to resuscitate New Sweden. The Swedish Council of State appointed Johann Printz governor, and he ruled during what turned out to be the heyday of New Sweden between 1643 and 1653.[34] A huge man physically, a veteran of many wars, a man of action both "furious and passionate" according to John Winthrop, he set out to checkmate both the Dutch and the English. He built several forts to control the river and block off Fort Nassau, and he arrested George Lamberton for trading without authorization. Learning that there was much sickness among the New Haven settlers on Salem Creek, he did not disturb them, reasoning that they could cause no harm. New Haven's interest revived in 1649, when the Delaware Company attempted to renew its activity. Stuyvesant, the Dutch governor, while pretending to be friendly toward the English, managed to cause their proposed expedition to be abandoned.

In June, 1634, an English eccentric named Sir Edmund Plowden talked Charles I into giving him a charter of doubtful legality granting him land that spread-eagled the whole of New Jersey.[35] Shortly after his release from debtor's prison that August, Plowden

---

[32] Clinton A. Weslager, *The English on the Delaware: 1610–1682* (New Brunswick, N.J., 1967), gives a good account of the various English ventures in the Delaware area.

[33] John H. Wuorinen, *The Finns on the Delaware, 1638–1655: An Essay in American Colonial History* (New York, 1938), p. 22, states that these Finns first migrated to Sweden and then came to America. Sweden and Finland formed a single nation during that period.

[34] For a biography of Printz, see Amandus Johnson, *The Instructions for Johan Printz, Governor of New Sweden* (Philadelphia, 1930), pp. 3–51. The same work contains the instructions given to him at the time of his appointment, his reports home in 1644 and 1647, and some of his correspondence.

[35] Father William Keller, "Sir Edmund Plowden and the Province of New Albion, 1632–1650," *Historical Records and Studies of the United States Catholic Historical Society*, XLI (1953), 42–70, and Clifford Lewis 3d, "Some Notes on Sir Edmund Plowden and His Province of New Albion," mimeographed booklet (1937) Library of Congress.

issued *A Description of the Province of New Albion* under the name of Beauchamp Plantagenet. Learning that there were already English colonists on Salem Creek, Plowden determined to settle there himself. With the blessing of Charles I, he took out a small expedition in 1642, but although he remained in America for six years, he never was able to establish a colony. While on the way from Virginia to the Delaware in the spring of 1643, his mutinous crew dumped him on a key near Cape Henry and sailed to the Delaware in the hope of finding a passage to England. Printz captured the mutineers and turned them over to their pursuers, but he became much annoyed when Plowden persisted in issuing free commissions from Virginia permitting ships to trade on the Delaware. Plowden was, if nothing else, persistent. After his return to England in 1648 he whipped up more enthusiasm for his project, and in June, 1650, the authorities granted him permission to transport 140 persons to New Albion, as he called his fief. By then, however, he was bankrupt, and he spent the years between 1653 and 1655 in debtor's prison, dying four years after his release.

The Swedish Governor Printz and Andries Hudde, commanding only twenty men at the Dutch Fort Nassau, managed to get along together, since Hudde was not strong enough to combat the Swedes, but this relatively amicable situation ended in May, 1647, when Peter Stuyvesant became director general of New Netherland. Printz and Stuyvesant, imperious commanders both, began to quarrel, but the Dutch West India Company advised Stuyvesant to exercise patience. The Dutch purchased more land from the Indians, but very few Dutch settlers appeared. In the spring of 1651 Stuyvesant, aroused by many complaints, led an expedition across New Jersey and founded Fort Casimir a half-dozen miles below Fort Christina. On its ramparts he planted the cannon from the abandoned Fort Nassau. But the Dutch found the Indian trade unrewarding, and only twenty-six families remained at Fort Casimir by April, 1653. Relations between the two rivals then settled down for a time.[36]

The Swedish colony failed to grow. Printz could account for three hundred souls in June, 1644, but by the fall of 1653 that number had dwindled to less than one hundred. No Swedish ships

[36] The Printz-Stuyvesant rivalry is described thoroughly in Ward, *Dutch and Swedes on the Delaware*, pp. 132–176.

reached the Delaware between 1647 and 1654. The New Sweden Company itself was in bad condition; there was little demand for imported fur in Sweden, and the colony, in spite of purchases in Virginia, could not meet the demand for tobacco in the homeland. Finally Queen Christina decided to reactivate interest in the colony and placed it directly under the Commercial College, whose minister, Eric Oxenstierna, was devoted to commercial enterprise. An expedition was formed under the direction of Johann Rising, secretary of the Commercial College, but before his arrival in New Sweden the discouraged and neglected director, Printz, had gone home. A commission was accordingly issued appointing Rising director.[37] The *Eagle* arrived in May, 1654, swelling the ranks suddenly by 250, or fivefold. Disease brought by the new colonists wrought havoc, and when the apprehensive Indians refused to bring food to them, the Swedes had to obtain provisions from distant Hartford. The winter of 1654–55 was a severe one, and there was much suffering.[38]

Rising could stave off the English but not the Dutch, and New Sweden was expiring. New Haven tried to renew interest in settlement on the Delaware in January, 1655, but though its general court voted to support the venture, the other New England colonies would not cooperate. Deputy Governor Stephen Goodyear appeared on the Delaware and reasserted New Haven's claims, but nothing more was done. Fort Casimir was an irritant to Rising, and in May, 1654, he recklessly seized it. This act aroused the Dutch West India Company, and Stuyvesant received orders to retake it, but action was delayed until he returned from a trip to Barbados. On August 18 the Dutch fleet arrived with seven craft and 317 soldiers, retook Casimir, and then moved up the river to Fort Christina, which surrendered without a fight. Since the terms of surrender did not call for the eviction of the Swedish settlers, most of them remained where they were instead of returning to Sweden.[39]

Stuyvesant's coup on the Delaware brought a moment of satisfaction to the Dutch, but on the whole these years were not happy

[37] For biographical information see Amandus Johnson, *Johan Classon Rising, the Last Governor of New Sweden* (n.p., 1915). Myers, *Pennsylvania, West New Jersey, and the Delaware*, pp. 131–165, reprints his reports of 1654 and 1655.

[38] The living conditions and economic difficulties of New Sweden are treated in depth in Wuorinen, *Finns on the Delaware*, pp. 81–109.

[39] Rising's account of his surrender is reprinted in Myers, *Pennsylvania, West New Jersey, and the Delaware*, pp. 167–176.

ones in New Netherland. Citizens complained in 1649 that the activities of selfish interests were more than counteracting the advantages of superior location and that in consequence the English to the north were outstripping them. To the extent that population was a measure of prosperity, they were undeniably right. When Stuyvesant arrived in 1647, there were about 2,000 people in New Netherland, while New England contained about ten times that many. By the time of the Dutch surrender in 1664, New Netherland had approximately 5,000 inhabitants, while the New England total had risen to 25,000. During the intervening years internal difficulties rendered New Netherland a dubious attraction for immigrants, but Englishmen were not only flowing into their own territory but crowding into land claimed by the Dutch.

The failure to attract colonists hurt Dutch prestige, but the deterioration of Anglo-Dutch relations in Europe had more immediate consequences. Determined to challenge Dutch commercial supremacy, England passed the "navigation act" of 1650, which prohibited foreign vessels from trading with its American colonies. A year later Parliament took a big additional step, adopting a comprehensive Navigation Act which in effect excluded the Dutch from the carrying trade between England and other countries.[40] Relations had been strained for years, and these new measures now precipitated the first Anglo-Dutch War, 1652–54. The English had the best of the fighting, and in the end the Dutch found it necessary to accept both the navigation restrictions and a settlement of English grievances. Dutch commerce with England was limited thereafter to direct trade, thus greatly reducing the opportunities available to the Dutch West India Company. Its stock fell from 150 to 40, and after 1654 the firm was wholly bankrupt. The States General refused to honor its promises of subsidies to the company, while poverty forced the latter to relinquish Brazil, its best market, and to neglect New Netherland. It would have lost that colony, too, if peace had not come in 1654, because at the end of the war Oliver Cromwell was completing plans to take it over by force.

New Netherland drifted into a state of increased unrest during these years, and only the Anglo-Dutch War saved Stuyvesant,

---

[40] See Lawrence Harper, *The English Navigation Laws: A Seventeenth-Century Experiment in Social Engineering* (New York, 1939).

whose employers in Holland were reluctant to make a change during a period of armed conflict. Recognizing the need for increased taxes, Stuyvesant called an assembly of delegates from the courts and villages, and he had to yield the power to impose excise taxes to the burghers of New Amsterdam. The English villages on Long Island also began to make demands. The Charter of 1640 had granted liberal local powers to these communities, composed of settlers from New Haven and nearby jurisdictions. In order to obtain land at that time, these people had cheerfully accepted Dutch citizenship and allegiance to the company. By 1653, however, their mood changed, and they complained about Stuyvesant's arbitrary rule and demanded the creation of a Landtag (assembly) with power over financial matters. They or at least their representatives, they insisted, should participate in the promulgation of all laws and orders. Stuyvesant disposed temporarily of this unrest by ordering the Long Island colonists not to meet again, under penalty of "arbitrary correction." When Indian troubles broke out again in 1655, he appealed to the magistrates to obtain contributions from leading New Amsterdam citizens, and he gave those officials power to tax anyone who refused to support the colony in time of danger. There were unifying as well as disunifying forces at work, because the growing crisis tended to bring the governor and the citizens closer together. In 1659, for instance, he gave the New Amsterdam magistrates permission to nominate their own successors. This concession and others raised local governmental power to the level prevailing in Dutch cities in the fatherland.[41]

The English drift into Dutch territory began in the 1630–40 decade, as New Englanders pushed west into Westchester or crossed the Sound and established homes on Long Island. A variety of privileges attracted these newcomers, including freedom of worship and the opportunity to operate their own petty courts and appoint their own magistrates, and they paricularly liked the offer of free land, tax-exempt for ten years.[42] Kiliaen Van Rensselaer predicted

[41] Van Rensselaer, *City of New York*, I, 346–378, gives a comprehensive description of the colonists' disputes and complaints, and the danger in which the colony found itself.

[42] Dixon Ryan Fox, *Yankees and Yorkers* (New York, 1940), narrates the long history of the New York–New England border controversies with urbanity and wit.

From *De Zeeuwsche Expeditie Naar de West Onder Cornelis Evertsen, den Jonge*
NEW NETHERLAND

as early as 1643 that the arrival of so many foreigners would cause trouble, but it did not occur at once. Guaranteed freedom from interference by their town charters, the English settlers remained silent during the early remonstrances against the Dutch West India Company. After the formation of the New England Confederation in 1643, however, some English-speaking settlers in New Netherland began openly advocating English conquest of that colony. The confederation and Stuyvesant attempted to resolve their several differences by the Treaty of Hartford in 1650, and the New Englanders won every point in dispute. The Dutch agreed to accept as their eastern boundary a line running ten miles east of the Hudson, and they retained only a small part of their original holdings around Hartford, forty miles east of the boundary line. Even after these substantial concessions, Connecticut remained unsatisfied, charging that the Dutch were urging the Indians to rise against them.

The English also threatened Stuyvesant's interests on the Delaware, and in June, 1658, he received orders to purchase land extending south to Cape Henlopen in order to strengthen the Dutch title. This seemed a wise move, because Josias Fendall of Maryland had managed the previous year to effect a truce between the Puritan and proprietary factions there and had begun a vigorous push of Maryland's charter claim of 40 degrees north. Colonel Nicholas Utie visited the Dutch settlements at New Amstel (New Castle) and Altena (Wilmington) with a small body of men in September, 1659, and warned their commanders that they must swear allegiance to Maryland. Stalling for time, Stuyvesant called for negotiation and informed the Dutch West India Company that Maryland would drive the Dutch out unless the Chamber of Nineteen provided a much stronger defense. Company officials asked the States General in November, 1660, to have the Dutch ambassador in London find means to prevent Baltimore from acting until Stuyvesant could negotiate a boundary line. Meanwhile Philip Calvert, Baltimore's half-brother, replaced Fendall and became so absorbed in rehabilitating Maryland that he had no time to pursue his colony's claims against the Dutch.[43]

The restoration of Charles II in 1660 revived interest in seizing New Netherland. The English advanced many reasons to justify conquest, a principal one being loss of revenue and trade. The Dutch, they pointed out, purchased as much tobacco as they could in Maryland and Virginia and shipped it to Europe via New Amsterdam, thus reducing British income from duties and cutting into the business available to worthy English merchants. The Council for Foreign Plantations, Sir John Berkeley presiding, appointed a special committee in July, 1663, to inquire into the feasibility of taking New Netherland. James, Duke of York and the king's brother, who was always interested in naval affairs and commerce—he was a large holder in the Royal African Company—

---

[43] The rise and fall of Fendall and his threat to the Dutch are described in Ward, *Dutch and Swedes on the Delaware*, pp. 278–337.

persuaded Charles to provide £4,000 to finance the expedition. Incredibly, in March, 1664, before the fleet sailed, the king also gave James a patent for huge grants of land in America, chief among which was the territory lying between the Delaware and Connecticut rivers. Influenced by the London merchants, Parliament did not oppose the project; in fact, it accepted a committee report in April declaring the Dutch the kingdom's greatest enemies to trade, thus justifying the king's remark that both houses were in good humor and ready "to pawn their estates to maintain a war." Charles was manifestly ready to fight, but he saw no need for any declaration of war, because New Amsterdam "did belong to England heretofore, but the Dutch drove our people out of it."

Events now moved fast. The Duke of York selected Colonel Richard Nicolls, a loyal Stuart follower, as his deputy governor, and King Charles shortly picked Nicolls, Sir Robert Carr, Colonel George Carteret, and Samuel Maverick to constitute a commission to visit America to settle disputes touching New England and also —and this part of their instructions was secret—to take New Netherland. Maverick, the former Boston merchant who hated Massachusetts Puritanism because of its attempts to regulate and circumscribe trade, was the one American on the commission. Just after Charles II became king, Maverick had written to Lord Clarendon, condemning the Massachusetts magistrates, who in his opinion were depriving the inhabitants of their rights as Englishmen and who completely disregarded the rights of the home country. Four frigates carrying Maverick and his associates and a military force of four hundred arrived in Boston harbor in July, 1664, prepared to descend upon New Amsterdam.

Stuyvesant's last months as governor were difficult and unhappy. The Hudson overflowed, destroying crops, and there was an earthquake. The Indians threatened trouble, and Connecticut was again advancing extravagant claims. The New Amsterdam magistrates were busy drawing up their usual remonstrances addressed to the States General and the company. Only a charter, wrote the director, "the sort of thing an Englishman dotes on as an idol," would satisfy them. Confronted by an Indian outbreak, Stuyvesant practically conceded Westchester to Connecticut and gave the English Long Island towns full autonomy. The Dutch West India Company informed Stuyvesant in the spring of 1664 that the English expedition intended only to bring New England under one government, and it said that henceforth there would be less trouble from the north. Neither Stuyvesant nor the New Amsterdam magistrates, however, believed this easy explanation. But in Holland, in spite of suspicion in some quarters, the States General accepted the report of the Dutch ambassador, who stated that King Charles had informed him that the expedition would in no way violate the alliance with the Dutch.

On August 18, 1664, the English fleet of four frigates entered New Amsterdam waters. Meanwhile, the Connecticut General Court had resolved that its charter embraced the whole of Long Island. Governor Winthrop crossed Long Island Sound with two hundred troops to make good that claim and to compel the English inhabitants there to take an oath of allegiance to the king. The Nicolls expedition reached the Narrows on August 28. Stuyvesant had once written prophetically, "Whosoever by ship or ships is master on the river will in a short time be master of the fort." Acting for Nicolls, Winthrop demanded that Stuyvesant surrender within forty-eight hours. New Netherlanders wishing to return to Holland would be at liberty to do so, but those choosing to remain would receive the same rights and privileges as His Majesty's own subjects. Nicolls published the king's patent, at which point Winthrop withdrew Connecticut's claim to Long Island. The English urged their opponents not to provoke needless fighting, but Stuyvesant nevertheless succeeded in prolonging negotiations for a few days. He hoped to prepare the fort to withstand an assault, but that proved impossible. Troops were few, munitions were short, and the chief men of New Amsterdam were reluctant to oppose such a formidable armada. Their patience exhausted, the English seized Brooklyn and moved their ships to Governor's Island. Stuyvesant ordered the fort to open fire, but the ministers, Johannes and Samuel Megapolensis, led him away from the ramparts. Then New Amsterdam surrendered on August 29 without firing a shot.[44]

The antagonists completed the treaty of surrender on September 7, Johannes Megapolensis and five burghers signing for the Dutch, and Nicolls, Carr, and Cartwright for the English. Signers representing special constituencies included John Winthrop, Jr., for New England, and the Springfield merchant Captain John Pynchon for the Massachusetts General Court. Stuyvesant could not bring himself to add his name to the document. Shortly afterward, Colonel George Cartwright took Fort Orange and Captain Robert Carr seized Fort Casimir on the Delaware. The name of New Amsterdam was changed to New York. Long Island became Yorkshire, and the name Albania was assigned to what soon became Nova Caesaria or New Jersey. On April 2, before the conquest, James had named Colonel Richard Nicolls as deputy governor of his domains, and Nicolls remained in New York to carry out this assignment.[45]

The conquest of New Netherland freed the Atlantic seaboard of non-English interlopers all the way from Maine to the Carolinas. The relationship between New England and Virginia became more intimate, and they could thereafter exchange their products without fear of interference. The time seemed right to plant settlements in this newly occupied land, but James in 1664 was not in a mood to act as colony builder. Rather, he hoped to derive some revenue from his territory and from New York's nascent commercial activity. Events in England left him little time to think out a philosophy relating to colonization, and so the actual course of action that he followed was devious. Almost at once, he gave away New Jersey to his loyal friends, Berkeley and Carteret, and he neglected the west bank of the Delaware until William Penn received his grant. In spite of this lack of a program of development, there was before long some settlement, as Quakers moved into West Jersey and Pennsylvania, New Englanders and Scots found their way into East Jersey, and tiny English hamlets sprang up in what eventually became Delaware.[46]

[44] "Report on the Surrender of New Netherland, by Peter Stuyvesant, 1665," in Jameson (ed.), *Narratives of New Netherland*, pp. 458–466.

[45] Van Rensselaer, *City of New York*, I, 491–530, is a thorough study of the fall of the colony. For a succinct account of the reasons for New Netherland's demise, see Richard B. Morris, "Why the Dutch Failed," in E. S. Miers (ed.), *The American Story* (Great Neck, N.Y., 1956), pp. 40–45.

[46] The key works on New Netherland, New Sweden, and New York are Van Rensselaer, *City of New York*; John R. Brodhead, *History of the State of New York* (2 vols., New York, 1853–71); Flick (ed.), *State of New York*; David M. Ellis, James A. Frost, Harold C. Syrett, and Harry J. Carman, *A Short History of New York State* (Ithaca, N.Y., 1957); Johnson, *Swedish Settlements*; and a fine chapter by Andrews in *Colonial Period*, III, 71–137.

CHAPTER 13

The Southern Periphery

D uring the earliest period of English colonial development on the mainland, adventurers and undertakers were also making efforts to establish settlements in the West Indies. The experiences of these island colonies in the years prior to 1660 paralleled in many respects events that occurred on the mainland. The colonists in the two areas were the same sorts of people, and the same kinds of men provided the planning and financing. In fact, entrepreneurs in England frequently had simultaneous interests in Virginia, Bermuda, and the West Indies.

The Somers or Bermuda Isles, lying 580 miles due east of Charleston, South Carolina, were well known at an early date, but they did not enter history until Sir George Somers was shipwrecked there in 1609. Brought to the attention of the Virginia Company in this accidental manner, Bermuda immediately acquired a fine reputation as a supply center and base of operations against Spanish shipping. David Quinn has discovered a newsletter dated June 29, 1611, written to enlist interest in Virgina, Bermuda, and Newfoundland, which suggests that the London investor, weary of supporting ventures in the Ulster plantations, might well look elsewhere. This document reminded the reader of the establishment of the Virginia Company in 1606, the Newfoundland Company in 1610, and the Bermuda Company, in association with the Virginia Company, in 1611. It pointed out that the Virginia Company Court had already begun successfully advertising Bermuda's fertility, and it mentioned

John Guy's successful founding of a colony, Cupers Cove, in Newfoundland and his plan to send out more colonists.[1]

Granted to the Virginia Company in 1612, Bermuda was handed
over to a subordinate group of enterprisers, and later in the year
the *Plough,* Richard More, master, carried a party of settlers to the
islands. The company promised to supply nets for fishing, while
Moore and his associates agreed to serve the king, obey the enterprisers, worship God, keep the Sabbath, and exclude heretics.
The colonists searched for pearls, ambergris, silkgrass, tobacco,
whale oil, and hardwood. They found no pearls, but the discovery of
a great piece of highly prized ambergris led to quarreling and bitterness. The company eventually realized £6,000 from this treasure,
enough to finance the first venture. Moore praised the climate and
fertility of the land, and since there were no hardships, the
colony attracted additional settlers and grew to six hundred people
by 1614. The enterprisers then applied for a separate charter of
incorporation, received it in 1615, and under the name of the
Bermuda Company entered upon a career that lasted nearly
seventy years.[2]

Bermuda may have been a healthy place, but early conditions
there satisfied few settlers. Moore proved so ineffective that he did
not last long as governor, and the six men who jointly took his
place when he left were so lax that conditions deteriorated rapidly.
The central problem was that the colonists, as was true in earliest
Virginia, had no land or livestock of their own but were merely
tenants at will of the company. Having no authority, they felt no
responsibility, and they spent less time looking after crops than
they did quarreling among themselves and grumbling at the company. Meanwhile, rats came in on a ship and added to the agricultural difficulties by overrunning the largest of the islands. Sir Thomas
Smythe of Virginia fame, governor of the Bermuda Company, de-

[1] David B. Quinn, "Advice for Investors in Virginia, Bermuda, and Newfoundland, 1611," *William and Mary Quarterly,* XXIII (Jan., 1966), 136–145.
[2] Henry C. Wilkinson, *The Adventurers in Bermuda: A History of the Island
From Its Discovery Until the Dissolution of the Somers Island Company in
1684* (London, 1958), gives an excellent account of earliest Bermuda, and pp.
27–71 deal specifically with the first settlement and the years up to 1615. John
Henry Lefroy (ed.), *Memorials of the Discovery and Early Settlement of the
Bermuda or Somers Islands, 1515–1685* (2 vols., London, 1877–79), reprints the
most important documents of the period.

cided on a general reorganization. He accordingly sent out Captain Daniel Tucker with orders to divide the land among the company members who were living there. Tucker created eight 1,250-acre districts, allotting twenty-five acres to each subscriber for every share he owned. He set aside land for the minister, the Reverend Lewis Hughes, and he leased such property as was not needed by the government to individuals who were known collectively as "the colony." These people paid the company quitrents at the rate of two pounds of tobacco per acre or £50 per share. This system prevailed to an extent until the dissolution of the company in 1684.[3]

The new arrangement brought about improved conditions. Colonists on company land felled timber, cleared the ground, and planted corn. Overseers worked these men from sunrise until nine and from three until sunset. Their pay took the form of meat, drink, clothes, and a base currency called "hog money," brought in by Captain Tucker. The system was later changed so that tenants worked their shares on half-profits, and this modification worked so well that it became compulsory in 1620. Bermuda colonizing methods were not unlike those in Virginia, since the two companies had the same leaders. The settlers began to construct their own houses, clear their ground, and sell the fruit and produce that they raised. There was a central store or magazine like the one in Virginia. The raising of tobacco received official encouragement, and by 1618 the colony was able to export 30,000 pounds of that crop to England.

The government of Bermuda was not without its early frictions. Governor Tucker was an overzealous and exacting man who managed to arouse considerable discontent, and the company accused him of arrogance, cruelty, and use of his position for personal profit. These charges provoked an unfortunate dispute among the joint founders of the Virginia and Bermuda companies that ended with the ouster of Sir Thomas Smythe as head of the Virginia Company. This victory for his enemies caused strife between the two enterprises and elimination of the Virginia Company from the Bermuda activity in 1615. Thomas Smythe, Robert Johnson, and Robert Warwick, the latter the largest Bermuda stockholder, then secured the election of Nathaniel Butler as governor. His instruc-

---

[3] Wilkinson, *The Adventurers in Bermuda*, pp. 71–76.

tions of 1619 were remarkably similar to those issued to Governor George Yeardley of Virginia earlier that same year. Butler and his council received orders to assemble the inhabitants, discuss grievances, and pass laws and constitutions for the general welfare. They were to adopt penalties for violations of the law, making sure that the penalties were moderate. Once adopted, new laws were to go to London for amendment and ratification by the company's general court. All laws had to conform to the laws of England, the orders of the general court, and the governor's instructions. The people were to meet together at least once a year. Sir Edwin Sandys thus had no monopoly on the idea of self-government for an American colony, even at this early date, and Smythe, Johnson, Warwick, and others were as friendly as Sandys toward establishment of a self-governing colony.[4]

Bermuda's first assembly, and the second in the New World, met at Georgetown (now St. George's) on August 1, 1620, a year after that of Virginia. This Bermuda body, gathering in a newly framed church, set a record for the continuity of its meetings, which lasted unbroken from 1620 to 1669. Its membership consisted of the governor, his council, the bailiffs of each district, and two members from each district elected by the inhabitants. The well-organized assembly followed the English parliamentary procedure more closely than did its Virginia counterpart. Unlike Virginia, however, it had no speaker, the secretary playing that role, and its members sat as a single house. Performing no judicial functions, its work was strictly legislative, but it passed a number of essential laws. The secretary read proposed bills three successive days, and the members had instructions to speak briefly to the point and to avoid all "nipping" remarks. A voice vote generally sufficed, a count being taken only when necessary. The laws then went to England for confirmation by the company.[5]

There was a good deal of dissension during Governor Butler's administration, in spite of the fact that he carried on his work with commendable skill. Favoring Warwick and opposing Sandys, he was always eager to show that Bermuda under Smythe, Warwick, and Johnson operated more effectively than did Virginia under

[4] *Ibid.,* pp. 102–145.
[5] *Ibid.,* pp. 189–202.

Sandys. This attitude did not make him universally popular in company circles, and some of the London officials accused him of highhanded and even illegal conduct. Butler was rough, but he was neither a brute nor a liar, and his *Historye of the Bermudaes* demonstrates considerable intelligence.[6] He also had to contend with altercations in Bermuda, mainly directed against the company. The colonists, as was true in Virginia, complained about the low price paid for tobacco, and they wanted the right to sell it directly to the Dutch. They were also upset because the early encouragement to raise sugar was withdrawn when it became clear that the boiling process consumed wood, which was very scarce. When his superiors in London dismissed Butler in 1622 after three years in office, he left a colony that was prospering, and he later became governor of Old Providence Island.[7] During the early years Bermuda was, on the whole, well managed, fairly prosperous, and relatively contented. The Jones Commission, appointed by the Privy Council in 1623 to look into conditions in Virginia and Bermuda, reported favorably on the latter area, and there was no attempt, as was done in Virginia, to abrogate its charter. The Bermuda Company thereby weathered the storm that wrecked the older organization.

Religious nonconformity found its way into Bermuda at an early date, and its subsequent growth added to the problems of governing the islands. Bermuda always harbored all shades of Puritanism, in this respect resembling Massachusetts Bay and Old Providence Island more than it did Virginia, where there were no people of that persuasion until 1642 and not many thereafter. One of the two Bermuda ministers wrote in 1617 that he did not use the Book of Common Prayer and that he had molded the government of his church upon the minister and four elders, who were chosen publicly. Governor Tucker disliked this arrangement but acquiesced because the minister was stubborn. After both of them had departed, the company sent out four new ministers in 1620, who carried instructions to put an end to laxity in church matters. Surprisingly, these new men all exhibited Puritan tendencies. Three

---

[6] This 363-page manuscript was published by the Hakluyt Society, 1882, and attributed to Captain John Smith. The British Museum Catalogue designates Governor Butler as its author.

[7] First settled in 1631 by the Providence Island Company and taken by Spain in 1641, it now forms part of Colombia and is known as Providencia.

of them were reprimanded, and two of their successors also proved to be nonconformist. Governor Philip Bell became alarmed in 1627 that the local vestries under the influence of Independency might undermine the government itself, and he warred openly with the ministerial group and its adherents. Succeeding governors were more urbane but no less bothered by aggressive nonconforming clergymen. In 1644 the two new ministers actually conspired to set up an independent church under the Reverend Nathaniel White free from any control by the state. They renounced their Church of England ministries and entered into a covenant to constitute a church establishment of their own. Neither the government nor the people sympathized with this degree of extremism, and so the officials were able to indict White and his co-worker, the Reverend Stephen Painter. The ministers appealed their case to the company, however, and obtained an acquittal. The fact was that because of the increasing influence of Puritanism in England, neither the Warwick Commission nor the Long Parliament was in a position to coerce the Puritans of Massachusetts Bay or those of Bermuda.

Nonconformity continued to make gains but then suffered a sudden setback. By 1645 the Independents, who were more tolerant and lenient than the Presbyterians, were in control of Parliament. To the amazement of the saints in Massachusetts, that body accorded Bermuda liberty of conscience free from any control by the civil magistrates. When the White and Painter cases came before it, the company refused to act contrary to the ruling of Parliament. The situation in Bermuda changed in 1649 when the royalists there rose against the local dissenters and proclaimed their loyalty to the recently beheaded Charles I. Taking control, the royalists banished White, Painter, and others, who departed with a former governor, William Sayle, to his plantation in the Bahamas, where "to enjoye Christ in the purite of his ordinances" they set up an independent church. This proposed settlement at Eleuthera, however, soon broke up.

Puritanism won back its losses in 1652 when the Commonwealth forces overcame their enemies in England. The company, royalist until this time, submitted to the government, and the Puritan party assumed control in Bermuda, as it also did in Virginia, Maryland, and Barbados. White and Painter returned, and the latter became a councillor for life. The Anglican Church received little attention, and religious life in the colony became "loose and lax, irregular and phanatique." Until his death in 1658, Warwick was the company's guiding spirit, and it was perhaps owing to him that the religious complexion of the islands was Puritan. It should not be forgotten that he was a graduate of Emmanuel College, Cambridge, a contemporary of John Cotton and George Downing, and a friend of John Winthrop, Sr. Perhaps it was not entirely accidental that Warwick bestowed church benefices upon a whole succession of Anglican ministers who were nonconformists in their sympathies.[8]

Bermuda was small and lacking in resources, and thus, in spite of slow growth from 2,000 in 1628 to 3,000 in 1656, it was by 1660 definitely overpopulated.[9] A limited supply of timber required strict regulation of its use. Growing tobacco became progressively less profitable, and the planters were turning more and more to the breeding of cattle. The population was a mixture of planters, tenants on half-shares, indentured servants, apprentices, Negroes, and Indian slaves. The several hundred planters, each holding property averaging £100 in value, were freeholders as well as members of the company. Some of the tenants-at-will lived on the estates, but the majority were on the company's public land. They all held their tenancies on the half-profit system, but eventually, as was true in other English colonies, tenancies by halves gave way to freehold. The economic limitations of Bermuda were manifest, and in time people drifted away to Antigua, Trinidad, Barbados, Tobago, St. Lucia, Jamaica, the Carolinas, and New England. Bermuda occupies a unique place in the history of English colonization because it is the only colony that remained for seventy years under the control of a corporation with its headquarters in England.[10]

Caribbean history in the period leading up to 1660 largely concerns efforts by other nations to reduce the Spanish control over the area. The end of open warfare between England and Spain in 1604

[8] Babette M. Levy, "Early Puritanism in the Southern and Island Colonies," American Antiquarian Society *Proceedings*, LXX (Apr., 1960), 164–200, is the most complete account of Puritanism in Bermuda.

[9] During the same period, Virginia grew from 7,500 to 20,000. Charles M. Andrews, *The Colonial Period of American History* (4 vols., New Haven, Conn., 1934–38), I, 237.

[10] A good coverage of early Bermuda history will be found in Andrews, *Colonial Period*, I, 214–248.

brought about a revival of trade. Privateering and piracy continued along the Spanish Main, however, as roving seamen attempted to prey on the Spanish establishment in South and Central America and the larger West Indian islands, which consisted of little more than villages serving as centers for mining, shipping, and proselytizing activities.[11] Sugar cultivation in the New World began in Brazil. Attracted to that region, Englishmen tried unsuccessfully to penetrate the territory between the Amazon and the Orinoco and in consequence became familiar with the West Indies and the mainland coast. London merchants wanted to establish plantations there, but their ambitions remained unrealized until 1624. In that year Thomas Warner, one of the Earl of Warwick's friends, landed a group of East Anglian colonists on St. Christopher (St. Kitts) in the Leeward Islands, where Ralph Merrifield and his associates began the first English settlement in the West Indies.[12] Charles I recognized the colony in 1626, granted liberty of trade to Merrifield and his fellow settlers, and appointed Warner the king's lieutenant for life. Before Warner died in 1649, the English had also established themselves on Nevis, Antigua, Montserrat, and Barbados.[13]

John Powell, captain of the *Olive,* landed at Holetown on Barbados on his way home from Pernambuco in 1625 and took possession in the name of the king. On his return to London he interested a wealthy trader, Sir William Courteen, who organized Courteen and Associates, a voluntary joint-stock company, which sent out ships, settlers, and supplies during the years 1627–29.[14] By the end of that time there were at least sixteen hundred people living on the island, all of them tenants maintained by the company. Whatever these workers produced went to the company, as was true in early Virginia, Bermuda, and Plymouth, three other colonies initiated by private enterprise. Barbados was the first English colony

11 Clarence H. Haring, *The Buccaneers in the West Indies in the Seventeenth Century* (London, 1910), pp. 1–28, describes the Spanish colonial system. For information on the Spanish settlements, see Philip A. Means, *The Spanish Main: Focus of Envy, 1472–1700* (New York, 1965), pp. 3–50.

12 See Aucher Warner, *Sir Thomas Warner* (London, 1933).

13 Vincent T. Harlow (ed.), *Colonising Expeditions to the West Indies and Guiana, 1623–1667* (London, 1924), pp. 1–17, reprints an eyewitness account of the first settlement at St. Kitts.

14 Courteen was a Netherlander whose father had settled in England, where he became a wealthy merchant. The name in Dutch is spelled Coerten.

established by an unincorporated group of merchants having no
higher aim than to make money. The Courteen Associates put
£10,000 into the project, a much larger amount than was invested
in Plymouth, where the religious motive was paramount.[15]

The Courteen interests undertook colonization without any royal
grant, and this weakness in their position proved very costly. Egged
on by Warner and Merrifield, the Earl of Carlisle obtained proprietary letters patent in 1627 for the countless islands stretching
from St. Eustatius to Barbados. To lighten his indebtedness to
Marmaduke Rawdon, a London merchant who helped him finance
his patent, Carlisle granted Rawdon 10,000 acres in Barbados. In
1628 Rawdon issued a commission as governor for three years to
Charles Wolverston. Thus threatened with displacement, Courteen
appealed to Philip Herbert, lord chamberlain and a power at court,
to aid him in obtaining a royal charter. In February, 1628, the
chancery obligingly issued him a royal patent to the "Montgomery
Province," an area covering much of the disputed territory. Before
the year was out, however, Carlisle, on appeal, was able to have the
Courteen charter set aside, and the Rawdon Associates thereby
emerged triumphant.[16]

The rival factions on the island soon engaged in a fierce fight.
Wolverston charged that Powell and his men had destroyed 30,000
pounds of Rawdon Associates' tobacco and had injured a number of
servants. He asked for assistance, but the Courteen faction seized
him and sent him back to England. The Rawdons then sent out
Henry Hawley, who ruthlessly restored Carlisle's interest. Now sure
of his title, the earl appointed Sir William Tufton governor and
Captain James Holdip receiver general of all rents and revenues, but
at the same time he ordered Tufton not to interfere with the Courteen merchants' 10,000-acre colony. These merchants elected Holdip
their agent and governor in 1649, thereby asserting the independence
of their private plantation. In this way Courteen gradually lost
control over the venture, and nothing remained for Sir William to
show for his pains and expenditures. From 1629 Barbados was a

---

[15] Arthur Percival Newton, *The European Nations in the West Indies, 1493–
1688* (New York, 1967), pp. 143–145. Harlow (ed.), *Colonizing Expeditions*, pp.
42–48, gives a contemporary description of Barbados in this period.

[16] Andrews, *Colonial Period*, II, 246–248.

proprietary colony, one of a number of islands that came within the Carlisle patent. Tufton, efficient but tactless, was ousted by Henry Hawley, and when Tufton resisted, he and three followers were shot. Carlisle died in 1636, leaving debts of £25,000 and many claims against his estate. His three trustees, who were instructed to pay the creditors first, governed Barbados until 1642, when the Carlisle family leased his proprietary rights to Lord Willoughby for a twenty-one-year period.[17]

In spite of all the turmoil over proprietary rights, the island somehow began to develop and prosper. Henry Hawley was responsible in 1639 for calling the first representative meeting of freeholders, and among his other measures he established the right of this assembly to initiate legislation. The several governors sent from London were none too satisfactory, although one of them, Philip Bell, did serve a long term, from 1641 to 1649. The years between 1641 and 1655 were a period of salutary neglect in the American colonies, and during this time Barbados assumed the status of an independent colony. Population grew from 1,800 in 1630 to 30,000 in 1650, and the people enjoyed a true measure of religious toleration, although the Church of England was officially established.[18] Government consisted of the governor, his council, and two burgesses from each of eleven parishes. The ministers received as tithes a yearly allowance of a pound of tobacco per acre on all cultivated land, besides the usual fees. Local governments and courts were well organized, and the local officialdom consisted of justices of the peace, constables, churchwardens, and tithingmen.

Barbados, only fourteen by twenty-one miles in extent, was more fertile than any other English island in the West Indies. Originally matted with jungle growth, the land when cleared yielded prodigious crops. The work of clearing the jungle was heavy and difficult. With rainfall limited to spring and autumn, water was

---

[17] James A. Williamson, *The Caribbee Islands under the Proprietary Patents* (Oxford, 1926), pp. 38–114, gives an excellent account of Barbados.

[18] Andrews, *Colonial Period*, II, 251. Carl Bridenbaugh, *Vexed and Troubled Englishmen* (New York, 1968), pp. 427–428, estimates the entire English West Indian population in 1642 at no more than 28,000, and warns that many of the accepted figures are wild guesses. For example the historian Sir Charles Lucas cites 12,000–13,000 for St. Kitts in 1637, while an English resident merchant estimated it as only 4,000 for 1635. Though there were Negroes in the islands at this time their numbers are unknown.

scarce, and fires were frequent and destructive. But the soil was rich and the climate healthful. The principal early staples were tobacco, cotton, indigo, ginger, dyewoods, and corn. Father Andrew White, the famous Maryland Jesuit, termed Barbados in 1634 the granary of all Caribbean islands, and a hundred ships a year reportedly arrived there by 1650. The earliest plantations were small and were situated on the leeward (western) side of the island. In spite of the 1632 Privy Council order restricting trade at English colonies to English bottoms, the Dutch conducted a brisk transatlantic commerce with Barbados. The Barbadians obtained provisions from Maryland and eventually from Virginia and New England. Tobacco culture began early but was never satisfactory, since the Barbados leaf was notoriously rank. Sugar became the chief export by 1650 and the basis of the island's prosperity. A Dutchman named Pieter Brower brought this lucrative plant from Brazil, and Colonel Richard Holdip experimented with it on his plantation. Barbados had its annual production up to three million pounds by 1650, and by then sugar had completely eliminated tobacco culture and had taken its place as the medium of exchange. Sugar cultivation radically altered the composition of the population. There were 36,600 white people and 5,700 slaves in 1650; ten years later there were reputed to be 20,000 whites with an equal number of slaves.

Barbados enjoyed unusual freedom during the period of the English civil war, but establishment of the Commonwealth brought discord to the island. As long as the fighting continued in England, Barbados was practically autonomous, being equally free from interference by the proprietors, Parliament, and the king. The planters, who were trading freely with the Dutch, wanted the situation kept the way it was, because they were making money and building up substantial estates. Assumption of control of England by the Commonwealth caused Cavaliers in some numbers to migrate to Barbados, where they joined with those planters who had royalist sympathies. The Walrond brothers and other like-minded men thereafter kept the island in an uproar, hoping to gain at the expense of the Roundhead element. Governor Bell, who had observed strict neutrality, soon became powerless to restrain the unruly but powerful group that proclaimed Charles Stuart king of England. These royalists forced laws through the assembly confiscating Roundhead estates and proclaiming free trade with Holland and Hamburg. Francis Lord Willoughby, lessee of the island and its revenues and the Earl of Carlisle's personal lieutenant, then superseded Bell. He promptly found himself opposed by the Walronds because he refused to strip the Roundheads of their property. Consequently, he sought and won the support of the moderate royalists, who above all wanted tranquillity and prosperity, and who knew that wholesale confiscation of estates and proscriptions would lead straight to chaos.

Events in Barbados, as well as similar acts in Virginia, Bermuda, and Antigua, drew unfavorable attention in London. Parliament decided that Willoughby's proclaiming of the king was treasonable, and it also, to oblige English merchants who resented unrestrained trade with the Dutch, passed an act in October, 1650, prohibiting foreign trade with the West Indian colonies. In the fall of 1651 it sent an expedition under Sir George Ayscue to reduce the rebellious islands. Willoughby decided to resist, and for a time he was successful. Colonel Thomas Modyford, leader of the Barbados moderates, defected, however, and then news of the Parliamentary victory at Worcester caused Willoughby to capitulate. Ayscue offered generous terms, and he kept his promise. When Parliament ratified the peace treaty in August, 1652, the Barbadians received liberty of conscience, control of taxation, restoration of Roundhead estates, and "as great a freedom of trade as ever . . . with all nations . . . in amity with England." Although Ayscue explained that this provision meant that trade was free under such restrictions as Parliament imposed, the islanders felt that they had been deceived. They disliked, too, the treaty provision that Willoughby, the Walronds, and others were to be spared banishment, an act of indemnity that they disregarded.[19]

Barbados was similar to Massachusetts, in that it gradually and by default attained a state of political and economic independence by 1655. Both the royalists and their opponents agreed that the liberties and privileges of freeborn Englishmen entitled them to noninterference from the mother country. In February, 1651, Governor Willoughby, the council, and the assembly issued a declaration

19 Williamson, *Caribbee Islands*, pp. 164–178, gives details of the Royalist Rebellion (1649–52) in Barbados.

asserting that the prohibitory act of 1650 was contrary to the safety and well-being of the people. They also questioned whether they could be bound by Parliament, since they had no representation in that body. As islanders, they were unaware of the mercantilist philosophy that was to shape England's policy in the future. Even when they found it necessary to capitulate in 1652, they still believed that freedom of trade meant unhampered trade, and they stubbornly held to this point of view for another decade. Actually, trade with the Dutch was vital to them, because Dutch imports were cheaper and credit terms were more liberal than those of English factors. Since 1632, when the Privy Council had forbidden ships sailing from plantations to ship their goods to foreign countries, Barbadians had ignored any regulation prejudicial to them. They closed their eyes to the Anglo-Dutch struggle for trade supremacy and to the London merchants' view that colonies lying on trade routes would soon desert English interests if they were allowed to trade freely. Not until the Navigation Act of 1660 renewed the earlier prohibitory act did they finally and grudgingly acknowledge that their dream of commercial independence was at an end.

The men of Barbados also treasured the notion of home rule and their agreement on the free trade issue did not prevent them from differing on the question of how their government should be organized. Under Philip Bell's easygoing regime from 1640 to 1650, they enjoyed great autonomy. When the English Commonwealth period began in 1649, some of the planters adopted its organization as a model and began to argue for a supreme assembly coupled with a weak governor and council. Governor Daniel Searle could do little to stem the resulting controversies, because his own commission issued by the Puritan government in London denied him the right to veto legislation, and Whitehall chose the members of his council. The assembly and council saw to it that the governor's power did not expand. The Barbadians wanted one of themselves as governor, and so they tried to get rid of Searle. Thomas Modyford led this movement and became speaker of the assembly, but he proved to be something of a trimmer and lost popularity when he supported Cromwell's expedition against Spain in the West Indies in 1654. The English fleet spent two months in Barbadian waters, from January to March, 1665, draining the island of provisions and men. The angered planters failed to reelect Modyford, so he went to England to try to get Searle removed and himself named as replacement. He engaged in two years of intrigue, supported by the Barbados "grandees" and opposed by the London merchants, and he was finally appointed governor in April, 1660. Because his commission came from outside Barbados, he had not brought home rule to the island, but he was at least the first planter to hold the governorship.[20]

The Restoration caused an immediate change in the government of Barbados, and gradual economic changes also began at about that time. Charles II took over the proprietorship and appointed Willoughby his governor and captain general so long as the latter's lease remained in effect. Under the terms of this arrangement, Willoughby received half the proprietary profits, with the other half going to pay off the Carlisle debts. This complex factional struggle continued until 1673 when the lease expired and Barbados became a royal colony. In the end it became a great sugar plantation owned by absentee planters and worked by Negro slaves. It adapted itself more and more to the mercantile system, sending its single staple to the mother country.[21]

British settlers on the four Leeward Islands—Antigua, St. Kitts, Nevis, and Montserrat—were also influenced by events in England during this period. The lieutenant general of the Caribbee Isles was the nominal governor of these small islands, though from his base in Barbados he was really in no position to interfere with their affairs. Antigua had excellent harbors and was consequently a port of call for many English ships, but its population was small. The island was valued by Barbadian planters, some of whom bought land there. Colonel Henry Ashton led the local planters in remaining loyal to Charles I, and he attempted in vain to persuade St. Kitts and Nevis to do the same. The English government gradually reduced Antigua by means of a four-year blockade that cut off all essential supplies, but it allowed the next governor, Colonel Christopher Kaynell, appointed in 1652, to have arms and ammunition for defense against the Spanish. Antigua, like other islands in the area, began by raising tobacco but then shifted to sugar. Because of its comparative religious freedom, many Irish Catholics settled there.

[20] *Ibid.*, pp. 178–187, 198–217.
[21] Vincent T. Harlow, *History of Barbados, 1625–1685* (Oxford, 1926), provides the best treament of that colony.

St. Kitts grew in spite of the fact that it was mountainous and contained relatively little land suitable for plantations. The energetic Sir Thomas Warner dominated the island as founder and governor until his death in 1649, and his promotion of immigration increased the population to 6,000. Because good land was scarce however, large planters gradually absorbed the smaller holdings and the dispossessed colonists moved away to neighboring islands. As was true in all the English Caribbean colonies, there was a governor's council and an assembly of all the planters. From 1625 on, French settlers occupied part of St. Kitts, but the two groups managed to live together peaceably in separate districts, principally because of fear of the Spanish.[22] This modus vivendi lasted until 1659, when the Spanish power was broken. In 1672 London combined all four of the Leeward Islands into a single royal colony.

Barbados and the Leeward Islands had much in common during their early years with the first colonies on the mainland, especially Virginia. They all enjoyed a modicum of popular government, especially during the period of neglect by the English government. As time passed and the mainland colonies became granaries and stock farms, there was a good deal of communication with the islands, and eventually mainland merchants became owners of profitable island plantations. Economic and monetary conditions in the mainland colonies would have been even worse than they were had not commerce with the islands flourished. The West Indies trade produced most of the hard money that made its way into the currency-starved mainland colonies. The West Indies were a very integral part of England's colonial enterprise in America.[23]

Unlike the islands already discussed, Jamaica's first white settlers were Spaniards rather than Englishmen, and its deliberate conquest by the English was an important event in Commonwealth history. Lying just south of Cuba's Oriente Province, Jamaica is approximately 150 miles long and 50 miles wide, and it is mountainous, with its small amount of level land restricted, for the most part,

[22] See Henry M. Crouse, *French Pioneers in the West Indies, 1624–1664* (New York, 1910).
[23] An old account with some continuing usefulness is Bryan Edwards, *The History, Civil and Commercial, of the British Colonies in the West Indies* (3 vols., London, 1793–94; 5th ed., 5 vols., New York, 1966). Andrews, *Colonial Period*, II, 241–273, is excellent for Barbados and the Leeward Islands.

to its southern coast. Columbus discovered Jamaica on his second voyage and spent a year there when he was ill in 1503–4. His son Diego inherited the island as part of the explorer's estate, and the king appointed him admiral of the Indies and absentee governor. Diego's deputy, Don Juan d'Esquivel, conquered Jamaica in 1510 and founded Oreston and New Seville on the northern coast. The capital moved in 1534 from New Seville to Villa de la Vega (now Spanish Town) on the south coast. Until 1655 Jamaica remained a proprietary of the dukes of Veragua, the descendants of Columbus, with the supreme authority remaining in the Spanish crown.

The successive proprietors did not find Jamaica particularly profitable. The chief staples during the early period were cassava, corn, beef, pork, and bacon, but the potentially valuable hardwoods, pimento, and annatto received little attention. Cattle and hogs ran wild, and the settlers killed them for their skins. The island exported a few of these hides, supplied various Spanish expeditions, and sent provisions and livestock to Cuba and other Spanish neighbors. Fifteen hundred people were living on the island in 1611, principally free Negroes, Negro slaves, and native Arawak Indians. In time, as a class of rich Spanish planters emerged, sugar plantations, cattle ranches, and cacao groves developed. Unruly runaway slaves receded into the impenetrable mountains, where they remained a permanent menace to the planters. Jamaica never equaled Barbados in agricultural wealth, but it enjoyed greater economic stability because of the greater variety of its products, and it was the only truly agricultural colony that Spain possessed in the entire New World. Its attractiveness to seventeenth-century England was not, however, based on its internal economy. The English lusted after Jamaica because it was located in the heart of Spain's colonial empire and could therefore be converted into a strategically located base from which to exchange English wares for Spanish precious metals.

The Puritan impulse in England began to lose its drive in the 1650's, and more secular matters, such as balancing the budget and stimulating trade, became of greater interest to the people. Impersonal forces, rather than Cromwell or the Puritans, brought about this new emphasis. Cromwell was not, in fact, particularly interested in finance and commerce, and he never did formulate a coherent commercial program. The merchants, of whom there were

more than two thousand, had little influence with the Commonwealth government, although Cromwell occasionally sought their
advice and deferred to them on colonial matters. Such effectiveness
as they might have had in suggesting policy was reduced by the
fact that they did not agree among themselves, some favoring war
while others opposed it. A number of them advocated free trade
with all ports open; others preferred monopolies and embargoes
designed to limit exports. Money was very scarce all through the
realm, and it was difficult to borrow on short-term loans, yet Cromwell needed increased revenue. Seeking a way to enhance England's
financial security, he hit on the idea of a surprise attack on the
Spanish Main.[24]

What became known as the Protectorate's "Western Design" was
an attempt to unify Britain's colonial possessions for a combination
of religious and financial reasons, and it started with a large expedition in 1654 to conquer Spanish territory in the Caribbean. Although
it marked the beginning of a new English colonial policy, Cromwell
saw it primarily as a device to supplant Spain in the New World.
There is no way of construing what he did as an act of honorable
statesmanship. Cromwell began by denying the validity of the line
of papal demarcation and asserting that England had to take
revenge on Spain for its depredations on English subjects in the
Caribbean. He cited the attack on the English on the island of
Tortugas (1635), the capture of Old Providence Island (1641), and
the murder of Englishmen on Santa Cruz (1637), and the final
seizure of that island. The notion that the Puritans were striking a
blow against the papacy by replacing Catholic with Protestant settlements was another justification for the attack. This idea lay behind
Cromwell's unsuccessful attempt later to persuade Puritans from
Boston and New Haven to emigrate to Jamaica. More immediately,
Cromwell needed money, and he believed he could capture Spanish
treasure ships, and in his need he was willing to overlook the fact
that he was then at peace with that nation. With a few notable
exceptions, English merchants did not favor the expedition, fore-
seeing that it would dislocate trade and incite retaliation. Those
who did support the adventure anticipated large supply contracts
and the acquisition of new sugar, tobacco, and other plantations.

24 Andrews, *Colonial Period*, III, 2–6.

By 1657, after immense expenditures, Cromwell came to rue what he had to recognize as a major error in judgment.

The Hispaniola (Haiti) expedition sailed secretly from the Isle of Wight in December, 1654, with Admiral William Penn in charge of the fleet and General Robert Venables in command of the troops on board. The ships reached Barbados in just six weeks but then frittered away the next two months waiting there for supplies. They finally sailed with 7,000 men and 1,200 auxiliary seamen, and from April 14 to May 4 Penn and Venables tried to seize the city of Santo Domingo, capital of Hispaniola. Although the English outnumbered the enemy by ten to one, they failed miserably and lost more than a thousand men in the process. Having failed in Hispaniola, they decided to take Jamaica, and on May 9 thirty-eight ships under Venables drew abreast of Kingston Harbor. The forts there contained only a few hundred defenders, and they surrendered promptly. The next day the invaders occupied Villa de la Vega six miles away. Under the harsh terms of capitulation, the English confiscated everything on the island, including the land, and the owners had to leave, taking only their clothing, provisions for the journey, and a few personal possessions. The conquerors permitted the remainder of the inhabitants to stay, provided they accepted English rule. Venables then set to work distributing the ranches and plantations that lay along the northern coast.[25]

Cromwell proclaimed Jamaica an English possession on October 10, 1655, and began efforts to promote immigration, but once the conditions prevailing there became known, few people wanted to go. The Spanish grandees repudiated the treaty at once, and although many of them did leave the island, a substantial number retreated into the mountains, where they carried on a fierce guerrilla warfare with the support of large numbers of Negroes and mulattoes.[26] These fighters fell on the English wherever they found them in small groups, and soon the occupiers had to contend with the added problem of dysentery and yellow fever. Men died by the hundreds, and within a year half the invading force perished. This toll of life continued for two and a half years until the invaders

25 Frank Strong, "The Causes of Cromwell's West Indian Expedition," *American Historical Review*, IV (Jan., 1899), 228–245.

26 Irene A. Wright, "Spanish Resistance to the English in Jamaica," Royal Historical Society *Transactions*, XIII (1930), 117–147.

finally became acclimated, and meanwhile the losses among the officers were as great as those among the enlisted men. Meanwhile Cromwell, as the second part of his Western Design, sent out Vice-Admiral William Goodson to intercept and loot Spanish treasure ships, but Goodson failed to capture a single important prize.

Considerable hard fighting was necessary before England was able to bring Jamaica under control. The able rebel leader, successor to Governor Juan Ramirez, was Cristóbal Ysassi Arnoldo. Supported by forces from Cartagena, Puerto Rico, Cuba, Mexico, and Hispaniola, his local insurgents devastated ranches, burned buildings, and drove the English from their new plantations. The invaders owed their final victory to General Edward D'Oyley, who forced Ysassi to retreat into the northern mountains. At that point the king of Spain directed the governor of Mexico, the Duke of Albuquerque, to recover Jamaica. Relief forces organized by Albuquerque reached Ysassi from various places in July, 1657, adding to the effectiveness of his guerrilla campaign. D'Oyley met this maneuver by sending a secret force over the mountains and following up with a flank movement from the sea, and he won a solid victory. The next year, 1658, he attacked Ysassi's camp at Rio Nuevo, broke it up, and scattered the Spanish forces into the woods. The English now held the initiative, but the condition of their forces remained precarious until the winter of 1660. Provisions were scarce, and with the accession of Richard Cromwell it was difficult for the bankrupt government to send help. As it happened, Spain was also in trouble, with its finances in even more desperate straits than those of England. Spain's failure to recapture Jamaica signaled that nation's decline as a great power, while England's retention of the island marked the beginning of its rise as a leading commercial and colonial kingdom.

Once the insurrection ended, Jamaica took its place as an important element in England's growing overseas realm. The insurgents decided to abandon the island in February, 1660, after their best fighters, the Negroes, deserted the cause. Defeated in his next engagement, Ysassi finally capitulated. He went to Cuba in May, hoping to get aid from Governor Don Pedro de Morales, but the governor turned him down and even forbade him to return to Jamaica. England proclaimed the end of the war with Spain on September 7, 1660. For the first time England had acquired territory by conquest in the New World situated in the heart of Spain's colonial empire. The House of Commons passed a bill practically unanimously in 1661 annexing Dunkirk and Jamaica, in spite of protests by the Spanish ambassador. D'Oyley, followed by Lord Windsor, Sir Charles Lyttelton, and Sir Thomas Modyford, administered Jamaica efficiently as a royal colony, and it became the largest and most important of Britain's West Indies possessions. The seizure of New Netherland and Jamaica put England on the road to empire. Fourteen sturdy colonies had come into being between 1607 and 1660, including Virginia, Bermuda, New Plymouth, Massachusetts, Barbados, St. Christopher, Jamaica, Connecticut, Rhode Island, New Haven, and Maryland. All of them would play their roles in the years ahead in the struggle for British supremacy in the New World.[27]

[27] The conquest of Jamaica is described in Andrews, *Colonial Period*, III, 1–34.

CHAPTER 14

Epilogue

And we look back, and see how the thing was done
And, looking back, think, "So, of course, it must be."
And are wrong by a million miles, and never see
The daily living and dying, under the sun.

For they did not know what would happen. No one knew.
No one knew, though the men in England planned,
Planned with cunning of brain and strength of hand,
And their plans were deer-tracks, fading out in the dew.

They planned for gold and iron, for silk and wood,
For towns and settled farming and steady things,
And an Indian pipe puffed out its blue smoke-rings,
And, where they had made their plans, the tobacco stood.

And those who came were resolved to be Englishmen,
Gone to the world's end, but English every one,
And they ate the white corn-kernels, parched in the sun,
And they knew it not, but they'd not be English again.

Stephen Vincent Benét, *Western Star**

History tries to explain what happened in the past to people living in the present and a good part of the difficulty is, as Benét points out, that what now seems to have been inevitable was once

* By permission of Brandt & Brandt.

not only unforeseen but actually unforeseeable. Many of the Englishmen who planned the colonization of America were intelligent, energetic, and persistent, yet even the most perceptive of them could not anticipate either the hardships or the opportunities that awaited the early pioneers. In particular, they could not predict the way in which environment would subtly but surely alter the institutions that the colonists brought with them and would even transform the colonists themselves. It would be a mistake to argue that the settlers had stopped being English by 1660, but even at that early date it is true that they were starting to become Americans.

The men who colonized North America and the West Indies had to overcome a variety of practical problems and face a host of grave perils, only some of which they could logically have anticipated. Inexperience always led to misconceptions about geography, agricultural and mineral resources, the chance for commercial exploitation, and actual living conditions. There was disease on the ships headed toward the New World and in the struggling young settlements. The climate and soil combined to hamper development of the northern areas, and even green Bermuda proved incapable of supporting its early population. The Indian aborigines were always a worry and sometimes a danger. The Spanish, French, Dutch and Swedish competed with the English and with one another for territory, and their rivalry sometimes turned into open strife. The English could not achieve complete cooperation among themselves. The West Country enterprencurs worked to keep settlers away from the Newfoundland fishing grounds. Virginia and Maryland haggled over boundaries and jurisdictional matters, as did Connecticut and New Haven, and the New England Confederation denied membership to Rhode Island. There were disputes even within colonies, particularly in Maryland, New Haven, Barbados, and the Leeward Islands.

In spite of all these difficulties, England had launched several dozen settlements by 1660, and its successes far outnumbered its failures. By then Englishmen knew the American coast all the way from St. George's in Maine to Norfolk County in Virginia, and they were familiar with the island network in the Caribbean. They had established outposts on a number of the islands and on the mainland had avoided only the sandy coast of New Jersey and the uninviting reaches of the upper eastern shore of Maryland and Virginia. During this period the Dutch occupied the Hudson Valley as far north as Albany, and the Swedes penetrated the Delaware to the falls at Trenton, and the English, whose settlers clung to the coasts and rivers, did not gain access to these fertile areas until the conquest of New Netherland in 1664. In Virginia plantations lined the James, the York, and the estuaries on the western shore of Chesapeake Bay, and in Maryland the settlements were close by the mouths of the Potomac and the Patuxet. The New England settlements were with one exception along the water's edge, on harbors or at most a few miles from the mouth of a river. Just as the Dutch had worked their way inland by following the Hudson, so New England pioneers had made their way to the valley of the Connecticut. Not all of them went by water, as the Dutch had done when founding Albany, for many undertook the hard trip overland from Boston and other coastal towns. In 1660 the great majority of Massachusetts colonists lived within fifty miles of Boston.

In addition to establishing itself over a wide area, England did an outstanding job of filling its settlements with people, considering the hardships involved. Estimates of early population can never be entirely reliable, but it now seems likely that in 1660 there were at most 70,000 Englishmen on the mainland, 30,000 of them in New England and the rest in Virginia and Maryland. Boston, with about 3,000 residents, was the largest English city in America. Although figures for the islands are even more elusive, one seemingly reasonable suggestion places the white population of Bermuda at 3,000 in 1656. Another calculation assigns 18,000 English colonists to Jamaica, Barbados, and the Leeward Islands in 1700, compared with 95,000 Negro slaves. Forty years earlier there would have been many more white men in those places and fewer Negroes, because the great expansion of sugar production during the last part of the century increased the need for slaves on large plantations and correspondingly reduced the need for small-scale agriculturists.

By contrast, neighboring New France developed slowly in spite of an early and advantageous start, so that in 1660 there were probably no more than 2,500 Frenchmen in North America, most of them trappers or missionaries. The French fishermen who dried their catch on the shores of Newfoundland and Cape Breton established friendly contacts with the Indians and soon began bartering implements for furs. Able and dedicated Samuel Champlain, representing the series of trading companies organized to pursue this commerce, explored far inland and set up posts at key locations, notably at Quebec in 1608. The St. Lawrence was the finest source of beaver on the continent, but the trade never became highly profitable, owing partly to indifference and confusion at home and partly to lack of manpower and organization in the wilderness. Champlain tried to counteract the shortage of French personnel by allying with the tribes living in the St. Lawrence Valley. In the long run this policy turned out to be a disastrous mistake, because it alienated the powerful Iroquois nations of upper New York, and the beneficiaries of the miscalculation were first the Dutch on the Hudson and then the English.[1] During the early years, the company permitted missionaries, but it did not welcome settlers. Recognizing the advantages of colonization as well as trade and conversion of the heathen, Cardinal Richelieu founded the Company of the Hundred Associates in 1627 to work toward all three objectives. Some settlers did begin to arrive after that date, but never in impressive numbers, and in 1643 New France contained no more than three hundred white men, excluding the several hundred inhabiting the trading stations on the Bay of Fundy. In 1665 there were only five hundred fifty persons at Quebec, a fourth of them priests and nuns. As long as there was a demand for fur, Canadians had no interest in raising corn or cattle. Factors lived at the trading posts, while *coureurs de bois* ranged the forests and streams hundreds of miles inland. Even after the crown assumed responsibility for the colony, there was no semblance of representative government or any desire for any. New France was and remained an absolutist colony. The French and English colonists had very little to do with one another in the years before 1660.

Spain, of course, continued to be active in the New World during this period, but it came into direct contact with England only in the West Indies. On the mainland the Spanish spent their time seeking Mexican treasure and looking for the fabled Straits of Anian (Bering Strait) which would lead them to India. Their

---

[1] Sigmund Diamond, "An Experiment in Feudalism: French Canada in the Seventeenth Century," *William and Mary Quarterly*, XVIII (Jan., 1961), 3–34.

explorers, the *adelantados,* ranged from Tampa, Florida, to the Mississippi River near Memphis and from Old Mexico into New Mexico as far as the Grand Canyon, and they moved by sea along the California coast to the Golden Gate. In 1609 the Spaniards conquered the Pueblos and established, Sante Fe. Nevertheless, in 1660 the Spanish population within the continental limits of the United States was negligible, and contact with the English colonies there was at a minimum.

England thus had a manpower advantage over its two principal rivals, but its colonizing success resulted less from shrewd advance planning than from experimentation and adaptation to local conditions. In Virginia, as Stephen Vincent Benét points out, "They planned for gold and iron, for silk and wood, . . . And, where they had made their plans, the tobacco stood." The necessities of tobacco culture caused Virginians and their neighbors in Maryland to live on isolated farms located for the sake of easy transportation along the innumerable riverbanks. They raised just enough food and livestock to satisfy their own needs, and they gave no attention to trade or shipping. In 1660 the plantation with its Negro labor force had not yet displaced the small family farm. Settlers in the British West Indies also developed tobacco as their original money crop but soon shifted to sugar, partly because the price of tobacco fell sharply. The other incentive to change was the fact that, as Richard Pares observes, tobacco murdered the soil, so that within twenty-five years new land was needed, and many of the islands had no cultivable reserve of land. The 1640's were the golden age in the sugar colonies, and by then Negro slaves were a necessity and large populations of white men had become superfluous.[2] Lacking a crop as remunerative as tobacco or sugar, New Englanders resorted to general farming, but Boston, a compact settlement with fine harbor facilities, soon found markets for the agricultural surpluses raised in the hinterland around it. Boston merchants achieved early wealth by organizing a complex system of trade with the inland agricultural towns and exporting cattle, grain, fish, and forest products to other mainland colonies, to the West Indies, and even to England, often utilizing locally built ships. The

[2] Richard Pares, *Merchants and Planters* (Cambridge, Mass., 1960), pp. 20, 21, 27, 35.

secularization of New England owes much to the activities and influence of the Boston merchant class.[3]

Proof of Benét's argument that the American environment altered English institutions and habits can be seen in the extent to which, even prior to 1660, the colonial social structure began to differ from its counterpart at home. The New World had no nobility at the top and no large vagrant population at the bottom. The relatively few members of the gentry who migrated did not always thrive, and in some places they tended to fade out both numerically and in point of influence as a class. Most of the colonists had been born into the middle orders, but the clear distinction between yeomen and their inferiors did not survive the transatlantic passage. Inasmuch as the majority of settlers eventually became landowning farmers, there was in fact if not in name a much larger yeomanry here than there was in England. Even indentured servants in America had a chance to improve their fortunes after they completed their terms of service. The merchant class could rise in status here as rapidly as it rose in wealth, whereas in England the position of such men remained ambiguous, because nobody could decide where to fit them into a hierarchy traditionally based on land ownership. In short, social mobility existed on both sides of the ocean, but there was more of it here, particularly during the first two generations. After 1660 the newly established American élite was generally able to hold its position during the rest of the colonial period.

Since the Negro slave formed a separate class by 1660 in the colonies the emergence of slavery as an institution requires a special note. The first Englishmen went to Africa in the mid-sixteenth century not to buy slaves but to trade with the natives. For years they regarded Africans only as a different sort of men—inferior, withal—because of their color, their features, their paganism, and their barbarous habits and customs. Their blackness, especially, aroused great curiosity and speculation, and they were generally believed to be descendants of Ham. However, it was not until the mid-seventeenth century that English traders regarded native Africans as beasts or chattels.

[3] This thesis is fully developed in Darrett B. Rutman, *Winthrop's Boston: portrait of a Puritan Town, 1630–1649* (Chapel Hill, N.C., 1965). The trend appeared earlier than is generally supposed.

The English trader, even with the example of the Portuguese and Spanish, and later the Dutch, before him, was slow to engage in the slave trade. As early as 1500 Portuguese ships were regularly supplying the Spanish settlements in America with slaves, and by 1550 slavery had become an institution in the New World. There are examples of English traders like Sir John Hawkins selling Negroes before 1600, but they were few in number.

Nor in this earliest age did all Englishmen approve of slavery, since they generally placed a high value on individual freedom. Villenage had practically disappeared in England except in the law books, and indenture was accepted as a contractual relationship. Slavery to an Englishman meant servitude for life, affecting even the offspring, and it originated from captivity. Sir Thomas Roe, special ambassador to the court of the Great Mogul (India) wrote in his *Journal* in 1616: "I returned thancks: that in England we had no slaues, neyther was it lawfull to make the Image of God fellow to a Beast." In the same vein, a year later he wrote that he would not purchase blacks as slaves, but only to save their lives and give them liberty. Since Roe's *Journal* was kept for the benefit of his employer, the East India Company, one can assume that this great company was not hostile to his views.[4]

Slavery in the English colonies first appeared as an institution in the British West Indies in the 1630's and 1640's, partly in imitation of the Spanish, especially when it was realized that the labor shortage could be solved more easily by using slaves rather than indentured servants. With the emergence of the sugar economy, by 1660 Negroes were displacing white inhabitants in all the English islands. Indeed, unless an Englishman had risen to the status of a sugar planter, there was little for him to do.

The response to slavery on the mainland followed, first in Virginia and Maryland, where there was a staple crop, tobacco, that necessitated cheap, unskilled labor. There was little interest in enslaving Indians, even Indian captives. Certainly, when, in 1619, the first Negroes were brought to Jamestown in a Dutch ship, no one had in mind the establishment of slavery in the colonies. Slavery developed slowly, and for twenty years little is known of slavery in the colonies. It is thought that before 1640 some Negroes

[4] Awsham and John Churchill, *Collections of Voyages and Travels.* (London, 1704), I, 772.

were slaves rather than indentured servants, since the earliest census records list the number of Negroes on each plantation. In any event there were both free Negroes and Negro servants. During the period before 1660 indenture was the common means of enlisting service in a region where labor was desperately needed.

By 1640, however, there is incontestable evidence of Negro slavery in both Maryland and Virginia. The slave codes were foreshadowed by this time and by 1660 were well developed. By 1660, also, the purchase and sale of Negroes had become common; the Negro women as well as men worked in the fields; and racial discrimination had set in. The contrast with indenture is marked: through indenture the servant ultimately became a free man. It was his labor, not his person, that was owned and sold.

Slavery existed in the New England colonies, but there were only a few hundred slaves as late as 1700. There was no compelling economic need for their type of labor. The first Negroes were brought by a Salem ship's captain in 1638 from Providence Island, a Puritan colony, where slaves were utilized as house servants. The Massachusetts Body of Liberties of 1641 actually endorsed slavery on two counts—as punishment for crime and captivity in war—but the general court applied these sanctions halfheartedly and sporadically. Men like Theophilus Eaton of New Haven justified the holding of a slave or two on Biblical grounds, citing Leviticus 25:45–46. Rhode Island, as mentioned, indignantly forbade enslavement in 1652, but the law remained a dead letter. On the whole, Negro slaves were better treated in New England than elsewhere, that is to say as well as white servants, except that they and their children served for life.[5]

Early New England architecture demonstrates how the colonists brought traditions with them and then made adaptations to meet local needs. For several years, carpenters erected dwellings exactly like those at home, but they rapidly made important changes in construction methods. To provide maximum warmth during the severe winters, they learned to cluster the rooms around one massive central chimney. To prevent fires that started in thatch dried in the hot summer sun, they went to shingle roof construction. Because timber was plentiful and lime scarce, builders abandoned half-

[5] See A. L. Rowse, *The Elizabethans and America* (New York, 1959), pp. 9–10 and Winthrop D. Jordan, *White Over Black* (Chapel Hill, 1968), pp. 3–98.

timber exteriors filled with wattle and daub in favor of clapboard siding.[6] Ecclesiastical design changed so fast that a distinct new style evolved by 1642, yet every element in the seventeenth-century New England meetinghouse derived from English models. The interior came largely from the Anglican church, but the Puritans naturally rejected such elements as conflicted with their religious beliefs. Their buildings had to serve the first generation as both places of worship and civic centers, and so English town halls and market halls logically made a major contribution to external appearance. The resultant rectangular structure surmounted by hip roof, balustraded platform, and turret reflected a style introduced into England from Flanders and Holland. The vogue for this four-square type of church did not survive the century, but some of the early ones were converted into town halls and schools and consequently influenced the design of those types of buildings.[7]

Culture is particularly susceptible to damage when transplanted from one place to another, and the frontier environment made it impossible to sustain in America the rich and varied life the settlers had known at home. Samuel Eliot Morison speaks of the "intellectual vacuity" characteristic of most of the colonies, where attention was directed toward the accumulation of wealth to the exclusion of all other activities. The exception was New England, which by 1640 had a college, a school system, and a printing press and which was producing literature in the form of sermons, histories, and poetry. By 1646 there were at least one hundred thirty university alumni in Massachusetts and the neighboring colonies, and these men, most of them ministers, gave the area an intellectual tone absent elsewhere. On the other hand, the Puritans saw fit to ban drama, erotic poetry, and religious instrumental music, three fields in which the English excelled, and they had so little interest in secular music that it did not thrive.[8]

The English naturally drew on familiar precedents in planning

[6] Thomas Jefferson Wertenbaker, *The Puritan Oligarchy: The Founding of American Civilization* (New York, 1947), pp. 116–120, 126–127.

[7] *Ibid.*, p. 111; Marian Card Donnelly, *The New England Meeting Houses of the Seventeenth Century* (Middletown, Conn., 1968), pp. 91–106.

[8] Samuel Eliot Morison, *The Intellectual Life of Colonial New England* (New York, 1936; 2d ed. Ithaca, N.Y., 1960), pp. 12–18; Wertenbaker, *Puritan Oligarchy*, pp. 128–129. For a comprehensive treatment of colonial culture see Louis B. Wright, *The Cultural Life of the American Colonies* (New York, 1957).

governments for their new colonies. Chartered business corporations, long accustomed to concentrating administrative power in the hands of a governor and council, resorted to that device in the ventures they promoted, and later colonizers copied it. Proprietors operating under royal auspices sometimes tried to establish feudalism in America, even though it had become obsolete at home, and although they were generally unsuccessful, they did manage to introduce feudal elements into the governmental systems in several colonies. The Pilgrims, forced by circumstances to land at Plymouth without any official sanction, undertook self-government but tried to legitimize it by basing it on a covenant, a contrivance borrowed from Separatist church organization. Connecticut and New Haven later solved the same problem in the same way.

Even though the colonies derived their forms of government from a variety of precedents, there was greater uniformity in political structure from jurisdiction to jurisdiction than has generally been recognized. There was everywhere a governor, a council or its equivalent, a general assembly, and a provincial court. There were, of course, many local variations. In Virginia, for example, the governor was appointed by the king after 1624; the proprietor always appointed that official in Maryland; and qualified voters elected him in New England. Elections occurred there annually, but there was a tendency to return the incumbent to office year after year. Similarly, there was an appointed governor's council in Virginia and Maryland, while in New England annual elections determined the council of assistants or magistrates. Councillors and assistants were the great men of every province, and they were usually retained in office for many years.

The general assemblies gained power progressively during the colonial period, and the trend was clear even before 1660. These assemblies all consisted of the governor, his assistants, and elected deputies representing their districts, and their original function was merely to give advice and approbation. All of them, however, soon won the right to initiate proposals, except Maryland, where the idea provoked a prolonged controversy. The colonists valued government by consent and looked to the deputies, who were allowed their expenses but paid no salaries, to speak in their behalf. By 1660 these elected representatives in Virginia, Maryland, and Massachusetts had been granted the privilege of meeting by themselves, making those legislatures bicameral and giving the deputies increased participation in the legislative process.

The business conducted by the assemblies was neither complicated nor particularly time-consuming. The New England legislatures scheduled two or more sessions a year, but one sufficed in Maryland and Virginia. A primary objective was to keep expenses to a minimum and to apportion taxes fairly among the towns. One economy device was the fee system, widely employed for the performance of innumerable public services. Except for a few recurring charges, the heaviest expenditure was for defense in time of danger, and even that outlay did not involve maintaining professional troops, because every able-bodied male had to belong to the militia and bring his own weapons to drills. Provincial taxes were consequently not onerous in comparison with those levied by counties and towns, but since they were paid in the produce of the country, collection was both a cumbersome and a costly process. The New England colonies collected general property taxes, poll taxes, excise taxes, and occasionally import-export taxes. The Chesapeake colonies relied chiefly on the poll tax, augmented toward the close of the period by an export tax on each hogshead of tobacco.

Local government below the provincial level derived from the English county system. The governor appointed justices of the peace, who met as the local court with civil and some criminal jurisdiction. The county justices enjoyed great authority in local administration, possessing the power to tax and the power to promulgate local ordinances. In Maryland, as the manorial system with its courts leet failed, the county court with its justices of the peace soon developed to take its place. In New England, where the town was the unit of government instead of the county, the freemen chose selectmen and lesser local officers to administer the town. In Rhode Island and Plymouth the town had the field of local government to itself, but in Massachusetts, New Haven, and Connecticut the superior provincial authority intervened in certain matters. Indeed, Massachusetts proved similar to Virginia, establishing counties and county courts at an early date, and there the governor's assistants or resident magistrates sat as the county court. In fact, as Wesley F. Craven points out, "Massachusetts had adopted the office of justice of the peace in every essential but the name." The county arm, in dealing with civil and criminal jurisdiction, in acting as a probate court, in its care for the poor, in its jurisdiction over highways, and in the regulation of taverns, shared many tasks of local government with the town. All in all, self-government made remarkable progress during the period before 1660.[9]

Voting requirements varied from colony to colony. All freemen took part in elections in Maryland from the start and in Virginia after 1646. The franchise was theoretically limited to church members in Massachusetts and New Haven, but in time many exceptions developed, especially arrangements allowing participation in local government.[10] Connecticut, Plymouth, and Rhode Island had a broader base for voting, but in none of these colonies or in the West Indies was democracy, in our sense of the term, either valued or sought. As a matter of fact, many qualified male inhabitants avoided voting because of the obligations entailed in serving on juries or in holding petty offices.

The Anglican Church suffered from serious weaknesses in England, and it had even greater problems in Virginia, Maryland, and the West Indies, where it was the dominant faith. The organization lacked vigor, the members lacked zeal, and it was impossible to recruit devout and learned clergymen in sufficient numbers. Complicating the latter situation was the fact that only bishops could ordain ministers, and there were no bishops in the New World. Archbishop Laud considered sending one to Virginia as early as 1638, but political troubles in England kept him from taking action. Virginia could have been the focus of Anglican effort in America, and so the Church's poor record there was particularly damaging. The bishop of London assumed spiritual jurisdiction over that colony's churches in 1620, but his privileges were meaningless, because the all-powerful Virginia Company chose the clergy, while its governor and assembly dealt with such matters as compulsory church attendance. Anglicanism did become established there in 1624, when the province became a royal colony, and it had the good fortune to be allowed to continue using the Book of Common Prayer during the Commonwealth period, but nothing could prevent further deterioration. The general assembly instituted

---

[9] Wesley Frank Craven, *The Colonies in Transition, 1660–1713* (New York, 1968), Chap. I.

[10] Rutman, *Winthrop's Boston,* pp. 161–163, 198.

an English type of parish government with elected vestries in 1641, preparing the way for dominance by the planter class. Because vestries thereafter made one-year appointments and could at will reduce a minister's salary, the clergy fell more and more under lay influence. By 1660 there were only ten clergymen in all of Virginia.[11]

There was an entirely different atmosphere in New England, because most of its settlers had rejected episcopacy in favor of the congregational principle and had crossed the Atlantic filled with religious zeal and a high sense of mission. In their passionate desire to build their lives around their meetinghouses, they huddled together in compact towns and made an imperfect distinction between civil and ecclesiastical authority. Thus town selectmen played some part in the operation of the churches, while ministers frequently gave advice to their congregations on public matters. Church members selected their own pastors, and because they did not consider marriage a sacrament, they had civil officials rather than clergymen conduct weddings. There were Independents in Rhode Island and Separatists both there and in Plymouth, but the Puritans formed by far the largest group, and all three of these denominations accorded generally shabby treatment to Quakers and people affiliated with other small sects. Puritanism with its closed system of church membership became more and more restrictive, and although it refined its theology, it gradually lost the support of the inhabitants, and even adoption of the Half-Way Covenant did not arrest this decline.[12] Nevertheless, the Puritan Church played a major role in the development of early America, and this cannot be said for the Anglican Church in Virginia.

The Restoration of 1660 began an era of vast change throughout England's overseas empire. Much of the transformation occurred because the later Stuarts aspired to bring their American possessions into a closer relationship with the realm, both politically and economically. They worked to curb the growing independence of the legislative assemblies, and whenever possible they transformed

11 Raymond W. Albright, *A History of the Protestant Episcopal Church* (New York, 1964), pp. 16–22.

12 Perry Miller, "The Half-Way Covenant," *New England Quarterly*, VI (Dec., 1933), 676–715, and Rutman, *Winthrop's Boston*, pp. 268–273, 276–279.

proprietary and corporate colonies into royal colonies. Within a generation the crown had personal control over Newfoundland, Nova Scotia, Maryland, and the Leeward Islands, which had all been proprietorships, and over Bermuda, Massachusetts, and Plymouth (by then part of Massachusetts), which had been founded under the auspices of business firms. New colonies, Jamaica and New York, entered the empire as possessions of the royal family. The new regime also attempted to regulate colonial trade for the benefit of the mother country, and it created new administrative agencies to help execute this program. These attempts to enforce political subservience and mercantilism raised issues not destined to be resolved for more than a century, and such traces of feudal land control as survived in the colonies, particularly in the Chesapeake area, provided an additional basis for gradually rising discontent.

England founded an American empire in the years between 1607 and 1660, and thereafter this collection of colonies grew in number, in population, and in economic and social complexity. New colonies appeared: the Carolinas, the Jerseys, Pennsylvania, and Delaware. Huguenot, German, Scottish, and Scotch-Irish immigration made the population ethnically more heterogeneous. Strange new religious sects appeared, especially in the middle colonies. The frontier practically everywhere along the mainland pushed beyond the fall line into the seemingly limitless wilderness. Wealth derived from shipping, commerce, and plantation agriculture created capital and produced a larger class of colonial merchants, industrialists, and plantation owners. The introduction of cotton in the South gave added impetus to the cruel slave trade and laid the foundations for the institution of slavery. Sugar brought slavery into the West Indies at an even faster pace and gave birth to a way of life completely unsuitable for the perpetuation of British institutions and values. New wealth, coupled with the rise of cities, provided opportunity for the pursuit of inquiry, learning, and culture —antidotes to superstition and credulity. In this new, exciting age, the colonies became aware of one another and drew closer together. As the struggling, isolated settlement of the first-generation immigrants began to disappear, the inhabitants, no longer landbound, no longer restricted to familiar shores, no longer homogeneous, were becoming, if not Americans, at least Americanized.

Selected Bibliography

The amount of writing on the early American colonies, both general and special, is extensive. Most of the works mentioned here should be available in any good academic or historical research library.

Bibliographical Guides and Printed Records

Oscar Handlin *et al.*, *Harvard Guide to American History* (Cambridge, Mass., 1954) supersedes earlier guides. Useful also are Henry P. Beers, *Bibliographies in American History: A Guide to Materials for Research* (2d ed., New York, 1942), and Grace Gardner Griffen, *Writings in American History* (33 vols., Washington, D.C., 1906–49). Griffin's invaluable annual listings of all books and periodical articles were preceded in 1902 and 1903 by similar volumes. Following a gap, 1941–47, the project was resumed under the editorship of J. M. Masterson in 1952 with the publication of the *Writings* for 1948. Thomas L. Bradford, *The Bibliographer's Manual of American History* (5 vols., Philadelphia, 1907–10) is of value, and the *Cambridge History of the British Empire*, Vol. I, ed. J. H. Rose (Cambridge, England, 1929), contains the best single bibliography of the early period. J. N. Larned, *Literature of American History, a Bibliographical Guide* (New York, 1902), has brief critical estimates, and Milton Waldman, *Americana: The Literature of American History* (New York, 1925), discusses the older historical writings.

For books relating to America before 1900, see Joseph Sabin (ed.) (and after Sabin, Wilberforce Eames and Robert W. G. Vail), *Bibliotheca Americana: A Dictionary of Books Relating to America, from Its Discovery to the Present Time* (19 vols., New York, 1868–91, but not completed until 1936 with Vol. XXIX); Charles Evans, *American Bibliography, A*

Chronological Dictionary of all Books, Pamphlets, and Periodical Publications Printed in the United States . . . down to . . . 1820 (12 vols., Chicago, 1903–34), especially Vols. I–IV; J. Franklin Jameson, "Guide to the Items Relating to American History in the Reports of the English Historical Manuscripts Commission . . . ," American Historical Association *Report* (1898); David C. Douglas (ed.), *English Historical Documents,* especially Vol. VII, Merrill Jensen (ed.), *American Colonial Documents;* Godfrey Davies, *Bibliography of British History,* 1603–1714 (Oxford, 1928). For examples of bibliographers' bibliographies of rare imprints for individual colonies, see Clarence S. Brigham, *Bibliography of Rhode Island History* (Boston, 1902), supplemented by "List of Books on Rhode Island History," *Rhode Island Educational Circulars,* Hist. Ser. I; and Elizabeth Baer, *Seventeenth Century Maryland: A Bibliography* (Baltimore, 1949).

The important historical journals are given with the first year of publication: *American Historical Review* (1895); *Agricultural History* (1927); *English Historical Review* (1886); *Mississippi Valley Historial Review,* now *The Journal of American History* (1914); *New England Quarterly* (1928); *Journal of Economic History* (1941); *William and Mary Quarterly* (1892), devoted entirely to early American history; and *Journal of Southern History* (1935).

Selected historical society publications constitute a long list: *Virginia Magazine of History,* 1893– ; *Virginia Historical Register,* 1848–53; *Virginia Historical Reporter,* 1854–60; *Virginia Historical Collections,* 1882–92; and *Tyler's Historical and Genealogical Magazine,* 1919–52. Earl G. Swem has compiled the valuable *Virginia Historical Index* (2 vols., Roanoke, 1934–36) to the *Register* and *Magazine* through 1930, and "A Bibliography of Virginia," Virginia State Library *Bulletin,* VIII, Nos. 2–4; X, Nos. 1–4; and XII, Nos. 1–2 (1915–32). For Maryland there are the Maryland Historical Society Fund *Publications,* 1867–1901, and the *Maryland Historical Magazine,* 1906–

The principal New England society publications are *The New England Historical and Genealogical Register,* 1847– ; Connecticut Historical Society *Collections,* 1860–1932, and *Bulletin.* 1934– ; New Haven Historical Society *Papers,* 1865–1918; Maine Historical Society *Collections,* 1831–1906; American Antiquarian Society *Proceedings,* 1850– ; Colonial Society of Massachusetts *Publications,* 1895– ; Massachusetts Historical Society *Collections,* 1792– ; *Proceedings,* 1879– ; Rhode Island Historical Society *Collections,* 1827–1941; *Proceedings,* 1872–92, 1900–14; *Publications,* 1893–1900; and *Rhode Island History,* 1942–

Materials relating especially to Dutch and Swedish colonization are found in New York Historical Society *Collections,* 1811–59; *Proceedings;* 1901– ; *Quarterly Bulletin,* 1917– ; and *Quarterly Journal,* 1919–31; *New*

York History, 1932–   ; Historical Society of Pennsylvania *Memoirs*, 1826–1895; *Pennsylvania Magazine of History and Biography*, 1877–   ; and *Pennsylvania History*, 1934–

The great biographical dictionaries are *Dictionary of American Biography* (21 vols., New York, 1928–44) and *Dictionary of National Biography* (22 vols. and supplements, Oxford, 1937–49). Both are invaluable. An atlas of American history is badly needed. Some useful maps may be found in Charles O. Paullin, *Atlas of Historical Geography of the United States* (Washington, 1932) and, for the earliest settlements, in James T. Adams (ed.), *Atlas of American History* (New York, 1943).

The printed records are voluminous. Selected works are as follows: W. L. Grant and James Munro (eds.), *Acts of the Privy Council, Colonial Series, 1613–1783* (6 vols., London, 1908–12); Danby Pickering (ed.), *The Statutes at Large . . .* (46 vols., Cambridge, England, 1762–1807); Vol. VII begins with the year 1607, but this series does not include the Commonwealth period; Leo F. Stock (ed.), *Proceedings and Debates of the British Parliaments Respecting North America, 1452–1727* (3 vols., Washington, 1924–30); Wallace Notestein *et al.* (eds.), *Commons Debates . . .* (7 vols., London, 1935); Charles H. Firth and R. S. Rait, *Acts and Ordinances of the Interregnum, 1642–1660* (3 vols., London, 1911); Frances G. Davenport (ed.), *European Treaties Bearing on the History of the United States and Its Dependencies* (4 vols., Washington, D.C., 1917–37), Charles O. Paullin (ed.), Vol. IV for the colonial period; Clarence S. Brigham (ed.), *British Royal Proclamations Relating to America,* American Antiquarian Society *Transactions* (Worcester, 1911); Charles M. Andrews, *British Committees, Commissions, and Council of Trade and Plantations, 1622–1675* (Baltimore, 1908); *Calendar of State Papers, Colonial Series, America and the West Indies, 1574–1711* (20 vols., London, 1860–1903), with excellent editing by W. Noel Sainsbury *et al.;* Ebenezer Hazard (ed.), *Historical Collections Consisting of State Papers and Other Authentic Documents* (2 vols., Philadelphia, 1792–94); Peter Force (ed.), *Tracts and Other Papers Relating Principally to the Origin, Settlement, and Progress of the Colonies in North America . . .* (4 vols., Washington, D.C., 1836–46; reprinted, New York, 1947), contains rare materials; Francis N. Thorpe (ed.), *The Federal and State Constitutions, Colonial Charters, and Other Organic Laws . . .* (7 vols., Washington, D.C., 1909), supplants Benjamin P. Poore's work on the same title (2 vols., Washington, D.C., 1878); and William MacDonald (ed.), *Documentary Source Book of American History, 1606–1775* (3d ed., New York, 1926), the most convenient edition.

Earl G. Swem's *Virginia Historical Index*, as cited, is the best guide to the printed sources for a single colony. For Virginia, see also Susan M. Kingsbury (ed.), *The Records of the Virginia Company of London: The*

Court Book, from the Manuscript in the Library of Congress (4 vols., Washington, D.C., 1906–35); *Journal of the London Company (1619–1624), Virginia Historical Society Collections,* N.S., VII (1888), I and II; William W. Hening (ed.), *The Statute at Large, Being a Collection of all the Laws of Virginia, from . . . 1619* (13 vols., Richmond, Philadelphia, and New York, 1823); H. R. McIlwaine and John P. Kennedy (eds.), *Journals of the House of Burgesses of Virginia, 1619–1776* (13 vols., Richmond, 1905–15); and T. S. Wynne and W. S. Gilman, *Colonial Records of Virginia, 1619–1680* (Richmond, 1874). For Maryland, see Thomas Bacon, *Laws of Maryland, 1637–1763* (Annapolis, 1765); *Archives of Maryland,* William H. Browne *et al.* (eds.) (67 vols., Baltimore, 1883–   ), which include the Proceedings and Acts of the General Assembly, 1637–1774, the Proceedings of the Council, 1636–1770, and the Proceedings of the Provincial Court, 1636–77; and *Calendar of Maryland State Papers,* I (1636–1785) (Annapolis, 1943).

The New England records are as follows: Charles T. Libby and Robert E. Moody (eds.), *Province and Court Records of Maine* (3 vols., Portland, 1928–47); A. S. Batchellor and H. H. Metcalfe (eds.), *Laws of New Hampshire . . . , The Province Period* (3 vols., Manchester and Bristol, 1904–15); Nathaniel Bouton *et al.* (eds.), *Documents and Records Relating to the Province . . . of New Hampshire, 1623–1800* (49 vols., Concord, etc., 1867–1943); Nathaniel B. Shurtleff and David Pulsifer (eds.), *Records of the Colony of New Plymouth in New England, 1620–1692* (12 vols., Boston, 1855–61); Nathaniel B. Shurtleff (ed.), *Records of the Governor and Company of Massachusetts Bay in New England, 1628–1686* (5 vols. Boston, 1853–54); *Records of the Court of Assistants of the Colony of Massachusetts Bay, 1630–1692* (3 vols., 1901–28); George F. Dow (ed.), *Records and Files of the Quarterly Courts of Essex County, 1636–1683* (6 vols., Salem, 1911–21; Charles J. Hoadly (ed.), *Records of the Colony and Plantation of New Haven from 1638 to 1649* (Hartford, 1857); John R. Bartlett (ed.), *Records of the Colony of Rhode Island and Providence Plantations in New England, 1636–1792* (10 vols., Providence, 1856–65); *Rhode Island Court Records, 1647–1670* (2 vols., Providence, 1920–22); Record Commissioners, *Early Records of the Town of Providence* (21 vols., Providence, 1692–1915); Charles J. Hoadly, *The Public Records of the Colony of Connecticut, 1636–1776* (15 vols., Hartford, 1850–80).

For the Middle Colonies, see Edmund B. O'Callaghan and Berthold Fernow (eds.), *Documents Relative to the Colonial History . . . History of New York* (15 vols., Albany, 1853–71), especially Vols. I–III, ed. O'Callaghan, and Vols. XII (The Delaware), XIII (The Hudson Settlements), and XIV (Early Long Island), ed. Fernow; Berthold Fernow, *The Records of New Amsterdam from 1653 to 1674* (7 vols., New York, 1897);

and Edmund B. O'Callaghan, *Laws and Ordinances of New York, 1638–1675* (Albany, 1868). For pre-English New Jersey, see Vol. I of William A. Whitehead *et al.* (eds.), *Archives of the State of New Jersey*, F.S., *Documents Relating to the Colonial History of the State of New Jersey* (33 vols., Newark, etc., 1880–1928).

Selected Manuscript Guides and Manuscript Materials

Philip E. Hamer (ed.), *A Guide to Archives and Manuscripts in the United States* (New Haven, 1961), supersedes earlier guides; see also Charles M. Andrews, *Guide to Materials in American History to 1783 in the Public Record Office of Great Britain* (2 vols., Washington, D.C., 1912–14); Charles M. Andrews and Frances G. Davenport, *Guide to the Manuscript Materials for the History of the United States to 1783, in the British Museum, in Minor London Archives, and in the Libraries of Oxford and Cambridge* (Washington, D.C., 1908); Grace G. Griffen, *A Guide to Manuscripts Relating to American History in British Depositories Reproduced for the Division of Manuscripts of the Library of Congress* (Washington, D.C., 1946); *Handbook of Manuscripts in the Library of Congress* (Washington, D.C., 1918), now outdated, is supplemented in various ways; and *A Guide to the Microfilm Collection of Early State Records* (Washington, D.C., 1948, and supplement, Washington, 1951) describes the compilation and microfilming of 2,500,000 pages.

The manuscript holdings of various depositories are listed as follows: *Handbook of the Massachusetts Historical Society, 1791–1948* (Boston, 1949); *A Guide to the Resources of the American Antiquarian Society* (Worcester, 1937); Evarts B. Greene and Richard B. Morris, *A Guide to the Principal Sources for Early American History, 1600–1800, in the City of New York* (2d rev. ed., New York, 1967); *Guide to the Manuscript Collections of the Historical Society of Pennsylvania* (2d ed., Philadelphia, 1949); William E. Ewing, *Guide to the Manuscript Collections in the William L. Clements Library* (Ann Arbor, 1953); Alice E. Smith, *Guide to the Manuscripts of the Wisconsin Historical Society* (Madison, 1914); Norma B. Cuthbert, *American Manuscripts in the Huntington Library for the History of the Seventeenth and Eighteenth Centuries* (2d pr., San Marino, 1964); Library of Congress, *Manuscript Collections in Public and Private Collections in the United States* (Washington, D.C., 1924); Charles M. Andrews, "List of Journals and Acts of the Councils and Assemblies of the Thirteen Original Colonies . . . Preserved in the Public Record Office in London," American Historical Association *Annual Report* (1908), Vol. I; and Adelaide R. Haas, "Materials for a Bibliography of the Public Archives of the Thirteen Original Colonies," American Historical Association *Annual Report* (1906), especially Vol. II.

English Background

The standard bibliography is Godfrey Davies, *Bibliography of British History, Stuart Period* (Oxford, 1926), and the standard history is Sir George N. Clark, *The Seventeenth Century* (Oxford, 1929). The American historian Edward P. Cheyney wrote *The European Background of American History* (New York, 1904) for the older *American Nation Series,* now superseded by Wallace Notestein, *The English People on the Eve of Colonization, 1603–1630* (New York, 1951) for the New American Nation Series. The latter should be used with Carl Bridenbaugh's newer, well-researched *Vexed and Troubled Englishmen, 1500–1642* (New York, 1968). Ralph H. Tawney, *The Agricultural Problem in the Sixteenth Century* (New York, 1912), and John U. Nef's two books, *Industry and Government in France and England, 1540–1640* (Philadelphia, 1940) and *The United States and Civilization* (Chicago, 1942), further explain the intricate economic revolution of this period. John W. Allen's two books, *Political Thought in the Sixteenth Century* (New York, 1951) and *English Economic Thought* (London, 1938), are useful. Joseph R. Tanner, *English Constitutional Conflicts of the Seventeenth Century* (Cambridge, Eng., 1928), augments these volumes. For contemporary material, one should consult the writings of Sir Simonds D'Ewes, *A Complete Journal of all the Parliaments during the Whole Reign of Queen Elizabeth of Glorious Memory,* ed. Paul Bowes (London, 1962), and his other works.

There are a number of good studies relating to the colonial system. Noteworthy are E. Lipson, The *Economic History of England* (3 vols., Cambridge, Eng., 1920–31); Hugh E. Egerton, *The Origin and Growth of English Colonies and Their System of Government* (Oxford, 1903); George L. Beer, *Origins of the British Colonial System, 1758–1660* (New York, 1908); Klaus E. Knorr, *British Colonial Theories, 1570–1850* (Toronto, 1944); Eli F. Hecksher, *Mercantilism* (2 vols., London, 1935); G. D. Ramsay, *English Overseas Trade during the Centuries of Emergence . . .* (London, 1957); Oliver M. Dickerson, *The Navigation Acts and the American Revolution* (Philadelphia, 1951); and especially Lawrence A. Harper, *The English Navigation Laws: A Seventeenth-Century Experiment in Social Engineering* (New York, 1939). More specialized are Arthur P. Newton, *The Colonizing Activities of the English Puritans* (New Haven, 1914); George Edmundson, *Anglo-Dutch Rivalry during the First Half of the Seventeenth Century* (Oxford, 1911), the best introduction to the subject; Violet Barbour, "Dutch and English Merchant Shipping in the Seventeenth Century," *Economic History Review,* II (1930), 261–290; Sir Charles Firth, *Oliver Cromwell and the Rule of the Puritans in England* (New York, 1900); George L. Beer, "Cromwell's Policy in Its Economic

Aspects," *Political Science Quarterly*, XVI (1901), 582–611, and XVII 1902), 46–70; and Sir George N. Clark, "Navigation Act of 1651," *History*, N.S., VII (1923), 282–286.

Religious backgrounds are treated in the following standard works: Champlin Burrage, *Early English Dissenters* (2 vols., Cambridge, 1912); Marshall M. Knappen, *Tudor Puritanism* . . . (Chicago, 1939); Wilbur K. Jordan, *The Development of Religious Toleration in England* (4 vols., Cambridge, Mass., 1932–40); William Haller, *The Rise of Puritanism* . . . *1570–1643* (New York, 1938); *Liberty and Reformation in the Puritan Revolution* (New York, 1955); Alan Simpson, *Puritanism in Old and New England* (Chicago, 1955), a stimulating work; Gertrude Huehns, *Antinomianism in England* (London, 1952); and William C. Braithwaite, *The Beginnings of Quakerism* (2d ed., rev. by Henry C. Cadbury, Cambridge, Eng., 1955).

The Period of Exploration

J. Holland Rose *et al.* (eds.), *Cambridge History of the British Empire* (7 vols., Cambridge, Eng., 1929–30), Vol. I especially. Other standard works are James A. Williamson, *Maritime Enterprise* (Oxford, 1913); Arthur P. Newton (ed.), *The Great Age of Discovery* (London, 1932); John H. Parry, *The Age of Reconnaissance* (2d ed., New York, 1964); Arthur P. Newton, *The European Nations in the West Indies, 1493–1688* (London, 1933; reprinted, New York, 1967); Sir Charles P. Lucas, *Beginnings of British Overseas Enterprise* (Oxford, 1917); Arthur D. Innes, *The Maritime and Colonial Expansion of England under the Stuarts, 1603–1714* (London, 1931), and the requisite chapters in Sir Charles P. Lucas, *A Historical Geography of the British Colonies* (7 vols., Oxford, 1888–1920). A. L. Rowse, *The Expansion of Elizabethan England* (London, 1959) and *The Elizabethans and America* (London, 1959), are vividly written. See also Nellie M. Crouse, *In Quest of the Western Oceans* (New York, 1928); J. Bartlet Brebner, *The Explorers of North America, 1492–1806* (3d ed., Cleveland, 1964); Franklin T. McCann, *English Discovery in America* (New York, 1952); and Charles H. Livermore (ed.), *Forerunners and Competitors of Pilgrims and Puritans* . . . (2 vols., Brooklyn, 1912).

Richard P. Hakluyt, *The Principal Navigations, Voyages, Traffiques & Discoveries of the English Nation* . . . (London, 1589; reprinted in full, 12 vols., Glasgow, 1903–5), is a classic work. See also Eva G. R. Taylor, *The Original Writings and Correspondence of the Two Richard Hakluyts* (2 vols., London, 1935), skillfully edited; and George B. Parks, *Richard Hakluyt and the English Voyages* (2d ed., New York, 1961), is excellent. W. Nelson Francis comments on Hakluyt's voyages in *William and Mary Quarterly*, 3d ser., XII (1955), 446–455. Also contemporary is

Hakluytus Posthumous or Samuel Purchas, *His Pilgrimage . . . of the World* (London, 1613); there were four editions by 1616. For the pre-Elizabethan period see Henry Harrisse, *John Cabot . . . and Sebastian His Son . . . 1496–1557* (London, 1896); Charles R. Beazley, *John and Sebastian Cabot* (New York, 1964); and James A. Williamson, *The Cabot Voyages and Bristol Discovery Under Henry VII* (Cambridge, Eng., 1962), the most scholarly.

There is a vast literature of Elizabethan discovery. Among many works are Edward J. Payne and Charles R. Beazley (eds.), *Voyages of Elizabethan Seamen* (Oxford, 1907); Douglas Bell, *Elizabethan Seamen* (Philadelphia, 1936); Sir William Foster, *England's Quest for Eastern Trade* (London, 1933); William Francis, "Elizabethan Finances of Discovery," *William and Mary Quarterly*, 3d ser., XIII, 184–201; Sir Eric St. John Brooks, *Sir Christopher Hatton: Queen Elizabeth's Favourite* (London, 1947); and Ralph M. Sargent, *At the Court of Queen Elizabeth: The Life and Lyrics of Sir Edward Dyer* (London, 1935).

The activities of Elizabethan discoverers fall into a separate category. A selected list would include James A. Williamson, *Sir John Hawkins: The Time and the Man* (Oxford, 1927) and *Hawkins of Plymouth . . .* (London, 1949); Sir Clements R. Markham (ed.), *The Hawkins' Voyages . . .* (London, 1878). On Sir Francis Drake see Sir Julian S. Corbett, *Drake and the Tudor Navy* (2 vols., London, 1898–99; reprinted, New York, 1965); Henry R. Wagner, *Sir Francis Drake's Voyage Around the World: Its Aims and Its Achievements* (San Francisco, 1926); Zelia Nuttall (trans. and ed.), *New Light on Drake . . . 1577–1580* (London, 1914); William Wood, *Elizabethan Sea-Dogs: A Chronicle of Drake and His Companions* (3d ed., New Haven, Conn., 1921); James A. Williamson, *The Age of Drake* (4th ed., London, 1960) and *Sir Francis Drake* (2d ed., London, 1966); and Edward F. Benson's briefer *Sir Francis Drake* (2d ed., New York, 1927).

The best works on Sir Walter Raleigh are Edward Edwards, *Life of Sir Walter Raleigh* (London, 1868); William Stebbing, *Sir Walter Raleigh: A Biography* (Oxford, 1899); Milton Waldman, *Sir Walter Raleigh* (New York, 1943); David B. Quinn, *Raleigh and the British Empire* (London, 1947); Ernest A. Strathman, *Sir Walter Raleigh: A Study in Elizabethan Skepticism* (New York, 1951); A. L. Rowse, *Sir Walter Raleigh, His Family and Private Life* (New York, 1962); and Willard M. Wallace, *Sir Walter Raleigh* (Princeton, 1959), a useful recent biography. See also William S. Powell, "John Pory on the Death of Sir Walter Raleigh," *William and Mary Quarterly*, 3d ser. (1952), 532–538. A notable publication is *American Drawings of John White* (Chapel Hill and British Museum, London, 1964).

Works on other Elizabethan explorers are William McFee, *The Life of*

Sir Martin Frobisher (New York, 1928); Vilhjalmur Stefansson (ed.), *The Three Voyages of Martin Frobisher . . . A.D. 1576–8* (2 vols., London, 1938), reprints contemporary records; William G. Gosling, *The Life of Sir Humphrey Gilbert* (London, 1911); David B. Quinn (ed.), *The Voyages and Colonizing Enterprises of Sir Humphrey Gilbert* (2 vols., London, 1940), with documents; George B. Manhart, *The English Search for a Northwest Passage . . .* (Philadelphia, 1924), discusses projected routes to the Orient; Sir Albert H. Markham, *Voyages and Works of John Davis the Navigator* (London, 1880); Sir Clements R. Markham, *Life of John Davis* (London, 1891); A. L. Rowse, *Sir Richard Grenville of the Revenge* (2d ed., London, 1949) and *Shakespeare's Southampton, Patron of Virginia* (London, 1965); Henry Stevens, *Thomas Hariot . . . and His Associates* (London, 1900); Warner Gookin, "Who Was Bartholomew Gosnold?" *William and Mary Quarterly*, 3d ser., VI (1949), 398–415; John Brereton, *A Briefe and True Relation* (London, 1602), describes the Cape Cod voyage; Llewelyn Powys, *Henry Hudson* (New York, 1928), the best life; Lawrence J. Burpee, "The Fate of Henry Hudson," *Canadian Historical Review*, XXI (1940), 401–406; and Sir Clements R. Markham (ed.), *The Voyages of William Baffin, 1612–1622* (London, 1881).

On the international situation see David B. Quinn, "Some Spanish Reactions to Elizabethan Colonial Enterprises," Royal Historical Society *Transactions*, 5th ser., I (1951), 1–23; Irene A. Wright (trans. and ed.), *Spanish Documents Concerning English Voyages to the Spanish Main, 1527–1568* (London, 1929), *Documents Concerning English Voyages to the Spanish Main, 1569–1580* (London, 1932) and *Further English Voyages to Spanish America, 1583–1594* (London, 1951); and Max Savelle, "The International Approach of Early Angloamerican History," in Ray A. Billington (ed.), *The Reinterpretation of Early American History* (San Marino, Calif., 1966), pp. 201–229.

David B. Quinn, who does his researches *in situ* wherever possible, has contributed, *inter alia*, *The Roanoke Voyages, 1584–1590: Documents to Illustrate the English Voyages to North America under the Patent Granted to Sir Walter Raleigh in 1584* (2 vols., London, 1955). Note also Edwin C. Rozwence, "Captain John Smith's Image of America," *William and Mary Quarterly*, 3d ser., XVI (1959), 23–36; Philip Barbour, *The Three Worlds of Captain John Smith* (Boston, 1964), and Jarvis M. Morse, "John Smith and His Critics," *Journal of Southern History*, I (1935), 123–137.

Earliest Settlements

These have been discussed by America's greatest historians in the early chapters of general histories and in the early volumes of multivolume works. Among the leading general histories are George Chalmers, *Political*

Annals of the Present United States . . . to the Peace of 1783 . . . (London, 1780); George Bancroft, *History of the United States* (10 vols., Boston, 1834–74); Francis Parkman, *France and England in America* (9 vols., Boston, 1865–92); a number of John Fiske's works including *The Beginnings of New England* (Boston, 1889); *The Dutch and Quaker Colonies in America* (2 vols., Boston, 1899); and *New France and New England* (Boston, 1902); Justin Winsor (ed.), *Narrative and Critical History of the United States* (8 vols., Boston, 1884–89), which contains valuable bibliographical notes; Alexander Brown, *The Genesis of the United States . . .* (2 vols., London, 1890), includes important documentary material, and *The First Republic in America* (Boston, 1898); Edward Channing, *A History of the United States* (6 vols., New York, 1905–25); Herbert L. Osgood, *The American Colonies in the Seventeenth Century* (3 vols., New York, 1904–7), introduces rigorous historical research; Charles and Mary Beard, *The Rise of American Civilization* (2 vols., New York, 1927), stimulating and controversial; and Charles M. Andrews, *The Colonial Period of American History* (4 vols., New Haven, 1934–38), unsurpassed in dealing with the earliest settlements.

There are five cooperative works of merit, not including the New American Nation Series, all with accounts of the early period: *The American Nation: A History,* ed., Albert B. Hart (27 vols., New York, 1904–9); *Original Narratives of Early American History,* ed. J. Franklin Jameson (19 vols., New York, 1906–17); The Chronicles of America Series, ed. Allen Johnson and Allan Nevins (56 vols., New Haven, 1918–51); *A History of American Life,* ed. Arthur M. Schlesinger and Dixon Ryan Fox (13 vols., New York, 1927–48); and *The Pageant of America,* ed. Ralph H. Gabriel *et al.* (15 vols., New Haven, 1926–29).

Other general works touching this period are Evarts B. Greene and Virginia D. Harrington, *American Population before the Federal Census of 1790* (New York, 1932); Stella H. Sutherland, *Population Distribution in Colonial America* (New York, 1936); Albert P. Brigham, *Geographic Influences in American History* (New York, 1903); Ellen C. Semple, *American History and Its Geographic Conditions* (Boston, 1903), still useful; and Donald D. Brand, "The Origin and Early Distribution of New World Cultivated Plants," *Agricultural History,* XIII (1939), 109–117.

Jarvis M. Morse, *American Beginnings: Highlights and Sidelights of the Birth of the New World* (Washington, D.C., 1952), discusses contemporary histories. Well-known general accounts of the early period are Herbert I. Priestley, *The Coming of the White Man* (New York, 1929); Marcus L. Hansen, *The Atlantic Migration* (Cambridge, 1940); Carl Becker, *The Beginnings of the American People* (Boston, 1915); Marcus W. Jernegan, *The American Colonies* (New York, 1929); Charles M. Andrews, *Our*

Earliest Colonial Settlements (New York, 1933), fine interpretative essays; Daniel J. Boorstin, *The Americans: The Colonial Experience* (New York, 1958), a rich synthesis; Edward K. Chatterton, *Seed of Liberty* (Annapolis, 1929), excellent on early English-American relations; Clinton Rossiter, *Seedtime of the Republic: The Origin of the American Tradition of Political Liberty* (New York, 1953), important; Louis B. Wright, *The Cultural Life of the American Colonies, 1607–1763* (New York, 1957) (a volume in The New American Nation Series), *The Atlantic Frontier: Colonial American Civilization* (New York, 1947), and *Religion and Empire: The Alliance Between Piety and Commerce in English Expansion, 1580–1625;* Thomas J. Wertenbaker, *First Americans, 1607–1690* (New York, 1927); and Clarence ver Steeg, *The Formative Years, 1607–1763* (London, 1965).

Thomas J. Wertenbaker's *Founding of the American Colonies: The Middle Colonies* (New York, 1938), *The Old South* (New York, 1942), and *The Puritan Oligarchy* (New York, 1947), contain materials not easily found elsewhere. Wesley Frank Craven has written *The Southern Colonies in the Seventeenth Century, 1607–1689,* the standard work; and James M. Smith has edited *Seventeenth-Century America: Essays in Colonial History* (Chapel Hill, N.C., 1959), which includes several valuable articles. Ray A. Billington, *The Reinterpretation of Early American History, Essays in Honor of John Edwin Pomfret* (San Marino, Calif., 1966), contains a number of bibliographical and substantive articles dealing with seventeenth-century America.

The following works on constitutional history touch on the early colonial period: Andrew C. McLaughlin, *The Foundations of American Constitutionalism* (New York, 1632); William R. Scott, *The Constitution and Finance of English, Scottish, and Irish Joint Stock Companies to 1720* (3 vols., Cambridge, Eng., 1910–12); Thomas Pownall, *The Administration of the Colonies* (London, 1764); Louise P. Kellogg, "The American Colonial Charter," American Historical Association *Report* (1903), I, 187–341; W. C. Morey, "The Genesis of a Written Constitution," *Annals of the American Academy of Political and Social Science,* I (1891), 529–557; Benjamin F. Wright, "The Early History of Written Constitutions in America," in *Essays in History and Political Theory in Honor of Charles Howard McIlwain* (Cambridge, Mass., 1936); Herbert L. Osgood, "The Corporation as a Form of Colonial Government," *Political Science Quarterly,* XI (1896), 502–532, and "The Proprietary Province as a Form of Colonial Government," *American Historical Review,* II (1897), 644–654, and III (1898), 31–55.

General works on colonial government are Leonard W. Labaree, *Conservatism in Early American History* (New York, 1948); Percy L. Kaye,

The Colonial Executive Prior to the Restoration (Baltimore, 1900); Evarts B. Greene, *The Provincial Governor* . . . (New York, 1898); Mary P. Clarke, *Parliamentary Privilege in the American Colonies* (New Haven, 1943); Thomas F. Moran, *The Rise and Development of the Bicameral System in America* (Baltimore, 1895); Cortlandt F. Bishop, *History of Elections in the American Colonies* (New York, 1893); Herbert Philips, *The Development of a Residential Qualification for Representatives in Colonial Legislatures* (Cincinnati, 1921); Frank H. Miller, "Legal Qualifications for Office in America, 1619–1899," American Historical Association *Annual Report* (1899), I, 87–153; Ralph V. Harlow, *The History of Legislative Methods in the Period before 1825* (New Haven, 1917); Albert E. McKinley, *The Suffrage Franchise in the Thirteen English Colonies in America* (Philadelphia, 1905); Cyrus H. Karrakar, *The Seventeenth Century Sheriff: A Comparative Study of the Sheriff in England and the Chesapeake Bay Colonies, 1607–1698* (Chapel Hill, N.C., 1930); Kenneth Colgrove, "New England Town Mandates: Introduction to the Deputies in Colonial Legislatures," Colonial Society of Massachusetts *Publications*, XXI (1920), 441–449; Paul S. Reinsch, *English Common Law in Early American Colonies* (Madison, Wis., 1899); Richard B. Morris, *Studies in the History of American Law* (New York, 1930); Michael G. Kammen, "Colonial Court Records and the Study of Early American History," *American Historical Review*, LXX 1965), 732–739; Edward Channing, *Town and County Government in the English Colonies* (Baltimore, 1884); and George A. Billias, *Law and Authority in Colonial America: Selected Essays* (Barré, Mass., 1965).

General and special works on economic topics are: Edgar A. Johnson, *American Economic Thought in the Seventeenth Century* (London, 1932); Joseph Dorfman, *The Economic Mind in American Civilization* (3 vols., New York, 1946–49); Edward C. Kirkland, *A History of American Economic Life* (New York, 1932); Richard Pares, *Merchants and Planters* (Cambridge, Mass., 1960), a critical work that challenges many generalizations; Carl Bridenbaugh, *Cities in the Wilderness* (New York, 1938), presents much original material; Clive Day, "Capitalistic and Socialistic Tendencies in the Puritan Colonies," American Historical Association *Annual Report* (1920), 222–235; Gaillard T. Lapsley, *County Palatine of Durham* (Cambridge, Eng., 1924); Marshall D. Harris, *Origin of the Land Tenure System in the United States* (Ames, Iowa, 1953); Viola F. Barnes, "Land Tenures in English Colonial Charters," in *Essays in Colonial History Presented to Charles McLean Andrews* (New Haven, 1931); Edith Abbott (ed.), *Historical Aspects of the Immigration Problem* (Chicago, 1926); and Beverly Bond, *The Quitrent System in the American Colonies* (New Haven, 1919).

Other works treating economic subjects are Charles J. Bullock, *Essays on the Monetary History of the United States* (London, 1900); Emory P. Johnson *et al., History of the Domestic and Foreign Commerce of the United States* (2 vols., Washington, D.C., 1915); James L. Bishop, *History of American Manufactures, 1608–1860* (3 vols., Philadelphia, 1866–68); Walter S. Clark, *History of Manufactures in the United States* (rev. ed., 3 vols., Washington, D.C., 1929), important; Harold Innes, *The Cod Fisheries* (New Haven, 1940), a major study; Charles B. Judah, *The North American Fisheries and British Policy to 1713* (Urbana, Ill., 1933), an excellent survey; Raymond McPortland, *A History of the New England Fisheries* (New York, 1911); Rolla M. Tryon, *Household Manufactures in the United States, 1640–1860* (Chicago, 1917); Carl Bridenbaugh, *The Colonial Craftsman* (New York, 1950), first-rate on the artisan class; also Davis B. Dewey, *Financial History of the United States* (New York, 1922); Curtis P. Nettels, *The Money Supply of the American Colonies before 1720* (Madison, Wis., 1934), indispensable; Percy W. Bidwell and John I. Falconer, *History of Agriculture in Northern United States, 1620–1860* (Washington, D.C., 1925), a standard work; Lewis C. Gray, *History of Agriculture in the Southern United States* (2 vols., Washington, D.C., 1933), valuable; Lyman Carrier, *The Beginning of Agriculture in America* (New York, 1933); and Joseph Schafer, *The Social History of American Agriculture* (New York, 1938).

A number of works deal with ethnological and social problems: Almon W. Lauber, *Indian Slavery in Colonial Times* . . . (New York, 1913); Edward E. Edwards, "American Indian Contributions to Civilization," *Minnesota History,* XV (1904), 255–272; Wilcomb E. Washburn, "A Moral History of Indian-White Relations: Needs and Opportunities for Study," *Ethno-History,* 4 (1957), 47–61; Wilcomb E. Washburn, "The Moral and Legal Justifications for Dispossessing the Indians," and Nancy O. Lurie, "Indian Cultural Adjustment to European Civilization." The last two are articles in *Seventeenth-Century America: Essays in Colonial History,* ed. James M. Smith (Chapel Hill, N.C., 1959).

On the Negro and Negro slavery see Elizabeth Donnan, *Documents Illustrative of the Slave Trade to America* (4 vols., Washington, D.C., 1930–35), especially Introduction; John Hope Franklin, *From Slavery to Freedom: A History of American Negroes* (New York, 1947); David B. Davis, *The Problem of Slavery in Western Culture* (Ithaca, 1966); and Winthrop D. Jordan, *White Over Black: American Attitudes Toward the Negro, 1550–1812* (Chapel Hill, N.C., 1968), an important book with illuminating chapters on the origin and rationale of slavery in the American colonies. See also Stanley Elkins, *Slavery: A Problem in American Institutional and Intellectual Life* (Chicago, 1959); Carl N. Degler, "Slavery and the Genesis of American Race Prejudice," *Comparative Studies in Society and History,*

II (1959), 49–66; and Milton Cantor, "The Image of the Negro in Colonial Literature," *New England Quarterly*, XXXVI (1963), 452–477.

Important also are Marcus Jernegan, *The Laboring and Dependent Classes in Colonial America* (Chicago, 1931); John R. Commons, *et al.*, *History of Labour in the United States* (4 vols., New York, 1918–35); and Abbot E. Smith, *Colonists in Bondage: White Servitude and Convict Labor in America, 1607–1776* (Chapel Hill, N.C., 1947); and Richard B. Morris, *Government and Labor in Early America* (New York, 1946).

Early works dealing with cultural and religious topics are: Vernon L. Parrington, *Main Currents in American Thought*, Vol. I, *The Colonial Mind* (New York, 1927), is still challenging, but in part has been superseded by recent work. Louis B. Wright, *The Cultural Life of the American Colonies* (New York, 1957), is a comprehensive statement. Bernard Bailyn pioneers in his book *Education in the Forming of American Society* (Chapel Hill, N.C., 1960), but note the comments of David J. Rothman in "A Note on the Study of the Colonial Family," *William and Mary Quarterly*, XXIII (1966), 626–634. Thomas C. Hall, *The Religious Background of American Culture* (Boston, 1930), emphasizes the tradition of dissent. For the several denominations see James S. M. Anderson, *History of the Church of England in the Colonies* (3 vols., London, 1845–1856); Arthur L. Cross, *The Anglican Episcopate and the American Colonies* (Cambridge, Mass., 1902); William S. Perry, *History of the Protestant Episcopal Church* (2 vols., Boston, 1885); Raymond W. Albright, *A History of the Protestant Episcopal Church* (New York, 1924), a modern synthesis; and Francis R. Hawks and William S. Perry (eds.), *Documentary History of the Protestant Episcopal Church in the United States of America* (2 vols., Philadelphia, 1863–64); Perry Miller and Thomas H. Johnson, *The Puritans* (New York, 1938); Babette Levy, "Puritanism in the Southern and Island Colonies," American Antiquarian Society *Proceedings*, LXX, I (1960), 122–154; William W. Sweet, *Religion in Colonial America* (New York, 1942); Herbert W. Schneider, *The Puritan Mind* (New York, 1930); Williston Walker, *The Creeds and Platforms of Congregationalism* (New York, 1893) and *A History of the Congregational Churches in the United States* (New York, 1898), a standard work; Leonard J. Trinterud, *The Forming of the American Tradition: A Re-Examination of Colonial Presbyterianism* (Philadelphia, 1949); Rufus M. Jones, *The Quakers in the American Colonies* (New York, 1911), a classic; Anita L. Lebeson, *Jewish Pioneers in America, 1492–1848* (New York, 1931); and Jacob R. Morris, *Early American Jewry* . . . (Philadelphia, 1951).

Literature, architecture, and science are dealt with in the following: Arthur P. Quinn, *The Literature of the American People* (4 vols., New York, 1951), Vol. I, ed. Kenneth P. Murdock, treats the colonial period;

Moses Coit Tyler, *A History of American Literature, 1607–1765* (2 vols., New York, 1878), still useful; and Robert R. Spiller *et al., Literary History of the United States* (3 vols., New York, 1948). There are two fine works on the architecture of the colonial period: Hugh Morison, *Early American Architecture* (New York, 1952), and S. Fiske Kimball, *Domestic Architecture of the American Colonies* (New York, 1922). Samuel E. Morison deals with intellectual and scientific aspects in *The Puritan Pronaos* (New York, 1936) and in *Harvard College in the Seventeenth Century* (2 vols., Cambridge, Mass., 1936). Highly suggestive is Whitfield J. Bell, Jr., *Early American Science: Needs and Opportunities* (Williamsburg, Va., 1955), with an excellent bibliography. An unusual treatment of a special subject is *Symposium on Colonial Medicine* (Richmond, Va., 1957), reprinted from *The Bulletin of the History of Medicine*, XXXI. For a comprehensive bibliography of the entire field of early American culture, see Louis B. Wright's bibliography in *The Cultural Life of the American Colonies* (New York, 1957).

Virginia

Many of the early documents and narratives have been printed. See Lyon G. Tyler (ed.), *Narratives of Early Virginia* (New York, 1927); Edward D. Neill's works, *The Virginia Company of London* (Washington, D.C., 1868), *Virginia Carolorum* (Albany, 1886), and *Virginia and Virginiola* (Minneapolis, 1878); William Strachey, *The History of Travaile into Virginia* (Hakluyt Society, London, 1849); Ralph Hamor, *A True Discourse of the Present State of Virginia* (London, 1615, reprinted, 1957); Alexander Whitaker, *Good News from Virginia* (London, 1613, reprinted, 1936); and Captain John Smith, *Travel and Works,* ed. Edward Arber and Arthur G. Bradley (2 vols., Edinburgh, 1910), the most recent edition. The 1910 edition is a reprint of Arber's 1884 edition with introduction, corrections and notes by Bradley. Captain John Smith, *The Generall Historie of Virginia, New-England, and the Summer Isles* (London, 1624), is the most important of Smith's works. See also Robert Tyndall, "Broughte of Virginia, 1608," *Massachusetts Historical Proceedings*, LVII (1925), 244–247; Louis B. Wright and Virginia Freud (eds.), *The Historye of Travell into Virginia Britania, 1612* (New York, 1953); David B. Quinn, "Advice for Investors in Virginia, Bermuda, and Newfoundland, a Newsletter, 1611," *William and Mary Quarterly*, 3d ser., XXIII (1966), 136–145; John Rolfe, *True Relation of the State of Virginia* (reprinted in *American Nautica Series*, 1951); Sir William Berkeley, *Discourse and View of Virginia* (London, 1663, reprinted in 1914), Robert Beverley,

The History and Present State of Virginia (London, 1705; modern edition, by Louis B. Wright, Chapel Hill, N.C., 1947); and Susie M. Ames, *County Court Records of Accomack-Northampton, Virginia, 1632–1640* (Washington, D.C., 1954), meticulously edited.

Among the general histories of Virginia are William Stith (ed.), *History of the First Discovery and Settlement of Virginia* (Williamsburg, Va., 1747), making use of some materials now lost; Alexander Brown, *The First Republic in America* (Boston, 1898), containing documentary material, and *The English Politics in Early Virginia* (Boston, 1901); Mary M. Standard, *The Story of Virginia's First Century* (Philadelphia, 1928); Matthew P. Andrews, *Virginia, The Old Dominion* (New York, 1937) and *The Soul of a Nation: The Founding of Virginia and the Projection of New England* (New York, 1943); Richard L. Morton, *Colonial Virginia* (2 vols., Chapel Hill, N.C., 1960), with Vol. I, *The Tidewater Period, 1607–1710*, supplanting earlier general accounts; John Fiske, *Old Virginia and Her Neighbors* (2 vols., Boston, 1897); and Thomas J. Wertenbaker's three research works, *Patrician and Plebean in Virginia* (Charlottesville, 1910), *Virginia Under the Stuarts, 1607–1688* (Princeton, 1914), and *The Planters of Colonial Virginia* (Princeton, 1922). Percy S. Flippin deals with *Royal Government in Virginia, 1624–1775* (New York, 1919), and see also Clarence W. Alvord and Lee Bidgood, *The First Explorations of the Trans-Allegheny Region . . . 1650–1674* (Cleveland, 1912).

Among the works on Captain John Smith are Bradford Smith, *Captain John Smith: His Life and Legend* (Philadelphia, 1953), a laudatory but balanced account; Edward K. Chatterton, *Captain John Smith* (New York, 1927), brief and interesting; John G. Fletcher, *John Smith* (New York, 1928), well written; Arthur G. Bradley, *Captain John Smith* (New York, 1905); and Philip L. Barbour, *The Three Worlds of Captain John Smith* (Boston, 1964), carefully researched, excellent bibliography.

Like Connecticut and New Jersey, Virginia has published a founding-anniversary series, Earl G. Swem (ed.) *The Virginia 350th Anniversary Celebration Publications* (Williamsburg, Va., 1957). A number of these pamphlet volumes exhibit modern scholarship and fresh viewpoints. Especially useful for this volume are Ben C. McCary, *John Smith's Map of Virginia . . . ;* Samuel M. Bemiss, *The Three Charters of the Virginia Company . . . 1606–1621;* Charles E. Hatch, Jr., *The First Seventeen Years . . . ;* Wilcomb E. Washburn, *Virginia Under Charles I and Cromwell . . . ;* and the volumes on land grants, government, agriculture, fishing, shipping, architecture, religious life, domestic life, justice, medicine, the Indians, and tobacco. Earl G. Swem, John M. Jennings, and James E. Servies have constructed *A Selected Bibliography of Virginia, 1607–1699* as Vol. I of this series.

The leading special works on early Virginia are as follows: Robert C. Johnson, "The Lotteries of the Virginia Company, 1612–1621," *Virginia Magazine of History*, V. 74, 260–290; Wesley Frank Craven, *Dissolution of the Virginia Company* (New York, 1932); Kenneth R. Andrews, "Christopher Newport of Limehouse, Mariner," *William and Mary Quarterly*, 3d ser., II (1954), 28–42; Nathaniel C. Hale, *Virginia Venturer: A Historical Biography of William Claiborne, 1600–1677* (Richmond, Va., 1951); Stanley M. Pargellis, "The Procedures of the Virginia House of Burgesses," *William and Mary Quarterly*, 2d ser., VII (1927), 73–86, 143–157; Edward Ingle, *Virginia Local Institutions* (Baltimore, 1885); J. A. C. Chandler, *Representation in Virginia* (Baltimore, 1886) and *The History of Suffrage in Virginia* (Baltimore, 1901); Albert O. Porter, *County Government in Virginia: A Legislative History, 1607–1904* (New York, 1947); George L. Chumbley, *Colonial Justice in Virginia* . . . (Richmond, Va., 1938); Oliver P. Chitwood, *Justice in Colonial Virginia* (Baltimore, 1905); Arthur P. Scott, *Criminal Law in Colonial Virginia* (Chicago, 1905); Philip A. Bruce, *Economic History of Virginia in the Seventeenth Century* (2 vols., New York, 1895) and *Institutional History of Virginia in the Seventeenth Century* (2 vols., New York, 1910), both standard studies; Percy S. Flippin, *The Financial History of the Colony of Virginia* (Baltimore, 1915), needs revising; William Z. Ripley, *The Financial History of Virginia, 1609–1776* (New York, 1893), discriminating, but dated; John S. Bassett, "The Relation between the Virginia Planter and the London Merchant," American Historical Association *Annual Report* (1901), I, 551–575; and Manning C. Voorhis, "Crown vs. Council in Virginia Land Policy," *William and Mary Quarterly*, 3d ser., III (1946), 499–514, valuable.

Economic and social studies are Charles M. MacInnes, *The Early English Tobacco Trade* (London, 1926); Arthur P. Middleton, *Tobacco Coast: A Maritime History of the Chesapeake Bay in the Colonial Era* (Newport News, 1953), principally eighteenth century; Lewis C. Gray, "Market Surplus Problems of Colonial Tobacco," *Agricultural History*, II (1928), 1–33; Avery O. Craven, *Soil Exhaustion as a Factor in the Agricultural History of Virginia and Maryland* (Urbana, Ill., 1926); Susie M. Ames, *Studies of the Eastern Shore in the Seventeenth Century* (Richmond, Va., 1940); Louis B. Wright, *The First Gentlemen of Virginia* (San Marino, Calif., 1940); John Duffy, "The Passage to the Colonies," *Mississippi Valley Historical Review*, XXXVIII (1951), 21–38; William Randel, "Captain John Smith's Attitudes toward Indians," *Virginia Magazine of History*, XLVII (1939), 218–229; Sigmund Diamond, "From Organization to Society," *American Journal of Sociology*, LXIII (1958), 457–475; James C. Ballagh, *History of Slavery in Virginia* (Baltimore, 1902) and *White Servitude in the Colony of Virginia* (Baltimore, 1895), both pioneer works;

Winthrop D. Jordan, "Modern Tensions and the Origins of American Slavery," *Journal of Southern History*, XXVIII (1962), 18–30; James H. Brewer, "Negro Property Owners in Seventeenth-Century Virginia," *William and Mary Quarterly*, 3d ser., XII (1955), 575–580; Oscar and Mary Handlin, "Origins of the Southern Labor System," *William and Mary Quarterly*, 3d ser., VII (1950), 199–222; and Bernard Bailyn, "Politics and Social Structure in Virginia," in James M. Smith (ed.), *Seventeenth-Century America*, pp. 90–115, excellent.

Studies pertaining to religion in Virginia are George M. Brydon, *Virginia's Mother Church* . . . (2 vols., Richmond, Va., 1947); H. R. McIlwaine, *The Struggle of Protestant Dissenters for Religious Toleration in Virginia* (Baltimore, 1894); William T. Thom, *The Struggle for Religious Liberty in Virginia: The Baptists* (Baltimore, 1900); Charles F. James (ed.), *Documentary History of the Struggle for Religious Liberty in Virginia* (Lynchburg, Va., 1900); Hamilton J. Eckenrode, *Separation of Church and State in Virginia* (Richmond, Va., 1900); and William H. Seiler, "The Anglican Parish in Virginia," in James M. Smith (ed.), *Seventeenth-Century America*, 119–142.

Maryland

For some original sources of early Maryland history, consult *Calvert Papers* (Maryland Historical Society Fund *Publications*, Nos. 28, 34–35 (1889–99); Clayton C. Hall (ed.), *Narratives of Early Maryland, 1633–1684* (New York, 1910), indispensable; and Lawrence G. Wroth, "Maryland Colonization Tracts," in *Essays Offered to Herbert Putnam* . . . (New Haven, 1929), 539–555.

There are many general histories of Maryland; among them are: Matthew P. Andrews, *The Founding of Maryland: Province and State* (New York, 1933); John L. Bozman, *The History of Maryland, from Its First Settlement in 1633 to the Restoration in 1660* (2 vols., Baltimore, 1837), is a mine of information; William H. Browne, *George Calvert and Cecilius Calvert, Barons Baltimore of Baltimore* (New York, 1890), *Maryland, The History of a Palatinate* (Boston, 1884), and *History of Maryland* (New York, 1893), all with a strong bias in favor of the Calverts; Clayton C. Hall, *The Lords Baltimore and the Maryland Palatinate* (2d ed., Baltimore, 1904); John V. L. McMahon, *An Historical View of the Government of Maryland* (Baltimore, 1831); James McSherry, *History of Maryland . . . from 1649 . . .* (Baltimore, 1849); Newton D. Mereness, *Maryland as a Proprietary Province* (New York, 1901), detailed but good; Edward D. Neill, *Founders of Maryland* . . . (Albany, 1876); John D. Scharf, *History of Maryland . . .* (3 vols., Baltimore, 1879), quotes sources; and Bernard C. Steiner, *Beginnings of Maryland, 1631–1639* (Baltimore, 1903), *Maryland During the English*

Civil War (2 vols., Baltimore, 1906–7), and *Maryland Under the Common-wealth: a Chronicle of the Years 1649–1658* (Baltimore, 1911), all products of painstaking research.

Among the special works on Maryland are many Johns Hopkins University studies: John H. Latané, *The Early Relations Between Maryland and Virginia* (Baltimore, 1895); St. George L. Siousatt, *The English Statutes in Maryland* (Baltimore, 1903); Edward Ingle, *Local Institutions in Maryland* (Baltimore, 1885); Lewis W. Wilhelm, *Maryland Local Institutions* (Baltimore, 1885); George Petrie, *Church and State in Maryland* (Baltimore, 1892); and Daniel R. Randall, *A Puritan Colony at Annapolis, Maryland* (Baltimore, 1886).

Other special studies are Edward B. Mathews, *Maps and Mapmakers of Maryland* (Baltimore, 1898); Bernard C. Steiner, "Baltimore and His Colonial Projects," American Historical Association *Annual Report* (1905), I, 109–122; John C. Claiborne, *William Claiborne of Virginia* (New York, 1917); Bernard C. Steiner (ed.), "Religious Freedom in Provincial Maryland," *American Historical Review*, XXVIII (1923), 258–259, an excellent note; Albert L. Werline, *Problems of Church and State in Maryland During the Seventeenth and Eighteenth Centuries* (South Lancaster, Mass., 1948); Eugene I. McCormack, *White Servitude in Maryland* (Baltimore 1904); James M. Wright, *The Free Negro in Maryland, 1634–1860* (New York, 1921); William A. Reavis, "The Maryland Gentry and Social Mobility, 1637–1676," *William and Mary Quarterly*, 3d ser., XIV (1957), 418–428; Arthur E. Karinen, "Maryland Population, 1631–1730," *Maryland Historical Magazine*, LIV (1959), 365–407; and Clarence P. Gould, *Money and Transportation in Maryland* (Baltimore, 1916).

The Northern Fringe

Charles E. Banks, "Popham Expedition Documents," American Antiquarian Society *Proceedings*, N.S., XXXIX (1929), 307–334; George P. Winship (ed.), *Sailors' Narratives of Voyages Along the New England Coast, 1524–1624* (Boston, 1905); Louis D. Scisco, "Kirke's Memorial on Newfoundland," *Canadian Historical Review*, VII (1926), 46–51; Ralph G. Lounsbury, *The British Fishery at Newfoundland, 1634–1763* (New Haven, 1934); Daniel W. Prowse, *History of Newfoundland* (London, 1895); John D. Rogers, *Newfoundland* (new ed., Oxford, 1931); G. C. M. Smith, "Robert Hayman and Newfoundland," *English Historical Review*, XXXIII (1918), 21–36; Gillian T. Cell, "The Newfoundland Company," *William and Mary Quarterly*, 3d ser., XXII (1965), 610–625, excellent; Henry J. Berkley, "Lord Baltimore's Contest with Sir David Kirke over Avalon," *Maryland Historical Magazine*, XII (1917), 107–114; George P. Insh, *Scottish Colonial Schemes, 1620–1886* (Glasgow, 1922); Henry Gardiner,

358 SELECTED BIBLIOGRAPHY

New England's Vindication (London, 1660; Gorges Society edition, 1884); and Robert G. Albion, *Forest and Sea Power* (Cambridge, Mass., 1925).

George M. Wrong, *The Rise and Fall of New France* (1928), is a classic study; see also Reuben G. Thwaites, *France in America* (New York, 1905), in the older American Nation Series. Related works are Henry P. Biggar, *The Early Trading Companies of New France* (Toronto, 1901); Sigmund Diamond, "An Experiment in Feudalism: French Canada in the Seventeenth Century," *William and Mary Quarterly,* 3d ser., XVII (1960), 3–34; Sir Edmund F. Slafter, *Sir William Alexander and American Colonization* (Boston, 1873); J. Bartlet Brebner, *New England's Outpost, Acadia before the Conquest* (New York, 1927); William I. Morse (ed.), *Acadiensia Nova, 1598–1779* . . . (London, 1935); and David B. Quinn, "The First Pilgrims," *William and Mary Quarterly,* 3d ser., XXIII (1966), 359–390, suggestive.

There are two scholarly works on Gorges: James P. Baxter, *Sir Ferdinando Gorges and His Province of Maine* (3 vols., Boston, 1890); and Richard Preston, *Gorges of Plymouth Fort: A Life of Sir Ferdinando Gorges* (Toronto, 1953). See also Henry S. Burrage, *Gorges and the Grant of the Province of Maine, 1622* (Portland, 1923); and James P. Baxter, *George Cleeve of Casco Bay, 1630–1667* (Portland, 1885). Other works relating to early Maine are James F. Baldwin, "Feudalism in Maine," *New England Quarterly,* V (1932), 353–357; Charles E. Banks, *History of York, Maine* (Boston, 1931); William Willis et al., (eds.), *Documentary History of the State of Maine,* Maine Historical Society *Collections,* 2d ser., 24 vols. (Portland, 1869–1916); Henry S. Burrage, *The Beginnings of Colonial Maine, 1602–1658* (Portland, 1914); William D. Williamson, *History of Maine* (2 vols., Hallowell, Mass., 1832); and Wilbur D. Spencer, *Pioneers on Maine Rivers* (Portland, 1930).

Early New Hampshire is treated in the following: John S. Jenness, *Transcripts of Original Documents in the English Archives Relating to the Early History of the State of New Hampshire* (New York, 1876); Charles W. Tuttle, *Captain John Mason, Founder of New Hampshire* (Boston, 1887), includes documents; P. E. Moyer, "Settlements of New Hampshire," *Granite Monthly,* LIV (1922), 153–166; Jeremy Belknap, *History of New Hampshire* (Philadelphia and Boston, 1784–1813), an early work, but still the best; Charles T. Libby, "Who Planted New Hampshire," *Granite Monthly,* LIV (1922), 364–368.

New England

See especially the older standard work, John G. Palfrey, *History of New England* (5 vols., Boston, 1858–1890).

Introductory studies are Raymond P. Stearns, "The New England Way in Holland," *New England Quarterly*, VI (1933), 747–792; Henry F. Howe, *Prologue to New England* (New York, 1943); Charles E. Banks and Samuel E. Morison, "Persecution as a Factor in Emigration to New England, 1630–1640," Massachusetts Historical Society *Proceedings*, LXIII (1930), 136–154; Charles K. Bolton, *The Real Founders of New England* (Boston, 1929); James T. Adams, *The Founding of New England* (Boston, 1931); Perry Miller, *Errand into the Wilderness* (Cambridge, Mass., 1956), reprints a number of Miller's searching essays; Francis A. Christie, "The Beginnings of Arminianism in New England," American Society of Church History Papers, 2d ser., III (1912), 153–172; Henry M. Dexter, *Congregationalism in the Last Three Hundred Years as Seen in Its Literature* (New York, 1880), contains a detailed bibliography; Paul E. Lauer, *Church and State in New England* (Baltimore, 1892); Ola E. Winslow, *Meetinghouse Hill, 1630–1783* (New York, 1952), treatment not found elsewhere; George L. Kittridge, *Witchcraft in Old and New England* (Cambridge, Mass., 1929), a classic study.

New England Puritanism in its many ramifications has fascinated a host of scholars. Robert J. Chaffin, "American Puritan Studies in the 1960's," *William and Mary Quarterly*, Vol. XXVII (1970), 36–67 provides a valuable commentary on the most recent. Some of these studies are: Raymond P. Sterns, "Assessing the New England Mind," *Church History*, X (1941), 246–262; Alan Simpson, *Puritanism in Old and New England* (Chicago, 1955), excellent; Edmund S. Morgan, *Visible Saints: The History of a Puritan Idea* (New York, 1963), a penetrating study; Charles E. Park, "Puritans and Quakers," *New England Quarterly*, XXVII (1954), 52–74; George L. Mosse, "Puritanism and Reason of State in Old and New England," *William and Mary Quarterly*, 3d ser., IX (1952), 67–81, specialized topic; Robert S. Michaelson, "Changes in the Puritan Concept of Calling or Vocation," *New England Quarterly*, XXVI (1953), 314–336; Alan Heimart, "Puritanism, the Wilderness, and the Frontier," *New England Quarterly*, XXVI (1953), 360–382; Perry Miller, "The Half-Way Covenant," *New England Quarterly*, VI (1933), 676–712; Edmund S. Morgan, "New England Puritanism: Another Approach," *William and Mary Quarterly*, 3d ser., XVIII (1961), 236–243; Darrett B. Rutman, "God's Bridge Falling Down, 'Another Approach' to New England Puritanism Essayed," *William and Mary Quarterly* 3d ser., XIX (1962), 408–421; Herbert W. Schneider, *The Puritan Mind* (New York, 1930); Norman Pettit, *The Heart Prepared: Grace and Conversion in Puritan Spiritual Life* (New Haven, 1966), well written; Clifford K. Shipton, "Puritanism and Modern Democracy," *New England Historical and Genealogical Register*, CI (1947), 181–198; and James F. Maclear, " 'The Heart of New England Rent': The Mystical Element in Puritan

History," *Mississippi Valley Historical Review*, XLII (1956), 621–652.

The culture of early New England is treated in Kenneth B. Murdock, *Literature and Theology in Colonial New England* (Cambridge, Mass., 1949); Thomas G. Wright, *Literary Culture in Early New England, 1620–1730* (New Haven, 1920); Peter Gay, *A Loss of Mastery, Puritan Historians in Colonial America*, (Berkeley, Calif., 1966) and Edmund S. Morgan's essay "The Historians of Early New England" in Ray A. Billington (ed.), *The Reinterpretation of Early American History* (San Marino, Calif., 1966), as well as in Morison's The *Founding of Harvard College* (Cambridge, Mass., 1935); *Harvard College in the Seventeenth Century* (Cambridge, Mass., 1936); and *The Puritan Pronaos* (New York, 1936), already mentioned. John L. Sibley *et al., Harvard Graduates* (Boston, 1873–   ), is a mine of information. Clifford K. Shipton has written "Secondary Education in the Puritan Colonies," *New England Quarterly*, VII (1934), 646–681.

Studies in special topics are Morrison Sharp, "Leadership and Democracy in Early New England Defense," *American Historical Review*, L (1945), 244–260; Lawrence Towner, " 'A Fondness for Freedom': Servant Protest in Puritan Society," *William and Mary Quarterly*, 3d ser., XIX (1962), 201–219; Lorenzo J. Greene, *The Negro in Colonial New England, 1620–1776* (New York, 1942); Lois K. Mathews, *The Expansion of New England* (Boston, 1909), a pioneer work; William Haller, Jr., *The Puritan Frontier: Town Planning in New England Colonial Development, 1630–1660* (New York, 1951); Melville Egleston, *The Land System of the New England Colonies* (Baltimore, 1886); Roy H. Akagi, *Town Proprietors of the New England Colonies* (Philadelphia, 1924), an excellent study; William B. Weeden, *Economic and Social History of New England, 1620–1789* (2 vols., Boston, 1890); Robert R. Walcott, "Husbandry in Colonial New England," *New England Quarterly*, IX (1936), 218–252; John W. McElroy, "Seafaring in Seventeenth Century New England," *New England Quarterly*, VIII (1934), 331–364; Raymond McFarland, *A History of the New England Fisheries* (New York, 1911); Marion H. Gottfried, "The First Depression in New England," *New England Quarterly*, IX (1936), 655–678; Bernard Bailyn, *New England Merchants in the Seventeenth Century* (Cambridge, Mass., 1955), excellent; Arthur H. Buffington, "New England and the Western Fur Trade, 1629–1675," Colonial Society of Massachusetts *Publications*, XVIII (1917), 160–192; Francis X. Maloney, *The Fur Trade in New England, 1620–1676* (Cambridge, Mass., 1951); Herbert M. Sylvester, *Indian Wars of New England* (3 vols., Boston, 1910); Alden T. Vaughan, *New England Frontier: Puritans and Indians, 1620–1675* (Boston, 1965), supersedes earlier studies, and his "A Test of Puritan Justice," *New England Quarterly* XXXVIII (1965), 331–339, asserts that the Indians were treated fairly; Douglas E. Leach, *Flintlock and Tomahawk: New England in King Philip's War* (New York, 1958), the early chapters; and Harry M. Ward, *The United Colonies of New England: 1643–1690* (New York, 1961).

Plymouth and Massachusetts

Henry M. and Morton Dexter, *The England and Holland of the Pilgrims* (Boston, 1905), valuable; Daniel Plooij, *Pilgrim Fathers from the Dutch Point of View* (New York, 1932); Charles E. Banks, *The English Ancestry and Homes of Pilgrim Fathers* (Boston, 1952); Samuel E. Morison (ed.), *Of Plymouth Plantation, by William Bradford* (New York, 1952), the best edition; *Bradford's Letter Book, 1629–1650*, Massachusetts Historical Society *Collections*, Ser. I, III (1794), 27–84; Nathaniel Morton, *New England's Memorial* . . . (Boston, 1669, and the modern edition in facsimile with notes by Arthur Lord, Boston, 1903). Morton borrows freely from Bradford, the prime source. See also Alexander Young, *Chronicles of the Pilgrim Fathers of Plymouth* (Boston, 1844), an excellent source book; W. Sears Nickerson, *Land Ho—1620* (Boston, 1931); Champlin Burrage (ed.), *John Pory's Lost Description of Plymouth Colony* . . . (Boston, 1918); Edward Arber, *The Story of the Pilgrim Fathers, 1606–1633, as Told by Themselves, Their Friends, and Their Enemies* (London, 1897), a collection of source material; Sydney V. James, Jr. (ed.), *Three Visitors to Early Plymouth: Letters* . . . (Plymouth, Mass., 1963); John A. Goodwin, *The Pilgrim Republic* . . . (Boston, 1888), the best account; Bradford Smith, *Bradford of Plymouth* (Philadelphia, 1951); Thomas W. Perry, "New Plymouth and Old England: a Suggestion," *William and Mary Quarterly*, 3d ser., XVIII (1961), 251–265; Darrett B. Rutman, "The Pilgrims and Their Harbor," *William and Mary Quarterly*, XVII (1960), 164–179; Samuel E. Morison, *By Land and by Sea* (New York, 1966), "New Light Wanted on the Old Colony," *William and Mary Quarterly*, XV (1958), 358–364, and "The Pilgrim Fathers: Their Significance in History," Colonial Society of Massachusetts *Publications*, XXXVIII, 364–379; Arthur Lord, *Plymouth and Pilgrims* (Boston, 1920); Roland G. Usher, *The Pilgrims and Their History* (New York, 1918), scholarly; George F. Willison, *Saints and Strangers* (New York, 1945), excellent; Douglas E. Leach, "Military Service of Plymouth," *New England Quarterly*, XXIV (1951), 342–364; David Bushnell, "The Treatment of Indians in Plymouth Colony," *New England Quarterly*, XXVI (1953), 193–218; John Demos, "Notes on Life in Plymouth Colony," *William and Mary Quarterly*, 3d ser., XXII (1965), 264–286, excellent social history; the same author's *A Little Commonwealth: Family Life in Plymouth Colony* (New York, 1970); Darrett B. Rutman, *Husbandmen of Plymouth: Farms and Villages in the Old Colony, 1620–*

1692 (Boston, 1968); and George D. Langdon, Jr., "The Franchise and Political Democracy in Plymouth Colony," *William and Mary Quarterly,* XX (1963), 513–526, and his definitive study, *Pilgrim Colony: A History of New Plymouth: 1620–1691* (New Haven, 1966). For an interesting historians' conference on "Plimouth Plantation" and a useful biography by George D. Langdon, see *Occasional Papers in Old Colony Studies* (Plymouth, 1969), pp. 1–50.

Massachusetts affords a long list of printed source materials. Works of this nature are William H. Whitmore (ed.), *Biographical Sketch of Massachusetts Colony from 1630–1686* (Boston, 1900); William Wood, *New England's Prospect* (London, 1634; reprinted, 1865); Thomas Prince, *A Chronological History of New England . . . from 1602 . . . to 1750* (2 vols., Boston, 1736, reprinted, Boston, 1826); John Wetering, "Thomas Prince's Chronological History," *William and Mary Quarterly,* 3d ser., XVIII (1961), 546–557; Alexander Young (ed.), *Chronicles of the First Planters of Massachusetts Bay from 1623–1636* (Boston, 1846); Thomas Hutchinson (ed.), *History of the Colony of Massachusetts Bay* (Boston, 1769, reprinted, Albany, 1865); Allyn B. Forbes (ed.), *Winthrop Papers* (5 vols., Boston, 1929–47); Robert C. Winthrop, *Life and Letters of John Winthrop* (2 vols., Boston, 1864–67); James K. Hosmer (ed.), *Winthrop's Journal* (2 vols., New York, 1908); J. Franklin Jameson (ed.), *Edward Johnson's Wonder-Working Province . . . 1628–1651* (New York, 1910); William Ames, *Cases of Conscience [De Conscientia]* (London, 1639) and *Marrow of Sacred Divinity* (London, 1627); Charles F. Adams (ed.), *Thomas Morton, The New England Canaan* (Boston, 1883, first issued in Amsterdam, 1627); Max Farrand, (ed.) *Laws and Liberties of Massachusetts,* reprinted from the 1648 edition (San Marino, Calif., 1949); and "Record of the Council for New England," American Antiquarian Society *Proceedings,* 1867, 59–131.

The list of works on early Massachusetts is a large one. Selected titles are as follows: Reverend William A. Hubbard, *A General History of New England . . .* (Cambridge, Mass., 1815, and other editions), more valuable than Mather; Thomas Hutchinson, *The History of the Colony and Province of Massachusetts Bay* (3 vols., London, 1764), with a modern edition by Lawrence S. Mayo (Cambridge, Mass., 1936), indispensable; John G. Palfrey, *A Compendious History of New England* (4 vols., Boston, 1884), learned; *Cotton Mather, Magnalia Christi Americana* (London, 1702; reprinted, 2 vols., Hartford, 1853–55), uncritical; Peter Oliver, *The Puritan Commonwealth* (Boston, 1856), anti-Puritan; Charles E. Banks, *The Planters of the Commonwealth* (Boston, 1930); George E. Ellis, *Puritan Age and Rule, the Colony of Massachusetts* (Boston, 1888); Charles Francis Adams, *Massachusetts, Its Historians and Its History* (Boston, 1893), and *Three Episodes* of *Massachusetts History* (2 vols., Boston, 1892); Brook Adams, *The Emancipation of Massachusetts* (Boston, 1886), critical of the oligarchy; Albert B. Hart, *Commonwealth History of Massachusetts* (5 vols., New York, 1927–30); H. F. Howe, *Prologue to New England* (New York, 1943), social life; and Richard S. Dunn, *Puritans and Yankees: The Winthrop Dynasty of New England, 1630–1717* (Princeton, 1962), especially good on John Winthrop, Jr.; and Robert C. Black III, *The Younger John Winthrop* (New York, 1967).

Special works on Massachusetts are as follows: Frances Rosé-Troup, *The Massachusetts Bay Company and Its Predecessors* (New York, 1930); Stewart Mitchell (ed.), *The Founding of Massachusetts . . . 1628–1631*, Massachusetts Historical Society *Proceedings*, LXII (1930), 225–273, reprints original documents; Charles H. McIlwain, "The Transfer of the Charter to New England and Its Significance in American Constitutional History," Massachusetts Historical Society *Proceedings*, LXIII (1929), 53–65; Charles F. Banks, *Winthrop Fleet* (Boston, 1930); Robert E. Moody, "The Mayflower Compact," *Old South Leaflet*, No. 225 (Boston, 1951); Nellis M. Crouse, "Causes of the Great Migration," *New England Quarterly*, V (1932), 3–36; Samuel E. Morison, *Builders of the Bay Colony* (Boston, 1930), a basic study; Herbert L. Osgood, "The Political Ideas of the Puritans," *Political Science Quarterly* VI (1891), 1–28; and Darrett B. Rutman, *Winthrop's Boston* (Chapel Hill, N.C., 1965), emphasis on commercial aspects, excellent bibliography.

There are numerous studies of the Bay Colony leaders: Frances Rosé-Troup, *John White . . . Founder of Massachusetts, 1578–1648* (New York, 1930); Stanley Gray, "The Political Thought of John Winthrop," *New England Quarterly,* III (1930), 681–705; Edgar A. Johnson, "The Economic Thought of John Winthrop," *New England Quarterly*, III (1930), 235–250; Edmund S. Morgan, *The Puritan Dilemma: The Story of John Winthrop* (Boston, 1958); Larzer Ziff, *The Career of John Cotton: Puritanism and the American Experience* (Princeton, 1962); Jesper Rosenmeier, "The Teacher and the Witness: John Cotton and Roger Williams," *William and Mary Quarterly*, XXV (1968), 408–431; Lawrence S. Mayo, *John Endecott: A Biography* (Cambridge, Mass., 1956); Augustine Jones, *The Life and Works of Thomas Dudley* (Boston, 1900); George L. Kittredge, "Dr. Robert Child, the Remonstrant," Colonial Society of Massachusetts *Publications*, XXI (1919), 1–146; Charles H. Bell, *John Wheelwright* (Boston, 1876); Thomas Shepard, "Autobiography," Colonial Society of Massachusetts *Publications,* Sixth Report (1889); George P. Winship (ed.), *The New England Company of 1649 and John Eliot* (Boston, 1920); Helen Augur, *An American Jezebel, the Life of Anne Hutchinson* (New York, 1930); Edith Curtis, *Anne Hutchinson* (Cambridge, Mass., 1930); Winnifred K. Rugg, *Unafraid: A*

Life of Anne Hutchinson (Boston, 1930), all partially superseded by Emery Battis, *Saints and Sectaries: Anne Hutchinson and the Antinomian Controversy in the Massachusetts Bay Colony* (Chapel Hill, N.C., 1962); Raymond P. Stearns, *The Strenuous Puritan: Hugh Peter, 1598–1660* (Urbana, Ill., 1954), valuable; and Ellen Brennen, "Massachusetts Council of Magistrates," *New England Quarterly,* IV (1931), 54–93.

Special studies on a variety of topics include Perry Miller and Thomas H. Johnson (eds.), *The Puritans* (New York, 1938); Justin Winsor, *The Memorial History of Boston* (4 vols., Boston, 1880–81); Charles J. Hilkey, *Legal Development in Colonial Massachusetts, 1630–1686* (New York, 1910); F. W. Grinnell, "The Bench and Bar in Colony and Province," in Albert B. Hart (ed.), *Commonwealth History of Massachusetts* (5 vols., New York, 1927–30), Vol. II; Richard B. Morris, *Studies in the History of American Law* (New York, 1930), Chaps. II and IV, and "Massachusetts and Common Law," *American Historical Review,* XXXI (1926), 443–453; L. T. Wolford, "Laws and Liberties in 1648," *Boston University Law Review,* XXXVIII (1948), 426–463; George L. Haskins, *Law and Authority in Early Massachusetts* (New York, 1960), excellent; Jules Zanger, "Crime and Punishment in Early Massachusetts," *William and Mary Quarterly,* 3d ser., XXII (1965), 472–477; Joseph H. Smith, *Colonial Justice in Western Massachusetts, 1639–1702: The Pynchon Court Record* (Cambridge, Mass., 1961); George H. Haynes, *Representation and Suffrage in Massachusetts, 1620–1691* (Baltimore, 1894); Kenneth A. Lockridge and Alan Kreider, "The Evolution of Massachusetts Town Government, 1640–1740," *William and Mary Quarterly,* 3d ser., XXIII (1966), 549–574; John F. Sly, *Town Government in Massachusetts, 1620–1930* (Hamden, Conn., 1967), concise; Sumner C. Powell, *Puritan Village: The Formation of a New England Town* (Middletown, Conn., 1963); Henry M. Burt, *The First Century of the History of Springfield* (2 vols., Hartford, 1898); B. Katherine Brown, "Freemanship in Puritan Massachusetts," *American Historical Review,* LIX (1954), 865–883, interpretative, and "Puritan Democracy: A Case Study," *Mississippi Valley Historical Review,* L (1963), 377–396; Richard C. Simmons, "Freemanship in Early Massachusetts: Some Suggestions and a Case Study," *William and Mary Quarterly,* 3d ser., XIX (1962), 422–428; Edmund S. Morgan, *The Puritan Family* (Boston, 1944); Robert C. Twombly and Robert H. Moore, "Black Puritan: The Negro in Seventeenth-Century Massachusetts," *William and Mary Quarterly,* XXIV (1967), 224–242, reveals little discrimination as yet against the Negro; Darrett B. Rutman, "Governor Winthrop's Garden Crop: The Significance of Agriculture in the Early Commerce of Massachusetts Bay," *William and Mary Quarterly,* 3d ser., XX (1962), 396–415; Richard A. Preston, "Fishing and Plantation, New England in Parliament in 1621," *American Historical*

Review, XLV (1939), 29–43; and Alden T. Vaughan, "Pequots and Puritans," *William and Mary Quarterly,* 3d ser., XXI (1964), 256–269, suggestive. The Massachusetts version of Puritanism has absorbed the interest of many scholars. Among their works are Aaron B. Seidman, "Church and State in the Early Years of the Bay Colony," *New England Quarterly,* XVIII (1945), 211–233; Perry Miller, *Orthodoxy in Massachusetts, 1630–1650* . . . (Cambridge, Mass., 1933), a study in depth and a book he intended to rewrite; and Edmund S. Morgan, *Visible Saints: The History of a Puritan Idea* (New York, 1963), an indispensable work written with clarity and charm. Perry Miller's articles on this subject have been conveniently reprinted in his *Errand into the Wilderness* (Cambridge, Mass., 1956), except for "Half-Way Covenant," *New England Quarterly,* VI (1933), 676–715; and see also his important *The New England Mind: From Colony to Province* (Cambridge, Mass., 1935), a sequel to his *Orthodoxy in Massachusetts.* Additional works are Emil Oberholzer, Jr., *Delinquent Saints: Disciplinary Action in the Early Congregational Churches of Massachusetts* (New York, 1956); and Marion L. Starkey, *The Devil in Massachusetts* (Boston, 1949). Isaac Backus, *History of New England with Particular Reference to the Baptists* (3 vols., Boston, 1777–96), and William Kellaway, *The New England Company, 1649–1776: Missionary Society to the American Indians* (New York, 1961), are also useful. In addition to earlier references to cultural manifestations see also R. F. Seybolt, *The Private Schools of Colonial Boston* (Cambridge, Mass., 1935); and George H. Martin, *The Massachusetts Public School System* (New York, 1894).

Rhode Island

General histories of Rhode Island are John Callender, *Historical Discourse on* . . . *Rhode Island* (Boston, 1739), reprinted in Rhode Island Historical Society *Collections,* IV (1938), 45–176; Howard M. Chapin, *Documentary History of Rhode Island* (2 vols., Providence, R.I., 1916–19); James G. Arnold, *History of Rhode Island and Providence Plantations* (2 vols., Providence, 1878); Edward Field, *The State of Rhode Island and Providence Plantations* (3 vols., Boston, 1902); Thomas W. Bicknell, *History of Rhode Island* (5 vols., Providence, 1920), quotes sources; Irving B. Richman, *Rhode Island: Its Making and Its Meaning* (2 vols., New York, 1902), the most useful; and William B. Weeden, *Early Rhode Island: A Social History* (New York, 1910), an early attempt at social history.

Roger Williams dominates Rhode Island historical writing. His *Writings* appear in Narragansetts Club *Publications,* 1866–74, Vols. I–VI; now superseded by *The Complete Writings of Roger Williams,* ed. James H. Trumbull *et al.* (New York, 1963). The first six volumes are facsimiles of the Narragansetts Club edition, with the introductions of the nineteenth-century editors; Vol. VII contains several new tracts, but no new letters. See Edmund S. Morgan's perceptive comments in his review of Vol. VII (ed. Perry Miller), "Roger Williams: His Contribution to the American Tradition, 'Miller's Williams,' " *New England Quarterly*, XXXVIII (1965), 513–535.

The principal works on Williams are Titus M. Merriman (ed.), *The Pilgrims, Puritans, and Roger Williams Vindicated . . .* (2d ed., Boston, 1892); Samuel H. Brockunier, *The Irrepressible Democrat: Roger Williams* (New York, 1952); Henry M. Dexter, *As to Roger Williams* (Boston, 1876), pro-Williams; Emily Easton, *Roger Williams, Prophet and Pioneer* (Boston, 1930), quotes letters; Perry Miller, *Roger Williams: His Contribution to the American Tradition* (Indianapolis, 1953), clarifying; Ola E. Winslow, *Master Roger Williams, A Biography* (New York, 1957), a standard work; James E. Ernst, *The Political Thought of Roger Williams* (Seattle, 1929); Edmund S. Morgan, *Roger Williams: The Church and the State* (New York, 1967); and Cyclone Covey, *The Gentle Radical: A Biography of Roger Williams* (New York, 1966). Leading articles are Alan Simpson, "How Democratic Was Roger Williams?" *William and Mary Quarterly*, XIII (1956), 40–67; George A. Stead, "Williams and Massachusetts Bay," *New England Quarterly*, VII (1934), 235–257; Henry B. Parkes, "Cotton and Williams Debate Religious Toleration," *New England Quarterly*, IV (1931), 735–756; and James E. Ernst, "Roger Williams and the English Revolution," Rhode Island Historical Society *Collections*, XXIV (1931), 1–58.

Works on other Rhode Island leaders are Henry E. Turner, *William Coddington* (Providence, 1878); Samuel Gorton, *Simplicities Defence Against Seven-Headed Policy* (London, 1646), presents the case against Massachusetts; Adelos Gorton, *The Life and Times of Samuel Gorton . . .* (Philadelphia, 1907), uncritical, but cites sources; and Kenneth W. Porter, "Samuel Gorton," *New England Quarterly*, VII (1934), 405–444.

Special studies on early Rhode Island are Elisha R. Potter, *Early History of Narragansett* (Providence, R.I., 1835), still of value; Edward Channing, *The Narragansetts Planters* (Baltimore, 1886); William D. Miller, "The Narragansetts Planters," American Antiquarian Society *Proceedings*, XLIII (1953), 49–115; and William E. Foster, *Town Government in Rhode Island* (Baltimore, 1886).

Connecticut

General works on Connecticut are: Benjamin Trumbull, *A Complete History of Connecticut* (2 vols., Hartford, 1797); Charles M. Andrews, *Connecticut's Place in Colonial History* (New Haven, 1924) and *The River*

Towns of Connecticut (Baltimore, 1889); George H. Hollister, *History of Connecticut* . . . (New Haven, 1855); George L. Clark, *A History of Connecticut, Its People and Institutions* (New York, 1914); and two important books, Albert E. Van Deusen, *Connecticut* (New Haven, 1961), and Mary Jeanne Anderson Jones, *Congregational Commonwealth: Connecticut, 1636–1662* (Middletown, Conn., 1968).

There are a number of well-written and informative pamphlets issued by the Tercentenary Commission of Connecticut Publications (New Haven, 1933–1936), ed. Charles M. Andrews *et al.* Early Connecticut is treated in II, *Connecticut Intestacy Law;* III, *The Charter of Connecticut;* IV, *Thomas Hooker;* V, *The Story of the Pequot War Re-Told;* VI, *The Settlement of Connecticut;* XII, *Early Domestic Architecture of Connecticut;* XIII, *Milford, Connecticut;* XIV, *Roads and Road-Making in Connecticut;* XIX, *The Indians of Connecticut;* XX, *The Fundamental Orders of Connecticut;* XXXII, *The Beginnings of Connecticut;* XLVIII, *The Rise and Fall of New Haven Colony;* and LX, *The Achievement of Religious Liberty in Connecticut.*

Thomas Hooker looms large in Connecticut history. See George L. Walker, *Thomas Hooker* (New York, 1891); Warren S. Archibald, *Thomas Hooker* (New Haven, Conn., 1933); Clinton Rossiter, "Thomas Hooker," *New England Quarterly,* XXV (1952), 459–488, an excellent inquiry; Perry Miller, "Hooker and the Democracy of Early Connecticut," *New England Quarterly,* IV (1931), 663–712, also published with an explanatory note in *Errand into the Wilderness,* pp. 17–47. George L. Walker, *History of the First Church, Hartford, 1633–1883* (Hartford, Conn., 1884), analyzes Hooker's writings. Other Connecticut biographies are: John M. Taylor, *Roger Ludlow, The Colonial Lawmaker* (New York, 1900); Samuel E. Morison, "William Pynchon, The Founder of Springfield," Massachusetts Historical Society *Proceedings,* LXIV (1932), 67–107; and Ruth McIntyre, *William Pynchon: Merchant and Colonizer* (Springfield, Mass., 1961).

Special studies are Charles M. Andrews, "The Beginnings of Connecticut Towns," *Annals of the American Academy of Political and Social Science,* I (1890), 165–191; Dorothy Deming, *The Settlement of Connecticut Towns* (New Haven, 1934); David H. Fowler, "Connecticut's Freemen: The First Forty Years," *William and Mary Quarterly,* 3d ser., XV (1958), 313–333; Herbert L. Osgood, "Connecticut as a Corporate Colony," *Political Science Quarterly* XIV (1899), 251–280; Nelson P. Mead, *Connecticut as a Corporate Colony* (Lancaster, 1906); Charles J. Hoadly, *The Warwick Patent* (Hartford, 1902); Bernard C. Steiner, *A History of Guilford* (Baltimore, 1897); William de Love, *Colonial History of Hartford* (Hartford, 1914); Chard P. Smith, "Church and State in Wethersfield, 1636–1639," *New England Quarterly,* XXIX (1956), 82–87; Henry M. Burt, *The First Century of Springfield* . . . (2 vols., Springfield, Mass., 1898–99); Henry A. Wright,

The Genesis of Springfield . . . (Springfield, Mass., 1936); Richard S. Dunn, "John Winthrop and the Narragansett Country," *William and Mary Quarterly*, 3d ser., XIII (1956), 68–86; Alden T. Vaughan, "Pequots and Puritans," *William and Mary Quarterly*, 3d ser., XXI (1964), 256–269; John Mason, *A Brief History of the Pequot War* (Boston, 1736); Clarence W. Bowen, *The Boundary Disputes of Connecticut* (Boston, 1882); and Maria L. Greene, *The Development of Religious Liberty in Connecticut* (Boston, 1905), excellent; Curtis P. Nettels, "Beginnings of Money in Connecticut," *Wisconsin Academy of Science Transactions*, XXIII (1927), 1–28; and Frederick R. Jones, *History of Taxation in Connecticut, 1636–1776* (Baltimore, 1896).

New Haven

The principal references for New Haven Colony are: Rollin G. Osterweis, *Three Centuries of New Haven, 1638–1938* (New Haven, 1953), good general history; Edward E. Atwater, *History of the Colony of New Haven* . . . (Meriden, Conn., 1902), quotes sources; Charles H. Levermore, *The Republic of New Haven* (Baltimore, 1886); Isabel M. Calder, *New Haven Colony* (New Haven, 1934), the best book; Henry White, "The New Haven Colony," *Papers of the New Haven Colony Historical Society*, I (1865), 12–16; Sarah D. Woodward, *Early New Haven* (New Haven, 1929); and Isabel M. Calder, "John Cotton and the New New Haven Colony," *New England Quarterly*, III (1930), 82–94. Biographies of early leaders are Franklin P. Dexter, "Sketch of the Life and Writings of John Davenport," *Papers of the New Haven Colony Historical Society*, II (1877), 205–238, and Simon E. Baldwin, "Theophilus Eaton, First Governor of the Colony of New Haven," *Papers of the New Haven Colony Historical Society*, VII (1908), 1–33. See also Elijah C. Baldwin, "Branford Annals," *Papers of the New Haven Colony Historical Society*, III (1882), 249–270, and Leonard Labaree, *Milford, Connecticut: The Early Development of a Town as Shown in Its Land Records* (New Haven, 1938); and for New Haven's aspirations on the Delaware, Epher Whitaker, "New Haven's Adventure on the Delaware Bay," *Papers of the New Haven Colony Historical Society*, IV (1888), 209–230.

New Netherland, New York, and the Delaware

The rise and fall of New Netherland has been treated by many writers: Henry C. Murphy, *Henry Hudson in Holland* (The Hague, 1900), excellent; Edgar M. Bacon, *Henry Hudson: His Times and his Voyages* (New York, 1907); Llewelyn Powys, *Henry Hudson* (New York, 1928), well-written, with new material; J. Franklin Jameson (ed.), *Narratives of New Netherland, 1609–1664* (New York, 1909), important source material; Edmund B. O'Callaghan, *History of New Netherland* (2 vols., Philadelphia, 1846–48), valuable; Petrus A. Blok, *A History of the People of the Netherlands* (5 vols., New York, 1898–1912); Pieter Geyl, *The Netherlands in the Seventeenth Century* (rev. ed., 2 vols., New York, 1961–64), a classic work; William E. Griffis, *The Dutch in the Making of America* (New York, 1921); Ellis L. Raesly, *Portrait of New Netherland* (New York, 1945), interestingly written; Victor H. Palsits, "Founding of New Amsterdam in 1626," American Antiquarian Society *Proceedings*, N.S., XXXIV (1924), 39–65, excellent; Harold C. Syrett, "Private Enterprise in New Amsterdam," *William and Mary Quarterly*, 3d ser., XI (1954), 536–561; Maud W. Goodwin, *Dutch and English on the Hudson* (New Haven, 1919); Samuel G. Nissenson, *The Patron's Domain* (New York, 1937), challenges older conceptions; Mrs. Schuyler Van Rensselaer, *History of the City of New York in the Seventeenth Century* (2 vols., New York, 1909), basic and broader than the title indicates; John H. Innes, *New Amsterdam and Its People* (New York, 1902); William R. Shepherd, *The Story of New Amsterdam* (New York, 1926); I. N. Phelps Stokes, *Iconography of Manhattan Island, 1498–1909* (6 vols., New York, 1915–28), a unique contribution.

On Peter Stuyvesant see Bayard Tuckerman, *Peter Stuyvesant . . .* (New York, 1898); Henry H. Kessler and Eugene Rachlis, *Peter Stuyvesant and His New York* (New York, 1959), replaces Tuckerman's life; and Dixon Ryan Fox, *Yankees and Yorkers* (Port Washington, New York, 1940), an able work.

Much has been written of the Dutch and the early English settlement of New York. The best works are as follows: John R. Brodhead, *History of the State of New York* (2 vols., New York, 1853–71), informative but almost unreadable; William Smith, *The History of the Late Province of New York* (London, 1957); and Alexander C. Flick, *History of the State of New York* (10 vols., New York, 1933–37), topical, uneven.

Special studies are Albert E. McKinley, "English and Dutch Towns of New Netherlands," *American Historical Review*, VI (1900), 1–18; Benjamin F. Thompson, *History of Long Island* (New York, 1839; new ed., 4 vols., New York, 1918, ed. C. J. Werner), Long Island's fascinating history obscured by lack of records; Isabel M. Calder, "Earl of Stirling and the Colonization of Long Island," in *Essays . . . Presented to Charles McLean Andrews* (New Haven, 1931); Allen W. Trelease, *Indian Affairs in Colonial New York: The Seventeenth Century* (Ithaca, 1960), basic research; Wilbur C. Abbott, *Colonial John Scott of Long Island, 1634–1696* (New Haven, 1918), dissects this shadowy adventurer; Lillian T. Mowrer, *The Indomitable John Scott: Citizen of Long Island* (New York, 1960), revisionist;

370 SELECTED BIBLIOGRAPHY

Thomas J. Condon, *New York Commercial Beginnings* (New York, 1968); and Edgar J. McManus, *A History of Negro Slavery in New York* (Syracuse, N.Y., 1966).

The first settlements on the Delaware, in addition to materials in Vol. XII of *Documents Relating to the Colonial History of New York*, are discussed in Christopher Ward, *The Dutch and Swedes on the Delaware, 1609–1664* (Philadelphia, 1930), a detailed work; Clinton A. Weslager, *Dutch Explorers, Traders and Settlers in the Delaware Valley, 1609–1664* (Philadelphia, 1961), specialized, with some fresh material; Evelyn Page, "The First Frontier—The Dutch and Swedes," *Pennsylvania History,* XV (1948), 276–304, an application of the Turner thesis; John H. Wuorinin, *The Finns on the Delaware, 1638–1655* (New York, 1938); Amandus Johnson, *The Swedish Settlements on the Delaware . . . 1614–1638* (2 vols., New York, 1911), excellent work based on a lifetime of research; and *The Instructions for Johan Printz* (Philadelphia, 1930), contains an excellent biographical sketch; Benjamin Ferris, *History of the Original Settlements on the Delaware* (Wilmington, 1846); Albert C. Myers (ed.), *Narratives of Pennsylvania, West Jersey and Delaware, 1630–1707*); Father William Keller, "Sir Edmund Plowden and the Province of New Albion, 1632–1650," *Historical Records and Studies of the U.S. Catholic Historical Society,* XLI (1953), 42–70; and Clifford Lewis 3d, "Some Notes on Sir Edmund Plowden and His Province of New Albion," mineographed pamphlet (1937) in the Library of Congress. John E. Pomfret, *The Province of West New Jersey, 1609–1702* (Princeton, 1954) and *The Province of East New Jersey, 1609–1702* (Princeton, 1962) summarize Dutch and Swedish activities in the region from Manhattan to Delaware Bay.

The Southern Fringe

Much has been written of the early British settlements in the West Indies. See Frank Cundall, *Bibliography of the West Indies* (Kingston, Jamaica, 1900), and "List of Works relating to the West Indies," *New York Public Library Bulletin,* XVI (1912), No. I, 3–8. General works are Philip A. Means, *The Spanish Main: Focus of Envy, 1472–1700* (New York, 1965); Arthur P. Newton, *The European Nations in the West Indies, 1493–1688* (New York, 1967); Bryan Edwards, *The History, Civil and Commercial, of the British Colonies in the West Indies* (3 vols, London, 1793–94); Aucher Warner, *Sir Thomas Warner* (London, 1933); Clarence H. Haring, *The Buccaneers in the West Indies in the Seventeenth Century* (London, 1910); Vincent T. Harlow (ed.), *Colonising Expeditions to the West Indies and Guiana, 1623–1667* (London, 1925); James A. Williamson, *The Caribbee Islands under the Proprietary Patents* (Oxford, 1926); and

David B. Quinn, "Advice for Investors in Virginia, Bermuda and Newfoundland, 1611," *William and Mary Quarterly,* 3d ser., XXIII (1966), 136–145.

More specialized writings are John Henry Lefroy (ed.), *Memorials of the Discovery and Early Settlement of the Bermuda or Somers Islands, 1515–1685* (2 vols., London, 1877–79), includes important documents; Wesley Frank Craven (ed.), "Lewis Hughes, 'A Plaine and True Relation of the Somer Islands,'" *William and Mary Quarterly,* 2d ser., XVII (1937), 56–89; Henry C. Wilkinson, *The Adventurers in Bermuda* . . . (London, 1958), a basic work; Vincent T. Harlow, *A History of Barbados, 1625–1685* (Oxford, 1926), standard; Frank Strong, "The Causes of Cromwell's West Indian Expedition," *American Historical Review,* IV (1899), 228–245; Charles H. Firth (ed.), *The Narrative of General Venables* . . . *to the West Indies* (London, 1900); Irene A. Wright, Spanish Resistance to the English Occupation of Jamaica, 1655–1660" Royal Historical Society *Transactions,* 4th ser., XIII (1930), 117–147; Henry M. Crouse, *French Pioneers in the West Indies, 1624–1664* (New York, 1910); Babette M. Levy, "Early Puritanism in the Southern and Island Colonies," American Antiquarian Society *Proceedings,* LXX (1960), 69–348; and Winthrop D. Jordan, "The Influence of the Origins of New England Slavery," *William and Mary Quarterly,* 3d ser., XVIII (1961), 243–251.

Excellent summary accounts of early British West India history are found in Andrews, *The Colonial Period of American History,* especially I, Chaps. XI and XII; II, Chap. VII; and III, Chap. I.

Index

harper 🔥 torchbooks

American Studies: General

CARL N. DEGLER: Out of Our Past: *The Forces that Shaped Modern America* CN/2
ROBERT L. HEILBRONER: The Limits of American Capitalism TB/1305
JOHN HIGHAM, Ed.: The Reconstruction of American History TB/1068
JOHN F. KENNEDY: A Nation of Immigrants. *Illus. Revised and Enlarged. Introduction by Robert F. Kennedy* TB/1118
GUNNAR MYRDAL: An American Dilemma: *The Negro Problem and Modern Democracy. Introduction by the Author.*
Vol. I TB/1443; Vol. II TB/1444
GILBERT OSOFSKY, Ed.: The Burden of Race: *A Documentary History of Negro-White Relations in America* TB/1405
ARNOLD ROSE: The Negro in America: *The Condensed Version of Gunnar Myrdal's* An American Dilemma TB/3048

American Studies: Colonial

BERNARD BAILYN: The New England Merchants in the Seventeenth Century TB/1149
ROBERT E. BROWN: Middle-Class Democracy and Revolution in Massachusetts, 1691–1780. *New Introduction by Author* TB/1413
JOSEPH CHARLES: The Origins of the American Party System TB/1049

American Studies: The Revolution to 1900

GEORGE M. FREDRICKSON: The Inner Civil War: *Northern Intellectuals and the Crisis of the Union* TB/1358
WILLIAM W. FREEHLING: Prelude to Civil War: *The Nullification Controversy in South Carolina, 1816-1836* TB/1359
HELEN HUNT JACKSON: A Century of Dishonor: *The Early Crusade for Indian Reform.* ‡ *Edited by Andrew F. Rolle* TB/3063
RICHARD B. MORRIS, Ed.: Alexander Hamilton and the Founding of the Nation. *New Introduction by the Editor* TB/1448
RICHARD B. MORRIS: The American Revolution Reconsidered TB/1363
GILBERT OSOFSKY, Ed.: Puttin' On Ole Massa: *The Slave Narratives of Henry Bibb, William Wells Brown, and Solomon Northup* ‡ TB/1432

American Studies: The Twentieth Century

WILLIAM E. LEUCHTENBURG: Franklin D. Roosevelt and the New Deal: 1932-1940. † *Illus.* TB/3025
WILLIAM E. LEUCHTENBURG, Ed.: The New Deal: *A Documentary History* + HR/1354

Asian Studies

WOLFGANG FRANKE: China and the West: *The Cultural Encounter, 13th to 20th Centuries. Trans. by R. A. Wilson* TB/1326
L. CARRINGTON GOODRICH: A Short History of the Chinese People. *Illus.* TB/3015
BENJAMIN I. SCHWARTZ: Chinese Communism and the Rise of Mao TB/1308

Economics & Economic History

PETER F. DRUCKER: The New Society: *The Anatomy of Industrial Order* TB/1082
ROBERT L. HEILBRONER: The Great Ascent: *The Struggle for Economic Development in Our Time* TB/3030
W. ARTHUR LEWIS: The Principles of Economic Planning. *New Introduction by the Author°* TB/1436

Historiography and History of Ideas

J. BRONOWSKI & BRUCE MAZLISH: The Western Intellectual Tradition: *From Leonardo to Hegel* TB/3001
WILHELM DILTHEY: Pattern and Meaning in History: *Thoughts on History and Society.° Edited with an Intro. by H. P. Rickman* TB/1075
J. H. HEXTER: More's Utopia: *The Biography of an Idea. Epilogue by the Author* TB/1195
ARTHUR O. LOVEJOY: The Great Chain of Being: *A Study of the History of an Idea* TB/1009

History: Medieval

F. L. GANSHOF: Feudalism TB/1058
DENYS HAY: The Medieval Centuries ° TB/1192
HENRY CHARLES LEA: A History of the Inquisition of the Middle Ages. ‖ *Introduction by Walter Ullmann* TB/1456

---

† The New American Nation Series, edited by Henry Steele Commager and Richard B. Morris.
‡ American Perspectives series, edited by Bernard Wishy and William E. Leuchtenburg.
ü History of Europe series, edited by J. H. Plumb.
§ The Library of Religion and Culture, edited by Benjamin Nelson.
‖ Researches in the Social, Cultural, and Behavioral Sciences, edited by Benjamin Nelson.
⅃ Harper Modern Science Series, edited by James R. Newman.
° Not for sale in Canada.
+ Documentary History of the United States series, edited by Richard B. Morris.
# Documentary History of Western Civilization series, edited by Eugene C. Black and Leonard W. Levy.
▲ The Economic History of the United States series, edited by Henry David et al.
¶ European Perspectives series, edited by Eugene C. Black.
** Contemporary Essays series, edited by Leonard W Levy.
* The Stratum Series, edited by John Hale.

History: Renaissance & Reformation

JACOB BURCKHARDT: The Civilization of the Renaissance in Italy. *Introduction by Benjamin Nelson and Charles Trinkaus. Illus.* Vol. I TB/40; Vol. II TB/41
JOEL HURSTFIELD: The Elizabethan Nation TB/1312
ALFRED VON MARTIN: Sociology of the Renaissance. ° *Introduction by W. K. Ferguson* TB/1099
J. H. PARRY: The Establishment of the European Hegemony: 1415-1715: *Trade and Exploration in the Age of the Renaissance* TB/1045

History: Modern European

MAX BELOFF: The Age of Absolutism, 1660-1815 TB/1062
ALAN BULLOCK: Hitler, A Study in Tyranny. ° *Revised Edition. Illus.* TB/1123
JOHANN GOTTLIEB FICHTE: Addresses to the German Nation. *Ed. with Intro. by George A. Kelly* ¶ TB/1366
H. STUART HUGHES: The Obstructed Path: *French Social Thought in the Years of Desperation* TB/1451
JOHAN HUIZINGA: Dutch Cviilization in the 17th Century and Other Essays TB/1453
JOHN MCMANNERS: European History, 1789-1914: *Men, Machines and Freedom* TB/1419
FRANZ NEUMANN: Behemoth: *The Structure and Practice of National Socialism, 1933-1944* TB/1289
A. J. P. TAYLOR: From Napoleon to Lenin: *Historical Essays* ° TB/1268
H. R. TREVOR-ROPER: Historical Essays TB/1269

Philosophy

HENRI BERGSON: Time and Free Will: *An Essay on the Immediate Data of Consciousness* ° TB/1021
G. W. F. HEGEL: Phenomenology of Mind. ° ‖ *Introduction by George Lichtheim* TB/1303
H. J. PATON: The Categorical Imperative: *A Study in Kant's Moral Philosophy* TB/1325
MICHAEL POLANYI: Personal Knowledge: *Towards a Post-Critical Philosophy* TB/1158
LUDWIG WITTGENSTEIN: The Blue and Brown Books ° TB/1211
LUDWIG WITTGENSTEIN: Notebooks, 1914-1916 TB/1441

Political Science & Government

C. E. BLACK: The Dynamics of Modernization: *A Study in Comparative History* TB/1321
DENIS W. BROGAN: Politics in America. *New Introduction by the Author* TB/1469
KARL R. POPPER: The Open Society and Its Enemies *Vol. I: The Spell of Plato* TB/1101 *Vol: II: The High Tide of Prophecy: Hegel, Marx, and the Aftermath* TB/1102
CHARLES SCHOTTLAND, Ed.: The Welfare State ** TB/1323
JOSEPH A. SCHUMPETER: Capitalism, Socialism and Democracy TB/3008
PETER WOLL, Ed.: Public Administration and Policy: *Selected Essays* TB/1284

Psychology

LUDWIG BINSWANGER: Being-in-the-World: *Selected Papers.* ‖ *Trans. with Intro. by Jacob Needleman* TB/1365

MIRCEA ELIADE: Cosmos and History: *The M} of the Eternal Return* § TB/20
SIGMUND FREUD: On Creativity and the Unco scious: *Papers on the Psychology of A Literature, Love, Religion.* § *Intro. by Be jamin Nelson* TB/
J. GLENN GRAY: The Warriors: *Reflections Men in Battle. Introduction by Hann Arendt* TB/12
WILLIAM JAMES: Psychology: *The Brie Course. Edited with an Intro. by Gord Allport* TB/10

Religion

TOR ANDRAE: Mohammed: *The Man and h Faith* TB/
KARL BARTH: Church Dogmatics: *A Selectio Intro. by H. Hollwitzer. Ed. by G. Bromiley*
NICOLAS BERDYAEV: The Destiny of Man TB/
MARTIN BUBER: The Prophetic Faith TB/
MARTIN BUBER: Two Types of Faith: *Inte penetration of Judaism and Christiani* TB/
RUDOLF BULTMANN: History and Eschatalog *The Presence of Eternity* TB/9
EDWARD CONZE: Buddhism: *Its Essence and D velopment. Foreword by Arthur Wale* TB/
H. G. CREEL: Confucius and the Chinese Wa TB/6
FRANKLIN EDGERTON, Trans. & Ed.: The Bha gavad Gita TB/1
M. S. ENSLIN: Christian Beginnings TB/
M. S. ENSLIN: The Literature of the Christia Movement TB/
HENRI FRANKFORT: Ancient Egyptian Religion *An Interpretation* TB/
IMMANUEL KANT: Religion Within the Limi of Reason Alone. *Introduction by Theodor M. Greene and John Silber* TB/6
GABRIEL MARCEL: Homo Viator: *Introduction a Metaphysic of Hope* TB/39
H. RICHARD NIEBUHR: Christ and Culture TB/
H. RICHARD NIEBUHR: The Kingdom of God i America TB/4
SWAMI NIKHILANANDA, Trans. & Ed.: Th Upanishads TB/11
F. SCHLEIERMACHER: The Christian Faith. *In troduction by Richard R. Niebuhr.* Vol. I TB/108 Vol. II TB/10

Sociology and Anthropology

KENNETH B. CLARK: Dark Ghetto: *Dilemmas o Social Power. Foreword by Gunnar Myrda* TB/131
KENNETH CLARK & JEANNETTE HOPKINS: A Rele vant War Against Poverty: *A Study of Com munity Action Programs and Observable So cial Change* TB/148
GARY T. MARX: Protest and Prejudice: *A Stud} of Belief in the Black Community* TB/143
ROBERT K. MERTON, LEONARD BROOM, LEONARD S COTTRELL, JR., Editors: Sociology Today: *Problems and Prospects* ‖ Vol. I TB/1173; Vol. II TB/117
GILBERT OSOFSKY: Harlem: The Making of a Ghetto: *Negro New York, 1890-1930* TB/138
PHILIP RIEFF: The Triumph of the Therapeutic: *Uses of Faith After Freud* TB/1360
GEORGE ROSEN: Madness in Society: *Chapters in the Historical Sociology of Mental Illness.* ‖ *Preface by Benjamin Nelson* TB/1337